hundred members of the U.S. House of Representatives were beneficiaries of special, low-interest bank loans, and the following year over a hundred Congressmen were found to be holders of bank securities. At meetings of the American Bankers Association, the financial elite gathers under yards of American flags to hear its favorite U.S. administration officials—who afterward receive handsome honoraria.

Christopher Elias also probes the sovereign leadership of the Federal Reserve and includes many provocative close-ups of well-known bankers, such as David Rockefeller, chairman of New York's Chase Manhattan Bank; San Francisco Bank of America Corporation's A. W. Clausen; Walter Wriston, chairman of New York's First National City Bank; and David Kennedy, former president and chief executive officer of Chicago's Continental Illinois National Bank and Trust Company.

It is Congressman Wright Patman who has waged the longest and hardest battle against the "dollar barons." In his Foreword he declares, "[This book] raises a very serious question about the extent to which our legislative and regulatory bodies—and the public—have allowed the power of the commercial banking industry to expand virtually unchecked . . . a danger which has too often been overlooked in a daily press."

CHRISTOPHER ELIAS has been a financial editor and reporter for more than two decades. He has been w
Herald Tribune, The W
and *Business Week* and
Fleecing the Lambs.

WHO ARE THE DOLLAR BARO

Bankers have become a ruling class—the powerful core of the nat
establishment that incites awe, timidity, and even puts fear into re
agencies, financial reporters and editors, politicians and legislator
President himself. To belong somewhere in the banking system, t
carved out a niche, has its rewards, both in terms of money and p
It is doubtful that any other group in the United States has as mu
say over the economy.

THE DOLLAR BARONS

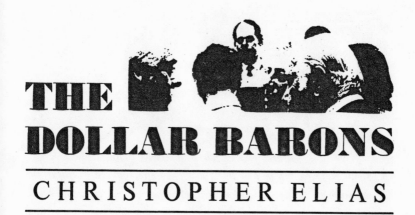

THE DOLLAR BARONS

CHRISTOPHER ELIAS

Macmillan Publishing Co., Inc.

NEW YORK

Macmillan Publishing Co., Inc.

866 Third Avenue, New York, N.Y. 10022

Collier-Macmillan Canada Ltd., Toronto, Ontario

Library of Congress Catalog Card Number: 73–6056

First Printing 1973

Printed in the United States of America

Contents

The banks in this country
are remote from the people and the people
regard them as not belonging to them
but to some power hostile to them . . .

—WOODROW WILSON
in a speech before
the American Bankers Association
Denver, 1908

Foreword

The question of concentration of economic power used to be a popular topic for political debate in this nation. Slowly we came to believe that the trust-busting of the early 1900s combined with the regulatory reforms of the New Deal had put this old bugaboo to rest for all time.

But the giant has not been sleeping. Today, the economic resources and the decision-making are more concentrated than ever before, all the reforms notwithstanding. Nowhere is this truer than in the financial community, and *The Dollar Barons* recounts some of the more ambitious power plays which have characterized this industry in recent years.

In a complex nation, operating within a complicated world economic system, power is a fact of life in the corporate society. The real question is not whether this power exists but whether it can be controlled and guided so that it supports the broad interests and needs of the people. *The Dollar Barons* raises a very serious question about the extent to which our legislative and regulatory bodies—and the public—have allowed the power of the commercial banking industry to expand virtually unchecked to the detriment of the public interest and the economic health of the nation.

This nation has 13,500 commercial banks scattered across the land and in the nooks and crannies of the fifty states, but the money lords are few in number and amazingly concentrated. Half the deposits of all the banks—all 13,500—reside in just fifty institutions—roughly three-tenths of 1 percent of all the banks in the country.

These are the dollar barons, the bankers who make the basic

decisions for this entire industry and for huge segments of our economy. These are the dollar barons who greatly influence economic decisions at all levels, and these are the dollar barons who play an increasing role in the political decision-making process at both federal and local levels.

The commercial banking system today controls $580 billion in deposits and, through manipulation of holding company devices, has made boardinghouse reaches into a variety of non-banking enterprises. In addition to these massive deposits and the overriding power of the credit mechanism—the loan-making powers—trust departments operated by the banks control another $350 billion of other people's money. These trust departments as a group are the largest single source of institutional investment, and the decisions made in these bank departments have a tremendous impact on the entire economy as well as on individual corporations.

Pension funds, a rapidly growing source of capital, are largely controlled by commercial banks. By 1980, the experts expect that the private pension funds will have amassed more than $300 billion, and at least 70 percent of this will be controlled by commercial banks.

All of this spells power. It would be wrong to say that all of this power is misused, but no one can question what this massing of economic power means in terms of potential danger to our entire society. It is a danger which has too often been overlooked in a daily press which reports banking legislation and financial developments as routine affairs followed by only a handful of in-house experts. But these developments and the growing concentration of power affect the hopes and well-being of every citizen and the very structure of our economic system. It is unfortunate that the popular press has failed to pursue these issues with vigor and for the most part has been content to add to the mythology and secrecy which have surrounded discussions of the financial community.

This is why *The Dollar Barons* is so valuable. It pulls together and gives significance to major banking incidents which have been largely overlooked in the popular press. Efforts like *The Dollar Barons* are essential in cutting through the complexities which have served as a prime bulwark for the banking community's successful effort to avoid real regulation and reform through the years.

In discussing these power plays among the money lords, the author draws a number of conclusions and, in contributing this foreword, it is not necessary for me either to endorse or to argue with each one of these findings. This remains for the author and his readers to argue out, but *The Dollar Barons* lays out the facts and raises some extremely provocative questions. In the process of raising these issues, the author also discusses the activities and possible motivations of some of my Congressional colleagues, and here again these are the author's own conclusions about which the readers will make their own judgments.

The important fact—as I see it from forty-five years of work on banking legislation—is that *The Dollar Barons* raises issues of vital importance to the nation, issues that should have been raised in a variety of forums long ago. It is an extremely valuable contribution to the public's understanding of some of the most misunderstood questions before the nation.

WRIGHT PATMAN
Chairman
House Banking and Currency Committee

Introduction

One day in April, 1972, David Rockefeller, the chairman of New York's Chase Manhattan Bank, stood before a group of newspaper editors convening in Washington, D.C., and during a speech entitled "A Crisis in American Values" told a story that alluded in jest to the legendary hardheartedness of bankers. The story was about heart transplants, and Rockefeller related how a very high priority had been assigned when the first transplants were undertaken to donors who were bankers. The reason for the high priority, was that bankers' hearts had almost never been used.

In a way it was a strange story for Rockefeller to tell, since he undoubtedly was still feeling the sting of "Banks and the Poor," a National Educational Television program which in vivid color and prose had portrayed the Chase Manhattan Bank as a backer of gambling casinos in the West Indies and an exploiter of the poor at home. Rockefeller himself came off poorly in the film, appearing as a well-fed, obviously very rich and powerful banker who tended to sweat when he explained his bank's lending practices.

As he spoke before the assembled editors Rockefeller might also have been remembering a just-published, especially hostile biography entitled *David,* whose author, William Hoffman, described David Rockefeller as one of the world's "most savagely disliked" bankers. The basis for this and other observations was a Rockefeller life-style that removed him (and his family) from sight and sound of most people, yet permitted him as head of the

Chase Manhattan Bank to exert extraordinary influence over the lives of hundreds of millions of people in the United States because of Chase Manhattan lending policies. *David* accorded Rockefeller more real power than that held by the President of the United States, suggesting that holding that office would be a demotion for him.

Both *David* and "Banks and the Poor" were greeted by David Rockefeller as might be expected. An initial sour reaction emerged from the Chase Manhattan Bank through a spokesman upon publication of the book. The TV program, which was a powerful and accurate indictment of banking, produced an initial reaction of rage, as reported by producer and writer Morton Silverstein. (It also generated a lot of fear among the managers of television stations who felt it would offend local bankers.) Rockefeller had agreed to participate in the filmed program, which was aired nationally over the nearly two hundred affiliates of the Public Broadcasting Service, but claimed that the ground rules as he understood them had been violated. For example, Silverstein reports Rockefeller objected strongly to the juxta-position of his remarks in defense of his bank's lending practices in housing and gambling with those of Wright Patman, the chairman of the House Banking and Currency Committee and the nation's leading skeptic so far as big-banker motives are concerned.

Silverstein insists, however, that Rockefeller had been told Patman's remarks would be contained in the film, though the technique of alternating first his view then Patman's on the same subject had not been explained.

But rage is not a characteristic of David Rockefeller, whose public bearing is that of the cool, reasonable man, and it is worth noting that he could refer to the hard hearts of bankers with humor after his own rough treatment. His entire speech, in fact, was a call to reason and "creative compromise" between supporters of revolutionary change and supporters of evolutionary change, the latter being the position of most bankers.

Few bankers would have responded to criticism as caustic as that aimed at Rockefeller with reasonableness so sweet. Much of banking, with the exception of the City National Bank and Trust Company, Columbus, Ohio, which recommended seeing the film in an ad, was livid. Banker opposition to the program, in fact, forced it off the air in many cities as bankers put pressure on the boards of local stations affiliated with the Public Broadcasting Service. Most bankers took their cues from the Washington-based American Bankers Association which had been given a pre-broadcast screening of "Banks and the Poor." Quietly and insidiously the word was spread among public television stations, often by their banker directors, that the program "presents a one-sided picture of the banking world" (a phrase used by a station in Virginia) and that bankers "saw no way to answer it." Closer to the truth was that some of the brutal collection practices of the banks, such as selling the home of a co-maker for a tiny sum that was overdue, had never really been told by journalists anywhere. The banks were also depicted as the supporters of loan sharks. The facts presented were the kind that had always been smothered by the financial press and the kind that had concerned Congressman Wright Patman for years.

Publicly, the banking industry was generally silent, preferring to work from within. Bankers greeted the criticism as they have always greeted criticism, with stony silence, taking their cues from the American Bankers Association. As the chief banking organization, the ABA prefers to say practically nothing on issues, as shown in the chapter "Banks as Lobbyists," and is generally opposed to change.

Helping the ABA and its member bankers is the mystique that has grown up around banking and kept inquirers in the press and Congress alike ignorant. It is this ignorance that precludes the asking of truly pertinent questions. Invariably, banking's public representatives, whether they are employed by the ABA or the Federal Reserve Board, intimidate inquirers almost immediately by questioning their knowledge of banking. Many a member of the House Banking and Currency Committee has even prefaced a question with an apology to the banker being interrogated for the Congressman's own admitted ignorance of banking matters. The practiced reaction of many of banking's public information officers to an inquiry by a reporter from the general press (as differentiated from those handmaidens of banking, the financial press) is to pull open a series of file drawers and stuff the reporter's arms full of sanitized, irrelevant material that brings home to him his own ignorance. Obviously, if someone with the right to inquire—a Congressman or a reporter—is faked out by banking's mystique, then the result can only be an enormous lack of information, which is what we have today.

Banks operate away from the people, and really do not answer to the people, but to agencies that in most cases tinker with the mechanism of banking, a mechanism that does not serve the needs of all the people. Far from it. The issue of ignorance so disturbed Wright Patman that he once wrote, "For many years, I have been deeply concerned by the general absence of economic news on the major television and radio networks. These are issues which touch the lives of every single citizen of the nation, but they are given only the most surface treatment on most news programs and little or no attention on the longer special news programs. Many of the subjects in the banking, monetary, and economic fields cannot be adequately dealt with on spot news programs and this makes the need for special news programming even more imperative."

The technique of using the banking mystique to quell inquirers was developed first by the Federal Reserve Board in Washington. The Board's machinations in controlling the money supply, one of its main functions as a central bank, are so secret that its determinations must be deduced (nothing is announced) from figures that appear weeks and months later. At one time the actions of the board were so secret that even Congress received no information for five years. On the insistence of a number of Congressmen, including Wright Patman, this was reduced to three months, though the reports, authored by the Federal Reserve, remain highly censored and reveal very little.

When a banker wraps himself in the banking mystique it produces a freezing, awkward atmosphere in which any inquirer can be rattled and put off. Then, having successfully deflected his inquirer, the banker retreats to his preferred silence.

It may be that silence is the correct ploy for bankers—it may even be golden—since few bankers are truly good public communicators, so remote have they become from the public they supposedly serve. Bankers are men at the top, the core of the establishment, which for the most part in the United States is composed of businessmen. Bankers do not like to respond to questions from outsiders, and as members of the most powerful economic block in the United States do not generally answer those who question their decisions. Rather it is they who conduct the inquisitions or require others to do their bidding. Bank tables of organization are much like military chains of command, with discipline as strict or even stricter. It can be death for a man's career if he disobeys, and his advancement depends on how good a soldier he is in the bank's wars.

By the time a banker gets to the top he has become an imperious, generally close-mouthed individual who feels, if his bank is in a small community, that he kind of runs the town. If he is the head man of one of the giants he may feel compelled to impress the world—which is easily enough done by a David Rockefeller or a Walter Wriston (chairman of New York's First National City Bank). He also feels answerable to hardly anyone.

It takes great power, in fact, to make a banker talk when he doesn't want to talk, and to convince him that the rules are made for him too. One of the best examples of this developed some years ago in the person of David Kennedy, the highly regarded chief executive of Chicago's Continental Bank. Kennedy was appointed Secretary of the Treasury by President Nixon, but floundered badly in an office that required persuasion and cooperation rather than issuing orders. Kennedy had rarely answered to anyone but himself and his closest peers, and in the give and take of Washington he was ineffective. Once when he appeared before the House Banking and Currency Committee, which was holding hearings on bank holding company legislation (the details are in Chapter 4), Kennedy lapsed into an angry silence when confronted with the fact that he still owned shares in Continental Bank, though he was now a regulator of banks, and at the hearing was testifying favorably on legislation that would benefit his bank.

When bankers do decide to speak out, they sometimes tend to castigate their critics, painting them almost as enemies of the state, or at the very least enemies of the free enterprise system. A good run-of-the-mill sample of how bankers generally respond to critics is a statement by William Renchard, who until his retirement on February 1, 1973, was chairman of New York's Chemical Bank (a bank, incidentally, whose role in controversies nearly always seems to be that of the heavy, as the chapters on merger and one-bank holding legislation will show). In his last letter to stockholders early in 1972, a letter signed by his successor, Donald C. Platten, Renchard took the view that critics, especially those faulting business for polluting the environment and for deceiving consumers, were undermining the free enterprise system itself. At least one statement in the Renchard letter suggested that the critics lacked integrity, and the letter even hinted that they were unpatriotic. "Critics of private enterprise," Renchard said, "in recent years have become increasingly vociferous in calling for permanent and pervasive controls over business and industry as a means of solving the problems arising from economic and social change. Lately, these extremists, some in the guise of consumer advocates, have been attacking our profit-oriented productive system as the chief cause of all socio-economic problems and as the chief impediment to their solution."

Renchard to the contrary, the leading critics of business, including banking, have not called for abolishing the profit-oriented economic system of the United States. They have, instead, called on business to be held more accountable for its actions.

Wright Patman, for example, is banking's most formidable and effective critic since he largely controls the serious consideration of legislation affecting banking and his committee's powers of subpoena can procure information about banking not possible for others to get. Patman is not antibanking; he is antibankers who, he says, do not act in the public interest. One thing Patman would do is hold banking accountable by making its chief regulator, the Federal Reserve Board, respond to the will of the President, or more precisely, act in accord with economic policies of the President.

Though another critic, Ralph Nader, would require corporations, including banks, to reveal such confidential information as tax returns—he charges that corporations make special deals with the Internal Revenue Service out of public view—he would leave the basic structure pretty much as it is. In other words, banks would continue as profit-making organizations. But, Nader believes, corporations, banks included, will not be responsive to the public interest no matter what their structure unless corporations becomes less secure than they are now. The way to insecurity would be through accountability. For example, coincidentally with the report of new, fat earnings, a corporation would also have to disclose just how much waste it had emptied into the local river in the last quarter. That kind of report is responsive to the public interest. Too much dumping, or any dumping at all, would result in top executives losing their jobs, or in a six-month prohibition on advertising products, for example. Each of these penalties, incidentally, already exists in the securities industry, where executives are held directly accountable. In the banking industry similar penalties against the bank or its executives could be applied for not disclosing the vast stock market activity of the bank's trust department, for example, or if there was evidence that the bank had harassed individuals whose loan payments were overdue.

The reaction of banks to such criticisms and suggestions is not limited to raising the banner of free enterprise and disparaging the critics, as Chemical's Renchard did. In 1971 a Ralph Nader task force directed by a former Justice Department lawyer named David Leinsdorf produced a scathing report on the practices of the First National City Bank of New York, especially in lending to individuals. The report said, for example, that First National City had sued 10,000 of its individual, small borrowers in 1969 and 15,000 of them in 1970. In relation to the total number of the bank's borrowers the numbers produced a *rate* of suit more than double that of any other bank.

The bank's executives were understandably enraged by the report, especially since the bank had cooperated with the task force to a great extent. The bank's chairman, Walter Wriston, was especially irate, and the bank issued a rebuttal, saying the statement covering its suit against borrowers was a distortion. It supported this with the non sequitur that First National City Bank makes "almost as many personal loans as all four of its major competitors put together."

But even as it was issuing a public rebuttal, the bank was moving against the report in another, overt way, by trying to enlist allies among the New York press. The move came during the once-a-year, off-the-record press conference and dinner First National City holds annually for the New York press. The dinner is a clubby kind of affair with the invited guests representing every faction of New York's writers and editors on finance and business. After dinner, cigars are passed out, amiable talk commences, and First National City Bank's executives agree to give responsive answers to pertinent questions, though without attribution.

When the question period began on this particular night, the report attacking the bank had not yet been made public. The bank's executives knew what charges it contained, however, and vindicating the bank was obviously on their minds. It is not clear how the appeal was made. Certainly, it was stealthy, since one of the editors, at least, suddenly realized that he was not only being told the contents of the report, but was also being asked to attack Nader. "What would they, the editors and reporters who were there, what would they do to fight Nader," the editor recalls being asked, "if Nader were doing to them what he was doing to the bank?" The bank's executives explained how the bank had opened doors everywhere inside its organization to the Nader investigators, and how scores of bank executives had given up many hours of their valuable time to answer questions. Sure, there was always a public relations executive or some other third party present when the Nader investigators were interviewing the bank's personnel. But so what?

"Many of those present took umbrage at the question," says the editor reporting the incident. "We answered by saying it's not up to you to ask us how to deal with Nader. That's your problem." The more important lesson of the incident, however, is that the First National City Bank attempted to enlist the aid of what is supposedly a free and independent press. As the editor who repeated the story said, "Practically everyone in the financial press in New York who was anyone was there."

For the most part, bankers are more successful than this in surreptitiously recruiting others to their causes—as a number of chapters in *The Dollar Barons* will show. Nor do banks have any real antagonists among the financial press, a fact that may have caused First National City to overstep the usual bounds. While the financial press may report every minor adjustment of the banking mechanism, only a handful stoop to taking up banking's cudgel. Indeed, many reporters never learn enough about banking to discover its ills or to question its operations philosophically —to raise queries such as whom banking should serve, the prosperous only or everyone. Unwittingly, many financial reporters and editors become the handmaidens of banking, serving their source first, their readers second, and the general public last. Some reporters and editors truly regard banking as a noble calling and are clearly its allies. Still others bask in talking to some of the most powerful men in the nation, while others are overly impressed, even bought, by the attention banking can lavish on reporters—as the First National City Bank dinner—one of the purposes of which was to establish and cement cozy relationships. Some reporters also work for publications that are nothing less than mouthpieces for the industry, soliciting their advertising and in turn espousing banking's aims as though they were necessary to the public good. Bank holding, for example, which could produce monopolies dwarfing anything seen so far, has not been handled as a controversy by the press, though it figuratively rocked the hearing halls of Congress when it was discussed. The cashless society, which would be a boon to the prosperous but a plague for the less than prosperous since easy access to credit would be all-important, is generally blandly described in all its hoped-for detail by the financial press. Thus, that extraordinary power of banks to determine who shall succeed in business—which is really what lending amounts to—will be extended to the individual as well. For without credit he will flounder in a cashless society.

To oppose the will of banks, however, can be costly, as many legislators have found. Many a Congressman has learned how impotent he is when introducing or supporting bills opposed by the banks. One reason is that his fellow legislators often own bank stocks or are connected as lawyers or investors with corporations that are customers of banks. Many a lawyer turned legislator has had banks and bank customers as clients, and he knows he may have to go back to practicing law some day. Thus he is in conflict—though usually he solves the conflict in favor of the banks and his own peace of mind. For years the word to new Congressmen in Washington has been, in effect, "Don't oppose the banks, at least in full view." In the opinion of Wright Patman, who has been in Congress for nearly half a century and is the most senior man in the House, the warning has worked well. Even for legislators who do not have direct connections with banks and their customers, timidity and awe seem to be major factors in dealing with bank legislation, and generally they raise little opposition to bank interests.

But fear of banks and fear of upsetting a business relationship are only a few of the weapons banking uses to sway legislators. More than once bank lobbyists have been charged with trying to influence members of Congress directly, especially new members, with special loans whose terms are simple in the extreme. The Congressman merely has to write out a check and it will be honored—immediately.

Banks have also been accused of trying to influence Congressmen with shares of bank stocks, with directorships on bank boards, and with illegal campaign contributions. In some cases, bank organizations have sent unsolicited campaign contributions to incumbent members of both houses who are sympathetic to bank interests—in defiance of the Corrupt Practices Act. Particular targets were those members serving on committees originating or considering legislation affecting banking.

Banking also has infiltrated successfully the majority of the regulatory agencies overseeing banking, both state and federal, either with men who are bankers or with men who though not bankers are probank. Happily for the public interest a few men do appear now and then, such as the Federal Deposit Insurance Corporation's Frank Wille, to adjudicate bank interest and the public need. Many a regulator, though, especially on the state level, has found himself fired or rendered ineffectual after opposing bank interests, as the reader will see.

Banking has always hovered at the core of government, from which it gets much of its real power. Banks financed World War II, for example, with loans to the Treasury totaling $84 billion by 1945. But banking's major job has been lending to business. Without a banking system creating money and controlling its supply, commercial life could come to a near standstill, as the early colonists and then independent America found out. In the commerce-minded United States of the eighteenth and nineteenth centuries banking flourished, with state-chartered banks being founded in large numbers and a central bank being founded twice. It was not until the 1930s that consumer credit had any place of importance in banking.

For their service to business and government, bankers have extracted and accumulated extraordinary power that expresses itself at all levels. In the early 1970s the banks euchered the United States into guaranteeing a loan of $250 million to a near-dying Lockheed Aircraft Corporation—at a time when some pretty brutal collection practices were going on among the poor. The accumulation of power has insulated banks against such forces of change as public opinion, hostile legislators, and, unless it is flagrantly violated, the law.

Though bankers today are loudly vocal defenders of the free enterprise system, too often they seem to be defending a system more accurately described as survival of the fittest. Unlike Darwin's thesis, however, which was based on natural selection, a process of unnatural selection is at work here. A good commercial idea does not automatically attract bank loans, even after a fervent pitch by the entrepreneur. On the human side, home building languishes and stalls despite great need when bankers choose to put money where they find the greatest return. The ability to lend or not to lend, to foreclose or call a loan, gives bankers power next to God, as one of their number has described it. Control of money and credit permits bankers to decide who is going to succeed and who is not. This might be acceptable if there were established standards of determining who should be extended money and credit and who should not be. Of course, systems do exist. Philadelphia's First Pennsylvania Bank maintains a system in which applicants for loans respond to a series of questions. The answers are evaluated on the basis of a point system, and it has been bank policy to grant loans to people scoring between 50 and 60 points out of 100 (the actual number of necessary points hinges on how tight money is, i.e., how much money the bank has available to lend). If an applicant accumulates the required points, he must be granted the loan—else the loan officer is reprimanded or even fired. But this same bank, like many others, also makes loan decisions, especially those involving large loans, on grounds far less precise. Literally, the way a man parts his hair, his speech habits, the wine he chooses at lunch when entertaining his banker, are among the thousands of superficial, though very real, factors ground into a decision to lend or not to lend. In a nation that has always required great supplies of money and credit, and where today credit is as essential as mail service or electric power, such practices are unacceptable in the view of many critics. The likelihood, too, is that the power of bankers to choose will increase as the basic world capital shortage continues to grow.

It goes without saying, of course, that in judging who shall make it bankers consider first how high their own return will be. In recent years that return has included not only interest but, often enough to be alarming, ownership in the borrower's firm as well. Whether banks have an inalienable right to high profits, of the kind detailed in Chapter 14, is a question well worth debating if credit is indeed essential to everyone but now denied to vast segments of the population. The basic conflict, of course, is whether a banking system geared to very high profits and an obsessive urge to expand fulfills its mission. Is such a system actually in conflict with the credit needs of the vast public by helping the rich get richer? Most people in lesser circumstances cannot get loans, and when they do, they pay the highest interest rates of all. In fact, it is undeniable that the lower a borrower's financial circumstances, the more he will pay for money. For a large portion of the population, even those of middle income, this can mean paying interest rates so high, not only to banks but also to loan companies and loan sharks, that a kind of servitude develops.

Bankers are well aware of the widening schism between them and the public. Further, since consumer credit is a burgeoning part of lending these days and banks are actively pursuing it, a few have begun to try to lessen the gap of distrust that exists.

Unfortunately, many of the attempts are window dressing and rhetoric.

David Rockefeller, for example, has called for "massive collaboration" by all business, banks included, to achieve social objectives, e.g., housing for the poor, jobs, financing minority businesses. Chase Manhattan even financed ghetto housing and made loans to minority businessmen, but the few millions put into housing were so minor alongside Chase Manhattan's enormous size (assets in 1971 were $24.5 billion) and the effort so well publicized that it amounted to not much more than public relations.

Even so highly profit-motivated a bank as New York's First National City recognizes the need "to make a constructive contribution to society," a statement made by Chairman Walter Wriston. More pragmatically, and perhaps more honestly, Wriston has said that every time banking has "refused to respond to legitimate financial needs of the community" it has created a competing monster. When the banks walked away from housing many years ago savings and loan institutions, which generally have a lock on home-building finance, were born. (Wriston and every other banker now complains that the associations are not regulated as strictly as banks.) Bankers also avoided investing the average man's money, saying there was no profit in it. The result was the birth of the mutual fund industry. Insurance, too, which is regarded as a traditional bank business by Wriston, was taken over by specialized companies because banks failed to develop it. Today, Wriston's First National City Bank is in the vanguard of consumer lending.

It may well be that only those banks away from the money centers of the Northeast can really close the gap between themselves and the people around them. (Northeastern banks, especially in New York, are based on lending to business. A recent study has shown that more than 80 percent of their loans are made to business.) Elsewhere, though, banks were formed for different reasons, though business loans still played a major part. In

San Francisco, for example, the Bank of America was formed just after the turn of the century for the benefit of Italian immigrants. Other banks would have little or nothing to do with them, and today the Bank of America still claims close ties with individuals by pointing to its 4 million depositors. Like other banks, the Bank of America argues that "profits are and must continue to be the central concern of any responsible corporate enterprise," a statement that is at least arguable when it comes to banks. But the Bank of America has also said in a public statement that "in the long pull, nobody can expect to make profits, or have any meaningful use for profits, if our entire society is wracked by tensions." The statement was made shortly after one of the bank's branches was set afire by a radical group of youths.

In January, 1972, Bank of America developed a formal organization within its management with the responsibility of tailoring its lending programs to promote the general welfare, even if it meant foregoing some profiit. An executive vice president named G. Robert Truex, Jr., was put in charge of "social policy" and given functional responsibility. This meant that he had as much power as executives overseeing such major bank activities as lending, branch administration, and international banking.

There is also at least one case in which bankers got out of their offices, physically, to go to bat for people. This occurred in Atlanta when a bank vice president named Ashton J. Albert fired up the officers of his own bank, the Trust Company of Georgia, and officers from eight other banks, including the Federal Reserve Bank of Atlanta, to find jobs for people. The bankers literally manned telephones in a twenty-four-hour marathon and called businesses in the Atlanta area, using their persuasive powers to demand jobs for young people. On April 25, 1972, the bankers called 320 businesses and landed 2,104 pledges of jobs, going far beyond their goal of 1,500. The banks participating, in addition to Albert's Trust Company and the Federal Reserve, were Citizens and Southern National, Fulton National,

the National Bank of Georgia, Citizens Trust Company, Georgia
Savings Bank and Trust Company, First Georgia Bank, and
Peachtree Bank and Trust.

Unfortunately the flexibility suggested by the Atlanta bankers
is not characteristic. The inflexibility suggested by Walter Wriston
is, unfortunately for everyone. Bankers are highly resistant to
change. As for genuine reform, which is what some critics say
is badly needed, that may be unthinkable and impractical to
propose. Calls for what passes as reform do exist, as Chapters 14
and 15 show, but these efforts amount merely to tinkering with
the banking mechanism, not satisfying human needs and making
banking more responsive to people. Bankers will accept some
tinkering, of course, providing it involves some kind of advantage,
say permitting commercial banks such as Chase Manhattan to
establish beachheads in somebody else's market, e.g., savings bank
customers. Banks are also ecstatic over the prospect of a cashless
society. Though consumers really have no need for this bank
service, which is being thrust upon them—the bank would automatically receive the customer's paycheck and then pay all his
bills—banks desire it mightily since it would reduce their costs
and raise their profits. Customers would no longer write several
checks every month, which would reduce work for the bank, at
the same time it allowed them to charge additional fees.

The Dollar Barons is likely to be branded muckraking, since
one of its intents is to uncover abuses. And since abuses exist
in huge numbers, bankers will receive more knocks than plaudits.
But it is my contention that the knocks are well-deserved ones,
as anecdotes and other documentation attest. Like other critics
of banking, I am not anxious to help do in the free enterprise
system. On the contrary, like others I only ask that banking
serve everyone, not just the well off. Today the treatment meted
out to people unable to contribute to bank profits is sometimes
contemptible. Banking has also undermined the legislative process
and may well have corrupted generations of lawyers, whose
services are indispensable to bank practices. Since bankers

themselves seem especially vulnerable to corruption and self-dealing, the latter on a widespread and growing basis, *The Dollar Barons* begins with the subject of self-dealing. Perhaps no other practice demonstrates so well the spirit of bankers, which severe critics label arrogance.

C. E.

PART ONE

Privilege

1

Heritage

S O L O N G as there has been a banking system of one kind or another bankers have been permitted to operate in a private world of personal privilege as a kind of price governments and people pay to maintain their economies, for without banking no economy can flourish and grow. In the United States banker privilege began early, simultaneously almost with the first Bank of the United States, which was founded February 25, 1791, at the urging of Alexander Hamilton, Secretary of the Treasury, over the strong objections of James Madison, then a member of the House of Representatives, and Thomas Jefferson, Secretary of State. The establishment of the Bank of the United States provoked one of the first great fights over the implied and delegated powers of the federal government. Those who opposed the bank were tied generally to the land and to agriculture, and clearly feared the power of a central bank. Jefferson, for example, said it was of "deadly hostility, existing against the principles and form of our Constitution." He feared the United States itself would come under the "vassalage" of such a bank. Those in favor of the bank were the commerce-minded, monied interests of the Northeast cities.

Scarce gold and silver, in addition to narrowly circulating paper currencies of a few states, were the chief mediums of exchange, though notes and even land were sometimes used to make payments. In fact, the absence of a widely circulating legal tender was felt across economic lines and became a problem so acute that homes and lands were sold out from under debtors who were well off, but cash-short. In Massachusetts the problem even instigated rebellion when Daniel Shays, a former army captain, took a position that was clearly reasonable. If the state insisted that debts and taxes had to paid, he said, in effect, then the state had the responsibility of providing a legal tender.

Hamilton believed his bank would go a long way toward increasing the currency supply through its extensions of credit—the nub of commercial banking. Payments not only would be made with a sound legal tender, but also be made punctually. It was a plan that pleased the merchant interests, many of whom could see other, more direct benefits. Many of Hamilton's closest supporters, for example, had lent money to the government during the Revolutionary War, and could see that among the chores that would be required in order to set up a central bank would be the satisfying of old debts.

Like so many other insiders throughout history, though, some of Hamilton's supporters also saw a way to capitalize on a government action. The government would have to settle its debt with veterans of the Revolutionary War, who had been paid with a scrip that became worthless. Hamilton planned to redeem the scrip under a Redemption Plan, and in a day when communications were rare or nonexistent, his insider supporters were able to send agents throughout the United States to buy up the scrip for pennies on the dollar. Hamilton was so determined to get his bank founded that apparently he tacitly agreed to the exploitation, fearing perhaps that defections would hurt his cause considerably. Thus some of the most prestigious people of the day took advantage of their inside information and made hundreds of thousands of dollars.

There is no question that Hamilton needed all the support he could get, and that only a last-minute appeal of his own saved the bank. His argument, based on federal sovereignty, was so eloquent that President Washington changed his mind about vetoing the bill creating the bank. Jefferson, however, did manage to extract a condition that the bank be situated in Philadelphia, not New York.

Hamilton's bank lasted only twenty years, the life of its charter. It was allowed to die despite indications that the banking system it had spawned through branches in the major cities was doing just what had been hoped—providing a stable currency. But the bank was doing something else, something no one, not even Hamilton, had foreseen. It was acting as a restraint and control on credit. As the main depository for government receipts, the bank and its branches were always holding large numbers of notes and checks drawn on the rapidly expanding number of state banks that were feeding credit into commerce. By pressing the state banks for payment the bank was controlling credit and the well-being of the lending banks. The more a bank lent, the more it was in debt. Forcing it to redeem its debt put pressure on it to restrain further lending.

Control of their operations went down hard, though, among banks whose owners were embarked on heady, euphoric expansion. State bank charters zoomed from just 3 prior to the founding of the central Bank of the United States to 90 when it died in 1811. In five more years the number jumped to 250, then to 300 by 1820. The central bank also represented competition, and so killing it off became a kind of dirty crusade, though the public denouncements by opponents of the bank took the old form of arguing its constitutionality, arguments laid to rest twenty years before. Aiding the owners of the state banks were two other facts. One, the central bank's stock was owned in large part by English investors, and the ill will against that country that would culminate in the War of 1812 was already high. Two, many state legislators held stocks in state-chartered banks or were willing victims of the bank's influence peddling.

Many of those early state banks became monuments to greed once it dawned on their founders just what the role of commercial banks was. Banks were never mere depositories of money. Their lending created money, as they lent three, four, and five dollars for each dollar of capital they were able to take in. That is, if the banks were operated honestly and ethically. Many were operated for the self-serving interest of their owners, and their capital and deposits used in schemes benefiting no one but the owners and favored stockholders. One classic case that came to light early and shamed the entire industry was that of the Farmers Exchange Bank in Glocester, Rhode Island. The bank was incorporated in February, 1804, and capitalized at $100,000. Bray Hammond, a writer of bank history and once assistant secretary of the Federal Reserve Board, describes the bank's activities as a "sort of musical comedy," beginning with its founding. At the time, banks were founded with infusions of specie, i.e., gold and silver, provided by stockholders. The idea was to have the capital of a bank based in hard money, not paper. The stockholders of the Farmers Exchange Bank followed the prescribed routine, but in a few days replaced the specie with promissory notes. Then the bank embarked on a lending program, issuing its own notes to such an extent that by March, 1808, it had $22,514 in notes circulating and $380.50 in specie on hand in its vault. Though this seems an extraordinary creation of currency, which is what bank notes were in those days, it was not really, as a Boston financier named Andrew Dexter was soon to demonstrate.

Dexter was the owner of the Boston Exchange Office, one of a number of firms that bought up bank notes, like those of the Farmers Exchange Bank, at a discount and then presented them to the issuing banks for payment. All in all, operations like Dexter's were healthy. To be sure, Dexter made a profit, but his activities acted as a restraint on a bank's tendency to issue too many notes and thereby overextend itself. With fewer of them circulating, a bank's notes did not depreciate so much, either, and inflation was checked. But Dexter's eye fell on the Farmers Exchange Bank, probably after buying up some of its notes, and he saw in it the means of making huge personal profits—not by holding in check the number of notes it could issue but by doing just the opposite and expanding vastly the number of its notes in circulation.

In taking control of the bank Dexter used techniques still used in takeovers today, and the ethics and honesty of which are highly questionable. Basically, the technique results in a company paying for its own acquisition by an outsider. In recent times (as later chapters will show) conglomerate corporations have acquired companies by borrowing money from banks, then, when in control, using the assets of the acquired company to pay off the banks. In Dexter's day the technique was similar. After persuading the bank's eleven directors to sell him their equity, he used the assets of the bank to pay them off. After becoming the bank's chief stockholder and guiding force, he became its biggest borrower, taking as much money as he thought he needed and determining his own terms, e.g., interest rate, collateral, the length of time involved. Dexter, in fact, opened up a kind of Pandora's Box of self-serving schemes.

Dexter's chief claim for being included in this brief history of scheming bankers, however, was established when he left for Boston sometime in 1808 carrying the dies used by the bank to print its notes. In Boston he printed small-denomination notes, since they tended to stay in circulation longer and not be presented for payment, at a rate that approached $20,000 a day. He paid the bank's cashier $400 a year to sign the notes, which had to be sent to Glocester, then distributed them among speculators in Boston or exchanged them for the notes of other banks. To inhibit the notes from returning home and being presented for payment he sent them as far as possible—as far as Ohio, in fact. Eventually, Dexter's house of bank notes came tumbling down, and in fact became a subject for national discussion in Congress, where it was disclosed that Dexter had issued $800,000 in notes on a bank capital that totaled $45.

Though the Farmers Bank became a case dirtying all banks, it was far from the real headquarters of banker sin, a point documented by a generally unheralded founding father named

William Few. A contemporary and associate of Washington, Madison, Hamilton, and other prominent men of the period, Few was a man whose opposition to dishonesty among some of his peers may well have written him out of the history books, for his memoirs are biting testimony to the immorality of New York's bankers and its corrupt legislators.

Few was a judge and legislator. He had been a colonel in the militia during the Revolutionary War, defeating the British in Florida and the Carolinas and making peace between the Indians and settlers there. He had also been a member of the Continental Congress, had helped write the Constitution and was one of its signers. He then became one of the first United States Senators. Apparently Few was honest and dedicated in the extreme. For example, he aligned himself with Washington and others in outraged opposition to a plan hatched by some writers of the Constitution to create a class of nobles. In his home state of Georgia he aborted one of the first nationwide land grabs and swindles, paying the price when the Georgia legislature refused to return him to the United States Senate in a move he described as "one of the greatest mortifications I have ever experienced."

The ground for the land grab was laid in the early 1790s when land speculation reached boomlike proportions. At the time, Georgia's boundaries were still uncertain and large tracts of unlocated land existed. It was this unlocated land that caught the eye of speculators, some of whom were members of the Georgia legislature. As Few saw it, "one of the most wicked and corrupt combinations was formed in the legislature to sell to a company of speculators all the unlocated lands of the state, which included territory sufficient for a kingdom, for only $600,000 to $700,000. Several members of the legislature were purchasers and others were bribed."

The legislation that emerged from the scheme was the Yazoo Act. After its passage people as far away as Massachusetts and Connecticut bought land in Georgia. William Few fought the giveaway by introducing and getting passed an act that repealed the Yazoo Act, but the corrupted legislators raised the fascinating

question of whether a legislature could repeal and act on the
basis of bribery and corruption of several of its members even
though proved. Soon the Yazoo party was formed and the issue
was in turmoil. One of the consequences was that the people who
had purchased the Yazoo lands could not get title to those lands
from Georgia, and were thus swindled.

When the legislature refused to return Few to the United
States Senate, though he had national stature unmatched in
Georgia, he moved to New York in 1799, bitter over events.
He had helped more than anyone else to create, defend, and
make Georgia a factor in the nation.

In 1801, Few became a member of the New York Assembly
—where he discovered corruption was a way of life, not just
an aberration, especially in granting bank charters. In 1804 the
opponents of a charter for the Merchants Bank, which Hamilton
was backing, charged that the New York legislature had been
bought off by the Merchants. Called by the Assembly to investigate the charge, Few could only concur. He found that "avarice,
intrigue and corruption had prevailed. The bank was incorporated," he concluded, "the dignity of the legislature had been
wounded, and several of its members charged with bribery." The
bribery Few referred to took the form of a technique bankers
used again and again. They arranged for legislators to buy stock
at low prices, then redeemed the stock at higher prices.

The granting of the Merchants Bank charter in 1805 was only
the tip of the iceberg of corruption. After further investigation
of bank chartering, Few said, "It was now demonstrated that
there was no integrity and virtue in the representatives of the
state sufficient to resist the spending influence of the large,
monied institutions, and it is to be lamented that no bank has
since been incorporated that has not dishonored the legislature
with base bargaining, intrigue and corruption. Nor is there any
reason to believe that the same course will not continue to
produce the same effect, so long as the creation of banks continues to be the object of legislation."

Few himself eventually turned to banking, accepting a direc-

torship with the Bank of the Manhattan Company in 1804, just
in time apparently to assist the Manhattan Company in its war
against a charter being granted to the Merchants Bank. It was a
bitter war, complicated by the animosity between Aaron Burr and
Alexander Hamilton. The Bank of Manhattan had been founded
in 1799 by Aaron Burr, who actually had been granted a charter
to found a water works company for the City of New York. In
petitioning for the charter Burr had gulled Hamilton into helping
him acquire a charter that carried a clause somewhat vaguely
written but clear enough to allow Burr to found the bank as
well. Four years later, in 1803, Hamilton sought a charter for the
Merchants Bank referred to by Few, and was bitterly opposed
by the Manhattan Company Bank. Apparently after confirming
the extensive bribery of the Merchants Bank, Few saw little
wrong with the Manhattan Bank acting in kind, since it offered
half a million dollars of its stock to the state of New York to
suppress the Merchants Bank. The Manhattan Bank also poured
vast amounts of money into the campaign of Thomas Jefferson,
long an opponent of Hamilton, so much in fact that some historians suggest the Manhattan Bank got Jefferson elected to the
presidency.

   Yet Few remained an unreconstructed enemy of bankers'
self-serving practices. In 1814, after ten years as a director for
the Manhattan Bank, he was offered the appointment as president
of New York's City Bank, which was founded in 1812, and was
the forerunner of the First National City Bank of modern times.
Few was soon "disgusted with the cupidity and partiality of the
directors. They had taken on discounts and applied them to their
own use," he said in his memoirs, "more than one third of the
capital of the bank, and had speculated in the stock of the bank
in a manner which I conceived to be injurious, unwarrantable
and by which the interest of the bank was sacrificed to the
cupidity of the directors, against which I remonstrated and laid
before them a report which contained statements showing their
errors and pointing out the evils that had resulted and would
continue if the system was not amended."

Needless to say, Few was not reappointed the bank's president, and remained with it only to the end of his term two years later. Once, when he was the bank's president, he drew up a statement of facts to be published, but like many in banking today, especially many regulators of banking, he refrained from publishing detrimental facts "because they would diminish public confidence in the bank and injure stockholders." As newspapers have proved time and again, though, exposure sends swindlers to deep cover and often to jail. At the very least, the practices they are called to account for are stopped. Yet Few feared that publishing such facts would appear an act of revenge for not being reappointed, and this, plus his mistaken concern for public confidence, caused him to file his report away. Yet his private opposition to corruption was so fact-filled and intense that in 1815 he was appointed to a committee of bankers investigating the very crisis of confidence in banking Few had tried to avoid creating. Confidence in banks had become so weakened that the industry itself convened its key members to sit down, examine, and prescribe for the ills. Interestingly, they met outside New York, in Philadelphia and Baltimore.

The conventions failed in at least one purpose, for the self-dealing practices of some bankers have been handed down and still flourish. Consider, for example, the practice of contributing to political, especially presidential, campaigns, as the Manhattan Company did during Jefferson's campaign to stamp out the opposition party's Merchants Bank. The practice still has its practitioners.

In August, 1972, Congressman Wright Patman, the chairman of the House Banking and Currency Committee, feared that a contribution of $25,000 to President Nixon's campaign of that year was influential in granting a national bank charter by the Comptroller of the Currency, a regulator of banks and in charge of the federal agency that grants national charters to banks. The proposed bank involved was the Ridgeway National Bank of Minnetonka, Minnesota, and among those proposing the charter as an applicant was Dwayne Andreas, a Minnesota Democrat turned Republican fund raiser. Andreas had contributed $25,000 to the Nixon presidential campaign that year, giving the money first to Kenneth H. Dahlberg, Nixon's Midwest campaign finance officer. Dahlberg, too, was one of the bank's charter applicants. Just as pertinent in the eye of critics was the presence on the application of the name Frederick L. Deming, who at one time was an Under Secretary of the Treasury for Monetary Affairs. (Under Secretaries of the Treasury, like the Comptroller of the Currency, are part of the Office of the Treasury of the United States.) It was the speed with which the charter was granted as well as the obvious conflict that impelled inquiry from Patman and raised eyebrows among others such as Edward Driscoll of the Minnesota Department of Commerce. Ordinarily, individual bank charter applications tend to languish, taking many, many months to process. In the case of the Ridgeway National Bank of Minnetonka, granting the charter required a mere three months.

William B. Camp, the Comptroller of the Currency at the time and a man regarded by banking's harsher critics as being probank, angrily denied there had been political influence peddling. Granting a charter so speedily, he said, was merely a matter of giving the "good guys" a charter. "If you're not a good guy you're not going to get a charter," he responded to criticism made by Patman. Still other critics, less well known than Patman, observed after the response that banking must be full of good guys, because of the great number of charters that had been granted, especially by Camp's predecessor, James Saxon. The real issue, of course, was the $25,000 contribution and the granting of a charter just about the time the contribution was made to the man who made it, and to a former Treasury Under Secretary. The episode clearly smacked of influence peddling, even if none was intended. At the very least it was bad timing.

Still, it was Camp who sounded the alarm about an outbreak of self-serving loans (a traditional practice of bankers discovered by William Few at the City Bank in the early 1800s, but clearly older than that). In October, 1970, Camp followed up a warning by the Criminal Division of the Justice Department that bankers were making loans to each other at preferential interest rates. Such loans are one of the privileges bankers exact for themselves, but they are neither ethical nor legal, since a banker uses his bank's funds as a base, or lever, for getting personal and even business loans that enable him to buy another bank, for example, or increase his equity in his own. The practice developed from the fact that small banks borrow from larger banks to help swing loans they are unable to make on their own, say to customers with large credit needs. But the larger or correspondent banks, as they are called, require that the smaller banks maintain deposits as "compensating balances," often a percentage of the loans required by the small bank drawing no interest.

In a practice described as widespread in 1970 by Will Wilson, then Assistant Attorney General in charge of the Criminal Division of the Justice Department, small bankers were maintaining compensating balances with larger correspondent banks, which would lend money to the smaller bankers for personal use. It was Camp who sternly repeated to bankers everywhere the Justice Department warning to bankers to discontinue the practice, saying, "We believe that where the facts demonstrate a clear detriment to the bank and a concomitant benefit to its officers, this activity would, at a minimum, constitute a breach of the fiduciary duty owed by the officials to the bank and might in certain situations warrant prosecution action." Only a few such actions were taken, but enough so that bankers got the very serious message. One such indictment sought by the Justice Department and handed up by a grand jury in Oklahoma involved Howard Lee Brookshire, president of the First Bank in Atoka, Oklahoma. The grand jury charged that Brookshire deposited $30,000 of his bank's money in the Grayson County State Bank of Sherman, Texas, then got a loan of $30,000 from the Grayson County State Bank "at preferential terms." Brookshire pleaded guilty and was fined $2,000 but has appealed. In September, 1972, Henry E. Petersen, successor to Will Wilson in the post

of Assistant Attorney General over the Criminal Division, said
the Justice Department was still investigating similar self-serving
loans and more indictments may be coming, but suggested that
the "practice has diminished since the regulatory agencies advised
the banking community that said practice may be in violation of
Federal criminal statutes."

Typically, and unfortunately, broad general warnings such as
those issued by Comptroller William Camp and even the Justice
Department do not expose details—names, dates, amounts of
money involved—that would go far toward preventing not only
self-serving loans but also other self-serving practices. There is
no real reason to believe that such practices are diminishing, as
the Justice Department says self-serving loans are diminishing.
On the contrary, the experiences of the Federal Deposit Insurance
Corporation, another regulator of banks but one that gets more
into the sordid side, suggests just the opposite.

Besides refunding the money of depositors of banks that fail,
the FDIC is the receiver and liquidator of failed banks. It also
maintains a running list of 250 or so banks that are considered
"problem" banks, or those that are playing games that might
cause them to fail. In its unique position the FDIC has accumulated irrefutable evidence that self-serving practices, including
loans to officers, directors, and owners of banks, are major causes
of bank closings. In a survey of fifty-six bank failures the FDIC
determined that thirteen, or 23.2 percent, failed because of self-
serving loans to bank management. Another nineteen, or 34 percent, failed both because of self-serving loans and other factors,
e.g., loans that should not have been made.

Self-serving practices that are more unethical than law-breaking
are just one side of the picture uncovered by the FDIC. Bankers
are just as likely as anyone else to succumb to temptation and
commit serious crimes, such as embezzlement and fraud. The
same FDIC survey of fifty-six bank failures revealed that fourteen
of the banks, or 25 percent, went under because of "defalca-
tions," the FDIC's term for embezzlement.

Since most banks can absorb such losses and stay alive, a better understanding of how widespread embezzlement is is revealed by another set of figures. In 1970, for example, there were 4,125 embezzlements reported to the Federal Bureau of Investigation. How many went unreported is unknown—obviously those that went undetected plus many that banks preferred to handle themselves. The amounts involved in the reported embezzlements totaled $73 million, a figure, which taken in conjunction with the number of embezzlements, suggests growth as compared with 1969. In that year embezzlements reported to the FBI totaled 3,773, and only $33 million was involved.

As for that other serious crime, fraud, it runs wild. Bank fraud, in fact, is a growth industry, a view supported by John J. Slocum, chief of the FDIC's Division of Liquidation. Slocum regards bank fraud as "one of America's fastest-growing enterprises." Though bank robbers get the publicity, the statistics that follow show that fraud is a lively enterprise easily outstripping in recent years the activities of burglars and bandits.

Years	Number of Frauds	Amounts Taken Through Fraud	Amounts Taken by Burglars, Bandits
1970	245	$32.7 million	$12.6 million
1969	180	$16.9 million	$ 9.1 milion
1968	146	$11.2 million	$10.5 million

SOURCE: Federal Deposit Insurance Corp.

Fraud, embezzlement, and the self-serving practices of bankers take a variety of turns, and in describing such "inside manipulations" the FDIC has written a lexicon of the things bankers do to cause bank closings and to get banks put into the "problem bank" category maintained by the regulators. Some of the specific acts are looting, check kiting (writing a check on an account with no funds, but depositing funds before the check clears), collusion with borrowers, forged notes, fictitious notes, fraudulent use of blank unissued stock certificates, deposit ledger shortages, loans to questionable borrowers (e.g., loan sharks), false loan collateral, cash shortages, excessive charges made against expense accounts, loans on nonexistent collateral, lax collection policies, forward loan commitments, overinvestment in securities, unwarranted payments of cash dividends to controlling stockholders based on projected but unrealized income, manipulation of correspondent bank accounts, loans in excess of the legal limits, loans to phantom borrowers, and the misuse of official blank checks.

One of the unfailing characteristics of banks that fail or get their names put on problem lists is the use of brokered funds (money bankers solicit from money brokers to increase the lending capability of their banks), a practice that is legal but clearly dangerous. When banks make forward loan commitments they cannot honor, as when the Federal Reserve Board restrains the money supply to cool off the economy, money to lend becomes scarce, or "tight," and banks often turn to brokered funds. At such times small banks, which may have been counting on their larger, correspondent banks for funds, find the funds just aren't available. The committed banker then turns to money brokers. Such brokers operate in the main cities of the country, especially where there is an elderly population anxious to be paid in inflation-ridden times a higher interest rate than that banks will pay on what may be life savings. Credit unions and labor unions have also been known to siphon their funds into the hands of brokers, who scoop up such savings by advertising a rate 2 or 3 percent higher than local banks pay, and turn the money over to the committed banker, who may be far from the money centers. The files of the FDIC, in fact, consistently turn up lists of residents of New York, Massachusetts, and Miami Beach, for example, with money on deposit in small banks in the Midwest, Texas, and Virginia.

Used this way, brokered funds bring only mild objections from regulators, sometimes even approval. But brokered funds have become the means by which special deals are made by bankers who solicit them, paying as much as 20 percent or more, in violation of Federal Reserve banking laws (Regulation Q), then lending the money out at far higher rates of interest to speculative enterprises, e.g., land buying. Brokered funds, however, are "hot" money and their return is demanded on very short-term notice. Thus the very least that can befall a banker using a large amount of such funds is a loss in liquidity. As the table on page 420 suggests (A Tale of Brokered Funds, Tie-In Loans, and Dead Banks), brokered funds are clearly a factor in bank failures.

As an example, there is the case of the People's State Savings Bank of Auburn, Michigan. This particular bank lent money out on special deals involving brokered funds at 34 percent interest rates, according to one computation. As the table on page 420 shows, People's States Savings Bank (which was not really a savings bank, but a commercial bank), with only $9.9 million in deposits, had taken in over $2.7 million in brokered funds. Its tie-in loans, the special deals in which the brokered funds whisk through the bank's front door and out the back to a speculator, totaled more than $2.3 million.

Brokered funds have even been used to fuel the activities of loan sharks, as in the case of the Crown Savings Bank of Newport News, Virginia, a commercial bank despite its name. This bank did not solicit brokered funds, but financed the operations of loan brokers in New York, Virginia, and Georgia, lending over $4 million between 1962 and 1964. The loan brokers, in turn, lent the money to borrowers who paid as high as 30 percent to the brokers—and another 6 percent to the Crown Savings Bank. So far as the House Banking and Currency Committee could determine in an investigation of Crown, the money eventually went to convicted criminals and bankrupts. The committee determined, too, that much of the money was used to finance large-scale criminal and other illegal activities, and that in the two-year period involved the total funds flowing in and out of the bank were $10 million or more. In September, 1964, the

FDIC recommended that the state of Virginia close down Crown after fifty-nine years of operation. With assets of only $8 million, it had sustained a loss of $946,000 on its loans and over $1.5 million of the money lent to brokers in two years was still unpaid, though overdue.

Because of what the FDIC calls a "startling correlation'" between brokered funds activities and bank failures, the FDIC has supported, even advocated, legislation such as that proposed by Wright Patman in 1971 to outlaw brokered funds.

In recent years, the transactions that revolve around brokered funds, as well as other self-dealing practices, have been the cause of a growing number of bank closings. In the three years 1969, 1970, and 1971 twenty-three banks failed, an average of 7.6 a year, far above the 3.7 average number of closings for the twenty-five years ending in 1971.

The rise in numbers of bank closings is being accompanied by a rise in the size of the banks that are closing down and by an increase, as well, in the payout of the FDIC to depositors. In January, 1971, the FDIC made the largest payout in its history—$50 million—to depositors of Houston's Sharpstown State Bank. One month after the Sharpstown payout, in February, 1971, the FDIC made the largest financial assistance loan in its history—$103.4 million—to form a new bank in Detroit to replace the defunct Birmingham-Bloomfield Bank. Perhaps even more significant is that the FDIC's biggest rescue of a bank occurred in very recent times, too—a $60 million loan to prevent the Bank of Commonwealth, also of Detroit, from going under. At the time it was the fiftieth largest among the 14,000 or more banks of the United States with assets of nearly $1.5 billion and deposits of over $1 billion.

The pace of bank closings is as well measured by the judgments of men as by numbers and statistics, since their first-person accounts often add up to a better understanding of what is happening than can be deduced from cold statistics. One such account comes from Irvine H. Sprague, one of three FDIC directors until early in 1973 reporting to Frank Wille, chairman of the FDIC.

Sprague was appointed to the FDIC post by President Lyndon B. Johnson on September 27, 1968. From the beginning he was swept up in a whirlwind of closings. When he arrived at the FDIC bank closings were just about to take off. Mild-mannnerd and with a subtle sense of humor, Sprague insisted when being interviewed that "my joining the corporation had nothing to do with what happened next. I was sworn in on September 27, 1968, and went up to the Supreme Court where my old friend, Earl Warren, was kind enough to swear me in. Then I went with my family to the White House to pay my respects to Lyndon Johnson. Then I came over to the corporation [the FDIC] and was here punctually . . . say at ten minutes to four. At four o'clock we had an emergency meeting. So I got a very rapid introduction to bank closings. Obviously, I didn't know what was going on, but the other two directors knew what should be done. That was the first one."

In the months that followed, especially in 1969, Sprague was indoctrinated as no director before him had been. "A very quick sequence of bank closings occurred," he recalls. "The first one came along and I went down to Texas. They had a little bank close in Dodson, Texas, just a crossroads. I was still in Texas when another bank closed in a place called Lovelady. The first one closed May 12, 1969; the second one May 28, 1969. Then I went back later in the year for a bank closing on August 25 in Big Lake, Texas. Before I got back to Washington another one closed in Aransas Pass, Texas. That was September 2, 1969. So you can see they came in clusters."

Sprague credits the recession during 1969–70 with "flushing out a lot of high flyers. As long as the economy was expanding and money was free and easy," he says, "land speculators and the other operator types made out on an expanding situation. When we had that recession money got tight and these fellows, the bankers, were overextended on speculation and on unsound loans. There were in oil drilling and real estate and in shopping centers, too. Banks should finance legitimate expansion, of course," Sprague maintains, "but if they put so much of their resources into speculations, the speculations can close the bank if they don't turn out right."

Sprague is also irked by loans bankers make to each other to buy greater control of their banks or to buy other banks, especially through stock purchases. Like so many regulators, Sprague prefers not to name names of live banks, but those in the story that follow could well be Detroit's Bank of Commonwealth and its former owner Donald Parsons, and the Chase Manhattan Bank. The story of their dealings is told later.

The FDIC lent $60 million to the Bank of Commonwealth, preventing it from failing. "There was a fairly large bank," Sprague began, "which was closely held by a small group. The group got its leverage to go into the banking business and to expand its control of it and other banks because the members of the group had fairly easy access to large amounts of money from a large bank. In other words, the large bank lent them money to expand. But in their expansion they pursued policies which our bank supervisory division construed to be extremely unsound. In the course of that they engaged in some self-dealing things I'm opposed to—loans to affiliates, loans to favored groups, loans to themselves. Well, of course, it's not against the law for a bank director to borrow money. There's no rigid formula of what's proper, but when an extraordinary percentage of a bank's loans are to insiders, well, they're not serving the public. They're running the bank for their own benefit. I think the larger banks, the ones that do the lending, have a function in exercising some caution in how they finance individuals expanding their banking business. They have a moral and a legal obligation to exercise some real judgment in making these loans." Such loans can boomerang badly, Sprague continued. "I know of one banking group that got burned very badly. They financed some acquisitions on a bank that closed, and they lost their ass on it. Now I understand they've changed their procedures and they're not so free and easy in these bank stock loans. Which is a good thing."

Sprague also argues against banks taking an equity interest when making loans, as some banks are beginning to do. He bluntly says he wants the practice outlawed. "I think legislation to outlaw it should be enacted in the public interest. The incentive to get into speculative deals is just magnified by equity kickers. You look at these bank closings where the speculation is just one step removed, where the bank would lend to a developer or a speculator in land. The bank would get a high rate of interest, the operator would share in the return. If the banks could speculate directly it would be a very unsavory situation. If you have an operator in a bank who has the ability to do that it would change the whole concept of a bank's business. Instead of serving the community he'd be looking around for a hot piece of action. Instead of serving the public the tone and the direction of banking would change."

No less a bank than the First Pennsylvania of Philadelphia denies that equity positions, small ones, are detrimental to banking. John Bodine, who became president of the First Pennsylvania in 1972, is one bank executive, at least, who approves of them. Small equity positions, by giving a bank a share of an enterprise's earnings, help justify loans to some marginal businesses. The bank, supposedly, has no control. "In my judgment," Bodine has said, "if the banks are going to do the job the community deserves from the banks, the banks have to be permitted to get in on a piece of the action. We're making loans we could not possibly make if we were not provided with some kind of equity. The kind I'm referring to is relatively minor. It would never be construed as control, which I consider to be 20 to 25 percent. We're not necessarily talking about ownership, either, but in equity, earnings." Nor would a bank favor lending to the borrower who hands over equity, Bodine asserts, saying banks would never favor one borrower because of a bank's equity interest, simply because the bank would be narrowing its own market.

Thus, unlike Sprague at the FDIC, Bodine sees the conflict as an academic one. Sprague, on the other hand, says, "Equity kickers are an opportunity to change the nature of banking, and you can get a good debate on whether it would be good or bad. My position is it would be bad."

Sprague, of course, is clearly conditioned by the dark side of banking. He copes with problem banks on a daily basis; he helps create marriages among them to save them from failing; and he —and the entire FDIC—are the ones called when a bank has died.

Such conditioning causes regulators to look for ways to cure banks before they get into deep trouble, much less die. In fact, the guiding philosophy of the FDIC is to keep a bank alive if it can. But even when a trouble bank is spotted, the authority of regulators is limited, and the FDIC seeks what it calls a "cease and desist" authority. Under it the agency could remove bank officers or fine them for willfully violating an FDIC order forbidding some of the self-dealing practices that destroy a bank. The FDIC already has cease and desist authority, but it can invoke it only where dishonesty clearly exists. Even then, though, a banker can be relatively sure that the FDIC won't seek the court approval that is necessary for enforcement, since the publicity might well cause a run on the bank and close it down. This is exactly what happened in the case of the Sharpstown State Bank of Houston.

The FDIC, of course, can also withdraw its insurance as a kind of club to keep straying bankers in line, but once again, such news would undoubtedly cause a run on the bank. The problem, obviously, is one of overkill, of having too much medicine and that administering it will hurry the bank along to oblivion. "What we need," Sprague says, "is a mechanism by which we can remove bank officers or fine them for violating a permanent cease and desist order. The authority would operate through private administrative hearings, rather than the public courts."

2

Seldom-Told Tales

NOTHING SUGGESTS more painfully to Irvine Sprague and others of the Federal Deposit Insurance Corporation the need for something less than a very big stick than the closing of the Sharpstown State Bank in Houston in January, 1971. Practically all the self-dealing practices that point to a bank in trouble were present. For example, the bank lent money to legislators and administration officials of Texas, including Governor Preston Smith, to buy the unregistered stock of a life insurance company controlled by the bank's chief executive, Frank W. Sharp. Sharp then arranged the sale of the stock, manipulating the price upward in a deal with a friendly Jesuit order, to insure a profit for the politicians. In return, Sharp expected passage of legislation that would eliminate the FDIC as a regulator of Texas banks, including his own.

Besides manipulating stock prices and trying to influence legislators with what was seen by the courts as plain bribery, Sharp engaged in many another classic self-serving deal handed down from the past. He lent the bank's money to friends to buy control in others' banks, specifically the City Bank and Trust Company of Dallas and the Dallas Bank and Trust Company, which had deposits over $20 million each. Sharp did not overlook himself, either. He borrowed enormous amounts to speculate in real estate. At one time he owed his bank $30 million. Such lending practices helped put his bank into a position where it had loans outstanding equal to 85 percent of its total deposits, which at the time of the bank's failure totaled $81.3 million. Regulators say that about 65 percent ought to be a maximum.

As the table on page 420 suggests, Sharp also steered his bank into soliciting brokered money, tying the funds nearly always into special high-risk loans such as land speculation. The table does not suggest, however, the true velocity of the soliciting. Since brokered funds characteristically are hot money, and, seemingly, often withdrawn on whim, they depart from a bank with a suddenness that can leave the banker scrounging for money to take their place. Brokered funds are often lent to a bank for relatively short periods, say a year, and a bank that issues, for example, certificates of deposit in great number finds itself on a merry-go-round of demands for payment as the certificates mature.

It was this kind of situation that confronted the Sharpstown State Bank, and as a result it was nearly always facing a liquidity, or cash-short, crisis. Sharp had managed to keep all the maturities from running him completely out of cash by soliciting even more brokered funds, but the liquidity crisis never really receded, and it was this that eventually pulled down the bank.

Two events triggered its failure. The first was a civil suit filed with Federal Judge Sarah T. Hughes on January 18, 1971, by the Securities and Exchange Commission charging Sharp and others with fraud and stock manipulation. The second event, which itself was triggered by the SEC suit, was a $15 million run on the bank by depositors that exhausted the bank's cash. In the weeks preceding both the run and the suit Sharp had been frantically paying out cash on maturing certificates of deposit that had come due in a crush. But in the days following the SEC suit the SEC took the position that the bank could no longer solicit brokered funds, contending in court that if it did it would be engaging in gross securities fraud since it was not disclosing its financial problems—i.e., that the only way it could pay back maturing certificates would be to issue more of them. Within Houston no bank wanted to come to the rescue of Sharpstown with funds, since Houston's bankers believed the run could not be checked that way and new infusions of cash would just be lost.

On January 25, 1971, just a week after the SEC suit had been filed, Sharp gave up trying to keep his bank alive with his round robin of brokered deposits and turned it over to Texas State Banking Commissioner Robert Stewart. Many times in the past Stewart had tried to persuade Sharp to change his ways, but Sharp saw the regulator as a bureaucrat to be ignored. Now Stewart called in the FDIC to act as receiver and to begin paying back the 27,300 depositors of the Sharpstown State Bank.

But the FDIC considered, too, whether it might be worthwhile to save the bank, perhaps through persuading an existing bank to step in with FDIC loan backing. Or the FDIC could create a new bank, lend it some money, and avoid a closing. In the end, though, the FDIC feared another bank, newly created or otherwise, would be subjected to expensive class action suits that could result from the scandal the FDIC knew would be emerging. The FDIC would then be in the position of guaranteeing the payment of any awards coming out the suits, since the FDIC accepts responsibility for a defunct bank's liabilities.

The SEC suit, which included 4,000 pages of depositions, told a story about Sharp that ran the length of banker self-dealing—fraud, stock manipulation, bribes, influence peddling, land speculation, and even "looting his bank." Besides Sharp, the suit charged twenty-seven other individual and corporate defendants, among them a former attorney general of Texas named Waggoner Carr who achieved some degree of national fame when he ran against but lost to U.S. Senator John Tower in 1968. Carr had also been a gubernatorial aspirant. Charged, too, was former State Insurance Commissioner John Osorio, a business and law partner of Carr's, and president between 1962 and 1970 of the National Bankers Life Insurance Company—the company whose stock had been manipulated by Sharp. Other defendants included Tom Max Thomas, once an associate in the law firm operated by Carr and Osorio; Joseph P. Novotny, president of the Sharpstown State Bank; Audy Byram, an officer of the Carr and Osorio business operations; and three brokers employed by a Dallas brokerage named Ling and Company: J. Quincy Adams, Phillip M. Procter, and James Farha. The corporate and business defendants named in the SEC suit were National Bankers Life Insurance Company, the Sharpstown State Bank, the Dallas Bank and Trust Company, the Olympic Insurance Company, the Employees Retirement plan of the National Bankers Life Insurance Company, and a handful of business enterprises that included Sharp's own, e.g., Sharpstown Realty Company, Oak Forest Realty Company, and Oak Forest Investment Company.

The cast of characters that truly raised eyebrows everywhere, however, was not the list of the accused, but the list of people in high political station who had benefited or tried to benefit from Sharp's maneuvering. Heading the list was Preston Smith, governor of Texas. According to the SEC papers supporting its suit and Smith's own later admission, the Texas governor bought 10,000 shares of National Bankers Life Insurance stock, which was unregistered with the SEC, at a price of $13.75 a share. The date was July 25, 1969. At the same time, Elmer C. Baum, an osteopath by trade, but more important, chairman of the state Democratic party, also bought 10,000 shares of the same stock. The Sharpstown State Bank lent $275,000 to make the transaction, and kept the stock as collateral. On September 8 Smith recommended that the state legislature, which was meeting in special session, take up a state bank deposits insurance bill Sharp wanted passed. Dutifully, Representative Thomas Shannon of Fort Worth introduced the bill. Shannon, too, according to the SEC suit, had bought the common stock of National Bankers Life Insurance Company with money lent by the Sharpstown State Bank, as had Gus F. Mutscher, Jr., speaker of the House of Representatives ($130,000); S. Rush McGinty, Mutscher's administrative assistant; F. C. Schulte ($22,000), another administrative assistant; Representative Thomas C. Shannon; and Representative W. S. Heatly, deemed by political observers in Texas as one of the most powerful members of the Texas House of Representatives at one time. (Nine months later a Texas grand jury handed up criminal indictments charging that Mutscher, Shannon, and Mc-Ginty had conspired to accept a bribe when they had accepted Sharp's loans to buy stock. The men were convicted on March 15, 1972.)

On September 12, 1969, less than two months after Governor Smith and Baum had bought their 20,000 shares, the SEC said in its charge, the Sharpstown State Bank sold their shares and those bought by Shannon, Mutscher, and the rest. The price was $20, determined by Sharp. In all, a total of $675,000 was paid over for 33,750 shares. In the public market the securities were selling for $15 or $16. Governor Smith, who had put up nothing, made $62,500. Baum made the same. Together, the two men had made $125,000 in seven weeks without advancing a cent of their own. In testimony developed during the bribery trial of Mutscher, Shannon, and McGinty, Joseph P. Novotny, the Sharpstown State Bank president, testified that a total of seven man had made $193,000. Novotny himself turned out to be a pawn of Sharp's with no real power. Though president, he was required to get Sharp's permission to grant loans higher than $10,000.

When Sharp chose the Jesuit order as the goat for the stock price manipulation, he had been especially cynical, for the members of the order were not strangers with a potful of investment money asking to be taken. On the contrary, Sharp had been regarded as so important a friend of the order that it had presented him to the Pope in Rome—a singular compliment for a Protestant. Indeed, it wasn't until March 10, 1972, two years after Sharpstown was closed down and going on three years after the Jesuits had bought the insurance company stock at a Sharp-inflated price, that a leading member of the order would bring himself to tell what had happened. Testifying in the bribery trial of Mutscher, McGinty, and Shannon, the Reverend Michael Kennelly told a story to an Abilene court that created a startling picture of Sharp.

At the time of testifying, Reverend Kennelly was president of

Loyola University in New Orleans, but in 1969 when Sharp advised him to buy the National Bankers Life Insurance Company stock at $20 a share, Reverend Kennelly was president of Strake Jesuit Preparatory College in Houston. He had known Sharp since the 1950s, he said, when Sharp had contributed land and financial aid, even to giving 20,000 shares of bank stock to the Jesuits, to help start Strake Jesuit Prep. Soon Reverend Kennelly and Stark were close friends—at least Reverend Kennelly saw it that way. "I generally sought his advice in matters financial," the priest told the court. The truth was that Reverend Kennelly put extraordinary trust in Sharp's advice. Besides paying higher than market prices for National Bank Insurance Company stock on Sharp's say-so, the order had put out a bond issue, also on Sharp's advice, the receipts of which the SEC charged had been converted into assets for the use of Sharp in his enterprises. In their naïveté, though, they had complete trust in Sharp, even rejecting, again on his advice, the need for legal counsel suggested by their law firm. (The firm had no less an associate than John Connally, President Nixon's Secretary of the Treasury for a time and once governor of Texas.)

Since they took no one else into their confidence, the precise relations between the Jesuit order and Sharp are vague, except that the order looked on him as a benefactor. Records suggest that Sharp gave the Jesuits land for construction of an auditorium, a fieldhouse, and other facilities at the Strake Preparatory College. He reportedly gave the order $3 million as well, but along with the other gifts this actually was part of a $6 million debt the order owed Sharp. Yet in appreciation of such generosity the Jesuits bestowed honor after honor on him. For example, for the first time in its four hundred–year history the order, which was part of the New Orleans Province of the Society of Jesus, named a Protestant—Sharp was a Methodist—a "provincial superior."

Considering the close relationship and his admitted ignorance of finance, Reverend Kennelly saw no reason not to agree to meet Sharp at the Sharpstown State Bank on September 11, 1969, to discuss the sale of the order's 20,000 shares of bank stock. It was at this meeting that Sharp advised buying the National Bankers Life Insurance Company stock with the proceeds from the sale. When Reverend Kennelly arrived at the bank that day, both Mutscher and Shannon were waiting with Sharp, who then asked the priest to write checks on the Jesuit Order account in prescribed amounts for Mutscher, Shannon, and McGinty. In addition, Reverend Kennelly wrote two checks to individuals he did not name during his testimony.

On the next day, September 2, 1969, Governor Smith and Baum sold their shares of National Bankers Life Insurance Company stock, too.

It had been a smooth enough deal for Sharp to make, but now in the state capital of Austin the legislation Sharp wanted passed so badly, which had been introduced by Representative Shannon just a few days earlier and passed in the final minutes of a second special session, was heading into trouble. Sharp had led Mutscher and other legislators to believe the legislation would merely permit Sharp to supplement FDIC insurance protection, and many in the legislature, believing this, had voted favorably. Actually the bill would let Sharp and other Texas banks give up the FDIC protection—and its supervision—and the real meaning of the bill was getting around. All that was needed was Governor Smith's signature, but Smith delayed signing the measure, and on September 29, 1969, instead vetoed the Texas Depositor Protection Act.

Behind the veto, though Governor Smith did not acknowledge it, was the opposition to the bill by bankers who were sour on the idea of Texas-based insurance companies insuring deposits in place of the FDIC. Once before, in the economic depression of the 1930s, there had been a Texas deposit guarantee, but it failed miserably and the bankers hadn't forgotten. The president of the Texas Bank Association in 1969 was a banker named Derrell Henry. As he recalled the events that led up to the veto, he said of the bill, "We in the association felt the present in-

surance offered by the FDIC adequately covered depositors'
needs, based on very low depositor loss over the years. I contacted the governor, or rather, he contacted me, and asked for a
recommendation. We felt that we needed to act fast. We had no
chance to go behind the bill and so we had no chance to obtain
any of the background. We knew only what was on the face of
the bill. Certainly we were not aware of any of the ramifications.
The bankers feared that the Texas bill would let smaller state
banks withdraw from the FDIC, which at the time was offering
coverage up to $15,000, and buy greater protection from Texas
insurance agencies."

Sharp's irritation with the FDIC began as early as 1967,
when the FDIC began questioning the quality of the loans he
was making: loans to himself to further his own business interests,
to his family, to the bank's other directors, and for his real estate
deals. Time and again the FDIC and Texas banking officials
urged Sharp to stop dealing for himself, to liquidate what they
considered bad loans, and to call for more collateral behind
others. But bad loans, instead of being liquidated, were often
transferred from bank to bank or to insurance companies Sharp
controlled. Robert E. Stewart, banking commissioner at the time,
told once how he "would go into Sharpstown and find a bad loan
and tell them they ought to get it off the books. Pretty soon it
would disappear. It would be paid. But soon it would show up
at one of the Dallas banks. We would complain and soon it
would show up at one of the two insurance companies, National
Bankers Life Insurance in Dallas or Olympic Life Insurance
Company in Fort Worth. Both were defendants in the SEC suit.
We were chasing the same loans in those three banks and in
those two insurance companies until we thought we were chasing
our tails."

Even after trying to "get the FDIC off my back," as Sharp
described his abortive attempt to set up a Texas deposit insurance
system, he continued to oppose the FDIC and other regulators.
He ignored Stewart, for example, who was relatively young and

new to his job as commissioner, as inconsequential in terms of real regulatory power. It was typical of Sharp as a wheeler-dealer to display such arrogance.

Even the FDIC was given the back of Sharp's hand late in 1970 and only a few months before his bank was closed. Sharp agreed, after FDIC prodding, to take on a new president in the Sharpstown State Bank, one recommended by the FDIC. The man was Dallas A. Johnson, a onetime agent of the Federal Bureau of Investigation, expert in bank fraud techniques, and a man who knew how to bail out a bank in trouble. In April, 1970, Johnson was hired to replace Sharp as chairman and chief executive at a salary of $50,000 a year for five years. Johnson set to work at once, attempting such remedial action as holding the line on loans to bank officers—Sharp included. Johnson's work was all in vain, though. Sharp countermanded his orders time and again in the months that followed and Sharp's own loans rose in this period from $22 million to $30 million. In November Sharp fired Johnson for getting in his way. The last straw apparently had been several million dollars lent to borrowers for stock purchases. They were the kind of loans that, though classified by the FDIC as "doubtful" and "substandard," had risen to a total of $15 million during Johnson's tenure, though all the while the value of the stocks bought with the money declined sharply in the bear market of 1970. The losses sustained, in fact, exceeded the capitalization of the Sharpstown State Bank.

With Johnson fired, the FDIC and Stewart examined the books of the bank. In a meeting with the bank's directors Stewart said the bank was insolvent and would have to be closed unless the capital loss caused by the loss in the value of stocks held by the bank was restored. Stewart and the FDIC also demanded that the bank find someone to replace Johnson. In response Sharp said he would give equity he owned in the Sharpstown Shopping Center, a realty business, to the bank. It was an unusual but acceptable solution to the bank's troubles, and Sharp began to look for buyers of his equity in the shopping center. He also began to interview candidates to replace Johnson. But in January, 1971, the SEC suit was filed.

A few months later, on June 14, Sharp himself was brought to trial on a federal information, a method of charging that by-passes grand jury action. Sharp waived a trial by jury and was allowed to plead guilty to minor charges. In one he admitted making a false entry in the books of the bank on December 17, 1968, a date seemingly chosen at random, since there were far more significant dates. In a second he admitted to selling un-registered stock of National Bankers Life Insurance Company. To the amazement of just about everyone who understood the extent of his maneuvers, Sharp was then found guilty by a U.S. District Judge named John V. Singleton who fined him $5,000 and put him on probation for three years. The judge reasoned that it was better to keep Sharp free "to remain a productive member of society." Next, Sharp was granted immunity from any state or federal prosecution growing out of the bank's operations and its stock deals—of which Sharp, of course, had been the author.

Under the law, Sharp could have been sentenced to as many as ten years in prison and fined up to $10,000, but he had agreed to testify before a federal grand jury investigating the bank's failure. So lean a sentence, however, provoked a great deal of conjecturing over his real influence.

The leniency shown Sharp was authorized in Washington by Richard Kleindienst, who resigned as President Nixon's Attorney General in 1973 during the Watergate furor. At the time of the Sharp trial Kleindienst was Deputy Attorney General and second in rank in the Justice Department. In a letter to Anthony J. P. Farris, the U.S. Attorney in Houston, Kleindienst wrote, ". . . You are hereby authorized to seek a grant of immunity for Sharp in the event he is called to testify before the grand jury in connection with the operation of the Sharpstown State Bank and assert his Fifth Amendment protection against self-incrimination."

Unquestionably, the deal was an extraordinarily good one for Sharp, who had, after all, been the eye of the hurricane. It had been negotiated for weeks by Sharp's attorney, Morton Susman, who even asked another judge, Sarah T. Hughes, who was scheduled to hear the SEC civil suit a few months later in August, 1971, to dismiss charges against Sharp. Susman's reasoning, which seems out of touch with reality, was that since Sharp had received immunity from "any prosecution, penalty or forfeiture," the immunity should apply to the civil case as well. In its complaint against Sharp and the other defendants the SEC was seeking an injunction forbidding the defendants from any further violation of the securities laws. Susman, in another interesting sample of reasoning, said that since the injunction was a penalty and forfeiture, Sharp was already immune from it.

Judge Hughes, however, was unimpressed by this reasoning and Sharp stood trial in the SEC civil suit, and along with eight other defendants, including Waggoner Carr, the former attorney general, was found guilty of violating federal securities laws. Judge Hughes then issued court orders prohibiting further illegal stock transactions.

Sharp's immunity from criminal prosecution was granted without the knowledge, much less the consent, of the SEC, which needless to say, was angry about it. James Sims, the attorney in charge of the SEC's Houston office, clearly felt betrayed. Sims and his staff had put in months unraveling Sharp's manipulations and Sims voiced his displeasure in plain enough language. "The SEC," he said caustically and in public, "was not a party to the negotiations leading to this plea and was purposely excluded by the Justice Department. Since the SEC developed the entire case the procedure was unusual." Sims then added in an obvious understatement that the Justice Department had been negotiating with Sharp "behind our backs."

Sharp's deal may have confounded the SEC, but it is a common enough practice that occurs when jails are overcrowded, when a judge has too many cases, or when a prosecutor has too many cases. It also occurs when a defendant has unusual power. In Sharp's case, it was the last. His deal was hatched by U.S.

Attorney Anthony J. P. Farris, according to Sims. Farris had said that SEC attorneys held too much "animosity" toward Sharp, a strange pronouncement for a prosecutor. Farris also said the pleas were accepted because they were based on charges "where we could make a case." This, too, is strange considering that the SEC had collected vast quantities of evidence. But Farris also believed that having Sharp, the kingpin, as a federal witness was a golden opportunity for prosecuting lesser fry involved in the scandal.

There is little doubt in the minds of anyone who followed the Sharpstown State Bank failure that a large political factor must be "folded in," as bakers describe the subtle mixing of ingredients in their oven dramas. It is a fact that one of the characteristics of banking is that it breeds incestuous relations among people regarded as the establishment.

Sharp was no country banker. He was a Texan in all that designation implies: a speculator who liked to see money whirl at its greatest velocity and who operated in the flamboyant manner and pattern admired in Texas. If his philosophy was to make money work faster than regulators like, it is a philosophy shared by many, many people, especially other Texans. The state was run by his close associates, who clearly admired him or were tied to him in some covert way. Many high-ranking Texans knew him personally, liked him, and were often involved with him. Any criminal trial would have exposed politicians, Republicans and Democrats alike, both state and national, to a glare of unwanted publicity.

As an example of how widespread bankers' roots can be there is Will Wilson, who, it will be recalled, as Assistant Attorney General of the Criminal Division of the Justice Department admonished bankers about making self-serving loans. Farris, the U.S. Attorney in Houston who made the deal with Sharp's lawyer giving Sharp immunity, did so on the orders of Richard Kleindienst. But Farris answered directly to Wilson who, when he had been practicing law in Texas between 1963 and 1968, had

had Sharp as a client. Before that, between 1956 and 1962, when he had been a member of the three-man Texas bank board (which issues the required charters for state banks) and the Texas attorney general, Wilson had approved the charter application of the Sharpstown State Bank.

To be sure, Wilson disqualified himself from the case and publicly disassociated himself from Sharp and the Sharpstown State Bank when the bank failed, but in October, 1971, barely nine months after the closing and only a month after the SEC suit had been tried, Wilson resigned from his job at the Justice Department amid a chorus of criticism. The criticism developed not over Wilson's past associations, but over his acceptance, according to news accounts, of large, unsecured loans from Sharp, and for advice he gave Sharp on how he might avoid banking regulations in Texas.

As for other well-placed individuals involved with Sharp, many of them suffered for their association. It is doubtful that Governor Preston Smith will ever rid himself of the humiliation. No charges were brought against him—except during campaign time when his opponent suggested that bankers were no longer petitioners of government in Texas but manipulators. Nor were charges brought against Elmer Baum, the Democratic state party chairman. Former Attorney General Carr was indicted, however, on fraud and conspiracy charges, while House Speaker Gus Mutscher and his two aides, Tommy Shannon and Rush McGinty, were sentenced to five years of probation. The convictions were felony convictions, which of course deprived them of ever again holding public office.

The shame of the Sharpstown State Bank case spread through Texas all during 1971, arousing its people and its legislature to the point that new strict laws now guide banks and bankers. Some of the new laws were precisely the kind the FDIC hopes to see adopted on a national level. They stem from an investigation launched by Lieutenant Governor Ben Barnes just days after the closing of the Sharpstown State Bank. Heading the investigation was Hubert W. Green, Jr., a lawyer who had been so stalwart a county prosecutor that the Texas Law Foundation had named him "Outstanding Texas Prosecutor." Perhaps more significant was that Green had not associated much with state officials.

Bankers throughout Texas welcomed the investigation, Green said later, not only because of the Sharpstown closing, but because bank closings in Texas were dominating the list of closings being compiled by the FDIC. The table (A Roster of Closed Banks) on pages 416–17 shows why the bankers were concerned. Just in 1969, five of the nine closings occurred in Texas.

Most of the banks being closed were state-chartered banks, and Green's investigation largely was aimed at determining whether state bank supervision and chartering routines were deficient. He soon found that force of will often counted far more than holding the office in regulating bankers. For example, when Robert Stewart succeeded J. M. Falkner as banking commissioner he was just forty years old and had been all but invisible as deputy banking commissioner. His predecessor, on the other hand, had become highly visible in a twenty-three-year tenure that lasted until illness forced him out at age seventy-nine. When Stewart, the unknown, ran up against Sharp, the all-powerful, the results could have been forecast. Falkner could telephone Sharp or any other banker and bark orders he had no legal right to bark. Nevertheless, the orders were obeyed. Though most bankers accepted Stewart, the Sharps of Texas would not. Sharp had never been frightened by the office and looked on Stewart as just another bureaucrat.

The lesson of the situation, of course, was that the regulatory agencies of Texas sadly needed new banking laws and regulations that could be realistically enforced even by a young, untried commissioner. What Falkner had done through force of personality had to be accomplished through laws. To be sure, the commissioner could remove an officer and even the directors of a bank, but the order doing so could be appealed to the Texas Banking Board, a politically vulnerable three-man group. The commissioner himself is a member of the board, but the other two members could easily be in the opposite corner since one is the state treasurer and runs for office every two years, while the other is a citizen appointed by the governor. The governor, too, runs for office every two years in Texas. Considering the effectiveness of Sharp in Texas politics, the commissioner ran a very real risk of undercutting his own authority if he insisted a bank's officers and directors be removed to solve the bank's problems.

When Green had finished his investigation he worked out eight bills for enactment by the legislature. Of the eight, seven were adopted. In one bill the commissioner acquired the right to issue cease and desist orders to stop self-serving practices. If the orders were ignored, the commissioner could levy fines. The law let him remove offending officers as well (something the FDIC succeeded in doing for only a short time in the Sharpstown State Bank), though it still gave bankers the right to appeal. The difference, though, was that appeals had to be made not through the three-man Banking Board, but through a six-man Banking Section of the Texas Finance Commission, the members of which are four bankers and two businessmen. Thus appeals would be decided by a banker's peers, a situation that really does not recognize the right of the public, i.e., depositors, since bankers might tend to favor fellow bankers and businessmen are much more closely allied with banks than with the general public. Still, the bill represented improvement.

Another bill gave the banking commissioner the right to put a bank under the control of a conservator if the bank's capital was threatened or if the bank violated banking laws and regulations. Fraudulent practices can bring on the appointment of a conservator, as can practices that threaten a bank's solvency—or dirty its reputation. If a bank resists the conservator's control and fails to get back on its feet, which is what happened in the Sharpstown State Bank, the commissioner can liquidate the bank. The law, however, also provides him with a smaller club than liquidation. Even before appointing a conservator he can attempt to straighten out a bank's affairs merely by having the officers adhere to a list of management practices he sets up. In this period the bank cannot dispose of any assets, lend or invest its funds, nor take on additional debts and liabilities.

The Texas legislature also gave the commissioner a number of other powerful options to control bankers, among them a string on brokered funds. The legislature required that bankers notify the commissioner in writing when brokered funds were being accepted, including such information as who was depositing the funds, who was borrowing them, and what the general conditions were that had caused the bank to solicit brokered funds. The law also gave the commissioner the power to limit the amount of brokered funds a bank can accept if he finds the bank is in jeopardy. He can even stop the bank from accepting brokered funds at all, or he can classify such funds as debt, i.e., a note or a bond of the bank's, and not as a deposit. Thus the brokered funds would not be covered by FDIC insurance.

With other laws the Texas legislature attacked the problems of disclosure in bank stock purchases, conflicts of interest among regulators, violations of cash reserve requirements, and the rights of bankers to appeal decisions of the commissioner.

Under the law governing disclosure the legislature required that buyers of stocks in banks must tell all. They must reveal under oath, for example, who the beneficial owners are, how the stock purchase is being financed, whether the stock is being used as collateral, whether the stock is being bought with borrowed money, and the source of that money. Such information reveals whether a stock purchaser is merely an investor in a bank or a front man serving some powerful individual or another bank trying to gain control.

In dealing with conflict of interest the legislature forbade Banking Board members to be connected with the management of a bank in any way, and directed that the "citizen" member of the three-man board must "represent the interests of the general public."

In recognition of bankers' rights, the legislature gave permission to oppose rulings in the courts, but it also determined that a $50-a-week fine for continuing violation of cash reserve requirements (it was Sharpstown's cash shortages that eventually caused it to go under) was too little a deterrent and raised the fine to $500 a week.

It will be years before anyone in banking forgets the Sharpstown State Bank and Frank W. Sharp, not only in Texas but in all the other states. The Sharpstown failure jolted everyone, bankers, regulators, and legislators alike, since it was such a classic case of how bankers can use a bank for self-serving reasons and destroy it. It also served to show how thoroughly banking is woven into American life.

It is maintained by the knowledgeable that the Sharpstown State Bank, despite the swinging practices of Frank W. Sharp, would still be operating if the SEC had not filed its suit. The bank was not insolvent, it was cash-short, and Sharp had promised to sell some real estate to meet the shortage, but the SEC suit aborted the move. Ignored in such arguments, however, are depositors. Sharpstown had 27,300 depositors, the great majority of whom were not wheeler-dealers. To be sure, depositors are protected by FDIC insurance in ever-increasing amounts to the point where 100 percent protection may not be too far off. But bank deposits are expected to be riskless and an out-of-control banker is unacceptable. Sharp, not unlike many other bankers, operated on a basis of what was good for him alone. The fact that he got off with so light a sentence as probation and a fine suggests how very real is the power of bankers, especially those who have built their banks up to a size that allows them to infiltrate the very governments of the people.

Not all bankers escape so lightly, of course. One in the northern section of New Jersey, a man named Douglas J. Schotte, drew fifteen years in a federal prison for the self-serving deals he made with his bank's money. Schotte, however, was not nearly so powerfully connected as Sharp.

It was on July 22, 1972, that he was sentenced (and fined $10,000 as well) for using the funds of his bank, the Eatontown National Bank of Eatontown, New Jersey, to trade in the stock market. Like Sharp, Schotte believed in making money whirl; in fact, it required a 169-count indictment to detail his activities and the employment of a computer for nine months to figure out his market trades.

The extent of his trading is suggested by the fact that four brokers used by Schotte earned $417,000 in commissions (meanwhile accepting $1.3 million in loans from him for themselves). They, too, drew severe sentences. One broker, James Perry of Paramus, New Jersey, was sentenced to four years and fined $10,000. Another, William Certilman of Scarsdale, New York, was sentenced to three years and fined $10,000. The remaining two, Bertram Cutler of Brick Township, New Jersey, and Emmet W. Cox of Oakhurst, New Jersey, were given one-year suspended sentences, two years of probation, and fined $10,000 each.

Schotte was convicted on only three counts of the 169-count indictment that charged him with using $245,000 of bank money to trade in the market. The three counts tell only a small part of the story, however, for Schotte actually applied $10,260,991 of his bank's money to trade in $200 million worth of securities.

Schotte got into the stock market with his bank's money in July, 1969. His timing could not have been worse, since one of the worst bear markets since the depression of the 1930s was about to begin. This bear market was basically his undoing, since he lost money consistently.

Schotte's technique was basically one of "kiting." He would issue "nonbook" cashier's checks drawn on his bank to cover his securities purchases, and when the securities were sold, usually just a few days later, use the proceeds to cover the previous purchases. Since the checks required so many days to clear, Schotte made use of what is called the "float." The key move was to delay payment of the cashier's checks until a profit on a stock could be realized. Then the appropriated funds would be replaced with no one's knowledge.

The kiting worked because of a rule in the stock market that permits securities buyers five days in which to make payment. The rules are even more lenient for banks, who do not pay for securities until they are delivered. In 1969 and 1970, when brokers were still delivering stocks to customers weeks late because of brokerage inefficiency, Schotte's scheme worked for a time. He would buy a security from one of his brokers and receive delivery along with a bill for payment. But the stock would be sent immediately to a second broker to sell, and the proceeds used to satisfy the bill of the first broker. Then a third broker would be used to buy more stock, and the round robin would commence again. Accounts were carried with a dozen brokerages in the name of "Eatontown National Bank, attention Mr. Douglas J. Schotte." As a result Schotte made hundreds, even thousands of trades. For instance, he traded just one stock, Telex Corporation, twenty-nine times, buying and selling 26,500 shares. As might be imagined, velocity was a critical factor in such transactions, and at times securities literally changed hands at interchanges on New Jersey's Garden State Parkway.

Schotte's scheme depended on a rising market, though, and between July, 1969, and August, 1970, when the Eatontown National Bank closed, the market was in the grip of a bear the likes of which had not been seen since the depression. On one hand, the United States was in an economic recession, business was poor, profits low. On the other hand, the small investor, on whom the stock market traditionally depended for its liquidity, had left the market after being victimized by poor advice and broker exploitation. For these reasons Schotte himself became a victim. Though he bought issues that were considered glamor and growth stocks, as the table on page 419 shows (On the Day of Reckoning), his losses mounted as stock prices receded. Yet he continued to plunge, trying to recoup by increasing his trading.

Just between July 10, 1970, and July 30, 1970, a period of twenty days, he issued eighty-seven cashier's checks totaling $4,927,212.36.

Yet it was not Schotte's market losses that flushed him out, but rather the curiosity of an employee of the National State Bank in Elizabeth, New Jersey. National State, as a correspondent bank, maintained some Eatontown accounts, and in routinely processing cashier's checks drawn on the Eatontown Bank the employee, whose expertise lay in computer data processing rather than in banking, recognized checks he knew had been presented before for payment. He reported his observations, and literally in hours Schotte's scheme fell to pieces.

The National State Bank, after a quick investigation, notified regional national bank examiners of the Comptroller of the Currency, the supervising agency of national banks (states supervise state-chartered banks), who turned up at the Eatontown Bank. In a quick examination of the books it was estimated that $5 million was missing, an amount not far off the mark. As shown by the table On the Day of Reckoning, the actual shortage was $5,760,004.76, but this was reduced by the unearthing of more than $500,000.

On the same day the bank examiners arrived—August 6, 1970—Schotte appeared at the local office of the Federal Bureau of Investigation with his attorney and confessed to embezzlement. On August 7, 1970, the Comptroller of the Currency declared that the Eatontown National Bank was insolvent and called on the FDIC to act as receiver. Eventually the FDIC paid out $13,561,000, though liquidations reduced the FDIC's own loss to $2,800,000. The First Merchants National Bank of Asbury Park bought the Eatontown National Bank building for $1,500,110 and the Farmers and Merchants National Bank of Matawan, New Jersey, bought a branch building of the bank for $382,000.

Unraveling Schotte's market actions proved to be so knotty a problem that it was nine months before a federal grand jury in Newark, New Jersey, could hand up an indictment. In the months of investigation it heard more than one hundred witnesses and was confronted with more than one million bits of paper concerning Schotte's high-speed market trading. Teams of accountants had to be put on the case and a computer had to be programmed to develop the tale of what had happened. At the end of nine months the 169-count indictment emerged. In its 177 pages it charged Schotte with buying stock for his personal use with bank funds in the bank name. It said Schotte paid for the stock with cashier's checks drawn on the bank, and further, that he managed to delay the clearing of checks given brokers for payment of the stocks he bought. The great majority of the counts were recitations of Schotte's market activities, naming the stock, the number of shares purchased, and the amounts involved. It was a dizzying list, as suggested by the fact that Schotte traded $200 million worth of securities.

The indictment also named the four brokers as conspirers who had accepted illegally-used bank funds as commissions and loans. William A. Certilman, a broker with TPO, Inc., received $197,560.24 in commissions between October 24, 1968, and June 6, 1970, and $568,698.61 in loans, the indictment charged. Bertram E. Cutler, employed by TPO, Inc., and by Filor, Bullard and Smyth, received $123,399.11 in commissions between November 1, 1968, and August 8, 1970, and $69,632.41 in loans. James Perry, also of TPO and once a partner in the investment firm of Singer, Kaplan, Ripple and Burley, received $11,727 in commissions between April 7, 1970, and August 12, 1970, and $150,764.82 in loans. Emmett W. Cox, Jr., employed by Thomson, McKinnon and Auchincloss and before that by Auchincloss, Parker and Redpath, received $82,752.14 in commissions between January 1, 1969, and August 8, 1970. Cox's loans totaled $345,590.12.

The original indictment and subsequent convictions spawned a whole series of other suits, both criminal and civil. It was discovered, for example, that Schotte had enlisted the aid of the superintendent of Monmouth Regional High School in New

Shrewsbury, New Jersey, to misapply his bank's funds as early as 1965. The educator, Patrick Parenty, accepted fraudulent loans from Schotte and used the money to buy stocks in his name through Certilman, the TPO broker. Parenty also used the loan money to cover a call on a short sale on an account he had with Cutler, the broker employed by Filor, Bullard and Smyth, Inc. On February 16, 1972, Parenty entered a plea of guilty to a two-count federal information, insisting that he had never used the funds he had borrowed for himself. Clearly he was viewed as a dupe by prosecutors, since on July 26, 1972, he was sentenced to a prison term of one year, of which all but sixty days was suspended. He was also fined $10,000.

Another case that sprang up was a civil suit filed by Eugene W. Landy, the main organizer of the Eatontown National Bank in August, 1964. Landy was a director of the bank at the time of its closing and was the largest holder of its stock among the bank's 330 shareholders with 33,180 of the 250,000 shares outstanding. His wife, Gloria Landy, owned another 5,547 shares, and an uncle, Harry Gross of Freehold, New Jersey, owned another 10,111 shares. Schotte, incidentally, owned a mere 432 shares.

Landy put the loss of shareholders after the bank closed at $5.5 million, an amount based on a price of $22 a share paid by some shareholders. His suit for damages was filed against the FDIC, as receiver, ten stock brokerage firms, the New York Stock Exchange, and the Eatontown National Bank's accountant.

Landy charged that the defendants were negligent or were violating federal laws and New York Stock Exchange rules by allowing Schotte's unauthorized stock transactions. He said that Schotte's scheme could not have been carried off without violations of those laws and regulations. It was a point reasonably made. A New York Stock Exchange rule requires broker-members to "know their customers" or not take orders for securities. Schotte's brokers certainly knew that Schotte's stock transactions were illegal.

The defendants, for their part, responded by saying that the loss shareholders sustained in the closing of the Eatontown National Bank could not be linked directly enough to their own actions to form grounds for a suit.

Landy was especially irked with the national bank examiners, maintaining they were at fault for not turning up deficits during audits. He was particularly frustrated because directors of the bank (of which he was one), though they maintained deposits in the Eatontown National Bank, were not covered by FDIC insurance as other depositors were. He could not convince the judge, however, and his suit, with the exception of three counts, was dismissed. However, he appealed.

Meanwhile, the FDIC determined that it, too, ought to be suing, and on February 16, 1972, seven months or so after the bank's failure, charged eleven securities firms with "aiding and abetting" Schotte. The list included in the complaint included some of Wall Street's most shining lights: TPO, Inc.; Filor, Bullard and Smyth; Merrill Lynch, Pierce, Fenner and Smith; Bache and Company; Goodbody and Company; Harris, Upham and Company; Thomson, McKinnon and Auchincloss; Halle and Stieglitz; Herold, Kastor and Gerald, Inc; Stern, Lauer and Company; Singer, Kaplan, Ripple and Burley. (Ironically, another Wall Street brokerage firm, Francis I. Dupont, had been a shareholder in the Eatontown National Bank, and on the basis of holding 2,242 shares worth $22 a share lost $49,324.) In its suit the FDIC asked that the firms be made responsible for Schotte's market losses. It was hardly an unreasonable request in the light of the know-your-customer-rule.

On April 30, 1972, Wall Street struck back, filing a suit against the FDIC, which as the bank's receiver was responsible for payment for stock bought by Schotte but still not paid for. That, at least, was Wall Street's view. TPO, Inc., wanted $684,610 from the FDIC and in fact succeeded in getting a judgment issued against the estate of the bank and against the FDIC. In all, five Wall Street firms filed suits.

When Schotte went off to prison on July 26, 1972, to serve his ten years (five years of the fifteen-year sentence could be served concurrently, said the judge), it was the end of a career in banking that had seemed promising. To his associates Schotte had projected the image of a man truly dedicated to his profession, which may well have been the reason he was never suspected of any wrongdoing, even by Eugene Landy who was an active vice president as well as a major shareholder. By the time he was discovered using the bank's funds to buy stock, Schotte had built a creditable career for himself. At thirty-nine, his age upon being sentenced, he had already been president of a national bank for three years.

Schotte began his career in banking after being graduated from New York University with majors in economics, finance, and accounting. The pattern of his early life might easily have been that of any other banker on the way up. After a four-year tour with the army he became an assistant bank examiner with the Federal Reserve Bank of New York, an institution that has served many a banker well as a springboard to better things. Schotte left his job with the Federal Reserve Bank of New York to become assistant cashier of the First Merchants National Bank in Asbury Park, the same bank that eventually bought the Eatontown National Bank building during the bank's liquidation. That move, too, was typical of a banker working toward better things. Schotte left First Merchants in 1964 to help Landy and others organize the Eatontown bank, and so well did he perform that by 1969 he was appointed its president. He was thirty-six years old.

Observers saw Schotte as imperturbable, though a sympathetic federal regulator who helped liquidate the bank believed that Schotte did not comprehend the enormity of his crime and that the fast-moving world of finance had "made him lose contact with the rest of us." A less sympathetic officer saw Schotte as "plain cool. He had the audacity to steal from the safekeeping accounts, which include those of the directors of the banks. That takes nerve."

A number of FDIC officials are also convinced it took inside help for Schotte to carry off his scheme. Among them are John J. Slocum, chief of the FDIC's Division of Liquidation, George W. Hill, the assistant chief, and George R. Davis, the FDIC's supervising liquidator. But being convinced is a long way from having proof, and the FDIC has kept an official silence, though in the privacy of their offices officials name names.

At times, the fall of bankers, who in most places in the United States are still considered "pillars of the community," is a tragedy of a classic kind. Bankers have not only betrayed their trust, but on occasion have themselves determined that their own deaths were the only possible penalty.

The story of one such tragedy began on Friday, March 26, 1971, in a tiny Colorado community named Cripple Creek. On that day the First National Bank opened its doors as usual, as it had done for seventy-eight years. First National was a little bank with deposits totaling only $1,200,000, a small sum as banking goes. But the bank's founders had been proud of their national bank charter, number 4845, which had been granted February 3, 1893, and for nearly all its years the bank had compiled an unblemished record. First National's business, like the business of thousands of other small banks in the United States, was relatively uncomplicated. It serviced the credit and deposits needs of a thinly populated area, it had no branches, and in fact was controlled by the owners of the Park State Bank, a slightly larger bank in terms of deposits ($2,752,400) in Woodland Park, Colorado, just twenty-three miles away.

First National did not even maintain a trust department. There was no need to. Though Crippled Creek was the county seat of Teller County, Colorado, it was overshadowed by Colorado Springs, twenty-five miles west. Though it served four other communities, the population of all five totaled a mere 900. The area's economy was a desultory one, tied to such income sources as pensions, welfare, county employment, and a few year-round retail and service stores. Summer tourists and fall hunters also injected funds into the local economy. Thus, so far as is known, First National operated in a routine, perhaps even humdrum, fashion and got into no trouble. That is until about 1963, when it became the pawn of absentee owners who viewed the bank merely as an investment. After the bank's being sold again and again a feeling of headlessness began to prevail among its employees and the bank eventually showed up on various trouble lists maintained by supervisory agencies. For a number of years in the late 1960s First National was assigned by the Comptroller of the Currency the lowest possible payoff rating (a rating that determines the ability of a bank to repay its depositors). The bank was also placed on a list calling for close supervision.

The official records of the FDIC, which insured the First National, suggest the bank's difficulties began in October of 1963 when control was sold to B. M. Jobe by the heirs of the former owner, A. E. Carlton. In September, 1965, the Jobe control, in the form of stock, was acquired by Jack C. Wells during a foreclosure proceeding between Wells and Jobe. Then in April, 1969, the controlling interest acquired by Wells was sold to Sweet River, Inc., a Texas corporation headed by J. D. Allen. In that same year, on September 12, 1969, Sweet River, Inc., sold its interest to C. J. Kehoe, a Texas banker who had controlling interest in the nearby Park State Bank in Woodland Park. Kehoe's purchase consisted of 360, or 72 percent, of the First National's 500 outstanding shares.

First National, despite being under the supervision of the Park State Bank, had its own slate of operating officers. There were Gordon D. Brown, president of both First National and Park State; Ralph A. Jones, vice president and cashier; Rollen L. Harshbarger, cashier; Youree Posey, a vice president; and Eugene R. Sitts, another vice president. For the most part, it was Jones and Harshbarger who managed the First National. Brown, the president, spent most of his hours at the Park State Bank.

On March 26, 1971, Brown decided to spend some time

routinely checking First National's operations. In the process he discovered that several Federal Reserve cash letters had been received but not paid for. It was an inexcusable oversight in Brown's view and he fired Rollen Harshbarger, who managed the bank's day-to-day operations, on the spot. But then Brown began to spot irregularities so numerous that he put the entire First National staff under suspicion and brought in an accountant from the Park State Bank four days later to run trials and to straighten out the cash letter problem. The accountant, a woman, arrived at the bank on March 31, 1971, four days after Harshbarger had been fired. Working at her side was Ralph Jones, vice president and cashier of the bank. Not long after she began—in fact, in the very first trial balance—the bank's demand ledgers showed a total $636,000, but the general ledger showed only $232,000 was actually available. The numbers indicated a shortage of $404,000, an astounding amount for so small a bank. New trials were run, and as the work went on it became clear an enormous shortage did indeed exist.

Jones seemed shocked by the disclosures, and discovering he was out of cigarettes, excused himself to go next door to buy some. He never returned. Instead, late that same day both his and Harshbarger's bodies were found, each man dead of gunshot wounds in the head and lying in a field on a ranch fifteen miles from the bank. The county coroner said both had died of self-inflicted wounds. Jones, forty-six, was the son of a local postmaster. Harshbarger, thirty-two, was the son of a sheriff. They died in a pact of mutual suicide, a grand jury later concluded.

On April 2, 1971, just two days later, a firm of auditors in Colorado Springs was asked to examine First National's books and records. About the same time national bank examiners from the office of the Comptroller of the Currency also arrived. Each confirmed the findings of the Park State Bank accountant. There was an enormous shortage, which at first was put at $448,000, but then went over $800,000 as new ledgers turned up short. In a bank with only $1,235,800 in deposits, the looting had been fantastic, as the Statement of a Looted Bank shows on pages 418–19.

The statement also showed a bank hopelessly insolvent, and whose affairs were so tangled that in the fall of 1972 accountants were still trying to unravel them. This may well have been the reason the Comptroller failed to close the First National of Crippled Creek until November of 1971. It was only then that a national bank examiner named Siegfried F. Seemann could feel competent to declare the bank insolvent. When the the FDIC was asked to act as receiver it found that every method of internal manipulation ever used to embezzle a bank's funds from the inside had been used. There were withheld deposits, pulled ledger sheets, false debits and credits, withheld notepayments, loans made to fictitious nondepositors directly from depositors' accounts with no notes being signed, withheld checks, and a string of miscellaneous manipulations. Indeed, chaos reigned. At the time of the examination of the bank's accounts late in 1971, a great number of unposted checks kept turning up, some of which were dated as far back as 1968. The examiners also found that statements sent to the bank's customers were different from the ledger balances maintained by the bank. As in the case of so many other banks that faced cash shortages, First National had maintained funds by soliciting brokered certificates of deposit. In April, 1971, the bank had sold $245,000, of which $225,000 were due for redemption in one year at an interest rate of 5½ percent. The money had come from a Houston firm, Hargrove, Brown and Associates.

The deaths of the First National Bank of Crippled Creek, the Eatontown National Bank in New Jersey, and the Sharpstown State Bank might suggest one of two assumptions: only the managements and owners of smallish banks indulge themselves by dealing out their bank's assets to themselves or by levering them to produce personal gain; or only smallish banks are closed down because of self-dealing by managers and owners.

Actually number two is true. As a look at the Roster of

Closed Banks shows on pages 416–17, no true giant of banking has been given last rites by the FDIC. This does not mean, though, that the managements of much larger banks do not indulge in self-dealing. On the contrary, the evidence suggests there is just as much self-dealing as in smaller banks. But large banks have large reserves, so large that they easily absorb the comparatively small-time deals of individuals. Further, the very size of some of the giants seems to dissuade regulators from being the tough cops they are with small banks.

Consider the case of the Chase Manhattan Bank, the nation's third largest with assets of $24.5 billion at the end of 1971, and Detroit's Bank of Commonwealth, one of the fifty largest banks with assets of nearly $1.5 billion in 1970.

In 1964 Chase lent $20 million in two loans to the so-called Parsons group, a partnership of investors led by Donald H. Parsons, a Detroit lawyer. The money was used to buy stock (and control) of the Bank of Commonwealth, in an obviously self-serving deal of a kind frowned on by regulators. As collateral Parsons put up 39 percent of the outstanding stock of the Detroit bank, using a technique of empire building like that of the corporate conglomerate, i.e., the acquired company ends up financing or collateralizing its own acquisition. In time, the Bank of Commonwealth became the cornerstone of an empire of the Parsons group of banks, nineteen in all, including the ill-fated Birmingham-Bloomfield Bank, which appears on the Roster of Closed Banks on pages 416–17. Parsons' banks were situated in four states and in Switzerland.

Parsons believed that banks should look for the highest gain, a philosophy not necessarily at odds with that of leading bankers, though clearly at odds with many bank regulators. Thus, the Bank of Commonwealth bought high-yielding bonds, for example, but at the sacrifice of quality. In the abnormally high interest rate period of the 1960s the prices of the bonds held by the bank, most of which were municipal and not readily disposed of because of the low liquidity of the municipal bond market, fell drastically.

So did the value of the bank's stock . . . and thus the value of the collateral being held by the Chase Manhattan Bank.

But far from being taken to task for its part in appeasing the appetite of Parsons for bank acquisitions, the regulators almost cheered when Chase Manhattan foreclosed in February, 1971, and later seized the stock it held as collateral in a special auction ordered by a U.S. District Court judge in Cincinnati. Chase Manhattan paid $5.5 million for the stock in the forced sale, and installed its own man, John A. Hooper, to replace Parsons as chairman. The Federal Reserve Board's vice chairman, J. L. Robertson, praised Chase for its "initiative in moving into this situation," though it was a situation Chase had clearly helped to create. The rationale of the FRB vice chairman and that of the FDIC as well was that the well-being of a section of the economy, Michigan, was at stake. Yet the evidence is vague that Chase Manhattan did much more than protect its loans and "reduce to ownership," as David Rockefeller described it, the collateral the bank held. During January, 1972, a year after Chase Manhattan seized control, the Bank of the Commonwealth was still in danger of insolvency and required a $60 million loan over a five-year period from the FDIC to keep it alive.

The "reduction" of collateral to equity was no ordinary feat. It required the resurrection of an obscure federal banking law even to permit regulators to justify and approve officially the irregular steps Chase Manhattan was taking. Not since World War II, in fact, had anyone thought of invoking a very old law which stated that when one bank takes the stock of another as collateral the lending bank can hold the stock for a period of up to two years. Interpreting this, too, as permission to hold a stock sale in opposition to the owner's interest, i.e., Parsons', also took some doing. Though Parsons argued that a United States district judge did not have the power or the right to order the auction of his stock, he was overruled.

By taking possession of the Parsons stock in the Bank of Commonwealth, the Chase Manhattan Bank put itself out of the status of ordinary creditor. If the Bank of Commonwealth had been liquidated, which was a real possibility, Chase Manhattan would have had to wait without, as do all creditors in a liquidation, until depositors are paid off. Often then there is nothing left for the creditors.

But in April, 1972, with ownership and control, Chase Manhattan said it was selling its shares—to the James T. Barnes family, which controlled one of the largest private mortgage banking companies in the United States. In September, 1972, the transfer of ownership was made at a price both Chase Manhattan and the Barnes family refused to disclose. It was a sale that highly pleased R. Frank Wille, chairman of the FDIC, but it revived questions of whether some banks are more equal than others in the eyes of regulators. Why, for example, did the FDIC engage in so massive a rescue operation, one that was controversial from a legal standpoint? Why did it extend a $60 million line of credit to the Bank of Commonwealth, a bank not far from insolvency, but refuse $1 million to the Sharpstown State Bank, which was not in danger of insolvency, but merely cash-short, especially in light of a stated FDIC policy of keeping banks operating? Are self-serving practices justified only for large banks? Was Sharp's personal war with the FDIC the reason his bank was folded—not by the FDIC, of course, which cannot close banks, but by the Comptroller?

The question of partiality was raised years before the Bank of Commonwealth crisis, in 1964 in the matter of the Crown Savings Bank, whose financing of loan share operations helped close it down. After investigating the operations of Crown Savings, the House Banking and Currency Committee concluded in a report that the FDIC had put a giant bank—again, Chase Manhattan—into a preferred position over general creditors. In collecting loans as the defunct bank's receiver the FDIC turned over 50 percent of what it collected on loans in which Chase had participated.

There are critics of banking who say that it is not mere

partiality that the FDIC and indeed all the other regulators show toward the giant banks. Rather it is awe, timidity, and even fear. The giant banks are the powerful core of the nation's economy and their banker heads the powerful core of the nation's establishment. They wield more economic, social, and political power than most heads of government. They have, in fact, become what Thomas Jefferson feared bankers would become—a group of men and institutions that operate separately and remotely from the people—a ruling class.

PART TWO

A Ruling Class

3

March to Power

WHEN THOMAS Jefferson, as George Washington's Secretary of State, opposed the creation of the first central bank, i.e., the Bank of the United States, he knew well enough the benefits such a bank might bring. The United States desperately needed a stable currency, and Hamilton's central bank was designed to produce one. But Jefferson feared the rise of a class of men who would have a kind of sovereignty, separate, remote, and serving principally themselves. As President, Jefferson once wrote Albert Gallatin, his Secretary of the Treasury, that the Bank of the United States was "of the most deadly hostility existing against the principles and form of our Constitution." Jefferson felt "no government [is] safe which is under the vassalage of any self-constituted authorities or any other authority than that of the nation or its regular functionaries." He saw the Bank of the United States as a potential army, "penetrating by its branches every part of the Union, acting by command and in phalanx, [able] in a critical moment [to] upset the government. Now, while we are strong, it is the greatest duty we owe to the safety of our Constitution to bring this powerful enemy to a perfect subordination under its authorities."

After eighteen years of operation the Bank of the United States still loomed as a menace in Jefferson's mind, and in 1809, he gave only halfhearted approval to the renewal of its charter, due to expire in 1811.

Clearly, the first Bank of the United States had done its job, and then some. It not only had helped produce a stable currency, but unexpectedly it had become a much needed controller of credit. As the general depository and collector of funds due the federal government, the bank had income consisting largely of the circulating notes of the state-chartered banks. Thus, it was an insistent creditor which frequently demanded payment for the notes it held issued by those banks. With offices scattered in the major cities, it became an efficient collector, since its representatives were close enough to enforce their demands. Generally the Bank of the United States pressed the state banks hard for payment, and was especially insistent upon payment from those state banks that issued large volumes of their own notes. Occasionally, but with growing frequency, the bank even became a lender of last resort, advancing its own funds to state banks that had gotten themselves into trouble by lending too much and found themselves short when demands were made for deposits. In this way, the central bank also prevented runs on the state banks.

Generally, the conservative bankers of the day responded to the controls that developed out of the bank's practices, recognizing a need for them. But speculative bankers, who were very clearly in the majority, resented the controls. Such men were not necessarily dishonest, though greed was a characteristic, since banking was an unusually profitable enterprise. Many bankers also saw the Bank of the United States, or national bank, as it was called, as nothing much more than another power block in opposition to their own. In support of this view, historians point out that the Bank of the United States was hardly an impartial institution. It was belligerent and wielded a large club over some banks that were slow to meet demands for payments, while bankers who were considered friends were allowed the luxury of so-called slow loans. And as Jefferson had feared, bankers had become a power group answerable to few people. They rarely petitioned the government. They preferred manipulating it, and both state legislatures and Congress bent, often quite willingly, before their wishes. They had become in a very few years a ruling class.

The officers of the Bank of the United States were as prone to manipulate the government as the officers of the state-chartered banks. Their political game was often quite successful. As Jefferson once wrote, the Bank of the United States made selected members of both houses of Congress bank directors. Naturally, in Congress these men always voted with the bank's views in mind. In tandem with other Senators and Representatives who were stockholders (many were), they could always achieve a majority.

The Bank of the United States did not always get its way, of course. In fact, it eventually became the victim of its own powerful class and lost the battle for its life. When its charter expired in 1811, a bill proposing renewal was killed in the Senate after Vice President George Clinton (significantly, a New Yorker with broad interests in state banks) broke a 17 to 17 tie not to renew.

There was not much question that the bank's foes were engaged in an intramural game and that the public good was not a significant factor in their opposition. State banks simply resented controls. At the time of the bank's death, James Madison, an old antagonist of the bank, was President, having succeeded Jefferson in 1809. But even Madison now felt it would be "expedient" to keep the Bank of the United States alive. To be sure, the bank did have some honest, unreconstructed opposition. Virginia's Senator Samuel W. B. Giles, for example, was a bitter opponent of the Bank of the United States, but not for reasons of personal gain. Giles was essentially fighting corruption, which he saw in the growing power of bankers and conflicts of interest. As a member of the House of Representatives during the formation of the Bank of the United States in 1791 he had advocated an amendment to the Constitution forbidding anyone holding office in the Bank of the United States to be a member of either the House or the Senate. Giles had even censured Alexander

Hamilton by introducing resolutions criticizing Hamilton's acts of expedience in setting up the bank.

But alongside critics of the Giles mold were men who clearly acted out of personal interest and perhaps were the very men Giles was thinking about. Senator Henry Clay, for example, was a vehement opponent of the bank, all the while holding interests in two Kentucky state banks. Senator Samuel Smith, another opponent, owned a bank in Baltimore. In the House of Representatives there was Andrew Gregg, who after leaving Congress became president of a state bank almost immediately.

The state banks themselves were thoroughly united in their opposition to renewing the national bank charter. Though there were hundreds of state banks in existence only five spoke up in favor of renewal.

Like so many arguments based on vested interest the arguments of the bank's opponents were couched in lofty terms. It was declared, for example, that the very existence of the Bank was unconstitutional, and that the control it exercised over state banks' lending activities flew in the face of states' rights. Although the constitutional issue had really been laid to rest twenty years before, it served as good enough cover, since it helped produce some of the uproar that dominated the issue.

Still another argument used against the bank, this one more pragmatic, was that substantial amounts of the bank's stock were owned by financial interests in Great Britain. In 1811, with the War of 1812 imminent, the argument was effective, though hardly honest. The bank's stock indeed had wandered abroad, being used by some Americans to settle debts, but British owners of the stock were denied any control over the bank's management. Further, since holding the stock really constituted an investment in the primitive economy of the United States, foreign ownership benefited the United States. On top of that, the United States held the option of cutting off dividend payments to foreigners.

Occasionally, the true spirit of the debate became apparent, as when Henry Clay sarcastically described the bank as a "splendid association of favored individuals invested with exemptions and surrounded by immunities and privileges." The remark expressed clearly the nature of the dispute: it was intraclass warfare over the spoils in a manner reminiscent of the feudal system. At stake was nothing less than the growing deposits of the federal government, deposits that grew as trade grew, since federal income was tied to duties. With the Bank of the United States out of the way, the state banks could become depositories—there was literally no place else to put the money—and thereby increase their own lending activities.

Lost in the fray was the voice of the public interest, which was reduced to a whisper. Though a U.S. Senator from South Carolina stood up in the Senate once to defend the Bank of the United States in the interest of the "clodhoppers" of the country, his argument was barely heard and nearly not recorded. In 1811 the first central bank of the United States was allowed to die.

The warfare among the bankers themselves resembled the resistance to central authority by the fiefs and vassals of Europe centuries before. Though a banker (a knight) who had become head of the central bank (king) by general agreement might well have established both order and law, he could look forward to rebellion. The bankers of the early nineteenth century in the United States had already developed a kind of kingdom of their own, as it had been feared, and members of its ruling class were battling each other for control. The events that followed the death of the Bank of the United States support this idea.

After the demise of the central bank state banks flooded the country with paper money, inflating the supply enormously with their own issues. As the War of 1812 began and the British invaded Washington and Baltimore, runs on banks closed down many of them, while others simply refused to pay and redeem their notes on demand—as the Bank of the United States had once forced them to do. One major and onerous result was that the federal government itself went without money—it didn't even have enough to pay its troops after the British blockaded U.S. ports and reduced import duties to hardly anything.

Out of this unbearable monetary situation, in April, 1816,

a second Bank of the United States was formed. Even the first bank's arch foe, Henry Clay, approved now of a new bank being founded.

But once again, internecine warfare killed off the second Bank of the United States. This time the lead was taken by New York banking interests who deeply resented being controlled by a central bank situated in Philadelphia to which New York's considerable import duties were sent. As a port, New York produced more duty revenue than all other ports put together. Philadelphia's bankers and New York's bankers were bitter rivals, and the New Yorkers once again fed the animosities of state banks around the nation with the same old lure—if the central bank were put out of the way, the government would be forced to make its deposits in the vaults of the state banks. In New York, of course, this would amount to a vast sum.

But though the motive for killing the second Bank of the United States was the same as for the first, the technique was different. New York bank interests, led by Martin Van Buren, nursed the prejudice of President Andrew Jackson against banks, especially Philadelphia banks, one of whose members had mistreated Jackson years before he became a public figure, and succeeded in getting Jackson to transfer federal deposits to the banks of friends of Van Buren's in New York. There were a number of supporting plots involved, including, for example, raids by New York banks on Philadelphia banks demanding large, abrupt withdrawals of cash or the payment of bills in specie. But Jackson's withdrawal of federal funds was a lasting blow, and in February, 1841, several years after he ceased to be President, the second United States central bank collapsed.

It was nearly seventy-five years before a central bank, the Federal Reserve System, appeared again. In the years between chaos often reigned. The state bankers, who had won the day, produced or helped produce a variety of inflationary periods and financial panics that built a basic fear and distrust of banks into the general population. So many bank notes were issued that at one point some 7,000 different kinds were being circulated. Many could be redeemed upon being presented at the issuing bank only with the help, literally, of a loaded gun.

The federal government itself was frequently short of money, and being without a fiscal agent, or central bank, at one point during the Civil War was forced to ask a private financier, Jay Cooke, to market its war bonds. At the same time an abortive attempt to print and circulate more than $430 million in paper, or fiat, money ended in a inflationary disaster as the notorious greenbacks, as they were called, fell to a value of practically nothing. Finally, in desperation, President Lincoln's Secretary of the Treasury, Salmon P. Chase, persuaded Congress to pass the National Bank Act.

Thought the act did not permit the kind of control a central bank might exert through regulation and the establishment of restrictive procedures, it did introduce reforms that propped up the currency and created a system of nationally chartered banks to act as orderly opposition to the chaotic disposition of the state banks. Strangely, bankers today hail the endeavor as the creation of the dual banking system, when in fact it was a counterattack against banks running wild. The national banks, though permitted to issue bank notes, had to back those notes with government bonds. These bonds, in turn, had to be held in the vaults of the banks issuing the notes. Each bank also had to maintain a specified amount of cash reserves against its deposits and to provide redemption center for its notes in a number of large cities. Further, at a time when note counterfeiting was a thriving business, the government began to print notes that were difficult to reproduce, and then made it a crime to counterfeit them. Counterfeiters became the special target of the newly established Secret Service. By 1865 Congress had also placed a 10 percent federal tax on the notes of state banks, and thus drove the notes out of circulation. As it turned out, however, the move was wasted. State banks had discovered and developed the checking account, which became a major source of bank deposits (as it still is today) and of lendable funds, and the number of state banks soared. Between 1870 and 1910, for example, their number grew from 335 to 12,000.

The National Bank Act did more than prop up the money supply and establish national banks. It also established the office of the Comptroller of the Currency as the first true regulator of banking. It was he who granted national bank charters. Still, the controls of the nineteenth century must have been rather benign (as, indeed, they are today), for by 1866, barely three years after the passage of the National Bank Act in 1863, 1,600 banks had been granted charters.

Constructive as the National Bank Act was, the highlights of the late nineteenth century—really, the pockmarks—were panics, the most severe of which occurred in the latter part of the century when all business and banking seemed out of control despite the presence of a Comptroller. Some of the most severe panics occurred in 1873, 1884, 1890, 1893, and 1903, and were characterized by bank failures preceded by that perennial indicator of loss of faith, runs on banks. As might be expected after such a series of conditioning panics, the public fear and distrust of bankers deepened. The bankers themselves seemed indifferent to the lessons the panics presented, for they changed their ways hardly at all. For example, every banker knew the weakness of a practice in which the smallest banks kept portions of their reserves as deposits with other larger banks in other cities. Those banks, in turn, kept portions of their reserves in banks in even larger cities, for example, in the money centers of New York and Philadelphia. The money-center banks encouraged the practice with high interest rates—they lent to Wall Street's stockbrokers and investment bankers to finance stock market transactions. When stock prices fell, banks called in vain for the return of the credit they had supplied, credit that had pushed stock prices up to unnatural heights, but which after the crashes no longer existed. In the runs on banks that developed, the entire system proved to be a house of cards again and again.

But nothing really was changed, at least by the bankers. They tended to blame the regulations of the day, complaining that the National Bank Act restrained them by restricting the supply of money, that the inelasticity of the regulations prevented bankers from being ready to pay out money on demand when runs developed. The bankers also complained that restrictions on credit, which are imposed by tying the limits of lending to reserves, prevented bankers from coming to the aid of each other when one or several of their number needed cash temporarily.

Then in 1907 the greatest of all banking panics up to that time developed. It was so severe that it produced a decline in the very supply of money. Country banks, as usual, demanded their deposits from city banks, which in turn pressed for their funds from the money-center banks, especially those in New York. Everywhere payments just stopped, and in the aftermath, in 1910, a National Monetary Commission was appointed to examine the entire banking structure. Among those who called out for reform was Woodrow Wilson, who as President would sign in 1914 the Federal Reserve Act creating the third central bank of the United States, one that would have more staying power than the preceding two. But another, perhaps more important, investigation than that of the National Monetary Commission got underway, which resulted in the famous-among-bankers Pujo Report of 1912. Whereas the National Monetary Commission examined the mechanisms of banking, the Pujo Report disclosed a whole series of incestuous business relationships between banks and investment houses; between banks and insurance companies; between banks and industrial corporations; between banks and railroads; between banks and utilities. In short, between banks and every facet of American business. Bankers were exerting their influence and control not only through financing, which can carry a great variety of covenants, but also by inserting themselves onto the boards of corporations everywhere and exercising voting power. To complete the circle of togetherness, the banks invited corporate executives onto their boards. It was a comfortable arrangement, if not one devised in the public interest, and in 1914 President Wilson asked Congress for new antitrust legislation, part of which was designed to put an end to the togetherness, or interlocking directorships. The result was the Clayton Act, which included prohibitions against such directorships. But it made exceptions, and those exceptions, in the opinion of the banks, included them. Thus the issue raised its head again in the 1960s and 1970s as will be discussed in a later chapter. Once again, bankers and businessmen were in bed with each other, attracted by their mutual understanding of business problems.

But the early part of the twentieth century saw some small success in reining in bankers' excesses. From the beginning the Federal Reserve's powers were so great that bankers regarded it with awe, though not necessarily with fear or with the realization that there were lessons to be learned. Bankers with the attitudes that had required resurrection of a central bank to control them infiltrated the system, and in its early years the Federal Reserve was an engine of inflation that produced enormous amounts of money. In the early 1930s it failed badly to prevent what it was expected to prevent—bank failure and panic. Instead, it is blamed by most bankers and economists today for causing the depression of the 1930s, the worst in American history. Among other things, the Federal Reserve stood by while banks pumped enormous amounts of credit into a stock market that clearly represented runaway speculation.

John R. Bunting, the chief executive officer of Philadelphia's First Pennsylvania Bank and Trust Company and once an economist with the Federal Reserve, is direct in his censure of the Federal Reserve and claims that a similar belief prevails among economists. "The banks were responsible for the great depression of 1929, 1930, and 1931," he asserts. "I think if you ask a hundred economists—any hundred, as long as they have the degrees and a reasonable amount of objectivity—they'll say that what happened in 1929 was absolutely stupid Federal Reserve policy. It caused the depression in 1929—that along with a

President of the United States who really didn't understand what was going on in 1929. There's no question that the monetary policy of that time was absolutely stupid. Now, it was carried out by the way of conventional wisdom. The Federal Reserve was not going against conventional wisdom. But conventional wisdom at the time was, by our standards today, just incredible."

If the Federal Reserve System and its board failed the public interest at first, among its own, the bankers, it was far more successful. It established its authority without challenge under an act that plainly gave it huge powers over banks—though only national banks are forced to become members of the Federal Reserve while state banks may join if they wish. There is no doubt that the Federal Reserve has evolved into an almost sovereign position, however, depending on the character of the chairman of the Federal Reserve Board since the act creating it made it financially independent of the administration, and in some minds indifferent to human need. Some of the board's independence was specifically granted; much of its power assumed. The Federal Reserve Act intentionally insulates the agency from the administration, especially as to its budget, which the President and Congress have no say over. The governors of the Federal Reserve Board, seven in all, are also immune to presidential pressure, since their terms are for fourteen years—long enough to prevent Presidents from packing the board since Presidents themselves are in office a maximum of eight years. It has been estimated that even a two-term President can appoint a maximum of four governors—unless, of course, some board members die. But the board has also determined it is immune to the desires of Congress, its creator, and it is that which irks legislators.

This relative immunity to being fired, even by the most powerful figure in the United States, has permitted the board to operate virtually in secret—for example, when it tinkers with the money supply. In fact, many Presidents, including Harry S. Truman and Lyndon Johnson, complained that Federal Reserve monetary policies were developed in opposition to economic policies of their administrations. When Johnson wanted to spend for both guns (the Vietnam war) and butter (the Great Society), he had to have the money to do it. Instead, he was subjected to a money crunch or credit crunch that originated at the Federal Reserve Board, under Chairman William McChesney Martin, a product of Wall Street and once president of the New York Stock Exchange, who disagreed with Johnson's economic policies. The board may have been right in believing the United States could not afford both guns and butter, but whether it should have produced a money crunch in opposition to a duly elected President is the issue. On the other hand, President Nixon has had the cooperation in his economic plans of Chairman Arthur F. Burns, whom he appointed, a man who has not hesitated to berate bankers for increases in interest rates that conflicted with presidential economic policies. Yet it is also true that President Nixon's plans for the economy did not include vast spending initiatives, with the exception of defense, which may well have jibed with Burns' own ideas. Still, Presidents can rightfully complain, as many have, that they have been elected by the people to, among other things, develop economic policy, and that the Federal Reserve Board in opposing them acts contrary to the will of the people. Bankers and the Federal Reserve Board, at least under the stewardship of Martin, have said that this kind of thinking was nonsense, that Presidents such as Johnson, Truman, Herbert Hoover, and Andrew Jackson were vastly ignorant of the monetary system and economics, and therefore incapable of developing sound economic policies. They claim the independence of the Federal Reserve Board was granted by Congress so the board could nullify presidential economic policies. The overwhelming arrogance of the argument has left many an inquirer dumbfounded, for it violates both the spirit and practice of democratic government and it emanates from an agency that operates in virtual secrecy on the premise that it alone knows best.

The argument does support the thesis that the Federal Reserve

Board sits atop a banking hierarchy which takes its cues from it and its system of banks (banks, incidentally, that deal only with other banks), and has become remote, aloof, and unreachable so far as most of the population is concerned. Even understanding the Federal Reserve System is a major task, since the Board has wrapped the entire thing in a mystique and secrecy that discourage inquiry. Information is released in thoroughly scrubbed, bland accounts written to depict the Federal Reserve as some sort of public guardian. Some of its most critical moves, actions that affect the supply of money and therefore the whole economy, are reported months later, though this is something of a reform since at one time the period was five years.

4

Trappings and Accountability

TO BELONG somewhere in the banking system, to have carved out a niche for oneself, carries rewards in terms of money and power. The governors of the Federal Reserve System, though they do not earn as much in salary—not nearly as much, in fact—as do the bankers they control (receiving $40,000 a year under the Federal Reserve Act, which has been amended a number of times to bring salaries up to that relatively low level; the chairman receives only $2,500 more than the other governors), have enormous prestige, since it is doubtful that any other agency in the United States has as much say over the economy. It is not just that the Federal Reserve controls the money supply; legislation in recent years actually gives it power to tell banking institutions whether they can unite in merger.

Bankers, on the other hand, receive substantial salaries. First Pennsylvania's Bunting outspokenly says what other bankers prefer not to discuss: "Nowhere can you make as much money as you do in a bank as easily as you do. There's no question about that. It's a great way. If you have a brain in your head, it's a great way to make a living." That bankers can earn huge salaries is clearly true. In fact, they may be said to belong to a $100,000-a-year club that is rapidly becoming a $200,000-a-year club.

Bunting's own salary and other rewards suggest that the living is indeed very good for bankers. As of April 24, 1972, his salary from the First Pennsylvania was $126,538, and even were he never to receive a raise he could look forward to $52,332 a year upon his retirement, provided he stays with his bank. Perhaps more significant, since salaries of that size are subject to income tax rates as high as 70 percent, were the options held by Bunting in 1972 on 15,000 shares of his bank's common stock at $29.11 a share—options that do not expire until October 24, 1974.

In 1972 First Pennsylvania's common stock rose as high as $51.62½ a share. If Bunting had exercised his options that year somewhere around the high he would have cleared well over $300,000.

Actually, the income, potential and actual, of First Pennsylvania's top officer is relatively modest when compared to that of one of the true rulers and aristocrats of banking, David Rockefeller. In 1971 the Chase Manhattan Bank paid David Rockefeller $230,000, an amount calculated to produce, under a formula tied to salary, $116,883 a year upon retirement. Rockefeller's real take-home pay from the Chase Manhattan, however, is tied to an enormous equity position. He himself was the owner in 1971 of 337,500 of the bank's common shares. Rockefeller's wife Margaret owned another 19,395 shares; and his children another 3,333 shares. Those shares alone provided Rockefeller and his family with an equity in the Chase Manhattan Bank that varied between $22,244,079 and $17,290,944 in 1971, depending on the high ($61.75) and low price ($48) of Chase Manhattan stock that year. In 1972 Rockefeller's direct ownership of the bank varied between $24,135,276, when the bank's stock reached a high of $67 a share, and $18,731,856, when it fell to a low of $52.

The real value of the shares becomes plain, however, when dividend payments are considered. In 1971 Chase Manhattan declared a $2 dividend on its common stock, meaning that the shares owned by David Rockefeller and his family produced $720,456. Thus, between dividends and salary Rockefeller collected $950,456 in 1971 from Chase Manhattan. The figures do not take into account Rockefeller's ownership that year of 20 percent of the stock of Hills Realty Company, Inc., a corporation liquidated in 1972, but which owned 4,000 shares of Chase Manhattan stock; or that Rockefeller was the beneficiary of a trust owning 17.7 percent of the stock of Rockefeller Center, Inc., a corporation that owns 193,928 shares of Chase Manhattan stock. Thus it can be estimated that Rockefeller's total income from the Chase Manhattan Bank is well over $1 million.

Interestingly, Rockefeller was receiving these enormous amounts in salary and dividends at a time when his fellow bankers, John R. Bunting among many others, were judging him as "running a third-rate bank" because of his neglect of Chase Manhattan in favor of "outside relations," as Rockefeller himself described his tendency toward being an international itinerant who ponders global questions. Of course, men who were considered more successful as bankers, that is, who raised their banks' profits or enlarged their business, were also being paid very large salaries, though nothing approaching the Rockefeller income.

For example, as the table Bankers' Salaries shows, A. W. Clausen, president of the largest bank in the world, San Francisco's BankAmerica Corporation, was paid $168,200 the year Rockefeller was getting a $230,000 salary and more than three quarters of a million dollars in dividends. Indeed, a fellow officer of Clausen's, Chauncy P. Medberry, was receiving a mere $126,350. Uptown from the Chase Manhattan Bank on New York's Park Avenue, the banker's banker, a name earned because of his aggressiveness and his bank's higher profits, Walter B. Wriston, the chief executive of First National City Bank, actually bested Rockefeller in terms of salary, being paid $235,000. But Wriston's options on his bank's common stock were far smaller at 65,040 shares (average option price: $31.83 a share) than Rockefeller's actual ownership of Chase Manhattan stock.

High salaries and other forms of remuneration are typical not only of the titans of banking, but also of relatively small city bankers as well, as the table on pages 421–24 suggests. For example, Lester W. Herzog, Jr., president and chief executive officer of First Commercial Banks, Inc., Albany, New York, was paid $86,297 in

1971, a salary calculated to give him upon retirement $45,596. First Commercial Banks, which consists of two affiliated banks (National Commercial and First Trust) operating in the northern counties of New York State, also makes loans to its officers at rates just slightly above the prime rate. (The prime rate of interest is that granted to the most credit-worthy business customers of banks, and though hardly ever available to individual customers, is readily available to officers of many banks.)

Many banks maintain investment plans in which a bank will match an employee's contribution, generally a percentage of his salary up to perhaps 6 percent. But the profit-sharing plans of upper management are far more likely to enrich their beneficiaries, tied as they are to the profits of the bank itself, then these investment plans designed for lesser employees will enrich them. Indeed, investing in the stock market in recent years has been a perilous undertaking and many bank employees who invested in a plan supervised by their bank have only losses to show.

At the same time, bank employees have had to make do with salaries that are generally low. In a Ralph Nader study of New York's First National City Bank, David Leinsdorf, the study's director, determined that the bank paid "notoriously low wages to the thousands of assembly line clerical employees who process tons of checks, securities and other papers each day." First National City Bank's officers were well paid, however, with "virtually all officers earning over $12,000." Wriston's salary, Leinsdorf said in an aside, was equal to the amount stolen from First National City by bank robbers in 1970.

The bank started brand-new clerical employees at $4,400 a year. Typists was paid $4,700 a year, while high school graduates with business training started out at $5,000. Leinsdorf concluded that the "vast majority of Citibank's clerical workers earned less than $6,500." In New York City, where the inflation rate generally far outstrips inflation rates elsewhere, these were low salaries indeed.

High salaries, secrecy, arrogance, mystique, stock options, and opposing the will of Presidents are not the only characteristics of the ruling class of bankers. Another characteristic, a dominant one, is an unwillingness to be called to account, or even to disclose what it is they are doing, especially if criticism is expected.

In 1972, for example, David Rockefeller passed the word that he would no longer see journalists who might be critical, or as a bank representative phrased it, "hostile." This came after Rockefeller had been criticized by "Banks and the Poor," a television documentary that just missed winning an Emmy award; by the biography *David*, and by *The New York Times* in an article suggesting that under David Rockefeller the Chase Manhattan Bank's fortunes were at "ebb tide."

"Banks and the Poor" was an example of advocacy journalism that shook up banks everywhere, and it was based on undeniable fact—banks figuratively take cudgels to the poor when they do not pay up. The author of *David* was a former financial writer whose book was indeed hostile, but was based on fact. The writer of *The New York Times* article was H. Erich Heinemann, a knowledgeable banking reporter, a former officer of the Morgan Guaranty Trust Company, and the son of a banker, who only pointed out what was well known in banking circles but not to the public. Chase Manhattan in recent years had lost its position as New York's largest bank, a meaningful indication to bankers and businessmen and especially to its arch-rival First National City Bank. Chase Manhattan had also lost its lead in correspondent banking, the system of vassalage that ties small banks to large ones, to a bank half its size, the Manufacturers Hanover Trust in New York. Heinemann had also reported that executives of Chase Manhattan were accepting offers from other banks they would ordinarily have ignored if they had been content with David Rockefeller's leadership.

All this suggested that Rockefeller was a poor banker and that Chase Manhattan, though hardly on the skids, was headed downhill. Rockefeller displayed his own dissatisfaction with things in October, 1972, only a few months after *The New York Times* article appeared, by firing Herbert P. Patterson, his president, and, more significant, the Chase Manhattan Bank's chief operating officer. Supposedly, observers were to construe it was all Patterson's fault—which could have been the case. Patterson had been a Chase Manhattan executive for twenty-five years, but was never regarded by people who watch such things as a strong man. A reporter for the *American Banker* magazine who met with Patterson many times said he was a man who seemed to be more interested in "making it in the 400, the social 400, than in working for the Chase. He spent a lot of time at the Hamptons on Long Island with his wife. He made the society pages, and did not work the sixty or eighty hours a week that bank executives on top normally work."

Most observers, however, including Rockefeller's fellow bankers, put the blame for Chase Manhattan's misfortunes on Rockefeller. Few were as outspoken as John R. Bunting, who says this about Rockefeller as a banker: "Not good at all. He's got the best name in the world, the absolute best name in the world, or at least the best name in this country. Rockefeller. Absolute best name in this country. He's got the bank with the—I would say—most prestige in the country going for him. And he's running a third-rate bank. Walter Wriston in First National City is beating the hell out of him. National City is beating the hell out of him."

In "Banks and the Poor" Rockefeller declared, "The banking industry recognizes fully that it has a very essential role to play, almost in the same sense that the doctor does in taking care of the personal needs of individuals who are in trouble as well as businesses—small businesses as well as large businesses. And in this period of time when there is a great deal of distress in our nation, when the economy is declining, the banking industry has paid special attention to the needs of the disadvantaged, to the needs of minority groups, to helping the unemployed find satisfactory jobs, and most importantly, to helping with the desperate housing problem that exists in the country today." The documentary's producer, Morton Silverstein, showed, however, that the Chase Manhattan Bank was far from being a doctor to the disadvantaged. As a member of a group of eighty banks pledged to lend $100 million for the rehabilitation through mortgages of homes in Brooklyn, the bank had committed a mere $700,000 more than two years after its initial announcement. The entire group of eighty banks had committed a total of $8 million.

In another part of the film Representative Wright Patman, chairman of the House Banking and Currency Committee, suggested that high mortgage interest rates of 7½ to 8½ percent had stopped home construction in its tracks, and that Chase Manhattan was really more interested in backing gambling casinos operated in the Bahama Islands by a company named Resorts International. To this charge Rockefeller replied that the investment in gambling had been made on behalf of a trust customers by Chase Manhattan's Fiduciary Investment Department, implying that the investment was an arms-length one in which the bank was concerned only with the well-being of its trusts customers. In a give-and-take sequence Patman retorted that the department was just as much a part of the bank's money-making operations as were its checking account services, personal loan department, and every other department. The retort went unanswered in the film, but official records show that the bank was far more interested in the possible return from gambling than it was admitting. According to testimony taken by the House Judiciary Committee, the Chase Manhattan Bank's Fiduciary Investment Department in January, 1969, planned to use trust funds to help Resorts International (known previously as the Mary Carter Paint Company) to take over, i.e., to raid, Pan American World Airways. A takeover attempt was denied, but the plan was for Chase Manhattan to sell 1.5 million shares of Pan American stock held in trust to Resorts International, which intended to buy another 900,000 shares of the airline's stock from a conglomerate corporation named Gulf and Western. The takeover attempt came to the attention of the House Antitrust Subcommittee, which began an inquiry to learn the "working relationship" between Gulf and Western, a seller of Pan American shares to Resorts International, and Chase Manhattan, also a seller to Resorts International, a company speculating in land and gambling. How deeply interested Chase Manhattan was in the gambling operation can be determined from its own analysis.

The bank estimated that hotel rooms and cabaret operations would be profitable enough, but the gleam in the eye of its Fiduciary Investment Department was put there by profit projections based on gambling. The bank's analyst said:

"All projects are currently making money; however, the Paradise Island Casino is by far the largest money maker. In addition to the 350 slot machines on Paradise Island, each earning a profit of $10,000 to $12,000 per year, gaming enthusiasts can play roulette, dice, black jack and chemin de fir [*sic*]. The casino and related areas employ 15 people and the operating costs per night, including top name entertainment, approximates $20,000. Based on one year operations, management estimates that each room on the island accounts for $30.00 in gaming net income per day. It has been estimated that $53 million to $54 million will be wagered at the casino in 1969 and of this 34 percent or $18 million will be gross winnings to the casino. After overhead, operating expenses and government taxes, $9 million in net income is projected. Another $3 million is projected from the hotel operations, golf course, beach and restaurants, etc. Management estimates that Resorts International (RTA) should net at least $3,000 annually per room from hotel and ancillary activities.

Looking out 3 to 4 years Resorts is planning on having 5,000 hotel rooms available. While only 1,500 or so will be owned and operated by RTA, it is estimated that the RTA hotels and related areas will contribute $10 million. With 5,000 rooms on the island, initial projections for the casino's gross win are placed at $50 million of which $30 million could conceivably be brought down to net.

In January, 1969, three research officers of the Chase Manhattan Bank visited Paradise Island, after which the bank agreed to sell its 1.5 million shares of Pan American World Airways stock to Resorts International and to become a major investor itself in Resorts International. The bank not only bought $15 million in notes issued by Resorts International, but also 1.5 million warrants to buy 1.5 million shares of the company's stock at $40 a share and another 1.5 million warrants to purchase the company's shares at $60 each. Then, using the trusts it held with full discretion, i.e., those it could buy and sell securities for without consulting the beneficiaries, Chase Manhattan sold stock in such going companies as Eastman Kodak, United States Time, Mack Trucks, Southern Railway, General Motors, and Standard Oil Company of New Jersey (now Exxon). The exchange of such stocks for so highly speculative an issue as Resorts International was clearly questionable, as was the bank's willingness to sell shares in Pan American World Airways to assist a company in which the bank had a major interest, i.e., Resorts International, to raid another company.

The question here, however, is whether bankers have the right, as David Rockefeller apparently believes, to closet themselves and refuse to reveal facts that are not necessarily complimentary. The public nature of banking and its intimate tie-in with the public economy suggests there should be public accountability. Banks, though public corporations, are unique because they are so vital to the nation's economic health. In return, banks have been permitted to deal for themselves at a profit in the nation's currency by lending it. Indeed, banks are permitted to create money to lend and thus profit by. The moment a bank credits the account of a borrower with a loan, the bank's own deposits are increased, since the act of extending credit in itself creates money, or a deposit the borrower can draw on. But the creation of money does not stop there. As the borrower draws on his loan by writing checks, the checks, as they are deposited in other banks, in turn raise the deposits of those banks and therefore their lending power. It has been estimated, in fact, that in the process a dollar can be increased thirty-three times, or to $33. Obviously, banks have been granted a very special mandate, one that separates them from the rest of U.S. business. That mandate also implies that banks act with public approval of their actions, and can act only as long as that public approval continues.

In David Rockefeller's case, the decision to grant audiences only to supporters of his bank's policies and to refuse to see those he judges hostile is especially questionable, since Rockefeller tends to address leaders of other nations as though he were speaking for the United States. For example, in 1970 at a meeting of the Council of Foreign Relations, he attempted to be the broker between the "sovereignties all over the world" (his own phrase), who were in conflict with the aggressive investment tactics of American corporations abroad, the so-called multinationals. It is this habit of his of addressing nations as an official of the United States that has led some observers to say that though Rockefeller would not want to be President of the United States because of the rough and tumble of politics, he would accept an offer to become Secretary of State. A journalist who knows David Rockefeller well says that "it is an open secret that Rockefeller would like to be Secretary of State. Once he confided that it was a thrill in 1972 to be called by a Russian trade delegation that was in the United States and asked to spend some time with them. I'm sure that though he achieved very little in the way of business for the bank, he was quite pleased that they thought of calling him, and my impression is that he probably spoke about business in general rather than how the Chase might help the Russians finance trade. Obviously to some extent the journalist was wrong for the Chase Manhattan was one of the first banks to establish itself in a trade deal with the Russians. Still another journalist with access to David Rockefeller sees him as "a fantastically decent human being with his own personal ethic, but the translation of his own principles into action so far has been something he is not yet willing to pay the price for." The journalist was talking about Rockefeller's unwillingness to become bloodied for the thing he has said he believes in, e.g., the housing in Brooklyn, that never got built.

In politics, however, Rockefeller would have to be accountable to the people. Actually his self-donned mantle of U.S. spokesman is consistent with a decision he made very early in his life. As a young man he was not quite sure which direction he should take and he consulted one of the most respected statesmen and politicians in the Western World at the time, Canada's Prime Minister William Lyon Mackenzie King. Rockefeller says that after the "conference," he rejected a role in government and opted for banking. Rockefeller himself tells the story in a way that implies that he opted for banking because bankers had more influence in world affairs than politicians.

That bankers fade badly in public life is an accepted fact even among bankers themselves. When asked about it they almost inevitably point to the short, unhappy public life of David Kennedy, once president and chief executive officer of Chicago's Continental Illinois National Bank and Trust Company. Unlike Rockefeller, Kennedy was regarded as a superb banker, and was frequently cited in glowing terms for his forward thinking. In his years as chief executive officer of Continental he made Continental over, through marketing techniques and merger, into a leading commercial bank and "the hub of one of the largest networks of correspondent banks in the country." (The accolades come from Donald M. Graham, Kennedy's successor.) But Kennedy proved that bankers are out of their depth in public life. As President Nixon's first Secretary of the Treasury—preceding John Connally, a nonbanker, and Connally's successor, George Shultz—Kennedy became a "tragic" figure, in the words of one banker. Kennedy's philosophy, which served him well in banking, was to maintain a low profile. But the philosophy hardly worked in public life, where give and take, as Connally proved later, counts. John R. Bunting of the First Pennsylvania Bank and Trust suggested when asked that Kennedy's problem was he could not be anything but "the typical banker, that is one who maintains a low profile." A journalist who knew Kennedy "pretty well" said he was "enlightened" as a person but unable to apply his principles—the same observation made by another journalist about David Rockefeller. But neither interpretation really explains Kennedy's refusal to answer questions put to him by a congressional committee, which had every right to ask them. Nor why Kennedy made no effort to clear up a blatant conflict of interest. While Treasury Secretary, Kennedy was proposing legislation that would benefit the bank in which he held a financial interest. Harsh critics have said it was arrogance, but there is no really satisfactory answer. Kennedy himself has remained mute about the question.

The incident occurred during hearing before the House Banking and Currency Committee, which in 1969 was considering a bill to amend the Bank Holding Company Act of 1956. The act regulated only holding companies controlling more than one bank; exempt from federal regulation were those controlling only one bank. Many large banks including Kennedy's, had created a holding company with the intention of buying up companies not only in the financial services, e.g., insurance, but in industrial activities as well, e.g., metal forming. It was a giant loophole that could lead to an extraordinary concentration of industry by the formation of financial conglomerates, as documented in a later chapter, and the hearings being conducted by Wright Patman were designed to develop legislation to plug it.

On Thursday, April 17, 1969, Kennedy made the first of two appearances as Secretary of the Treasury before the Patman committee. As Secretary of the Treasury he was a key witness in any banking legislation. Almost from the beginning Patman questioned Kennedy why he was retaining stock ownership in Continental Bank's own one-bank holding company, Conill Corporation, even as he was Treasury Secretary. Conill was a company that Kennedy himself had created.

Minutes after the hearings opened, Patman had this exchange of words with Kennedy, who was accompanied by Charls Walker, an Under Secretary of the Treasury at the time and a former executive vice president of the American Bankers Association:

> THE CHAIRMAN: This morning we have before us witnesses who are scheduled to present the Nixon administration's view on the various bills to regulate financial conglomerates. The prepared

statements of Secretary Kennedy and the Under Secretary, Charls Walker, refer only to one bill, number H.R. 9385, but I trust that they will lend us their wisdom on the other bills which relate to this subject, particularly the one the committee is studying. Secretary Kennedy, I know, has indeed given this subject a great deal of study. In fact, just recently one of Mr. Kennedy's letters on this subject came to my attention. It was dated December 13, 1968, and was addressed to the stockholders of Continental Illinois National Bank & Trust Co., It was signed David M. Kennedy, chairman of the board of directors, and I quote:

> After careful study, management is convinced that a one-bank holding company is the best means of serving present needs and meeting changing financial requirements of industry, government, and the public. This new corporate structure will permit management increased flexibility in establishing new services utilizing the bank's expertise in the financial field. . . . Your board of directors unanimously recommends your approval of this plan.

And as a result of Mr. Kennedy's persuasion, the bank did indeed become a one-bank holding company, known as the Conill Corp., a Delaware company. I place a copy of the entire letter in the record.

It is obvious, Mr. Secretary, that you come this morning, in effect, wearing two hats. One as an official of the U.S. Government; the other as a former official who was the guiding force behind one of the nation's largest one-bank holding companies. These comments I make here this morning, Mr. Secretary, are not personal in nature. I hope that you, this committee, and the general public understand this. In fact, I do not know of a single member of this committee who has any personal feeling against you. I certainly do not. I do not know of any member of this committee who dislikes you in any way and we all admire you for your great career of banking and finance, as one of our great leaders in the United States of America.

But it is the duty of this committee and its chairman to explore the qualifications of any witness who appears before us. It is essential that this Congress and the committee and the public fully understand from what vantage point you view this very important legislation. It is very much like selecting a jury in the trial of a case. A juror is selected because he doesn't have any interest and would not be influenced by anything except the law and the testimony. And this is comparable in many ways.

Mr. Secretary, I am sure that you are a man of high integrity, but you come before us today to testify on banking legislation at a time when you hold substantial interests in a bank. And more importantly, it is an interest in a one-bank holding company—the very subject on which you testify.

In recent weeks, Mr. Secretary, a great deal of information has come to me concerning your various financial arrangements with the Continental Illinois Bank and the Conill Corporation, of which it is a subsidiary. Based on this information, it is my opinion that you are very closely connected, through various financial arrangements, with the Conill Corporation and the Continental Bank.

This would greatly disturb me under any circumstances, but I am particularly concerned that such a situation exists when you are here to testify on what I consider to be and many other banks consider to be the most important piece of banking legislation since the early 1930s. It is a time when the Congress and the American people need a clear objective judgment from the executive branch unfettered by ties to the banking industry.

In fairness to you I do not want to generalize. I will list some of the specifics, and I hope that you will give careful consideration to making public your entire financial statement, particularly as it regards any bank holdings. Information that has come to my attention leads me to believe—I state these as facts:

1. That you and your wife hold at least 7,800 shares of Continental Illinois bank stock which was placed in a "blind" trust at Old Colony Trust of Boston, Massachusetts. While this stock was to be "diversified," there was no requirement that all of this stock, or even any substantial portion of the stock, be sold.

2. More importantly, it is my understanding that you have now exercised an option on 30,855 additional shares of Continental Illinois stock with a market value well in excess of $1,200,000. But it is my understanding, that this stock option of 30,855 shares has not been placed in trust and will not be placed in trust before August 15, 1969. So, you are, in effect, the owner of that stock at this time.

Mr. Secretary, it takes no financial expert to realize that the value of this huge stock option will fluctuate according to what happens to the legislation regulating one-bank holding companies. I mean the legislation before us here today; the legislation on which you are about to testify.

3. It is also my understanding, Mr. Secretary, that you had a very large holding in a profit-sharing plan at Continental Illinois.

And part of this holding has now been transferred to you in the form of Continental Illinois stock. But, unlike the stock listed in point one, your trustee is not obligated to "diversify" this holding. In effect, this block of stock remains intact and you know that the moment you leave the Office of the Secretary of the Treasury you will have in your possession a substantial holding in Continental Illinois Bank, or the Conill Holding Co. Under these circumstances, it would be extremely naive to say that you have no interest in the value of that stock at this moment.

4. Also, Mr. Secretary, it has come to my attention that Continental Illinois has promised you future financial remuneration of a sizable sum, something on the order of $200,000. It is money that will be paid to you when you leave office.

5. In addition, it is my understanding that on January 31 you started receiving a pension from the bank amounting to nearly $5,000 a month or roughly equivalent to your salary from the Federal Government. I understand, of course, that this is a pension which you were granted as a former employee and as a member of the bank's pension plan.

Mr. Secretary, I could talk at length about the various conflict of interest statutes that relate to your situation as Secretary of the Treasury, but I will not go into these in any great detail here this morning.

It is my understanding that section 208 of title 18 of the U.S. Code has been called to your attention. As you know, subsection [a] in substance requires an officer of the executive branch to refrain from participating in any matter in which he has a financial interest.

I hope that you are keeping this provision in mind. I would like to point out that should the definition of banking be broadened, as contemplated in the administration's holding company bill, the value of your stock in Conill Company—the Continental Illinois National Bank—will rise sharply. Surely when you recommended that Continental Illinois form a one-bank holding company you felt that this was a profitable venture for the corporation or you would not have so recommended.

This kind of question could be eliminated if you could tell the committee this morning that you were willing to revise your trust arrangement to provide for the immediate sale of all bank stock. Perhaps this would cost you money in the form of additional taxes, but I do not think this should be the overriding factor in meeting your obligations as Secretary of the Treasury. Living up to the spirit and the letter of the law is often costly to the average citizen and I do not think that it should be any different for Cabinet officers.

Unfortunately, Mr. Kennedy, your Under Secretary, who I understand has done much of the work on the administration's bill, likewise comes to us as a foremost advocate of the banking industry. Mr. Walker, of course, was for years the chief executive officer of the American Bankers Association, the principal lobbying arm of the banking industry. In the months before he took his present office, he participated in planning the position of the banks on bank-holding company legislation.

So, Mr. Walker faces similar difficulties in separating a lengthy career in banking and his present responsibilities as an official of the U. S. government.

Again, I repeat, I find this situation very strange. I think it is a sad state of affairs when an administration sends us bankers to comment on banking legislation.

Later, after Kennedy and Walker (and former Assistant Attorney General for Antitrust Richard W. McLaren) had read statements on bank holding, Patman resumed comment on the conflict of interest he saw:

PATMAN: Now, the statement that I read at the beginning, are you willing to answer that when you look over your transcript [of the hearings], or should I interrogate you about it? You would be willing to comment on it in your transcript, I assume?

KENNEDY: Comment on what?

PATMAN: Comment on the statement that I made. I made some allegations in my opening statement this morning about you getting about $60,000 a year.

KENNEDY: I have no comments, Mr. Chairman. No comments at all.

PATMAN: And other things about—

KENNEDY: No comment.

PATMAN: No comment at all?

KENNEDY: None at all.

PATMAN: Well unless you agree to comment on that in your statement, when you look over your transcript we will just have to interrogate you about it.

KENNEDY: Go ahead and interrogate. I have no comments.

PATMAN: You have no comment at all?
KENNEDY: None.

A week later, on Thursday, April 24, 1969, Kennedy appeared reluctantly and only upon the insistence of Patman, who again raised the question of Kennedy's conflict of interest. In the opening minutes Patman said:

Mr. Secretary, I raised some extremely serious questions about your holdings of bank stock at a time when you are serving as a public official and at a time when you are charged with making decisions affecting the banking industry. Mr. Secretary, you did not comment on these charges when you were here last week. As I remember, you simply had a "no comment" answer. While you may not have intended to do so, and I personally doubt that you did, for all practical purposes you pleaded the Fifth Amendment. I will not go back over these same charges here this morning because I want to see us get on with this hearing. I think this is the most important bill we have before Congress affecting banking, and I feel it is necessary that we get the bill passed. But as I pointed out last week, your bank stock and your other connections with the Conill Corporation—a one-bank holding company—do have a direct bearing on your presentations before this committee. Let me state very frankly and quickly what I expect from you: It is my understanding that you have in your possession a full and detailed financial statement which lists all of your bank stock and other holdings. I would like that statement along with any other pertinent information furnished the committee without delay and certainly before the hearings on the one-bank holding company legislation are concluded. This is one sure way, Mr. Kennedy, that you could very quickly exonerate yourself if you are right.

Second, Mr. Secretary, I urge you to confer with your lawyers and with the Justice Department attorneys and review in detail all of the Federal statutes and Executive orders dealing with conflicts of interest. I would want their findings reported to this committee. I also hope, Mr. Secretary, that you will confer with the President and other appropriate officials to determine whether your situation as a bank stockholder is indeed in keeping with the personnel policies of this administration.

President Nixon submitted one of the finest reports on crime I have ever heard in a message to Congress . . . but if that message is implemented by proper laws the Secretary of the Treasury will have the greatest responsibility in carrying out those laws. Therefore, it is necessary that we have a Secretary of the Treasury who is holding his office in accordance with the law and not in conflict with the law and has no ax to grind of any kind. From the facts that I have before me I can only conclude that you do indeed have a serious conflict of interest which can be remedied only through the immediate sale of your bank stock and through the severance of your other financial ties to the Conill Corporation. I hope you can come back before this committee in a few weeks and report unequivocally that you have disposed of your bank stock and removed any possible conflict of interest and that you are not serving in violation of the law.

Kennedy did not accept Patman's invitation to return, but only six days later, on Wednesday, April 30, 1969, Patman opened the Bank Holding Act amendments hearing with this comment:

PATMAN: The committee will please come to order. Before we hear from the witnesses this morning I want to make a brief report to the committee about some of the issues that have been discussed in earlier sessions concerning the Secretary of the Treasury, David Kennedy. Although the Secretary refused to comment when he was before this committee, he has now taken some partial steps in an obvious attempt to resolve his conflict of interest. As this committee remembers, I raised questions about Mr. Kennedy's stock option of 30,855 shares of Continental Illinois stock and about the 3,800 shares of the bank stocks which he received from a profit-sharing plan. As the morning newspapers report, Mr. Kennedy has now decided to sell the 30,855 shares in the stock option and has decided to take his profit shares in cash—$645,000— rather than in stock.

Both the *Wall Street Journal* and *The New York Times* carry detailed accounts of this latest move by the Secretary of the Treasury in this morning's editions. Unfortunately, another newspaper inadvertently left the impression that Kennedy had disposed of some of this stock before he took office. This is not factual. The facts are that he exercised the option after he took office and he sold the stock while he was Secretary. The disposition of the stock has come recently, only after the issue was raised in Congress. The Secretary's action is not sufficient to sever his ties with the Continental Illinois National Bank or the Conill Corp.—a one-bank holding company. As I have pointed out earlier, the Secretary has been promised a payment of $200,000 from the bank after he leaves office. This is a sum that was voted by the board of directors of Continental Illinois National Bank after it had learned that Mr. Kennedy was to become Secretary of the Treasury and that he would be in a position to take care of the bank's interests at the highest levels of this government. I understand that the Treasury Department has put forth a defense that the bank cannot revoke this $200,000 payment. This is no defense at all. If this is a defense, then we are setting a new standard for gifts to public officials and to Cabinet appointees. Under this logic, the gifts are all right as long as the donor cannot take them back. This is not acceptable. The Secretary should firmly and immediately revoke his interest in this gift from the bank. Also, the Secretary, as this committee well knows, continues to receive every month a $4,800 payment from the bank in the form of a pension. He also receives other benefits from the bank, including life insurance and health insurance payments. The Secretary should move to sever all of these ties to the bank and get on with the job of serving as a public official. He has to make a choice of whether he wants to be a public official or a banker.

As I insisted last week this committee should receive a full financial report from the Secretary of the Treasury. I do not think it is too much for the Banking and Currency Committee to ask this of a Cabinet official. This committee should make its own independent judgment on the serious issues raised by Mr. Kennedy's connections with the bank. I hope no member of this committee feels that it is sufficient to have an opinion from the general counsel of Mr. Kennedy's own Treasury Department. I think it would have been unusual, to say the least, if the general counsel, who is an employee operating under Mr. Kennedy's direction, had found his boss guilty of wrongdoing. His own employee has found him innocent. If there had been any other verdict we would have had a new general counsel of the Treasury.

A day later, on May 1, 1969, Patman revealed to his committee that Kennedy's counsel, Paul W. Eggers, had supplied the Banking and Currency Committee with a statement which Patman said was "highly confusing with a number of unsubstantiated claims." Patman had asked Eggers to appear before the committee to discuss the statement, which was "minus dates and documentation," but Eggers refused as had Kennedy.

Disturbed, Patman said, "If the Secretary has no financial

ties with the Conill Corporation, and if he is free of any conflict of interest in connection with the one-bank holding legislation he has proposed, then why should he not appear in open session and explain this fact? If he has nothing to hide why does he not appear? Why does he submit all of his statements through counsel and then refuse to answer inquiries either from the Congress or from the press? The Secretary of the Treasury is using an executive version of the Fifth Amendment to prevent the facts from being known about his financial arrangements with the banking industry."

Kennedy may well have felt that as a major banker he had a certain immunity. Critics said later he was genuinely surprised that he would be called to task on so basic a conflict, the implication being that it would be overlooked because of his origins, i.e., banking. Kennedy must have known, as most bankers know, that they are virtually immune to being charged with conflict, and even when charged nothing is done about it—as, for example, when many bankers made illegal political campaign contributions that were clear violations of the federal Corrupt Practices Act.

Under the act it is unlawful for national banks to contribute to election campaigns, but in 1970 Patman documented charge after charge of banks being actively and secretly engaged in fund raising. But despite the documentation, the outcome of the investigation was a victory for the bankers that clearly suggested their political power in the Nixon administration. This was the kind of immunity Kennedy felt he had—though finally he became an embarrassment to President Nixon and was replaced by John Connally.

Patman's charges of violations of the Corrupt Practices Act were made public in a letter in 1970 to John Mitchell, then Attorney General. In Seattle, said Patman, the League for Good Government, a front for bankers, had solicited funds from bank officers making $12,000 or more a year, using a memo carrying the name of nineteen top officers of the National Bank of Commerce, though not the name of the bank itself. Contributions, which could be directed to either party, were to be mailed to Box 3966, Seattle, the same box number held by the bank. The memo said:

> Each year political parties, candidates and committees promoting special legislation approach the bank for financial support. As you know, banks are prohibited by law from contributing to any political candidate's campaign for public office. As a result, for some years a relatively small number of officers have been attempting to carry the financial burden of these requests. In recent years these requests for political contributions have substantially increased in both number and dollar amount. It now has become apparent that a wider degree of participation is imperative and we want to extend a cordial invitation to you to join us in this important civic responsibility.

The memo was accompanied by a two-year pledge form and a "fair-share formula," and said, ominously, "records will be maintained of each individual's contribution."

At least one junior officer of the National Bank of Commerce who received the memo did not regard breaking the law as a civic responsibility and wrote to Patman, "If you were an officer of the National Bank of Commerce of Seattle how would you like to receive this letter from a group of your senior officers?"

In another case the Manufacturers Hanover Trust Company of New York required its top officers to kick back a portion of their salaries for a political fund, with checks drawn to the order of "Robert Isban Special Account." Robert Isban was the deputy controller of the bank. On April 8, 1970, an anonymously written letter turned up in Wright Patman's office accusing the bank of this illegal practice. The letter said:

> Dear Congressman Patman:
>   I believe it is illegal for banks to make contributions to political candidates. The Manufacturers Hanover Trust Company has gotten around this by forcing its 1,000 plus officers to kick back ½ of 1 percent of their salaries each year. Checks are drawn to the order or "Robert Isban Special Account." Mr. Isban is a

Deputy Controller. Disposition of the slush fund is not disclosed to those who contribute.

Still another instance involved the Marine Midland Bank of Buffalo, New York, which surreptitiously called a meeting at the Inn on the Park in Toronto, Canada, on November 8, 1969, to discuss establishment of a fund "from which contributions to political candidates can be obtained." The heart of the plan was contained in a bank memo from C. E. Berryman, senior vice president, to David J. Laub, president. It called for assessments on the salaries of Marine Midland's 107 officers receiving salaries of $15,000 or more, and it was estimated that on the basis of ½ of 1 percent $9,170 could be contributed from $1,834,000 assessable dollars. The memo said that bankers who have successful programs all state that it cannot be done on a voluntary basis. A certain degree of persuasion has to occur. The writer, Berryman, said that it should be the responsibility of each senior vice president to ascertain that each officer in his area of administration receiving $15,000 or more is made aware of the importance of this program and has the opportunity to contribute. It was a message whose substance was repeated in bank memorandums everywhere—in Detroit, in Cleveland, in East Lansing.

In at least one bank mere money was not enough. In 1971 in Security Pacific National Bank of Los Angeles, the nation's tenth largest bank at the time, a so-called Active Citizenship Program (ACT) was introduced to measure the "involvement inventory" of its employees. An involvement inventory questionnaire distributed by the bank sought answers on private organizations employees were associated with, e.g., the YMCA, including how much assistance the employee and his organizations received from the bank in terms of financial support, e.g., time off. The insidious part of the questionnaire were those questions regarding an employee's associations with elected or appointed officials and "others of prominence," including whether the employee had a close relationship with frequent contact and whether he or she knew the official well. The bank said it would use the information gathered in its public, community, and government relations programs, and that "contact with a legislator might be helpful in developing information on legislation which might affect Security Pacific National Bank, or the banking industry in general."

Such attempts at wielding political influence were generally done in a low-pressure way—but not always.

In Texas a handful of bankers developed a formula for political fund giving that did not try to sidestep the Federal Corrupt Practices Act by encouraging giving among its officers and employees. The bankers merely circulated a memorandum asking that contributions be made based on a formula tied to the dollar resources of the banks. The memo carried the names of a number of Texas bankers and asked that contributions be paid to A. C. Verner of Lubbock. Vernor was president and a director of the First National Bank of Lubbock. Though the bank's name was not included in the memo, its post office box number was.

Some of the most blatant attempts to raise political funds occurred in Ohio, where the Central National Bank of Cleveland worked out a formula, as many other banks had, for assessing its officers' salaries. The difference was that the bank sought the credit directly—in defiance, apparently, of the law. Its chairman, E. L. Carpenter, said to his bank officers, "If you have been making political contributions directly to others, it will be greatly appreciated if you will do it through the bank so that the bank will get credit for it on the goals assigned us." The goals had been assigned by economically powerful customers of the bank, and funds collected were handed over to a "Good Government Program."

Still another Ohio bank, the Bellefontaine National Bank of Bellefontaine, lent $20,000 to the campaign of a state auditor named Roger Cloud, the Republican nominee for governor. Bank records showed that a check had been made to the Cloud for Governor Committee. Cloud himself had at one time been on the board of the bank and had also been a vice president.

The Bellefontaine National Bank, as well as the Manufacturers Hanover Trust and the First National Bank of Lubbock, were especially referred to in the letter sent by Wright Patman to Attorney General John Mitchell. (The letter also pointed out that in New York State at least eight commercial bank exectuives, including David Rockefeller and Gabriel Hauge, president of Manufacturers Hanover Trust, were on the Republican state finance committee.) In the letter Patman asked Mitchell for an investigation of illegal contributions on the part of national banks and bank-backed political committees. In November, 1970, Will Wilson, the Assistant Attorney General who had been associated with Frank W. Sharp and the Sharpstown State Bank, wrote a noncommittal two-paragraph letter in response to Patman's lengthy six-page request for an investigation. Eventually the Justice Department did bring charges against five national banks —none of which were nationally prominent. Four of the five were Ohio banks: the First National Bank of Cincinnati; the Ohio National Bank of Columbus; the First Knox National Bank, Mount Vernon; and the Bellefontaine National Bank. The fifth was the Frost National Bank of San Antonio, Texas.

First National Bank of Cincinnati was charged in four counts with making loans totaling $60,000 for political purposes. Ohio National of Columbus was charged with making a loan to a political committee representing a state treasurer. First Knox National was charged with lending $2,000 to the Knox County Republican Finance Committee. The Bellefontaine bank was charged in four counts with making loans to the Cloud for Governor Committee. (Cloud was defeated despite the bank's support.)

The outcome of the charges, the first ever made under the Federal Corrupt Practices Act since it became law in 1925, was strange, suggesting once against the immunity bankers can frequently count on. In February, 1972, after the cases against the Ohio banks had been dismissed by federal district court judges but were being appealed, the Justice Department decided to drop the charges . . . not because of any admitted weakness in its case.

The department announced that the law itself had been amended by the Federal Election Campaign Act of 1972 to permit banks to make political campaign loans. The law had been supported by President Nixon and the Justice Department reasoned that even though it was not retroactive, the "interests of justice would not be served by continuing to seek convictions" for something now permitted.

5

Elitist Nabobs—and a Bit of Arm-Twisting

A S WITH all privileged systems and groups throughout history, banking is composed of an elite. The standards of admission to the fold are severe, if not impossible, for most people. There are probably only a handful of black bankers in the United States, for example, and few of these can be found in the executive offices of the major banks. When John R. Bunting, whose own background is Philadelphia's middle class, asked Henry G. Parks, a black businessman, to serve on the board of Philadelphia's First Pennsylvania Bank and Trust Company, the invitation was enough to collect headlines for Bunting. Bunting, however, is a banker who once described the free enterprise system bankers defend so vehemently when they feel they and their practices are under attack in this way: "The current economic system in America can be fairly described as being socialism for the rich and capitalism for the poor." It was a remark made in reference to special federal legislation in 1970 guaranteeing a $250 million loan to Lockheed Aircraft Company, a loan twenty-four major United States banks would not make without the guarantee though their loss reserves (money that banks can put aside from their net income and pay no taxes on) exist for just that purpose. One or two of the biggest banks could have absorbed the entire loss themselves, e.g., Chase Manhattan, which had over $300 million in its loss reserve account. Bunting has also said, "If you're a banker it's a revelation to see, hear, and be part of strategies that make it possible for people with

tremendous incomes to avoid paying much—if anything—in income taxes. Take Ronald Reagan and John Wayne, with their
cattle interests. John Wayne, the all-American, star-spangled
love-of-country guy, of all people. That really startled me. What
has happened is that the fellows like me, people whose income is
almost totally derived from the corporations they work for, are
really the ones who are carrying the load."

Such comments, of course, are unique in banking and have
helped earn Bunting the enmity of some of his fellow bankers.

It is not only blacks who are rare figures in banks. Jews are
scarce, too. Though they populate and even dominate investment
banking—raising capital through the public and private sales of
corporate securities—the management ranks of commercial banking in the United States are notable for their absence of Jews.
An aggressive Jewish Wall Street entrepreneur suggests that banking, despite its high salaries, really does not pay enough to satisfy
his own appetite for riches; thus it is natural for him and other
Jews to choose investment banking, where fortunes can be made.
Critics of bank hiring and promotion practices, though, say that
this is a convenient cover that has actually been used by banks
themselves. The Ralph Nader study of First National City Bank
noted that there were no Jews at all in top positions. A highly
respected banking editor of a major publication, a man who is
on a first name-basis with leading bankers, also asserts that Jews
are kept out of the upper echelons and tells this story, somewhat
bitterly, of a friend who was a leading candidate for the very top
spot in a New York bank—until it was realized he was a Jew:
"A friend of mine was working as a senior vice president. He
was someone I knew for ten years. I never knew, either, that he
was a Jew. He didn't have a Jewish name or a Jewish face. One
day earlier this year [it was 1972] he telephoned me and asked
whether I knew of any openings in banking. Two new men, two
senior vice presidents, were informed they would be promoted to
executive vice presidents, and ultimately become chief executive
and the number-two man. The first statement they made to the

board of the bank was that the first thing they wanted to do was to get rid of my friend because he was Jewish and they didn't want any Jews in top management."

Studies do tend to bear out the thesis that there are few Jews at the top of banking. One that was conducted by the American Jewish Commitee in 1966 (another was being conducted late in 1972) confirmed a lack of Jews. Named *Patterns of Exclusion from the Executive Suite: Commercial Banking*, the study reported a "virtual absence of Jews" in "executive posts in America's major commercial banks," though in the years since its distribution the study's director, Samuel Freedman, has seen "some improvement." The data were gathered by eighteen area offices of the American Jewish Committee and covered the nation's fifty leading commercial banks in terms of size of assets. Two levels of management were surveyed, senior officers and middle management, but no position lower than vice president was considered.

Among 632 senior officers included in the survey only eight, or 1.3 percent, were Jews, and four of these were employed by a single bank. Four other banks had one Jewish senior officer each, while the remaining forty-five banks had none.

Much the same condition existed at middle management levels, from which senior management generally is chosen. Jews were scarce. Among 3,438 executives only thirty-two, or 0.9 percent, were Jewish. Those thirty-two were employed by twelve of the fifty banks studied—meaning that many of the nation's banks did not have a single Jew either in middle or upper management.

The scarcity of Jews at banking helms was especially noticeable in New York, which is not only the banking capital of the world but also a city with an extraordinarily large Jewish population. Among the fifty banks in the survey, nine were situated in New York, and though the nine employed 173 senior officers, only one of these officers was a Jew. In middle management a mere 9 among 927 were Jews.

The reasons bankers themselves gave for Jews not appearing in executive suites ranged from a belief that Jews were dishonest, overly aggressive, too inclined toward wheeling and dealing (banking is a business for gentlemen), and too anxious to make substantial amounts of money in a hurry. Jews were also socially unacceptable, some executives felt, and at least one major banker admitted that the field was dominated by Anglo-Saxon Protestants who were "completely inbred in their social relations." Finally, many a banker admitted he feared the bogeyman of the "powerful Jewish banker."

Keeping Jews and blacks and others who are unacceptable out of banking's top hierarchy is not the only evidence that bankers are an ingrown group. There is, for example, the case of the attempted raid on the Chemical Bank and Trust Company in New York, a raid that was aborted by the Chemical's fellow banks. It is doubtful that the members of any other industry would perform in such a way to keep one of their number in control—if only for the reason that the Justice Department would descend on them with antitrust charges. In the case of the banks, however, what was clearly a violation of the antitrust laws was dismissed by an Assistant Attorney General, when asked about the violation, as follows: "What good would it do to throw the bankers in jail?" More realistically it might be asked whether the Justice Department would have been able, even if it wished, to throw the bankers in anybody's jail.

The story of the raid and its failure began in February, 1969, when a small conglomerate named Leasco Data Processing Equipment Corporation and its aggressive young chairman Saul Steinberg made plans to take over the Chemical Bank. Leasco had been founded in 1962 as the Ideal Leasing Company and in 1964, when it decided to become a public corporation, it was still a relatively tiny company with revenues of $8 million. By 1969, however, Leasco had grown 13,610 percent, thanks to a string of acquisitions financed in large part by banks. All the while Leasco was growing, such banks as the Chase Manhattan and Continental Illinois were purchasing Leasco stock for their trust accounts. In at least one case Leasco promised to buy back its own stock from the banks, paying sums equal to 12.5 percent for a riskless investment. This last was the kind of deal that made bankers truly friendly toward Leasco, and allowed Leasco, a corporate minnow, to swallow corporate whales. For example, when Leasco acquired a company named Reliance Insurance in 1968, Leasco's assets were $74.2 million, its 1967 revenues only $14.4 million. Reliance, on the other hand, owned assets worth $581.3 million and had revenues of $330.1 million in 1967.

When Saul Steinberg's eye fell on Chemical Bank Leasco's assets were $402.2 million. Chemical was the sixth largest bank in the United States, and owned assets of $8.97 billion.

Late in January, 1969, William S. Renchard, chairman of the Chemical Bank, received what he called "solid intelligence" confirming rumors that had been circulating for months of Leasco's planned takeover. By this time Leasco had accumulated 349,000 shares of Chemical Bank stock, or 4,000 more than its goal of 345,000 shares. Much of the stock had been accumulated secretly between November, 1968, and January, 1969, by Leasco's newly acquired subsidiary, Reliance Insurance Company, and kept in a numbered account in the First National Bank of Jersey City, New Jersey.

Secret purchases of the shares represented only one side of the takeover, however. Steinberg next planned to buy shares openly by offering Chemical Bank shareholders a deal to exchange their securities for Leasco securities. At one point Steinberg planned to offer warrants, which are options to buy stock, and convertible subordinated debentures, which represent debt that can be converted into common stock. The offer would have been such that Chemical Bank shareholders would have received $60 worth of Leasco securities for every $50 of equity, or common stock, they held in Chemical. Under the deal the market value of Chemical Bank's shares would actually have increased. At one point it was estimated by the bank itself that because the market price of Leasco shares was so high, under a one-for-one exchange of stock (another plan that had been considered)—the value of Chemical stock would be enhanced 86 percent.

It was an offer that could succeed, Chemical's Renchard knew, and he initiated a series of defensive actions described later by a House antitrust subcommittee as "frantic." Two of Wall Street's most effective proxy gathering firms, Georgeson and Company and Dudley King and Company, were hired by Chemical not only to solicit proxies among Chemical's share-holders but also to deny their services to Leasco. Renchard personally tried to influence on Chemical's behalf the New York State superintendent of banks. By February 19 Governor Nelson Rockefeller, brother of David, called on the New York State legislature to give the superintendent approval power in bank takeover attempts. Renchard also talked the matter over with the Federal Reserve Bank in New York and with William McChesney Martin, chairman of the Board of Governors of the Federal Reserve System. Chemical even made plans to draw the Justice Department into the fray, and indeed on February 18, 1969, the Justice Department did begin an investigation of Leasco.

Strangely, though, if there was cause to delve into antitrust the first place to have looked would have been Chemical, since the main battle plan, one that had been carefully worked out and written down, called for an "attempt to discourage the lending of funds to the potential acquirer." Since banks nearly always financed the acquisitions of fast-growing conglomerate corporations such as Leasco, Chemical decided that "through banking and other financial contacts the company officials may be able to prevent the company making the offer from obtaining sufficient funds to finance the purchase of the shares tendered."

In antitrust hearings Renchard denied that this plan had been followed. But his own statements refute his assertion. For example, Renchard admitted discussing the Leasco takeover attempt with Donald Graham, chairman of the board of Continental Illinois, requesting Graham to discourage Leasco. Continental, by no coincidence, was the lead bank in a group of forty banks holding major loan agreements with Leasco. Under questioning by Kenneth R. Harkins, chief counsel of the subcommittee, Renchard admitted trying to influence Graham:

HARKINS: On February 4 or 5, 1969, did you talk to Mr. Graham the chairman of Continental Illinois Bank and Trust Company of Chicago, concerning Leasco's efforts to take over Chemical?

RENCHARD: I believe my first conversation with Mr. Graham was on February 7.

HARKINS: What did you discuss at that time?

RENCHARD: I spoke to Mr. Graham and he told me he was planning to meet with the officials of Leasco. I suggested to him that he might consider discouraging them in their thinking about acquiring the Chemical Bank.

HASKINS: Did you ask Mr. Graham of Continental Illinois if he had been approached by Leasco for any additional funds?

RENCHARD: I don't believe so.

HARKINS: You knew that Continental was the lead bank for Leasco's loans, didn't you?

RENCHARD: Yes sir, that is why I called him.

HARKINS: You called him on February 7?

RENCHARD: I tried to reach him, I think, on the 6th. I found he was going to be in New York on February 7, and I reached him at the Barclay Hotel.

Graham, as it turned out, was not the only banker Renchard talked to about Leasco. Under questioning that came later the following testimony developed:

HARKINS: Do you recall any conversation with officials from Bankers Trust Company about this?

RENCHARD: At this time, no, not specifically.

HARKINS: Do you recall any conversations with officials from Manufacturers Trust Company about this?

RENCHARD: I may have. I went to a dinner.

HARKINS: What was the date at the dinner?

RENCHARD: The following Monday night, I guess. I must have talked to 300 bankers.

HARKINS: You would have talked to bankers about Leasco?

RENCHARD: No. I mean there was a dinner of the Reserve City Bankers Association on Monday evening, February 10. There must have been 300 bankers present and I am sure that everyone I bumped into had something to say about this.

HARKINS: And would you have discussed this with bankers from the United California Bank and the Wells Fargo Bank?

RENCHARD: Possibly.

HARKINS: And the First National Bank of Boston?

RENCHARD: Could be.

It was plain, too, that Renchard was hardly alone in conducting a quiet campaign among Leasco's lenders. Apparently, the entire officer corps of Chemical was at work in the campaign to destroy Leasco's credit:

HARKINS: Would any other representatives of Chemical discuss the Leasco situation with people from Bankers Trust Company, Manufacturers Trust Company, United California Bank, Wells Fargo Bank, First National Bank of Boston?

RENCHARD: I don't know of any specific discussions. You can't rule out conversations at social gatherings.

HARKINS: Did you at any time during your serving as chairman of the campaign against Leasco suggest that the officials of Chemical should discuss with other banks and make suggestions that Leasco should be discouraged.

RENCHARD: No sir. I don't think I had to tell them that.

Renchard had made his point well with other bankers. On the very day he had spoken to Graham, the chairman of Continental Illinois, Graham spoke to Steinberg and told Steinberg to stop his acquisition plans. The following testimony developed during Steinberg's appearance as a witness before the House antitrust subcommittee.

HARKINS (addressing Steinberg): Did Mr. Graham during his conversation tell you or indicate in any way that he had talked to Mr. Renchard?

STEINBERG: No. I don't believe that he did.

HARKINS: Did he in any way talk to you about the possible takeover of Chemical Bank by Leasco?

STEINBERG: Yes sir.

HARKINS: What did he say? Do you recall?

STEINBERG: He gave me his fair frank advice that he thought that this was not a good thing for the banking business even though he volunteered that he thought banking should be going in this direction, but he believed that this would not be a good thing for banking and confidence in banking.

HARKINS: Who arranged this meeting with Mr. Graham?

STEINBERG: Mr. Hines, I believe [a vice president of Continental Illinois not identified further in the official text].

HARKINS: What was the date of the meeting?

STEINBERG: The 7th, 7th of February.

HARKINS: How many of those chief executive officials of major banks discussed with you the possibility of the inadvisability of your attempting to take over the bank?

STEINBERG: I don't recall, sir.

HARKINS: Anybody other than Mr. Graham?

STEINBERG: Not chief executive officials? Others?

HARKINS: Other bank representatives.

STEINBERG: Other bank representatives, yes.

HARKINS: Any representatives of these banks?

STEINBERG: Yes.

HARKINS: Can you identify the banks?

STEINBERG: I don't recall exactly, sir, you will have to understand that. But it would be normal for me to speak to Bankers Trust Company, Manufacturers, United California, I think, Wells Fargo. Perhaps the First National Bank of Boston.

Renchard and Chemical also tried to destroy Leasco's takeover attempt by developing ways to drive down the price of Leasco's stock—at a time when Chemical's own Investment Analysis Department was recommending Leasco stock "as a purchase now." Obviously, the holders of Leasco's common shares, the general public, were of little concern to the embattled bank, for the battle plan of Chemical suggested that the "breadth of the market on Leasco stock" might not be great and "it might be possible to attack its value if need be." Between February 3 and February 27, 1969, Leasco's stock did indeed drop from $135 to $99. It was a significant tactic, since Leasco's tender offer to Chemical stockholders was based on the fact that Leasco was selling in the open market at a high price.

Under questioning by Harkins, Renchard, a man who railed at critics of banking as enemies of the free enterprise system, admitted that all the bank had to do to drive down Leasco stock was call attention "to the fact that the market [for the stock] was volatile," meaning that if large amounts of Leasco securities were offered for sale there would not be enough takers, and Leasco stock would drop in price. Renchard did not mention the letters from customers and corporate associates of the bank who assured him that in any takeover they themselves would hold onto their Chemical shares, even if a premium of $30 a share were offered, while at the same time they would cheerfully dispose of Leasco stock.

Perhaps the most insidious development in the entire shoddy affair occurred with an implication as late as 1971, two years after the takeover attempt, that a *New York Times* banking reporter, H. Erich Heinemann, had acted as a go-between for the Chemical. The bankers clearly had struck fear into Steinberg, who implied during his testimony that it was not a takeover he had been engineering, but "a merger into Chemical." He was not the aggressive corporate raider, but a malleable executive, willing to be absorbed and to work his way up in the corporation that would result from a merger, as distinguished from a takeover. The testimony that follows has Steinberg recalling a luncheon meeting with Heinemann, the *New York Times* reporter, then another luncheon with Chemical Bank's top executives, including Renchard:

> HARKINS: Did you have lunch with a Mr. Heinemann at which Chemical was discussed?
>
> STEINBERG: Yes, sir.
>
> HARKINS: And who is Mr. Heinemann?
>
> STEINBERG: Mr. Heinemann is a financial writer for *The New York Times*.
>
> HARKINS: And on what date did you have this lunch with Mr. Heinemann?
>
> STEINBERG: The article [one written by Robert Metz of *The New York Times*, an associate of Heinemann] came out on the

sixth in the *Times* and I had lunch on the seventh, and lunch had been arranged some weeks before.

HARKINS: Some weeks before?

STEINBERG: Some weeks before.

HARKINS: Had it been arranged at the request of Mr. Heinemann or at your request?

STEINBERG: At the request of Mr. Heinemann.

HARKINS: Now, we have a document that relates to your lunch with Mr. Heinemann. At that lunch did you discuss the Chemical Bank takeover with Mr. Heinemann?

STEINBERG: At the lunch we discussed what Leasco saw as the future role of banking, and then we discussed, naturally discussed —. I finally decided to meet with Mr. Heinemann and we discussed the Chemical Bank.

Later Steinberg said that he "was pleased" to have lunch with Heinemann because Heinemann was following proposed legislation on one-bank holding companies and one-bank holding was what he had in mind in a merger of Leasco and Chemical Bank.

HARKINS: Did Mr. Heinemann at this luncheon indicate to you he was going to report what you told him to Chemical Bank?

STEINBERG: No, he did not.

HARKINS: I show you a document we obtained from the Chemical Bank.

STEINBERG: Could you tell me whose writing it is on the bottom?

HARKINS: No, I couldn't tell you that.

STEINBERG: Could we have a copy of that?

HARKINS: It will be in the public record.

The typewritten statement suggested that Heinemann was an informer for Chemical Bank, though it is not uncommon for a reporter to develop information by restating to others information that has been given him by sources. Steinberg admitted that the document was basically correct in stating what had been talked about at his lunch with Heinemann. The important thing, however, was that at the lunch Steinberg had said he did not care "whether Leasco was merged into the bank and would be perfectly happy

to have his subsidiaries simply become subsidiaries of the bank."
It was an enormous departure from the original goal, and critics
of Heinemann suggested that instead of reporting this as news
he had gone to the bank first. For Chemical Bank the meaning
was that Leasco was capitulating, and three days later, on
February 10, 1967, Steinberg called Renchard and asked for
a luncheon meeting. The telephone call itself had to be con-
ciliatory, since Renchard sent his own car to pick up Steinberg
at a New York hotel, and a number of other high-ranking
Chemical executives were at the meeting.

> HARKINS: Did you discuss the possibility of a takeover of
> Chemical by means of a tender?
> STEINBERG: I made it very clear the way that we would like
> to see these two companies get together would be a merger of
> Leasco into the holding company of the bank.

Obviously Steinberg was talking about a very different thing,
and on February 20, 1969, Renchard notified his board members that Leasco had been beaten off. His telegram said:
"Pleased to report Leasco has announced withdrawal of plans
to press for affiliation with Chemical."

The testimony of Steinberg, which questioned the motives
and attacked the integrity of *Times* reporter H. Erich Heinemann,
understandably produced a rebuttal from Heinemann that does
not appear in the public record. The rebuttal came in the form
of a two-page letter from Heinemann to Kenneth Harkins, the
Antitrust Subcommittee's counsel, and read as follows:

> Dear Mr. Harkins:
>
> I wish to call your attention to a number of specific errors in
> your report on the Investigation of Conglomerate Corporations
> regarding my purported role in the abortive takeover attempt by
> Leasco Corporation of the Chemical Bank.
> One. Page 259, first complete sentence. Mr. Renchard did not
> "plant" or "leak" the story of the attempt with me. The story
> that appeared in *The New York Times* on Thursday, Feb. 6, 1969,
> under the by-line of Robert Metz was developed independently by
> Mr. Metz from sources whose identity has never been disclosed.

As *The Times* banking reporter, I called Mr. Renchard for comment on Mr. Metz's report, and conveyed the substance of that conversation to Mr. Metz in a memorandum—a portion of which was reflected in his published article.

Two. Page 266, bottom of the page. I did not serve as a "conduit" for information that was the "basis" for Mr. Metz's article. I reported Mr. Renchard's reaction to material that had already been developed by Mr. Metz—as he would be happy to confirm should you take the trouble to ask.

Three. Page 266, bottom of the page. I did not arrange my luncheon meeting with Mr. Steinberg in January. I was on vacation in Austria skiing during January, 1969. The luncheon with Mr. Steinberg was arranged on Feb. 3—my first day back at work after vacation—at the insistent request of Mr. Gershon Kekst, who at that time was an officer of Ruder & Finn, Leasco's public relations counsel. It was the juxtaposition of Mr. Kekst's insistence —on which he declined to elaborate at the time of our Feb. 3 conversation—that convinced me, even before I spoke to Mr. Renchard on the afternoon of Feb. 5, that Mr. Metz's information was essentially accurate. Mr. Kekst subsequently confirmed to me that the invitation was an attempt to secure favorable press treatment (presumably by explaining Leasco's case in advance) should a formal takeover bid be announced.

Four. Pages 266 and 267, the Maxwell memorandum. While the substance of Mr. Maxwell's summarization of my conversation with him late in the afternoon on Friday, Feb. 7, 1968, is accurate insofar as it goes, his (and your) characterization of it is totally false. *The Times*, as your report indicates, had already reported that a takeover battle was brewing. My judgment that afternoon what that Mr. Steinberg had said nothing to me during our meeting that would, in and of itself, justify any additional coverage. My telephone call to the bank was an attempt to elicit comment from Chemical, which—if set in contrast to Mr. Steinberg's charges and assertions—could have been the basis for a further story. This attempt was not successful, and no additional stories were written until the following Tuesday, when Leasco had its annual meeting.

Contrary to Mr. Steinberg's implication is his testimony I was neither asked for, not did I give, any assurance that the substance of the luncheon meeting with Mr. Steinberg would be held confidential. Thus, had there been disclosures that would have added significantly to what Mr. Metz had already reported, the entire conversation would have been aired in the *Times*.

Clearly, the only way for me to attempt to elicit comment from Chemical on Mr. Steinberg's charges and assertions was to indicate to the bank what the substance of those charges and assertions were. This is why I called Mr. Maxwell; not, as he incorrectly put it, to "pass on the results" of my meeting.

I should appreciate it if you would include the text of this Letter in any subsequent publication of material concerning this incident.

> H. Erich Heinemann
> Assistant to the Financial Editor, *The New York Times*.

If the power plays of the giant banks in which a reporter's integrity can be attacked, if the exclusion of Jews from their ranks, if the high salaries and the other trappings suggest a powerful ruling class, the annual convention of bankers reinforces this impression. Sponsored by the American Bankers Association, whose membership numbers 14,000 or so, the convention is a meeting at which little real work is done, either in the hallways and smoke-filled rooms or in the general sessions. In Dallas in 1972, for example, general sessions were froth-filled meetings characterized by speeches larded generously with self-praise and verbal rabbit punches for banking's critics. The background for this was an opening session in which enormous enlargements of America's battles were projected on vast screens to the accompaniment of "America the Beautiful."

The ABA convention is a social event, meeting as it does on a round-robin basis annually in different cities of the United States (New York, Chicago, San Francisco, Honolulu, Miami, and, in 1972, Dallas). It is viewed by reporters forced to cover it as a nonnews event and "a week-long drunk."

Approximately 5,000 to 6,000 bankers attend the convention, accompanied by their wives, to pay homage to, or to gawk at, the titans of the industry—who host lavish receptions that of orgies of eating and drinking. (So far as it is known sex, at least with strange partners, is not one of the major pursuits.) Indeed, the main purpose of the ABA convention is the hundreds of receptions held morning, noon, and evening. Stuffed with food, often staggering perilously, the nation's bankers wander from reception to reception, as many as half a dozen in a single day. The high point of the journey may turn out to be a handshake with the men at banking's top—men who stand with their wives at the entranceways of the vast reception rooms of the most lush hotels, shaking thousands of hands and acting like sovereigns.

The image of lords of the manor accepting the homage of vassals is not a far-fetched comparison. It has been made before. Invariably, the banker who shakes his host's hand is a link in his host's empire of correspondent banks—which can easily run into the thousands. Collectively, the business of small bankers is highly profitable for large banks, which perform a variety of services, for a fee, that small banks cannot perform. Thus, in effect, the large banks protect the small banks from competition. In turn, the large banks require the small banks to maintain deposits at no interest (compensating balances), as well as to pay fees. In presenting themselves at the receptions given by large bankers the executives of the small banks perform what can be construed as an act of fealty.

For the titans of the banking industry, hosting these lavish receptions is a wearying business, and many of them have moaned aloud when handed a duty roster that includes attendance at any number of small, private receptions as well as the great, general ones. In recent years the moans have grown into actual protests —one reason being that the bonds that have held the small banks and the large banks together are being abraded by the large banks' tendency toward branch banking, which undermines the small banks' business. To the more sensitive bankers the table they must set seems a symbol of utter waste and dissolution. The Dallas convention in 1972, for instance, was regarded as a dull one, contrasted to those held in Hawaii and San Francisco in other years. Yet a typical table of food included dozens of varieties of hot and cold hors d'oeuvres, baskets of shrimp prepared two or three ways, tubs of shelled crab claws, squares of sautéed filet mignon dipped in a white sauce, plus quarters of roast beef, corned beef, cheeses, French pastries, and literally thousands of bottles of the most expensive liquors. In Dallas' lavish Fairmont Hotel twenty-six receptions were going full tilt at one point, and over a hundred were held in a single day. At a bash in the Apparel Mart featuring songs by choir boys twenty-eight bartenders manned four bars to insure prompt refilling.

It would not be unfair to say that some bankers have begun to see the convention as a stomach-turning affair, and are beginning to question its need. The Bank of America, for example, became so disillusioned over the cost and the gluttony of the convention that in 1972 it refused to host a reception. (Significantly, this bank has been a leading proponent and founder of branch banking since the early 1900s.) The decision seemed at first a kind of heresy, but on examination it was consistent with the historical conduct of this bank, which time and again has failed to act like a lord. It is an old story, well known in the industry, how the Bank of America was founded because of the indifference of other banks to the average man. As one of the bank's executives describes it, A. P. Giannini founded the Bank of America because "his Italian brethren in San Francisco were not getting a fair shake from the other banks." The Italians of San Francisco were being ignored, but it would be a mistake to believe that the Bank of America was founded simply on altruism. The Bank of America was a successful, profit-making institution almost from the beginning. It grew by leaps and bounds, and today is the largest bank in the United States, not only because of its "retail" trade but also because of its vast commercial lending and financing transactions. Yet it would also be a mistake to believe that its founding did not represent some kind of optimum in the free enterprise system, since the "Bee of Ay," has rarely ignored its social responsibilities, and indeed in recent years may well have shown the way to other banks and bankers.

A number of the bank's officers might well shudder at the suggestion that they are liberals, since they are true believers in self-help as the only way to make it. But the officers of the Bank of America—along with, it must be said, a good handful of bankers across the nation—are helping to overturn many of the primitive, hardened attitudes of banking. In doing so they are bringing banking back from a "remoteness" charged by Woodrow Wilson in his speech before an ABA convention in 1908.

PART THREE

Expansion—
At All Cost

6

One-Bank Holding—
Story of a Loophole

FOR AS long as there have been commercial banks bankers have aspired to the roles of king and kingmaker, especially in the Eastern United States. The means used was to link the vast sums of money under the control of bankers to the current driving business force dominating the economy of the time. When the aspirations were successful, the result was a vast concentration of economic power accompanied by a disturbing abdication of ethical and moral responsibility, high profits, and finally, legislation written by a wrathful Congress to curb bankers and put an end to their abuses—until the next time.

At the turn of the century, when John D. Rockefeller and his peers dominated the economy with their oil, industrial, and rail empires, the banks were so closely allied with industry that a very small group of Eastern bankers, the infamous J. P. Morgan among them, controlled most of the credit and money supply of the United States. Typically, the monopoly was characterized by interlocking directorships. Indeed, they flourished as they do today, and bankers moved freely and incestuously from their chairs on bank boards to their chairs on industrial boards. Many could even remain seated physically in the same chair.

After the financial panics of 1903 and 1907 a concerned Congressman from Louisiana named Arsene Pujo in 1910 formed a congressional committee to investigate "The Money Trust," an apt label pinned on the bankers by the committee's counsel, Samuel Untermeyer. Later, in its recommendations to Congress, the committee said that "no part of the stock of any national bank should be permitted to be owned or held directly or indirectly by any other bank or by any trust company or holding company."

The Pujo Committee's recommendations and findings led directly in 1914 to the passage of the Federal Reserve Act. Significantly, though the act was designed to wrest away the means or mechanism of controlling money and credit from a few bankers, it also attempted to curb the ambitions and covetousness of those same bankers, since it put them under the purview of the Federal Reserve Board. For the first time bankers had to answer to someone. (The Pujo investigations also contributed to the passage of another famous piece of legislation, the Clayton Antitrust Act. It, too, was passed in 1914 and struck at industry, prohibiting anticompetitive and monopolistic mergers.)

Unfortunately neither the Federal Reserve Act nor the Clayton Act went far enough. Neither cut the alliances between the banks and Wall Street's investment banking houses, those firms that raise capital for industry by selling industry's securities to the general public. By the 1920s and even earlier the bankers were at it again. They extended credit in extraordinary amounts to investment banking firms they either owned or which owned them, often financing men whose sole aim was to monopolize various portions of the economy—as in the case of the Insulls with their utilities holding-company pyramids, or the Van Swearingens with their railroad empires. In lending money to the investment houses they were hitched to, the banks would be repaid with large shares of the profits. The money lent would be used by the investment banker, i.e., underwriter, to buy a company's securities, which in turn would be sold to the general public. In this underwriting of monopolies the irony was that it was the public which ended up financing it.

As in earlier years, it was a financial crisis, this time the stock market crash of 1929, that led to congressional investigations and a whole series of acts written once more in large part to curb the banks. One law, the Glass-Steagall Act, finally separated banks from the investment banking business and from dealing in securities.

Among the investigations the most revealing was that of Ferdinand Pecora, a staff investigator of the Senate Banking Committee which unearthed an unbelievable catalogue of ills. Among them was that in chasing underwriting profits the banks had made loans to affiliated investment banking houses no independent banker would ever have made. Bank solvency also had been impaired, since many of the loans to the investment bankers were tied to such poor securities that the securities were rejected even by the gullible public of the 1920s. The banks even sold securities themselves, doing this legally only by shielding themselves behind that traditional device of monopolists, the holding company. The holding company has been used by corporations and banks for all of this century and a large portion of the last. It has always been feared, and even before the investigations of the 1930s a warning had been sounded. In December, 1929, President Herbert Hoover, acting because of the alarm of the Federal Reserve and the Comptroller of the Currency over the growth of holding companies in banking, sent a message to Congress expressing his fears of concentration. "If allowed to expand without restraint," he said, "these methods would dangerously concentrate control of credit." The concerns of the Pujo Committee of two decades earlier were again raised, as Hoover referred to the dangers of "group" banking and "chain banking," in which individuals and partners bought one bank after another.

Congress did not share Hoover's alarm, apparently, or perhaps the message ran headlong into the opposition of banks, because four years passed before Congress enacted the Banking Act of 1933, the first federal legislation specifically designed to curb bank-holding companies. And it was a weak act.

Though banks themselves could not own nonbanking businesses, there were no restraints on bank holding companies organized by the banks to acquire nonbanking businesses. The act also allowed holding companies to own banks, a point enormously significant in the following years.

It was not until the Bank Holding Company Act of 1956 was passed that bank holding companies finally were subjected to any real restrictions. The bill was passed mainly because of the acquisition habits of Transamerica Corporation, a San Francisco–based bank holding company that had acquired forty-seven banks in five Western states under the guidance of its president and chairman, Frank N. Belgrano, Jr. In 1952 the Federal Reserve Board, which is authorized to enforce the monopoly provisions of the Clayton Antitrust Act as they apply to banks, ordered the Transamerica Corporation to divest itself of its holdings. But Transamerica went to court in what promised to be a long-drawn-out litigation. It was after this and a long series of hearings in Congress that the Bank Holding Company Act of 1956 was passed. Signed into law by President Eisenhower, the act required nearly all bank holding companies in control of 25 percent or more of the stock of two or more banks to register with the Board of Governors of the Federal Reserve. The heart of the act required the bank holding companies to divest themselves of control of all nonbanking or nonbank-related corporations. Further, before they acquired more than 5 percent of the voting stock of any bank, the holding companies had to get Federal Reserve Board approval. Nor were they permitted to control a bank outside a home state without permission of the other state.

For its part, the Federal Reserve administered the law strictly. When a bank holding company registered, it applied the test in the law. The Board scrutinized the bank holding company's history, its financial condition, its prospects, and the character of its management. The Board also determined whether an acquisition being proposed was closely related to the business of banking.

The Bank Holding Act of 1956, however much it did to

throw a rein over banks and bank holding companies inclined to gallop toward concentration through the bank holding device, contained exemptions, one of which proved to be an enormous loophole. It exempted from registering with the Federal Reserve Board those holding companies with only one bank in their tables of organizations. In other words, the act applied only to holding companies controlling two or more banks.

The exemption was no accident. Congress was especially concerned at the time with mergers among banks and the possible pyramiding of banking empires. It was not as concerned with keeping banking and commerce separated, and the legislators knew that in many small communities small one-bank holding companies were common since many small banks would founder without the income from the auto agency, the insurance agency, or the lumberyard that was part of their small conglomerate.

At first the thinking of Congress seemed right. For a number of years after the passage of the act generally small one-bank holding companies were formed at a nominal rate of about forty a year. Just before passage of the act in 1955 there were 117 one-bank holding companies. Total deposits of the banks involved were $11.6 billion. By 1965, just ten years later, the number of one-bank holding companies had reached 550, while deposits among the banks involved totaled $15.1 billion. The figures suggested clearly enough that it was still the small banks that were converting their corporate structure and that there was no real danger of concentration.

But then in the three years following 1965 an extraordinary growth occurred, not so much in numbers of banks as in size of the deposits they represented. While the number of one-bank holding companies grew from 550 to 783, the deposits figure soared from $15.1 billion to $108.2 billion. By the end of 1968 thirty-four of the hundred largest commercial banks in the United States had formed or announced plans to form holding companies. Among them were the Bank of America,

Chase Manhattan Bank, First National City Bank, Manufacturers Hanover Trust, Morgan Guaranty Trust Company, Chemical Bank New York Trust, Wells Fargo, Crocker-Citizens National Bank, and First Pennsylvania Bank and Trust.

The motives of the banks were clear enough and the conversions to one-bank holding hardly an idle exercise. The big commercial banks were determined to expand and to diversify by exploiting an exemption never intended for them. It was a classic case of how to find a loophole and a still more classic example of how banks could continue to find ways to thwart the will of Congress. For decades Congress had again and again declared its intent to keep banking separate. Yet here were the big commercial banks of the country poised to expand into commerce, including manufacturing, and into related financial functions such as insurance and mutual fund selling. It mattered not that as far back as the days when the Pujo Committee met the recommendation was to separate banks and, for example, insurance companies. Nor did it seem to matter that the Glass-Steagall Act that came out of the depression expressly forbade banks from selling securities after the debacle of 1929. In fact, it took a Supreme Court decision to turn aside the effort of New York's First National City Bank to begin selling shares in its own mutual fund in the early 1970s.

It was not as though Congress had not been warned of the trouble ahead. In 1955, during hearings held by the House Banking and Currency Committee, William McChesney Martin, chairman of the Federal Reserve Board at the time, strongly opposed the one-bank holding exemption, spotting it as a loophole. He said, "It seems clear that the potential abuses resulting from the combination under single control easily exist in a case in which only one bank is involved." Martin was pointing the finger at the big banks and said later, "If the one controlled bank [of a one-bank holding company] were a large bank, the holding company's interests in extensive nonbanking businesses might very well lead to abuses even more serious than if the company controlled two or more very small banks."

Fourteen years later, in 1969, the same fears were being expressed during hearings held before the same committee on amendments to plug the loophole. The committe's chairman, Wright Patman, went to the point minutes after the hearings opened on Tuesday, April 15, 1969:

> The one-bank holding company activity is a bank-centered conglomerate company. . . . [I see] bank holding company growth undermining and changing the entire economic structure of the United States. . . . Our economy cannot function properly without a sound, efficient and objective banking system which will allocate credit and provide other banking services on a fair and equitable basis. Therefore, it is, in my opinion, imperative that we continue to maintain the separation of banking activities from other businesses that has existed in Federal law since 1933.
>
> As the prime source of credit, banks are in a unique position. No other business activity can exert this type of pressure and influence against other businesses. It has an exclusive monopoly on bank deposits. No other financial institutions can accept [demand] deposits. Commercial banks have an exclusive, lucrative franchise on that. Clearly the banks are in a position to engage in unfair competition when they move into nonbanking businesses. The potential abuses are many but let me list some of the dangers when a bank becomes part of a one-bank holding company operation.

That list was a catalogue of fears that had dogged Congresses and administrations alike for nearly a century:

> One. Unsound lending decisions by banks feeding unwarranted amounts of credit to nonbank subsidiaries of the holding company.
>
> Two. Loan discrimination of banks in favor of enterprises owned by the holding company and against companies which compete with subsidiaries of the holding company and against companies which compete with subsidiaries of the holding company.
>
> Three. Banks forcing borrowers, particularly small businesses, to purchase nonbanking services and goods from other subsidiaries of the holding company in order to obtain banking services, thus further tightening control and forcing a greater concentration of economic power.

There is much at stake in this legislation for many interest groups and, therefore, the pressures brought to bear on various aspects of this problem by these special interests will be great. In spite of this, this committee must, and I know it will, under all circumstances keep in mind above all else, what is in the best public interest.

The very first witness, A. A. Berle, professor emeritus at Columbia University, zeroed in on the real issue. "The name of the game is power," he said. "What can be done is attainment of a power position by various individuals in the banking world, the world that controls banks." Berle feared the emergence in the United States of a form of Japan's so-called "Zaibatsu system."

> That means a feudal control of huge industrial combinations plus banks, analogous to what they have in Japan. It may be all right for Japan. . . . Here I think it is dangerous. The one-bank holding company, left unlimited, can go in all directions, and there is no limit. It crystallizes around itself, first, a concentration of financial power, and second, a concentration of industrial power beyond belief in the United States. There is no question that a one-bank holding company, with the resources of its bank, with the stock-holding power in the bank's trust department, and especially if it also acquires control of mutual funds which have further stock interests, can probably attain control of any corporation in the country it really wants to get, aside from a few of the very large giants that are too large. This is already beginning to happen.

It was Berle's opinion, too, that one-bank holding companies represented a kind of can't-win corporate device: "When these holding companies go full steam ahead, they face two possibilities. They may succeed, in which case you have a terrific financial and industrial concentration. Or they may fail, in which case you have a disaster damaging many, many people." Berle suggested, too, that the very size of such companies defied control by an ordinary human brain. "Unless we have suddenly developed a group of commercial geniuses of the first order," he said to the House Banking and Currency Committee, "it is simply impossible that a director of a holding company of this kind can understand all the intricacies both of a bank and of the various financial and nonfinancial operations they propose to engage in."

Still another witness, Professor Louis B. Schwartz of the University of Pennsylvania Law School, raised the issue of "tying," an illegal practice under antitrust laws in which a borrower patronizes the affiliated commercial enterprises, e.g., insurance, of the bank holding company to improve his credit position with the bank at the core. The possibilities of tie-in sales among one-bank holding companies, say with hundreds of subsidiaries, could be almost limitless. Those businesses outside the orbit of the bank, especially new businesses, would find themselves cut off from customers anxious to curry favor with the bank. "As the scope of these conglomerate enterprises extends," Schwartz warned the committee, "it becomes harder and harder for new enterprises to challenge these concentrations of capital."

Schwartz, like Berle, was concerned over the inability of the human mind, even a banker's mind, to "understand a billion dollars and to manage an extreme diversity of geographically unrelated and functionally unrelated operations." But he was also concerned about the difficulty of exerting "public control" over the one-bank holding companies:

I think a very important element is the added difficulty of public control. If you have a combination of unrelated enterprises, you are going to accumulate difficulties for the regulatory agencies. As far as the public is concerned, a general suspicion will arise that there are subterranean and improper influences affecting that critical function of banking. Much that I have said may seem alarmist, suggesting what might happen. I thought it would be interesting to the committee to take cognizance of what has actually happened in India. You have heard the Zaibatsu referred to. I do not have any personal acquaintance with the Japanese concentration, although reports which I have read do indicate a close resemblance between those vast families of enterprises and our own conglomerates. But as a special assistant to our ambassador in India 5 or 6 years ago I had occasion to talk to representatives of the giant conglomerates that dominate Indian trade. There are two overwhelming families there—I speak of families now not in the private family sense, but in the sense of families of corporations, conglomerates. One is the Tata group, and the other is the Birla group. . . . The salient feature is that these two families of enterprises control at least 20 percent of all India's industrial and financial activities.

Schwartz then quoted a study showing that at the cores of the two groups were India's biggest banks, and that the banks favored private business firms with which they were connected. The study showed that one conglomerate owned steel mills, utilities, chemical companies, tobacco companies, textiles, coal mines, insurance companies, and of course, banks. The Tata group was also the sole source of supply for locomotives and controlled 43 percent of auto production.

Admittedly, said Schwartz, "that is the end of the line," but he asserted that situation would result if nothing was done at the beginning to check the growth of conglomerates, especially those with a bank at their core:

> I point out that banks are the preeminent capitalist enterprises. Their sole business is to direct the flow of capital to others who come to them and who should be awarded some of this limited supply solely by reason of the fact that their productive and distributive enterprises meet real needs, are the most efficient. The danger here is of course that with a relationship through a holding company the flow of capital will not be handled that way, but it will be handled on the basis of favoritism. A second point is that whatever you can say about conglomerates among industrial and distributive enterprises involving no aspect in each of them of monopoly, the banks inevitably have something that amounts to monopoly oligopolistic power. They have it because entry into banking is limited by law on the grounds of preserving bank solvency, and assuring the reliability of the credit system of the country. Therefore they are inevitably in a special position, surrounded by both legal and practical barriers to competition, even though in principle, banking competition exists.

Witness after witness hit at the tie-in alluded to first by Schwartz. Milton Shapp, who had not yet become governor of

Pennsylvania, appeared as founder of Jerrold Electronics Company, a Philadelphia corporation and an investor in cable television, a radio station, and a company developing automated equipment for the apparel industry. Shapp had been a corporate borrower. Jerrold Electronics could not have grown to annual sales of more than $42 million at the time Shapp sold out his interest without millions being borrowed from a bank—specifically the Liberty Bank and Trust Company, which became part of Philadelphia's Fidelity Bank. Once in the early 1950s Shapp turned up at the bank to borrow $100,000. Jerrold Electronics was still an infant and the bank, not unreasonably, asked Shapp, who was chief executive officer, to take out a $100,000 life insurance policy to protect the loan. "When I agreed," said Shapp, "one of the bank's officers called me aside and suggested that the bank would consider it a favor, a sweetener, if I would purchase the policy from one of the bank's preferred insurance agencies, rather than from my regular agent. I needed the loan. I complied."

Still another businessman, an Indianapolis travel agent, related how he had been a victim of tying when he found himself in competition with a one-bank holding company. The travel agent was a man named Othmar G. Grueninger, operator of a travel agency bearing his name. Grueninger actually owned five agencies in Indiana and made the point he was "not afraid of business competition" but that bank travel bureaus "threatened the continued existence of independent travel agencies such as mine." Grueninger was afraid of being put out of business by Indianapolis banks that had opened up three new travel agencies in Indianapolis shortly after three independent agencies had gone out of business.

Grueninger documented the inroads of banks by saying that on January 1, 1968, there were forty-eight agencies in the state of Indiana. Only five were owned by banks. By year's end, a year in which banks rushed to form holding companies, nineteen of the travel agencies were owned by banks. Grueninger also complained that as soon as his bank became his competitor, arranging a loan became difficult. But banks had still another advantage, said Grueninger. Banks do not generally operate travel departments, though there are 200 or so who do, and are aggressive. In Indianapolis all the major banks had them. At the same time, independent agencies were forced, like any viable business, to maintain accounts with banks. "This meant that every time I deposited checks from my customers," Grueninger said, getting to one of the most basic conflicts, "I was providing the bank with the names of my best clients." The banks also had access to the records of their depositors and could make selective mailings to promote their travel services. Coupled with this was the ability of banks to determine who was credit-worthy merely by looking over the records of depositors.

"Bank travel agencies used their resources to my detriment in many ways," the travel agent complained in a story documenting how easily banks can intrude and penetrate, if allowed, the businesses of others. "A prospective customer came to me with a $10,000 steamship booking," Grueninger said. "Steamship industry regulations require the travel agent to collect 25 percent of the total amount in advance as a deposit to insure use of the space, but when I billed the client for the deposit—the amount was over $2,500—he advised me that the bank travel agency had never previously required a deposit. One must conclude that the bank agency either advanced the money for the customer or in some other manner underwrote the obligation. In any case, such action to circumvent the steamship requirements is in violation of the industry regulations. However, the customer returned to the bank travel agency because of the favorable terms.

"Perhaps the most significant aspect of bank travel agencies," Grueninger suggested, "is the fact that the bank has little regard for the profitability of its travel agency operations." This statement is confirmed by most banks. There is little or no profit in their travel service departments. But, as Grueninger pointed out, "the independent agency operator must make a profit to survive," while the bank travel agency is not concerned with such basic considerations.

As the hearings progressed it became clear that just about everyone who appeared felt the one-bank holding loophole had to be plugged. J. L. Robertson, vice chairman of the Board of Governors of the Federal Reserve System, characterized the one-bank holding company as a corporate device through which banks engaged in forbidden nonbanking activities. Nicholas Johnson, a commissioner of the Federal Communications Commission, feared domination of a community by banks when there were ownership links between the banks and the major publications or broadcast stations. Said Johnson: "Banks provide a variety of indispensable financial services and can often dominate the economic and political life of a comunity. When this power is supplemented with control over information and opinion, there may be a serious loss of diverse views in that community on local issues." Johnson referred then to "the situation in Rocky Ford, Colorado. . . . In that community, the Rocky Ford Investment Corporation owns the Rocky Ford National Bank and radio stations KAVI–AM and KAVI–FM. These are the only radio stations in that community." Then Johnson reminded the House Banking and Currency Committee of its own findings in Baltimore, Maryland. "In your staff study of banks' trust activities," he said, "the A. S. Abell Company in Baltimore is cited. Your figures show that the Mercantile-Safe Deposit and Trust Company holds 61.3 percent of the stock of the A. S. Abell Company, including the sole voting rights on 27 percent. A. S. Abell owns the *Baltimore Sun,* the *Evening Sun,* a major TV–FM station in Baltimore and a TV-AM-FM station combination in Salisbury, Maryland."

Even the American Bankers Association, which represents most of the nation's 14,000 banks, was not against plugging the one-bank holding loophole. Its president at the time, Nat Rogers, said to the committee, "The American Bankers Association is not opposed to reasonable legislation designed to prevent possible future problems. We do not believe that banks or bank-holding companies should operate in areas that are unrelated to banking or finance."

It was a position that must have made the executives of the nation's large banks react in anger, since they had every intention of invading businesses unrelated to banking and finance. In the aftermath of the ABA statement—in fact, even before public announcement of the ABA's position—a number of the major banks actually formed their own organization, the Association of Corporate Owners of One Bank, to advance their cause. Other banks withdrew their support of the ABA, financially and other-wise, labeling the trade and lobbying group "inept." Criticism of the ABA as a lobbyist grew so that it has spent the years since reorganizing its internal structure, placating the large banks, and moving to Washington from New York, supposedly because physical closeness to the seat of government would make it a more effective persuader.

Furious, many of the nation's large banks took to under-ground war, a move strongly suggesting their cynicism about the concerns of practically everyone else, from the President, who had called for curbing their expansion, to the small businessman, who was fearful of being swept away by banks expanding into his field. Only one or two of the major banks, most notably Bank of America, and Chase Manhattan, even deigned to send representatives to appear at the House Banking and Currency Committee hearings in April and May of 1969, though the issue was one of the most significant and the committee was the originator of federal bank legislation. A number of major banks or their holding companies, e.g., J. P. Morgan and Company, Chemical New York Corporation, and the First National Bank of Chicago, merely filed prepared statements characteristically carrying ringing phrases hailing the free enterprise system and suggesting that those opposing the expansion of banks into other businesses were opposed to honest competition. In only a very few instances had the committee's chairman, Wright Patman, sent invitations to testify, relying instead on public announcements and press stories to elicit the usual offers to testify.

As it was, witnesses who did appear were those opposed to bank expansion and those who feared what bank concentration might do. Those old enough invoked memories of the economic depression of the 1930s, the most severe in American history and one caused by bank expansion, tie-in sales, and vast credit infusions to favored subsidiaries or affiliates. These very same abuses were now feared again.

Other witnesses, such as executives of data processing companies, insurance companies, even less-than-giant-size banks, expressed fear of being driven out of business by large banks blanketing themselves in the holding company. Still other witnesses with a broader overlook, e.g., Federal Reserve Board members, urged that the one-bank holding loophole be plugged to insure the survival of small businessmen and the lonely entrepreneur who might be cut off from loans or forced to buy other services of a bank even to get a loan. Richard W. McLaren, Assistant Attorney General over the Antitrust Division at the time, said, "Most of the nation's largest banks have formed one-bank holding companies with the obvious objectives of forming unregulated financial, commercial, industrial power centers. This raises serious antitrust questions as well as being contrary to our traditional policy of keeping banking separate from other business activities."

Not so strangely, perhaps, since he has been an advocate of bank expansion, seemingly at all costs, a major regulator of banks, Comptroller of the Currency William B. Camp, raised a strong voice against any controls. From a speech by Camp introduced as testimony before the committee:

> The holding company device is not itself harmful to the public interest—but only some of the ways in which it may be used. Indeed, if this device represents the most effective and most efficient means of undertaking a prudent and useful expansion of

banking services, it should be lauded as beneficial to the public interest. Specific controls have already been imposed on the use of holding companies to effect the merger of competing banks. But this is obviously not the issue that concerns those who favor the regulation of one-bank holding companies. What does concern them is the desire to retard the expansion of banks into related financial fields by blocking the use of one of the more effective devices that may be utilized for this purpose. That is the real target and we must be aware of that fact.

Originally, Camp had made the speech on September 30, 1968, before an audience of bankers attending the ninety-fourth annual convention of the American Bankers Association.

The banks themselves took their arguments to the nation's press, often surreptitiously, since they were trying not so much to implant facts as to sway and influence. For example, one banker, who refused to be identified apparently since his name was not used, was quoted in *The New York Times* as responding to antibank-holding comments with this comment: "We're spending our time worrying about the problems of the 1930s. This is wrong. Times have changed." The real question, which went unanswered, was not whether times had changed, but whether bankers had changed. The evidence was that they had not.

At another time, New York's First National City Bank complained to the press through a spokesman that banks ought to be allowed to sell mutual funds, though the Glass-Steagall Act expressly forbade banks from selling securities. Again, the spokesman was unidentified. The subject, though, was plainly an obsessive one for the bank, which did start up a mutual fund and was turned back only by a Supreme Court decision.

Still another time, George S. Moore, chairman of the First National City Bank, made a secret trip to Washington with the express intent of privately influencing individual financial editors and editorial writers. Moore asked the journalists not to reveal his identity after meetings in the offices of *The New York Times,* the *Wall Street Journal,* and the *Washington Post.* Generally, Moore accused insurance agencies, savings and loan companies, and other competitors that solicit and accumulate money as their product of pressing for legislation against one-bank holding companies to "handcuff" the banks. The accusations were out-landish in the face of the tide of opposition, both pragmatic and intellectual, and, as is the practice of journalists in the face of foolishness, the accusations were largely ignored. Only one paper, the *Washington Evening Star,* published a story based on what Moore had said and abided by his request for anonymity by describing the story's source as a "leading banker." In publishing the story, however, the newspaper piqued the curiosity of the *American Banker,* a highly respected and much read daily news-paper for bankers that, in the words of its editor, Willard C. Rappleye, Jr., tells them what they ought to know and not just what they want to hear. The *Banker* told the story behind the story, identifying Moore in the process, undoubtedly to his embarrassment.

Even three years after the great debate of 1969 over one-bank holding it was a mystery why Moore and other bankers engaged in what could only be a futile exercise. Some kind of legislation was going to be passed; Moore and everyone else in banking knew the political realities. There was not only Wright Patman's bill (H.R. 6778), introduced in the House in February, 1969, and Patman's vigorous criticism of the very large banks and his determination to force one-bank holding companies to register to contend with. There was also the administration's own bill (H.R. 9385), introduced in the House in March, 1969, by William B. Widnall, a New Jersey Republican, and as a member of the House Banking and Currency Committee chaired by Patman, a frequent defender of banks and especially of bankers being grilled by Patman. Perhaps most significant was the message to Congress from President Nixon that accompanied the Widnall measure, since it was an unmistakable call for Congress to do something. Said President Nixon:

> The Secretary of the Treasury, with my approval, has today trans-mitted to the Congress proposed legislation on the further regula-

tion of bank holding companies. Legislation in this area is important because there has been a disturbing trend in the past year toward erosion of the traditional separation of powers between the suppliers of money, the banks, and the users of money, commerce and industry. Left unchecked the trend toward the combining of banking and business could lead to the formation of a relatively small number of power centers dominating the American economy. This must not be permitted to happen; it would be bad for banking, bad for business, and bad for borrowers and consumers. The strength of our economic system is rooted in diversity and free competition; the strength of our banking system depends largely on its independence. Banking must not dominate commerce or be dominated by it. To protect competition and the separation of economic powers, I strongly endorse the extension of Federal regulation to one bank holding companies and urge the Congress to take prompt and appropriate action.

In the upper house Senator William Proxmire, the Wisconsin Democrat and consumer advocate, had introduced a bill, too (S. 1052). But it was a bill out of touch with the prevailing mood. The Proxmire bill would have put all one-bank holding companies under the restraints of the Bank Holding Act of 1956, but only temporarily, until a presidential committee could be created to study the role of one-bank holding companies in the economy. This proposal, as might be expected, was endorsed by bank representatives. Carter Golembe, for example, a Washington-based consultant to banks, a former deputy manager of the American Bankers Association, and a man whose monographs on banking are must reading for many bankers, regarded the Proxmire proposal as "the only intelligent choice." The Patman and administration proposals were labeled "preventive legislation" being weighed "in an atmosphere which reeks with the attitude that they [bankers] must intend to do something wrong." This comment, in light of the intense concern being expressed by reputable critics in and out of government, was an understatement. The integrity of bankers, especially those directing the large banks of the nation, was being severely questioned.

But the die was cast. Legislation was going to be passed

and during 1969 and well into December of the following year the debate raging in Congress was over how restrictive the legislation should be, not whether there should be any.

Wright Patman's bill was far and away the more restrictive. Each bill extended the Holding Company Act to cover all one-bank holding companies, and each tightened the definition of control over a bank.

But the Patman bill would have required one-bank holding companies to divest themselves completely of companies whose business was unrelated to banking. Divestiture would not be immediate, and in fact, could take up to two years. Patman, at least, had no objection to amending the tax laws to forego taxes that would be due on any profits the holding companies might make on forced sales of their subsidiaries.

The administration bill, on the other hand, which was sponsored by the Treasury Department and introduced by Widnall, would have established a grandfather, or forgiveness, clause permitting one-bank holding companies founded by June 30, 1968, to retain their acquisitions. The proposed date was advanced to February 17, 1969, the day Widnall introduced the Treasury Department's bill.

Patman argued that any grandfather clause amounted to an exemption that defeated the whole purpose of the Bank Holding Company Act of 1956 to divorce banks and commerce. The clause would be another loophole. He argued further that a grandfather clause rewarded those bank holding companies formed before the cutoff date and penalized those that had been formed after. Patman suggested that advancing the cutoff date of the grandfather clause, as Widnall had proposed, would favor a number of large banks that had formed one-bank holding companies in anticipation that even though they might be forced to register as bank holding companies, another loophole, the grandfather clause, would let them keep their nonbanking subsidiaries.

One or two of these large banks that would qualify under the grandfather clause were among the nation's most aggressive and expansion-minded. Among them, for example, was one of the very largest, New York's First National City Bank, whose own George Moore had tried to recruit some of the nation's press in his cause. On October 31, 1968, when deposits totaled $16.6 billion, it formed the First National City Corporation, and thus qualified itself under the grandfather clause if it should be enacted. Next in line was Chemical Bank New York Trust Company, the same bank that had called on its fellow banks to fight off its acquisition by Leasco Data Processing Corporation. On December 20, 1968, Chemical Bank formed the Chemical New York Corporation. The bank's deposits totaled $7.6 billion. About a week after Chemical cloaked itself in the holding-company mantle, the U.S. National Bank of Oregon, whose home base is Portland and whose deposits then were $1.5 billion, went the way of one-bank holding by forming the U.S. Bank Corporation on December 31, 1968. Finally, a month later, on January 31, 1969, First Pennsylvania Bank and Trust Company, the Philadelphia bank headed by John R. Bunting, formed the First Pennsylvania Corporation. The bank's deposits were $2.2 billion.

A cutoff date of February 17, 1969, would do more than just let some very big banks slither in under a legislative forgiveness wire. It would also permit twenty-eight bank holding companies with eighty-two subsidiaries having nothing to do with banking to claim exemption and engage in a wide variety of businesses. Some were in ranching, others in department store and restaurant operations. Some manufactured textiles, others manufactured heating equipment, lawn mowers, and furniture. One or two were erectors of steel and operators of cable television. One subsidiary even operated a pizza parlor. At the very least, the array of businesses suggested an early stage of the concentration feared by most expert witnesses who turned up at the Patman committee hearings and which Congress had tried for decades to prevent.

As Patman pointed out many times to his committee members, to witnesses, and to the House of Representatives, the original Bank Holding Act of 1956 contained no grandfather clause. When the act was passed, twelve companies were forced to divest themselves of subsidiaries. Among them was Trans-america Corporation, which controlled the Bank of America as well as Occidental Insurance Company and a number of lesser-known banking and nonbanking businesses. "There is no evidence," Patman said in a message to the House of Representatives, "that any of the 12 companies suffered from any adverse effect from separating their banking and nonbanking activities. The evidence is to the contrary. The resulting businesses have grown substantially."

Patman's arguments had little effect, though, especially among a majority of his own committee, twenty-one of whose thirty-four members led by Widnall eventually gutted Patman's measure, H.R. 6778. As a result, the views of the House Banking and Currency Committee that were reported to the Committee of the Whole House on July 19, 1969 were not those of its chairman, Patman. Rather, they were those of Widnall, the defecting committee members, and the Treasury Department, whose own bill had been merged with Patman's. The defections were obviously humiliating for Patman, since the rump defectors had rewritten the bill to include the controversial grandfather clause as well as the advanced cutoff date espoused by Widnall. Patman's own, more restrictive views, along with those of a minority of eleven members of his committee, went to the Committee of the Whole House as "additional" views. In the New York headquarters of the American Bankers Association and among the individual Washington lobbyists employed by some of the major banks there was much contentment and relaxation. Patman had been outmaneuvered. But the relaxed mood turned out to be premature. On November 5, 1969, the bill reported out by Patman's committee went to the floor of the House. But then in a parliamentarian stroke that should have been expected from an old political professional, Patman went to the floor of the House that same afternoon and in four hours, as he describes it, "repaired" his bill. In persuasive appeals made directly to the full House of Representatives, Patman put back everything that had been taken out of his bill. Only three lines remained of the rewritten committee bill after he substituted thirteen pages of tough language based on his own original proposal, throwing in for good measure a laundry list of businesses that banks could not get into under any circumstances, e.g., data processing and insurance. By November 6, 1969, the bill as Patman had originally conceived it had been passed by the House and sent to the Senate.

The maneuver was a hammer blow for the banks and their lobbyists, most of whom were not even aware of what was happening until it was over. Only a handful of alert Washington lobbyists employed by the major commercial banks in New York learned of the Patman maneuver while it was going on. The American Bankers Association, which maintained its headquarters in New York at the time, didn't learn of Patman's repairs until the next day, despite having a major bureau in Washington close to the White House and the Capitol. Its reputation for incompetence, especially among the major banks which had felt for years that their interests came second in ABA planning to the interests of the thousands of small member banks, grew to the point where a deep split developed. Consequently, as mentioned earlier, the ABA moved its headquarters to Washington, presuming it would be more effective with a physical presence in the capital, and initiated a series of internal reorganizations that went on for years.

Furious now, determined as well, and hardly concealing their political clout, the banks turned to the Senate to kill a bill that most informed opinion in the United States believed was an absolute necessity. Without a bank holding bill, for example, four New York banks would have a green light for their announced plans to buy up four major insurance companies. By investing the vast liquid assets that would be merged, the banks could easily control massive portions of U.S. industry. There was no way of knowing, either, how many other banks would then follow. Said Patman, who feared the worst, "The half-dozen largest banks in New York could acquire the six largest insurance corporations and through fractional reserves could have enough money to then buy up almost all the profitable manufacturing and industrial corporations in America."

One tack of the banks in Senate lobbying was to try to dissuade Senator John Sparkman, chairman of the Senate Banking Committee, from holding hearings at all. This seemed practical since many bank lobbyists, especially those of the ABA, were alumni of the Senate Banking Committee staff of researchers and lawyers. The effect would be to kill the bank holding bill completely. At the same time, a plan was devised to euchre President Nixon into changing his stand on the need for a bank holding bill. Basically, the strategy involved getting the President to state in his annual Economic Message in January, 1970, that full-fledged deep reform was required in banking, and since one-bank holding was merely a part of that reform no action would be needed on the bank holding bill before other areas were dealt with. It was hardly a far-fetched strategy. Wide-ranging reform for the banking mechanism was on President Nixon's mind, and in June, 1970, some six months or so later, he would appoint a twenty-member Commission on Financial Structure and Regulation to "review and study the structure, operation and regulation of the private financial institutions in the United States for the purpose of formulating recommendations that would improve the functioning of the private financial system." (The commission was chaired by Reed O. Hunt, the retired chairman of the Crown Zellerbach Corporation, and became known as the Hunt Commission.)

The persuading of the President was to be done by Charls E. Walker, the Under Secretary of the Treasury who was a former executive of the American Bankers Association and onetime head of the ABA's Washington office. Walker, a persuasive, talkative man who was supposed to have the President's ear, aspired to, and was a favorite choice of some to become, Secretary of the Treasury. (As it turned out, he did not.) He was credited with being the architect of the plan, or plot, according to which side observers were on.

The plan to persuade the President failed even before its central argument could be broached, undoubtedly because of the arrogance (some say stupidity) with which it was devised and put into motion. In developing the plan, Walker failed to clear it with Arthur Burns, the man who was soon to succeed William McChesney Martin as chairman of the Federal Reserve Board. Under Martin, a majority of the board had favored a strong bank holding amendment, as Martin and a board governor, J. L. Robertson, had testified. There was no reason to believe Burns would have a different attitude. To slight him was foolish. But Burns was not the only one ignored. In the Justice Department a number of lawyers learned of the Walker plan, and becoming concerned that there would be no bill at all, went to the Council of Economic Advisers, that triumvirate of economists who advise the President, and warned its members to beware of Walker's "trickery." The lawyers also told Wright Patman, who had learned by this time of the attempt to influence Senator Sparkman not to hold Senate Banking Committee hearings on the one-bank holding bill.

Once again, Patman responded like an old political warrior. As vice chairman of the Joint Economic Committee of Congress, which held hearings on the Economic Report of the President to Congress, Patman called as witnesses Arthur F. Burns, who by this time (the winter of 1970) had become chairman of the Federal Reserve Board; Paul McCracken, the chairman of the President's Council of Economic Advisers; and David Kennedy, Treasurer of the United States. Each man publicly reasserted his belief there was a great need for a bank holding bill, and in doing so helped Patman "cut the rug out from Walker and Senator Sparkman," as a lawyer who was present describes the effect. The Walker plan died at birth, while Senator Sparkman, a target of small businessmen who were writing him to say they wanted a bank holding bill, announced hearings with unusual suddenness. In Chicago, one day in March, when asked by a reporter for the *Wall Street Journal* just when the hearings might be scheduled (four months had gone by), Sparkman replied he had scheduled them for the following month. The Senator did not reveal, however, that the Patman bill, H.R. 6778, had once again been rewritten, this time in Sparkman's Senate Banking Committee. What emerged aroused controversy and ill will rarely seen in Congress.

The Senate bill was riddled with exemptions. For example, it exempted family-owned holding companies, and retained exemptions for labor unions, agricultural, and horticultural organizations. Whereas the House version, in divorcing banking from nonbanking, listed particular activities, especially the sale of securities and mutual funds, that banks could not get into, he Senate bill permitted the Federal Reserve Board to approve nonbanking activities "functionally related to banking," subject to test under the antitrust laws. The Senate bill also carried the controversial grandfather clause, in which nonbanking businesses of bank holding companies acquired up to March 25, 1969, could be kept. The House bill allowed nonbanking subsidiaries to be kept only if they had been acquired before May 9, 1956, the date of passage of the original Bank Holding Act of 1956. The House bill would have given the companies five years to divest themselves of their nonbanking subsidiaries, or the amount of time specified in the earlier act. The Senate bill, on the other hand, set a divestiture period of ten years.

The most controversy-provoking change, however, was the so-called Williams Amendment, the "conglomerate exemption" introduced by Senator Harrison Williams, a New Jersey Democrat. Basically, the Williams Amendment exempted from regulation any one-bank holding company in existence up to the time legislation was passed if the net worth of the subsidiary bank was no larger than $50 million and represented less than 25 percent of the net worth of the holding company of which it was part.

But net worth is no measure of real economic power, especially among banks, where a more realistic measure is deposits, since this is one of the figures that basically determines how much a bank can lend to others. A rule of thumb is that a bank's total deposits tend to run about ten times its net worth; thus a bank with a $50 million net worth might well have $500 million or more in deposits. In turn, the holding company of which the bank was a subsidiary might have a net worth of $200 million, but again, this would be no measure of its real economic clout. Its sales, for example, could be anything from $1 billion to $2 billion, perhaps more, while its borrowing power could be as much or more.

Perhaps worst of all to the opponents of the Williams Amendment was the clause giving the Federal Reserve Board the power to waive even the $50 million net worth stipulation, thus leaving only the restriction that the bank's net worth had to be 25 percent or less of the holding company's net worth.

In the eyes of Patman and others in the House and Senate this was a loophole the proverbial truck could drive through—or more specifically, an enormous holding company. Though the good guard at the door was the Federal Reserve Board, which had sided with Patman, it was nonetheless a loophole which could, for example, permit a company the size of General Motors to become the holding company of a bank the size of Chase Manhattan, so long as Chase Manhattan's net worth did not exceed 25 percent of the net worth of its holding company. More specifically, some opponents of the Williams Amendment saw it benefiting CIT Financial Corporation, a diversified financial services holding company that in 1965 acquired the National Bank of North America, a New York bank with deposits of $1.3 billion during the time the Williams Amendment was introduced. Under the Williams Amendment such an acquisition would have qualified for exemption from registering with the Federal Reserve, since the net worth ratios of the two fell within the specified limits. The effect would have been to gut the bill.

Thus it was with extraordinary bitterness that those in the

Senate who wanted a strong bill fought to beat off the Williams Amendment. In the end they lost. Once again, it was a parliamentary maneuver that turned the tide, this time against the bill. Along with Senator Wallace Bennett, a conservative Republican from Utah, Sparkman had persuaded the Senate leadership to put back to two o'clock a vote on the Williams Amendment scheduled for five in the afternoon. As a result, twenty-nine Senators were missing at the earlier vote-counting time, including Ted Kennedy, and the amendment passed 37 to 34. But absenteeism was only part of the reason for the vote. Another was the defection of men regarded as liberals who voted in favor of the Williams Amendment. It was bitter medicine for the proponents of strict control, who for months afterward recalled with rancor the defections of such "red-hot liberals and populists," as they were characterized by disappointed opponents of the amendment, as Senators George McGovern, who was to become the Democratic presidential candidate in 1972. Quentin N. Burdick, a North Dakota Democrat, and Lee Metcalf, a Montana Democrat. "Their votes were a disgrace," says an attorney who helped write the bill, and was emotionally upset by the inclusion of the Williams Amendment. Indeed, the three were even accused, though not directly, of sacrificing their liberal principles at the request of Charles Brannan, former President Harry Truman's Secretary of Agriculture, to bail out the pension fund of the National Farmers Union.

The story goes that in the early 1960s the pension fund had bought into a potash mine as an investment just before the market for potash crashed. In deep trouble, the management of the pension fund's investments was taken over by a Denver bank, the Central Bank & Trust Co. The bank, in turn was acquired by the D. H. Baldwin Company's holding company subsidiary, Baldwin-Central Inc. Under the definition of control in the Bank Holding Act, divestiture would have been required. Brannan, a member of the board of the bank, approached McGovern, Burdick, and Metcalf, reminded them of their rural constituency, and, according to the accepted story, persuaded them to vote for the Williams Amendment.

The Williams Amendment and its political roots even provoked the Justice Department to comment caustically. On September 17, 1970, in a speech before the Federal Bar Association Convention, Donald I. Baker, deputy director of policy planning for the Antitrust Division, applauded the idea of specific bank holding amendments to separate banks and commerce, implying that the antitrust laws alone were not enough:

> Anyone who saw the success of a few of the nation's largest banks in promptly getting special legislation to reverse an adverse antitrust decision would think twice before allowing such a bank to combine with, say, General Motors, Lockheed, or CBS, even assuming there were no direct or immediate economic effect involved. Those with political power often have it within their capacity to secure exemption from competition on the basis of justifications which few economists can subscribe to. That simply is the fact of life in Washington, and in the state capitals around the country. It should not be ignored. Unfortunately, the Senate has just illustrated this point again by passing the so-called Williams Amendment to the pending bank holding company legislation, an amendment which would permit a group of individual conglomerates to keep control of banks they now hold. We in the Justice Department have strongly opposed this special interest rider, which is inconsistent with the whole thrust of the 1970 legislation and we urge the House-Senate conference to eliminate it.

Thus, amid almost unheard of acrimony, H.R. 6778 went to a joint conference of the House and Senate in the fall of 1970. Differences were so intense and the anger so great among members of the House and the Senate that there could have been no bill reported out at all—to the delight of more than a dozen bank lobbyists who had figuratively pitched tents to maintain a continuous watch in the corridor outside the Capitol conference room in which the House and Senate Conference Committee was meeting in sessions described by the *American Banker* as among "the most contentious ever held on banking legislation." On one side were the members of the Senate: John Sparkman, chairman of the Senate Banking Committee, William Proxmire, Harrison A. Williams, Wallace F. Bennett, and John G. Tower. On the other side, representing the House, were Wright Patman, William A. Barrett, Leonor K. Sullivan, Henry S. Reuss, William B. Widnall, Albert W. Johnson, and J. William Stanton.

The three weeks of meetings that followed proved to be just what the *American Banker* said they were. At one meeting when Patman began stating his reasons for wanting a restrictive bill, Senator Bennett of Utah berated him for making the "same old speech against bankers." At another point Bennett simply told Patman to shut up, that Patman was interrupting Senator Sparkman, who at the time was himself charging Patman with using the press for planted stories that smeared Bennett, Sparkman, and Senator John Tower, a Texas Republican with deep conservative roots.

What should be understood and appreciated is that the divisiveness in the committee occurred against a backdrop of documented conflict involving many members of Congress. During the two years it was taking to shepherd a bill through Congress to plug the one-bank holding loophole, scores of Congressmen were linked with bank interests. Though Senate rules do not require Senators to make public their financial interests, House rules do, and in 1970 more than a hundred members of the House admitted they owned $5,000 or more worth of securities issued by banks. But that was only part of the story. Members of the House were also substantial borrowers from banks at rates well below those paid by nearly everyone else. In 1969, for example, when the prime rate soared to 8½ percent (meaning that most people and corporations in the United States were paying a rate far, far higher than that) one Washington, D.C., bank was lending money to over a hundred House members at rates just over 6 percent. Because the Senate has no such public disclosure rule, it can only be speculated how many Senators had borrowed money at preferred interest rates or were investors in banks.

7

The Legislation That Emerged

I T W A S under a backdrop, then, of acrimony and suspicion that a bill regulating one-bank holding finally emerged from the Joint Conference Committee of the House and the Senate. In Patman's view, and in the view of many of his enemies, the bankers, Patman won the day. To be sure his laundry list of prohibited, specific businesses had been jettisoned and a grandfather clause allowed. The exemption date of June 30, 1968, finally agreed on was the one first proposed by Representative Widnall, the ranking Republican on Patman's House Banking and Currency Committee, two years before. But the loss of the laundry list became academic when the Federal Reserve Board, which had campaigned for restrictive legislation, became the administrator, regulator, and determinant of just what business banks through their holding companies could get into. (At one point, very early in the House Banking and Currency Committee hearing in 1969, supporters of the administration-sponsored bill had proposed a troika of regulators to administer one-bank holding: the Federal Reserve Board, the Federal Deposit Insurance Corporation, and the Comptroller of the Currency.)

The grandfather clause and its cutoff date, also became academic when Patman won a trade-off which in effect nullified the grandfather exemption. No exemption would be allowed based merely on the date of acquisition. Instead, the Federal Reserve was required to examine every holding company whose subsidiary bank claimed assets of more than $60 million, regardless of when the holding company was formed. As the administrator of the law, the Federal Reserve Board was required no more than two years after passage, specifically by December 12, 1972, to approve or disapprove nonbank acquisitions made before the June 30, 1968, grandfather date. The grounds for disapproval were undue concentration, unfair competition, a decrease in competition, and unsound banking practices. Those nonbanking subsidiaries acquired after the grandfather date of June 30, 1968, had to be divested unless they qualified as businesses closely related to banking. In recognition of the difficulty of separating companies that had been merged for some time, the separation process, the divestiture, could take as long as ten years.

That much was the law. At first, the Federal Reserve Board, in an administrative exercise of its own, determined as the regulator that if a one-bank holding company picked up another bank or two, or a handful of them, divestiture of nonbanking subsidiaries ought to be speeded up, and in this instance reduced the maximum period from ten years to two. Then the board reversed itself. Yet despite the confusion this suggested, one of the most important goals had been reached. One-bank holding companies were not covered under the law without any substantial broadening of the definition of just what was "closely related" to banking.

Patman said that the bill that emerged from the joint committee and was passed in December 31, 1970, "upholds the basic principles" of his original measure. The counsel of Patman's House Banking Committee, however, a contributing architect of the Patman version of the bill, went further. The counsel, Benet D. Gellman, said, "We accomplished almost everything. We got the one-bank holding companies covered, which was the main thing. There were no major exceptions, either, in the final bill, and everybody who formed a holding company after June 30, 1968, had to divest and the Federal Reserve began its case by case review after the bill was passed." Indeed, the bank-holding bill passed in 1970—which was really a series of amendments to the Banking Holding Act of 1956—carried some other tough clauses, not all of which were originated by Patman.

Patman had felt, for example, that so-called tie-in arrangements, in which the granting of a loan may hinge on the applicant's taking other, not necessarily needed services of a bank or its holding company should be specifically prohibited, but this had been knocked out of his bill early in the fight. Patman compromised then, seeing a prohibition in antitrust laws already on the books. But then, in an agreeable development, the Senate version of the one-bank holding bill amendments specifically prohibited tie-in arrangements. The final bill carried the specific prohibition, applying it to *all* banks, in fact, not just those connected with holding companies.

At the same time, both versions narrowed considerably what percentage of securities ownership constitutes control of a bank by a holding company. Under the 1956 act, control of 25 percent of the stock of a bank was considered working control, and thus only those holding companies with 25 percent or more of the stock of two or more banks needed to register with the Federal Reserve Board and be regulated. Many banks, however, especially the "chain banks" in the Midwest and in Texas, were held in working control with stock ownership just under 25 percent. The 1970 amendments, reflecting the versions of both the House and the Senate, recognized that as little as 5 percent ownership can mean control.

Typically, the one-bank holding bill emerged from the joint conference of the House and Senate only because of trading. For example, Patman's laundry list of prohibited businesses was traded for a clause requiring strict regulation by the Federal Reserve Board. If a bank holding company planned to buy a company and make it a subsidiary, the company had to be "so closely related to banking or managing or controlling banks as to be a proper incident thereto." The grandfather clause, as mentioned earlier, was traded for an examination by the Federal Reserve Board of every holding company grandfather acquisitions of banks with assets of more than $60 million, and if a finding, say of concentration or of decreased competition, emerged, the acquisitions made by the holding companies could be disapproved. Divestiture then would be mandatory.

But not all trades were made in an effort to produce legislation considered to be in the "public interest." At least one was made to benefit a vested interest and political supporter, according to congressional sources. This case in connection with the Williams Amendment. In turn for agreeing to drop the amendment, the Senate's conferees exacted a price of tacking on to the bank holding bill authorization for the minting of 150 billion commemorative one-dollar coins displaying a likeness of President Eisenhower on one side and Apollo 11 on the other, and containing 40 percent silver. On the surface, the Ike Dollar Amendment, as it came to be called, seemed little enough to give up for an amendment that might well have gutted the one-bank holding bill, or at least had the potential to. Though it was denied by Senator Williams, the Silver-Dollar Amendment was seen as a personal sop by opponents of his amendment, since a major political supporter of his in his home state of New Jersey, Charles Engelhard, headed a company, Engelhard Minerals and Chemicals, that "was anxious to get into the metallurgical process that would have produced the Eisenhower dollar." Under the Coinage Act of 1965, silver was being phased out as a component of coins. Coins being minted after 1965 had to have a core of copper and a surface of nickel. Under the tacked-on Silver-Dollar Amendment, the Secretary of the Treasury was authorized to issue 150 million silver dollars with a core of silver and copper and a surface mostly of silver. The amendment even transferred 25,500,000 troy ounces of silver from the national stockpile (in short supply for years) for sale at the low price of $1.29 an ounce. "It is understood by the conferees," said Wright Patman and three other conferees of the House (William A. Barrett, Leonor K. Sullivan, and Henry Reuss), "that 130 million of the new silver coins will be manufactured and sold as uncirculated commemoratives and 20 million of them as proof coins, under administrative arrangements through the Treasury Department assuring their widest possible distribution among citizens interested in acquiring a few each."

Patman had traded well, despite giving the Silver Dollar Amendment for the Williams Amendment. The Federal Reserve

Board, responding to broad, discretionary powers granted by the act, turned out to be a generally restrictive administrator. On November 3, 1971, Brenton C. Leavitt, program director for banking structure for the Board of Governors of the Federal Reserve, pointed out that the Bank Holding Act, as changed by the 1970 amendments, "defined a bank as an organization that does two things; namely, accepts demand deposits and makes commercial loans." Though Patman had always considered the Federal Reserve a day-in, day-out opponent, since he resented the fact that it answered to no one, not even Congress, he grudgingly acknowledged two years after the passage of the Bank Holding Act of 1970 that the board had done a reasonably good job in keeping banks and commerce separated. And he was not the only one who said so; in 1972 there was a consensus among those who watch such things. *American Banker,* for example, said, that the stampede of banks into the holding company form had been "sidetracked." No fewer than eighty-nine corporate conglomerates that had picked up banks as subsidiaries were being evicted from the banking business and being forced to divest themselves of the banks as of November, 1972. Another forty-four diversified corporations that had bought banks were under investigation. At the same time, the large banks that were creating one-bank holding companies with themselves as subsidiary in a tail-wagging-the-dog maneuver had been curbed by the Federal Reserve Board's own laundry lists. Banks were barred, for example, from mutual fund operations, an activity they coveted and were led in by New York's militant First National City Bank. They were barred from selling insurance that was not connected with a credit transaction. Real estate brokerage was ruled out as well as land development and management consulting.

But there was a positive side to the Federal Reserve Board list, too. By May 27, 1971, it had declared seven activities were closely enough related to banking for bank holding companies to get into. Later, three more were added. The holding companies could make loans for their own accounts or the accounts of others in various financial businesses, e.g., credit card operations, factoring, mortgage lending, and finance companies. They could operate as industrial banks, Morris Plan banks, or industrial loan companies, but in line with state laws and on the condition that no demand deposits were accepted and no commercial loans made. Both restrictions applied, too, if bank holding companies got into the trust business, acting as a fiduciary or custodian. They could also service loans and extensions of credit for anyone, and they could act as investment or financial advisers to mortgage and real estate investment trusts and to mutual funds. They could also lease personal property, lend money to corporations that were promoting the economically deprived areas of the communities around them, and sell such services as data processing and bookkeeping, if they had excess capacity.

But seven activities were denied by the Federal Reserve Board. The bank holding companies were barred from selling mutual funds, an activity many of them sorely longed for, and generally from selling or even underwriting insurance not connected with a loan, though some limited exceptions were spelled out, e.g., a holding company agent could sell insurance to the company's own subsidiaries or in towns with population under 5,000 if the company had an office in such a town. (Actually, the board regarded its ruling on insurance as a permissible activity, though many in the banking industry saw it as a denial.) To keep the bank holding companies out of land speculation they were told not to get into land development, real estate brokerage, real estate syndication, and even the management of property as a service. (The prohibition reflected a long-held fear in the United States about banks being the owners of real property.) To the chagrin of a leading consultant to banks, the Federal Reserve Board even turned down the proposed acquisition of such consultants by bank holding companies. The consultant, Carter H. Golembe Associates, Inc., of Washington, had made arrangements to be acquired by Marine Midland Banks, Inc., of Buffalo, New York. When the acquisition was denied, Golembe lectured the chairman of the Federal Reserve Board, Arthur F. Burns, on the subject, as he saw it: that being a consultant to banks was an activity closely related to banking. Undoubtedly it was, but consultants can also be links between commerce and banking.

The list of prohibited businesses established by the Federal Reserve hied closely to a philosophy spelled out by Burns while testifying before the Senate on bank holding legislation. At the time, he had opposed specific lists saying what bank holding companies could or could not do, but less than a month after the bank holding amendment became law the Federal Reserve Board developed its own laundry list of permissible activities. By May the Board list was complete. On only one major issue did the Board show doubt. There was a series of applications by bank holding companies to take over savings and loan companies. Clearly, such businesses were closely related to banking, one test the Federal Reserve Board was required to make under the law, but the gut issues of concentration of power and the public interest also were relevant. Many large banks drool over the prospect of taking over savings and loan companies with their large deposits, thus enhancing their own size and power. But since savings and loan companies were created to provide home financing, an activity ignored for the most part by large commercial banks, home-building activity might suffer even more than in recent years if controlling large banks diverted the funds into higher-interest-bearing investments. The Federal Reserve Board forewent a ruling on the applications by bank holding companies to take over savings and loan companies and looked to Congress for help, saying that the past "statutory pattern suggests intent on the part of Congress to maintain savings and loan associations as specialized lenders to finance housing, with specialized rules appropriate to that role. Acquisition of savings and loan associations by bank holdings companies could tend to blur this Congressionally-established structure." The Board then said that nothing would be done until Congress could consider the idea. Within Congress, and especially on the House Banking and

Currency Committee, there was much opposition to such a take-over. Savings and loan associations, some said, should be given even greater latitude—in fact, should be given all the prerogatives of the commercial banks—in order to create competition instead of concentration. In ducking a decision, the Federal Reserve Board undoubtedly also considered the opposition of the Federal Home Loan Bank Board, the agency that regulates the "S and L's."

As might be expected, the banks tried to exploit the list of permissible activities spelled out by the Federal Reserve Board to develop a new series of loopholes. For example, a Rhode Island bank holding company, R.I.H.T. Corporation, tried to invest in a commercial building being erected in a shopping center on the grounds that it was helping to promote community welfare. The Board said no, that the corporation was stretching the point, which R.I.H.T. Corporation management and lawyers knew well enough.

Occasionally, the Federal Reserve Board, even when a bank holding company applied to take on what was clearly permissible, became a horse trader, granting permission only for something in return. For example, when Boatmen's Bancshares, Inc., a St. Louis bank holding company, wanted to get into mortgage banking—a permissible activity—by acquiring a going company, Williams, Kurrus and Company, the Board approved the application on the condition that Williams, Kurrus and Company give up a real estate brokerage it was operating. In a similar case, the Board said that UB Financial Corporation, a Phoenix bank holding company, could keep its mortgage lending firm of H. S. Pickrell Company if Pickrell gave up real estate brokerage.

One of the better assessments of the Federal Reserve Board as the regulator of bank holding companies under the new amendments was made by the very consultant, Carter H. Golembe, who was denied permission to marry his firm to a bank. "An analysis of the . . . list of prohibited activities," Golembe said late in 1972, to his bank clients, "suggests . . . the

Federal Reserve is likely to be wary of any attempts to engage
in activities which involve real property . . . that the Board is
not likely to open up any new doors with respect to the securities
industry . . . that the Board will take a particularly hard look
at any activity of the development of conglomerations of financial
or economic power." Interestingly, the Federal Reserve Board
was applying two tests that had originated with Wright Patman to
the expansion plans of the bank holding companies. One was
whether the business the holding companies wanted to get into
was related to banking. The other was whether the business was
a "proper incident" to banking. In this second test the Federal
Reserve Board considered whether the public benefits to be gained
outweighed any detrimental public effect. Such a test might very
well be applied, for example, to the acquisition of savings and
loan associations by the bank holding companies. A question that
might be asked is whether such an aquisition would make the
savings and loan companies more effective financiers of housing.
The answer undoubtedly would be no, since the commercial banks
at the core of the bank holding companies have a far greater
interest in commercial lending than in home financing.

The Justice Department has been as interested in the two
tests of expansion as anyone, and time and again has acted almost
as a guide through an area that both proponents and opponents
of bank expansion have found murky. The Justice Department
view of things, in fact, is something no bank holding company
lawyer would wish to proceed without, for in the long run it is
the courts that have the final say, and in any court case the bank
holding companies would find themselves either faced directly
by a Justice Department lawyer or listening to the department's
views as a "friend of the court."

Thus in the summer of 1972 when the impact of the Bank
Holding Act of 1970 was being assessed, much attention was
paid to the views of the department's director of policy planning,
Donald I. Baker. As he had two years before during the bitter
Senate-House conference, Baker now spoke out again on the sub-

ject, defining the Justice Department position. On July 20, 1972, at a meeting of the American Bankers Association, Baker "offered a view that was something less than a passive spectator. I see the 1970 legislation," he said, "as reflecting several fundamental themes. First, the desirability of continuing our broad tradition of separating banking from general commerce and industry; second, recognition that the specific line that separated banking from other financial activities had been eroded by time and technology, most notably by the computer; third, banks are important potential competitors in many financial fields."

Baker lauded the Federal Reserve Board as an administrator of the Bank Holding Act as it was amended, and told the bankers that the legal burden was on them to show how and why it was in the public interest for a bank holding company to dip into some other line of business, even if financially related. The key tests bankers needed to apply were whether a new activity increased convenience to the public, whether it increased competition, and whether it produced gains in efficiency that outweighed such adverse effects as concentration, a reduction of competition, the emergence of unfair competition, conflicts of interest, and unsound banking practices. Those holding companies that entered some other line by starting from scratch (or de novo, as it is known) would be given greater leeway than those that tried to buy up going companies, because while new companies stimulated competition, the buying up of established companies, especially those operating in the same geographic area as the holding company, eliminated competition. Baker praised the Federal Reserve Board, because it "has clearly recognized the competition problem that acquisitions raise when the holding company seeks to expand into its bank's own geographic market."

Baker also warned the bankers against tying loans to conditions that loan applicants take other, unwanted services. The practice was illegal, generally, under the Sherman Antitrust Act when sufficient commerce was restrained by tying, but he pointed out that a section of the Bank Holding Act specifically made tying illegal. A bank holding company expanding into new markets with a so-called full service bank (one that offers a spectrum of services) at its core would be vulnerable to prosecution by the Justice Department and the payment of treble damages in suits brought by private parties if it were found, for example, that taking out insurance or buying data processing service were conditions of being granted a loan. Banks should price other services separately, Baker suggested, and even offer them somewhere else physically in the holding company organization rather than in the bank itself.

As though he were also trying to cheer up the bankers, many of whom believed they had been hobbled, Baker suggested that the Bank Holding Act of 1970 and the one of 1956 actually represented an opportunity to expand into other businesses, even though the banks had to stay close to things financially related, e.g., data processing.

It is doubtful that bankers really need cheering up. That they had only temporarily retreated is shown by the following remarks, which are taken from a registration statement of Manufacturers Hanover Trust but which appear in a similar form in the statements of other banks: "It is not presently contemplated that such activities [acquisitions of other companies] would involve non-financially oriented fields, although the registrant has, under existing law, broad corporate powers to engage in operations unrelated to traditional commercial banking and allied functions should its board of directors determine at some future time that such course of action is in the best interest of the registrant and the stockholders." No declaration of sovereignty could have been stated more clearly, though a critic might have the right to ask whether the best interest of a bank and its stockholders transcend the public interest.

It would be a mistake to characterize the bankers of today, especially those at the top of the major banks, as being the same as the one-dimensional corporate ogres of decades ago who built empires of pure economic muscle for no discernible public good.

The Insulls, who controlled the nation's utilities through holding companies, were not interested in bringing more efficient electric and gas services to anyone. Nor were the Van Sweringen brothers, who once controlled the railroads through the holding company device, interested in providing more efficient train service. Today's bankers are unquestionably able and inclined toward producing more efficient services—individual checking account charges, for example, have dropped away to practically nothing among many banks, and a few would even agree to paying interest on checking account funds if the banking industry worked to change the law prohibiting this. They won't.

But a comparison of today's leading bankers with the empire builders of the past is impossible to avoid. Though bankers insist they can bring vast new efficiency to just about any business they touch, whether it be insurance, data processing, or leasing, there is no public clamor for such efficiency. The cashless society, for example, in which someone's bank account would make payment almost simultaneously with the ringing up of a purchase miles away upon insertion into a machine of a credit card, is hardly a national need. Such automation, however, would help bank profits substantially, and in that fact lies the key to why bankers are injecting their organizations into the economy rather than just maintaining and improving traditional services, i.e., making the payments of customers, accepting deposits for safekeeping, extending credit, and acting as a fiduciary guard.

The trouble is bankers are not satisfied with being bankers, and since the early 1960s have decided to act more in their stockholders' interest and to advance their own personal ambitions and accumulation of power. It is in these roles that bankers may be compared with the pyramid builders of yesterday, and indeed with the corporate heads of today's conglomerates, whose purpose seems nothing less than vast growth for growth's sake, great personal power, and, at times, profit.

Some apologists for the banks claim that bankers were pushed into building empires resembling the worst side of American business. In the 1960s, it is argued, corporate treasurers stopped putting all their spare cash into checking accounts that paid no interest, and instead lent it out in such places as the commercial paper market, to the United States Treasury by buying Treasury bills, and in a turnabout, even to the banks. For the banks, the paying of interest for money they formerly received free meant a rise in costs, but a cost squeeze never materialized, for banks merely raised interest rates to extraordinary heights. Late in the 1960s the primate rate rose to 8½ percent. Thus, if banks were paying only 4½ percent for their money, especially in savings accounts, the markup was about 90 percent. For those customers without the highest credit rating, interest on loans was easily 12 percent to 18 percent, suggesting markups of up to 300 percent over the cost of funds. Thus, even in the recession years of the late 1960s bank profits were good, though obviously not for all banks. Typically, the aggressive banks, such as First National City of New York, rolled up substantial earnings. Not counting gains or losses in securities trading, First National City earnings rose from 1966 to 1971 at a compound growth rate of 9.7 percent, a percentage any industrial corporation gladly would accept. The Chase Manhattan rate was 8.1 percent in the same period, while the Chemical New York Corporation, an aggressive bank though dubbed "the Comical Bank" by some critics who see it as a fumbler for its role in stopping Leasco, had to be content with a mere 4.8 percent compound growth rate. The rate for Bank-America Corporation was 10 percent, and the somewhat silent Morgan Guaranty Trust on Wall Street had a resounding 11.5 percent compound rate.

Despite such earnings growth, the aggressive nature of modern bankers was far from satiated, and such leaders as Walter Wriston of the First National City Bank of New York and George A. Roeder, Jr., a vice chairman of Chase Manhattan in the 1960s, tried to justify what seemed to others to be a growing tendency toward gluttony. These two "free spirits" (the appellation was thought up by supporters of their position), and many others, spoke out in print and in public in a kind of poor-mouthing. Practically every banker demeaned the traditional role of banking, i.e., making money on commercial and industrial loans. National monetary policies, they complained, can adversely affect bank earnings. This was true, but banks have never had much trouble adjusting to "tight" conditions when money is scarce or to "easy" conditions when money is plentiful. In either case, and indeed in between, they have always earned and earned and earned. And while wages and prices have been subject to controls, interest rates have not, and even the usury laws of the states have been circumvented time and again by a whole clutch of devious devices, e.g., subtracting interest ahead of time or actually holding back a part of the sum being lent.

It is simple enough to understand why bankers wanted to be businessmen, said the bankers, though they did not express it that way. Banks could earn more by charging fees for services such as leasing, insurance, and factoring. First National City's Wriston bemoaned the fact that while "the number of zeros in our balance sheet is going up . . . our percentage of the market declines," seeking to justify First National City as "a financial service business" also selling mutual funds.

It was Roeder of Chase Manhattan, however, who suggested during the hearings on the amendments to the Bank Holding Act of 1956 that the "cost-price squeeze" of banks was "a problem." He added something else—a fear by banks of competition. Factoring organizations, the direct placement of commercial paper by industrial corporations, the activities of leasing companies, all these were hurting the traditional business of banks, lending. Everyone was beginning to compete against banks, Roeder suggested to the House Banking and Currency Committee. Even companies that made products were financing their own credit sales. This unfortunate circumstance of competition, he said, had forced banks to develop bank holding companies.

Only a very few bankers today still talk about putting their banks at the core of a huge number of subsidiaries, especially industrial subsidiaries. Most are tactfully quiet, preferring only to keep the door open with unostentatious assertions or discreet printed statements.

Yet one banker, aggressive, articulate, and anxious to speak his mind to all comers, and one who defied President Nixon in 1973 over lowering the prime rate, has maintained a position that there ought to be marriages between commerce and banks. The banker, who is First Pennsylvania's John R. Bunting, has said for years that the Zaibatsu system of alliances between Japanese banks and business was beneficial, at least in Japan. Says Bunting: "The Japanese have banks that can do this, tie in with industries. They're running a reasonably good show, and have been for the last thirty years. As a matter of fact, I don't know how we beat them in World War II when I look at what they're doing over there."

An iconoclast in an industry in which iconoclasm is rare, at least in public, Bunting insists that competition does not exist in the United States and that the will of banks to unite with commerce is a pragmatic one highly desired by the populace. "My own guess," he said in the summer of 1972, "is that the thing the Japanese are doing is very much in consonance with what our own society wants for banks. Let's just say corporations such as ITT. To have a variety of businesses within themselves, rather than to have the old-fashioned kind of competition which we never had in this country anyway, but which we hold up as a goal toward which we're working. I say that for this reason. People want security. They do not want unemployment. They do not want to go through layoffs. The large firm, indeed the whole essence of the one-bank company, is that in the down years for the bank, the mortgage company, for example, will be having a good year. In the down years for consumer loans, some other part will be having a good year. You see, a conglomerate is what I am talking about. The original conglomerate was the old ice and coal company. You sold ice in the summer and coal in the winter, and you kept the people that were your employees on duty all the time. You didn't have to disemploy them when the season changed. And this is still the essence and the best rationale for a conglomerate. I think the conglomerate movement in this country is inevitable. By stalling it the way the government is, by inhibiting it in every way, I think we are causing a lot of bloodshed, a lot of unemployment, a lot of dislocations that are unnecessary. I just don't think there is any question about it. I do think it's going to change the kind of economic system we have. It's changing now, to be sure, but in disarray. We just don't know where the hell we are. As for competition, it's a myth. Competition obviously isn't holding prices down anywhere that I know about. When did it ever? Only in textbooks. Who isn't immune to the laws of competition?"

Bunting's willingness to put his head in the lion's mouth in his pitch for conglomerates and banks marrying has given him a kind of underground fame among many of his fellow bankers. But he goes even further. In his world of conglomerate companies each one, large and small, would be assigned a bank to head off what he calls "unfair competition." Auto makers, steel makers, indeed, ice and coal companies, would each be backed by its own bank. "Put a bank behind each," Bunting has said. "That's what I want to do. Put a bank behind each. Let someone own Avis; let another one own Hertz. My bank owns U.S. Steel. Give somebody else Republic. Give somebody else Bethlehem. He takes Ford. Somebody else take General Motors."

Leading bankers have argued for years that a bank immersed in commerce is in the public interest. Though few bankers would become involved in industrial commerce such as steel, nearly all of them have maintained that hitching up with financially related businesses, i.e., becoming "congenerics" rather than "conglomerates," would give banks the kind of profits that would make them, as lenders, more viable and able to change. In fact, R. A. Peterson, president of Bank of America for many years, fought against the bank holding amendments of 1970 on the grounds that the rising cost of lending money was chewing into bank profits to so great an extent that it was "imperative" to find new sources of profits through the holding company. Like other bankers, Peterson also asserted that favoritism, say by granting soft loans to subsidiaries, was not possible. Law prevented this, as did the watchful eyes of bank regulators.

One business magazine, a perennial apologist, also went to bat for the banks, suggesting during the heat of battle that there were fewer risks to bank depositors when their bank got into new financial businesses that were not banking. It was the holding company that was involved, and thus the bank was shielded. Since the holding company generated its money from the sale of securities, from external borrowings (laws limit the amounts a single bank can lend to a single borrower), and from dividends paid to it from its own underlying, or subsidiary, bank, the money of depositors could not be threatened since it was not involved. This whole process of thought ignored the main point of the opposition to bank holding companies, however, which was to keep banking separated from commerce.

One of the main factors in the failures of banks, as pointed out in Chapter 1, has been runs on banks caused by depositor loss of confidence. If a bank's management becomes more concerned with nonbanking activities, even though they are financially related, an impairment of depositor confidence can occur. Banking's self-created mystique may even prevent most depositors from understanding that they are not in jeopardy and a run could easily get under way. To be sure, large American banks could weather just about any run, and the sophisticated depositors of a bank, the corporations, for example, would not necessarily withdraw funds. Still, a run on a bank, based on ignorance or not, clearly points up the basic conflict of a bank siphoning its energies and income into commerce.

That siphoning could be enormous, too, as in the case of New York's First National City Bank. In 1970, for example, to finance its nonbank business First National City paid its holding company, First National City corporation, $152.7 million in dividends, or $7.2 million more than the $145.5 million earned by the bank. Much of the money, was lent to the corporation's subsidiaries, e.g., the mortgage financing, travel, and traveler's check subsidiaries. At the year's end more than $112 million had been lent to the nonbank subsidiaries. Again in 1971 the bank's holding company sucked up enormous amounts of the bank's money, taking $160 million in dividends, this time from First National City Bank. Meanwhile, the holding company made loans to its nonbank subsidiaries totaling $356.5 million, much of it again going to the holding company's mortgage affiliate, Advance Mortgage Corporation. This example shows how, as opponents of bank holding had feared, the nonbank subsidiaries of bank holding companies hardly ever lack for money and have a leg up on competitors.

8

Merger and
Immunity to Antitrust Laws

ONE OF the more realistic measures of who's who in a society's pecking order is vulnerability to the law. Who goes to jail? Who is prosecuted? Who is restrained? Who, as the saying goes, pays the piper? Policemen bust a poorly dressed drunk or pot smoker faster than one neatly attired in the good gray herringbone shield of a Brooks Brothers topcoat, especially if they recognize the wearer's university club tie. Ambitious prosecutors seek out vulnerable entrepreneurs such as builders, a coarse lot who predictably tend to bribe local officials and commit fraud almost openly, rather than move against the likes of General Motors, a company whose defective automobiles may have been killing people for a while but which when found out was allowed to hound the investigator. (Nader eventually brought a successful suit against GM and obtained a large settlement.)

Position in the pecking order is everything. In fact, for a cock of the walk like the nation's commercial banking industry it can lead to an overbearing insistence that prosecution and being called to account are only for others.

Even when it was determined in 1963 by an authority no less than the United States Supreme Court that the banks were subject to the laws of the land, in this case the antitrust laws, a handful of banks that had decided to merge got a sympathetic United States Senator in 1965 to introduce legislation that would exempt them from the antitrust laws, in effect, vetoing the Court's decision. The handful of banks did get their special interest bill, and a few of their mergers were allowed to stand, but for the concession so many restrictions had to be accepted that a huge merger movement among the nation's major banks was all but stopped. Many bankers still exclaim over the extraordinary bungling in this case that allowed three mergers to go free of prosecution in return for banks everywhere becoming subject to the harshest antitrust laws on the books.

The story of how the banks killed off their own broad merger movement has its beginnings in the 1950s. During that decade and the first few years of the 1960s more than 4,500 mergers, consolidations, and acquisitions took place. Hundreds upon hundreds of banks disappeared, swallowed up by larger banks in what was a feverish drive to build economic clout by uniting deposits and assets. No banker seemed immune to the fever. In the tiny hamlet of Perry, New York, The Bank of Perry swept up the First National Bank of Perry, thereby eliminating competition much as its big-city broker bankers were doing. On a single day, December 1, 1954, twenty-three banks disappeared into the maw of San Francisco's First Western Bank and Trust Company, a bank that seemed to have unlimited digestive powers. In 1955 it swallowed six more banks, and in 1956 three more. Apparently satiated temporarily, First Western was able to absorb only one bank in 1957, none in 1958, and only one in 1959. In all, thirty-four banks disappeared as independent entities. To be sure, the banks First Western picked up were relatively small institutions, yet large banks also disappeared. In New York, for example, the Corn Exchange Bank Trust Company, with its $832 million or more of assets, became part of the Chemical Corn Exchange Bank. The New York Trust Company, with over a billion dollars in assets, became a part of Chemical Bank New York Trust Company, a bank that picked up the Bank of Rockville Centre Trust Company as well, with over $43 million in assets, the Bensonhurst National Bank of Brooklyn, with $39 million in assets, and the First National Bank of Mount Vernon, with nearly $56 million in assets. In this period such major banks as San Francisco's Bank of America and New York's First National City Bank and the Chase Manhattan Bank were also feeding on the assets of other banks.

Though the surviving banks swelled, mightily in some cases, there was little advantage to all the merging for the public, since the period was not marked by increased banking services. The mergers did reduce competition, however, and in Congress the alarm grew, for by the end of the 1950s increasing concentration was clearly an indisputable fact. Not only had large banks been acquired by larger banks, but the total number of banks in the United States had declined by 5 percent, though nearly 900 charters had been distributed to newly organized banks.

All the while they were absorbing each other, the banks maintained that they were immune to the antitrust laws, both the Clayton Act and the Sherman Antitrust Act. Unfortunately for the public interest, they had the agreement at the time of the Justice Department, supposedly the champion of the public interest in antitrust matters. The reasoning went: Though the Clayton Act forbade lessening competition, which is what the banks were doing, it did not cover banks. As it had been written early in the century, the Clayton Act was intended to ward off the empire builders of another day—men whose technique was to pick up banks and other businesses by buying up their stock issues. The bank mergers of the 1950s were accomplished by uniting assets, and thus one Antitrust Division head man of the time, Robert A. Bicks, said the Clayton Act was of "little help" in controlling mergers. Even amending the act in 1950 to include acquisitions of assets didn't help, for as it turned out, only corporations subject to the Federal Trade Commission were affected.

Meanwhile, that other famous antitrust legislation, the Sherman Act, was also left to languish, though its prohibitions against monopolistic practices and tendencies gave the government the right to act against mergers made on either a stock acquisition or marrying of assets basis. But only once, in 1959, was it invoked, and then in a civil suit.

It wasn't until late in the 1950s that a number of legislators in both the House and the Senate became alarmed over the immunity of banks to prosecution under laws that applied to everyone else. Their alarm produced the Bank Merger Act of 1960, to inhibit mergers, but in their haste they created a bill nearly everyone, proponents and opponents of bank mergers alike, considers weak, for the merging continued, though on a somewhat reduced scale. In the five years following passage of the act, 765 bank mergers were approved. The banks still claimed immunity, on the grounds that the act required the Federal Reserve Board and other bank regulatory agencies to evaluate the effects of bank mergers, including the competitive effects. It was this approval by regulatory agencies that provided the banks with their argument, which was that approval of a regulatory agency gave them immunity. The banks knew, too, that the Justice Department, especially its Antitrust Division, was less controlled by the banks than were the bank regulatory agencies.

It was a neat bit of reasoning and clearly one favoring the banks, considering the record of their regulatory agencies. In the nine years between 1950 and 1958 the Comptroller of the Currency approved 730 bank mergers and disapproved only 22, a point that was made in Congress and which has made the comptroller—no matter what man occupies the office—a target of justifiable criticism. The fact is that banking agencies, whether they are national or state, are expected to assure the financial health of banks, basically to protect depositors. If a bank can reduce competition, it obviously can maintain itself more easily. The cost to the public, however, is high interest rates on loans, low rates of interest paid on deposits, reductions of services, and a reluctance on the part of bank managements to be innovative.

The banks maintained that the Bank Merger Act of 1960 placed them under the exclusive and final jurisdiction of the regulatory agencies, i.e., the Federal Reserve Board, the Comptroller of the Currency, and the Federal Deposit Insurance Corporation. The Justice Department was to be only one advisory voice to be considered along with many other voices when the regulatory agencies made their decisions. In some minds the statement, which was made regularly by the American Bankers Association, was hard to believe since it removed the banks from control except by their own sympathetic regulators, and placed them beyond the law. Another argument of banks was simply a telling of half-truths. Because it was regulated, as were other industries such as airlines, shipping, railroads, and stock exchanges, the banking industry was immune to prosecution under the antitrust laws, just as these other industries were immune. The hole in the argument was that banking was hardly regulated as comprehensively as these other industries. Airlines, railroads, power companies, telephone companies—all must ask whether they can raise rates, for example, or reduce or add on services. Banks have always raised interest rates almost at will and in accordance with their own needs, just as they have always added on services or not offered them almost on a basis of their own needs. Significantly, banks can discriminate, too, about whom they lend money to, whereas power companies, telephone companies, and railroads must provide service.

In Congress the arguments of the banks hardly won favor, and during the debate over the Bank Merger Act of 1960 at least four Senators became angry. Disturbed that the Attorney General of the United States did not have more than an advisory voice, they warned the bank regulatory agencies that "their acts will be closely scrutinized by Congress and the country, and, if it should appear that they continue to disregard the need for competition in banking, then at least some Members of Congress will urge that stronger powers be provided to the Department of Justice." The men were Senators Paul H. Douglas, Joseph S. Clark, William Proxmire, and Edmund S. Muskie, all of whom extended their word of caution, as they phrased it, formally and on the record. At the other end, Senator Lyndon B. Johnson said that bank mergers "are now and will continue to be exempt from the anti-merger provisions of the Clayton Antitrust Act." Stronger powers for the Department of Justice were assumed, though interestingly it was the Attorney General himself —Robert Kennedy—who provided the impetus for change. After the election of John F. Kennedy in November, 1960, a number of Justice Department lawyers decided that many bank mergers were indeed in violation of the antitrust statutes, despite the recently passed Bank Merger Act of 1960, and said so in strong formal terms. A handful of mergers drew heavy fire and figured significantly in events that came later.

One example was the case of the First National Bank and Trust Company and the Security Trust Company of Lexington, Kentucky. On December 1, 1960, these two asked the Comptroller of the Currency for permission to merge. Though the Attorney General and even the other two regulatory agencies, the Federal Reserve Board and the Federal Deposit Insurance Corporation, filed adverse reports on the effect of the merger, the Comptroller approved it three months after the request was made—on February 24, 1961. It did not matter that several weeks earlier, on January 10, 1961, the Justice Department told the two banks it was about to launch an antitrust investigation. Just one hour after the merger was completed on March 1, 1961, the Justice Department filed a suit, asking for a temporary injunction. The court accepted the promise of the banks that if the Justice Department won its case they were prepared to separate themselves, and the two banks accepted an order from the court to maintain separate books and records in case they had to separate. The injunction was denied.

A second case involved the desire of Chicago's Continental Illinois National Bank and Trust Company to mate with the City National Bank Trust and Company, in a wedding that appeared incestuous as well as anticompetitive to some critics. The two banks, situated on the same block, had maintained a kind of cousinly relationship over the years, and now they wanted to get in bed together. On December 13, 1960, the banns appeared in the press, and on January 20, 1961, the Comptroller of the

Currency, Raymond Gidney, was asked to unite the two banks. (Under the Bank Merger Act of 1960 the Comptroller passed on mergers in which a national bank was the survivor; the Federal Reserve Board passed on a merger if the survivor was a state bank but a member of the Federal Reserve System; and the Federal Deposit Insurance Corporation passed judgment if the survivor was a state bank but not a member of the Federal Reserve. No matter which regulator decided, there was a Blue-beard factor in all the marriages, since one partner always died suddenly. In the case of Continental, it physically moved the assets and personnel of City National across the street, claiming its dowry almost immediately.)

This time the Justice Department was not alone in its opposition. The Federal Reserve was against the merger, too, though the FDIC was not. Needless to say, the Comptroller favored it, and on August 24, 1961, it was approved, even though the Justice Department had said on June 7 it would file suit, charging violations of both the Clayton Act and the Sherman Antitrust Act. In reply to the suit, which was filed on August 29, 1961 (less than a week after the merger approval), the banks told a judge they would agree to divorce and resurrect the corpse of City National—which, as Continental later revealed, was actually beyond resurrection, especially if it had to wait for the decision of a trial not scheduled until 1966, five years later.

A third case involved the Manufacturers Trust Company and the Hanover Bank, both of New York, and both anxious to unite as the Manufacturers Hanover Trust Company. After receiving the approval on May 23, 1961, of New York's superintendent of banks, the two banks then, as members of the Federal Reserve System, sought the permission of the Federal Reserve Board. After holding informal hearings, to which the Board strangely did not invite the Justice Department, the Board gave its approval on September 6, 1961. An advisory report of the Comptroller of the Currency had recommended approval and a report of the FDIC had been, in effect, an abstention. Just two days after getting approval, the two banks consummated their merger —minutes before a suit was filed by the Justice Department charging the banks with violating the Sherman and Clayton acts. For three days the Justice Department argued in a New York federal court for an injunction staying the merger, but the banks prevailed, promising that if the government won its case they would part. The promise of divestiture if the government won its case was again enough to deny the injunction.

In the few years that followed, the Justice Department brought three more cases against bank mergers. One involved the Crocker Anglo National Bank and the Citizens National Bank in California. These two, coming under the jurisdiction of the Comptroller, filed for permission to merge on May 3, 1963. Despite a strong adverse report from the Justice Department, and another from the Federal Reserve Board (the FDIC's three voting directors, one of whom was the Comptroller, could not agree), the merger was approved on September 30, 1963. Indeed, on July 8 the Justice Department had even warned the two banks at a formal meeting with their attorneys that a suit would result if they merged. Then the Justice Department sought an injunction, but again the banks argued successfully in court that the merger should not be delayed, since the Justice Department could always require divestiture if it won its case. On November 1, 1963, the banks merged, three weeks after the Justice Department had filed suit charging violations of the Sherman Act and the Clayton Act.

The following year brought still another case, this one involving the Third National Bank and the Nashville Bank and Trust Company in Tennessee. Although strong reports opposing the merger were filed by the Attorney General, the Federal Reserve Board, and the FDIC, the Comptroller approved the merger on August 4, 1965, permitting it to take effect on August 18. On August 10 the Justice Department sued, moving at the same time for a preliminary injunction, but the president of Third National convinced a court that divestiture, in case the Justice

Department won its suit, would be far less an ordeal than delaying the merger.

Two St. Louis banks argued their case in the same way. The Mercantile Trust Company National Association and the Security Trust Company, whose request to the Comptroller for permission to merge was approved June 24, 1965, successfully argued against a preliminary injunction. The two banks told a court that they were "far more willing to resolve the problems of divestiture" if the Attorney General won an antitrust suit than "endure the hardships of a preliminary injunction" that would keep them apart.

At first, it seemed as though the Justice Department had little to go on in its drive to show that banks, too, were subject to the antitrust laws. Lawyers and legislators everywhere felt the banks had an immunity. But then on June 17, 1963, a fateful day, a majority of the Supreme Court delivered a bombshell opinion that banks were, as the Justice Department under Robert Kennedy had maintained, subject to the Clayton Act. The decision came in a appeal by the Justice Department, which had opposed a merger between the Philadelphia National Bank and the Girard Trust Corn Exchange Bank, the second and third largest banks in Philadelphia at the time. As usual, the Comptroller of the Currency had permitted the merger, despite opposition not only from the Attorney General, but from the FDIC and the Federal Reserve Board as well, all of whom advised that a merger would sharply reduce competition in the Philadelphia area. The merger would give the two banks a 30 percent control over banking in the area.

For the customers of the two banks the merger meant higher costs and charges. Where interest rates varied, the surviving bank invoked the rate least favorable to the borrower. If a depositor had not paid for services before, say in checking, he did now. Each change made brought the bank a higher yield and the customer a higher cost with the elimination of competition.

In reversing a decision of a U.S. District Court, the Supreme

Court ruled that the Clayton Act made bank mergers unlawful if they tended toward monopoly or substantially reduced competition. In an opinion written by Justice Brennan the majority said, "We reverse the judgment of the District Court. We hold that the merger . . . is forbidden by Section 7 of the Clayton Act and so must be enjoined; we need not, and therefore do not, reach the further question of alleged violation of Section 1 of the Sherman Act."

That further question, whether bank mergers could also be in violation of the Sherman Act, was reached less than a year later, when the Supreme Court determined that the First National Bank and Trust Company and the Security Trust Company, two of that handful of banks that had agreed to divestiture if the Justice Department should win its case, were in violation. Obviously, the two banks were not giants as banks go, though in their own geographical area, a point hammered on by the Justice Department, they would control half the banking business. Banking was a local business in Fayette County, the home of the two banks, in an opinion written by Justice Douglas, since it was inconvenient for bank customers to go elsewhere. More than 95 percent of the combined bank's customers maintained officers in Lexington, Kentucky, in Fayette County. Further, the merged bank was larger than all four remaining, competing banks put together, and such bigness was a powerful attraction to potential customers. "The elimination of significant competition . . . constitutes an unreasonable restraint of trade in violation of Section 1 of the Sherman Act," the majority concluded, with Justice Harlan dissenting.

For the banks that had pledged to divest if the Justice Department won its cases, the Supreme Court decisions of 1963 and 1964 meant it was time to redeem those pledges. But it was clear that the pledges were merely a tactic in an overall strategy of delay. For example, almost a year elapsed before the two Lexington banks found in violation of the Sherman Act dissolved their merger, and even then they acted only after a

District Court on March 18, 1965, issued an order for them to do so. The Manufacturers Hanover merger, which had been consummated on September 8, 1961, over the strong objections of the Justice Department and well before the Supreme Court decisions, dragged its feet even after the Supreme Court decisions. It was not until March 10, 1965, that a New York District Court finally declared the merger violated both the Sherman Act and the Clayton Act.

The decision was hardly a victory for law and order, however. Five weeks later, on April 6, 1965, Senator Willis Robertson, chairman of the Senate Banking Committee, introduced S. 1698, an amendment to the Bank Merger Act of 1960, but which came to be called privately the Manufacturers Hanover Home Relief Act. The thrust of the bill was to forgive all past bank mergers, including the handful either being challenged by the Justice Department or already found in violation of the antitrust laws. Since the Justice Department had no intention of challenging the thousands upon thousands of mergers long consummated—to break them up would harm millions of customers and stockholders dealing with and investing in those banks—the bill was in reality a forgiveness bill for special interests, i.e., the banks being challenged or under orders to divest, and had the effect of vetoing the decisions of the Supreme Court in that handful of mergers. It also seemed to open the future for bank mergers in the form of a clause, the effect of which was misunderstood, added by Senator Proxmire. Basically, Proxmire wanted the Justice Department to institute antitrust actions against bank mergers within thirty days or forever hold its peace, except in rare exceptions—e.g., where a bank had lied in telling of its merger plans. To Attorney General Nicholas deB. Katzenbach, S. 1698 was the ultimate giveaway to the banks. Not only would past mergers be forgiven, even those of banks that had agreed to divest upon losing their cases, but also the Justice Deparment was being hobbled in future actions. "Our major objection to the thirty-day cutoff procedure," he said, "is that no convincing reason exists for according special treatment to banking. I have discussed the important role antitrust can play in maintaining a healthy banking industry; in this respect banking cannot and should not be distinguished from other industries for which no such special procedure is here proposed." Robert Kennedy, by now a Senator from New York, saw the major purpose of the bill as being "aimed at these six banks that had merged." He, too, felt that the thirty-day clause was not "critically needed."

Senator Philip A. Hart, whose opposition in the Senate to the bill was swept aside, complained that it "has the effect of imposing a thirty-day statute of limitations," and at the same time gave the Attorney General the right "to confer perpetual immunity on bank mergers, or even worse, compel a nervous Attorney General in charge of the antitrust department to file suit in every case lest somebody jump on him for missing one." Hart also pointed out that a merger's potential for harm might not become clear until long after it had been consummated.

There was no stopping action in the Senate on the bill, which cleared the Senate Banking and Currency Committee in a matter of days, on June 8, 1965, and passed the Senate three days later on a voice vote after ten hours of debate. It was railroading of a rare kind, a charge that can easily be supported in accounts of the way witnesses were handled. Attorney General Katzenbach, for example, was asked on the Wednesday before a Memorial Day weekend to testify the following Tuesday, the day after the holiday. Unprepared to testify on such short notice on a bill so significant, Katzenbach could not appear but asked for time to prepare a statement. This was granted, but the report could not be prepared in time, either, and the hearings adjourned without it.

Nor were any hearings held after the Proxmire amendment was tacked on. By mid-June two months after it had been introduced in the Senate, the bill was ready to go to the House Banking and Currency Committee. An aide of Chairman Wright Patman recalls that "the pressures continued and those on the House committee were enormous." The majority of Patman's own committee had introduced the Senate bill, not Patman, even before any hearings on it had even been thought about. We didn't have the votes to stop it, and there was only one thing left for us to do. That was filibuster. So we started the hearings in the middle of August, picking up a couple of months there. And those hearings ran and ran and ran and ran. For six weeks. This time Katzenbach did testify, magnificently. We gave him all the time he wanted, and he just demolished the bill. Bobby Kennedy, who had been elected to the Senate the year before, but had been Attorney General when the cases were brought, testified as well."

Patman's brand of filibustering was something to see. A long line of witnesses was called, not one of whose testimony could be considered as mere padding. Senator Hart appeared to get his substantial objections into the official record. Senator Proxmire appeared to explain the need of the thirty-day clause, pointing out that his views for years had been to give the Justice Department increased power to stop mergers when competition was reduced. The Robertson bill, before Proxmire's added clauses, would have exempted completely from the antitrust laws, including both the Sherman Act and the Clayton Act, thousands of mergers approved under the Bank Merger Act of 1960, i.e., by the Comptroller, the Federal Reserve Board, or other regulatory agencies. "My amendment," Proxmire said, "would give the Justice Department time to start a suit." With a suit under way —and this was the key meaning—a merger could not be completed until after the suit had been concluded. Only the courts could declare a merger exempt, after which, however, there could be no further legal blockades under the Clayton Act. (But then, if it wished, the Justice Department could turn to the Sherman Antitrust Act. The thirty days were actually sixty days, said Proxmire, since after the thirty-day waiting period, the Justice Department had thirty days to file its report.

The result of his amendment, Proxmire said, was that banks would have no immunity from prosecution. He would not concede, however, that other sections of the bill constituted special interest legislation for the relief of a few banks.

For six weeks the witnesses appeared, causing J. William

Stanton, a member of the committee (actually it was the Sub-committee on Domestic Finance), to complain that the hearings were getting more time than "major legislation." Nevertheless, the hearings went on. Donald M. Graham, vice chairman of the Continental Illinois, one of those the Robertson bill would give relief to, said that the City National Bank that had been absorbed by his bank "cannot be revived."

At one point the subcommittee unearthed a story of extraordinary conflict in the American Bar Association, some of whose more powerful members were representing the banks whose mergers would be protected and who had killed an inside report of a Bar Association committee opposing the legislation. On September 28, 1965, Patman revealed what had happened:

> The story before us here this morning is not pretty. It is a story of pressure. It is a story of intimidation. And most important it is a story of censorship and of a blatant lobbying effort to keep vital information from the Congress on pending legislation. Unknown to the Congress, an important task group of the American Bar Association, more than two months ago—weeks before this subcommittee opened hearings—issued a full report on S. 1698. That report flatly opposed enactment. The report pointed out that the Congress has not seen fit to grant immunity from antitrust laws—as proposed by S. 1698—except in cases of fully regulated industries such as utilities and railroads. This report was adopted unanimously by a five-member task group of the American Bar Association. The five lawyers who signed this report are all experts on antitrust law and top members of their profession. Presumably the American Bar Association's position as represented by this task group report would have an important bearing on S. 1698, but until today, this subcommittee, the Congress, the press, and the public have been kept completely in the dark about the ABA report. Only through the power of subpoena and the work of the staff of this subcommittee have we been able to pull this report to the surface. Frankly, I commend the five lawyers who bravely affixed their signatures to their honestly drafted opinion. Since their appointment to the ABA task group, these lawyers have been subject to a wide range of pressure, intimidation and wild charges of conflict of interest. The pressure was so severe that two members resigned even before the report was

drafted. As might be expected, this pressure has been directed from the offices of the law firms representing five of the six banks whose antitrust violations would be excused by this bill.

Then Patman ticked off the law firms and their clients. The first was Morrison, Foerster, Holloway, Clinton and Clark, a San Francisco firm representing the Crocker Citizens National Bank. The second was Mayer, Friedlich, Spiess, Tierney, Brown and Platt, a Chicago law firm representing Continental Illinois National Bank and Trust. Third was Thompson, Mitchell, Douglas and Neill, a St. Louis firm representing Mercantile Trust Company. Fourth was Hooker, Hooker and Willis of Nashville, Tennessee, representing the Third National Bank. Fifth was Simpson, Thacher and Bartlett, one of New York's more prestigious law firms and representative of Manufacturers Hanover Trust. "The ringleader in the effort was George Balamut, a partner in the law firm of Simpson, Thacher and Bartlett . . . the biggest beneficiary of the legislation before this committee," Patman said. Balamut had charged the Bar Association committee's chairman, George Reycraft, with bias because Reycraft had once worked for the Justice Department. At the time Reycraft headed the task force committee, however, he was member of Cadwalader, Wickersham and Taft, a Wall Street firm. As for Balamut, all the time he was working against disclosure of the report he and his firm were employed by Manufacturers Hanover.

In the report Reycraft and the other members of his American Bar Association committee said, "The subcommittee is opposed to the enactment of S. 1698 for the reason that it considers the bill to constitute an attempt to deal with only a small part of a much larger problem." The statement was followed by reasoning suggesting that "the overall problem" of bank mergers should be dealt with. Besides Reycraft's signature, there appeared the signatures of Richard E. Day, Arthur H. Kahn, Philip Patterson, and Melvin Spaeth, attorneys and law professors with unusual expertise in antitrust law. Some of the pressure brought to bear on the five was enormous. For example, besides Balamut's opposition there was the opposition of Whitney North Seymour, Sr., a partner of Simpson, Thacher and Bartlett. As a former president of the American Bar Association he was a man with enormous clout in the legal profession. It was participation and opposition such as his that impelled Wright Patman to discourse on the role of lawyers in American society. Speaking of how the report of the American Bar Association committee was quashed, and not revealed to its membership at a general meeting in Miami, Patman said, "It was a shameful case of censorship. It would seem that the fateful warning sounded by Louis D. Brandeis sixty years ago has come to pass." Then he quoted Brandeis:

> Instead of holding a position of independence, between the wealthy and the people, prepared to curb the excesses of either, able lawyers have, to a large extent, allowed themselves to become adjuncts of great corporations and have neglected the obligation to use their powers for the protection of the people. We hear much of the corporation lawyer, and far too little of the people's lawyer. The great opportunity of the America bar is and will be to stand again as it did in the past, ready to protect the interests of the people. . . . Such questions as the regulation of trusts . . . call for the exercise of legal ability of the highest order. . . . The leaders of the bar . . . have, with rare exceptions, been ranged on the side of the corporations. . . . The leaders of the bar have, with a few exceptions, not only failed to take part in constructive legislation designed to solve in the public interest our great social, economic, and industrial problems; but they have failed likewise to oppose legislation prompted by selfish interests. They have often gone further in disregard of the common weal. They have often advocated, as lawyers, legislative measures which as citizens they could not approve, and have endeavored to justify themselves by a false analogy. They have erroneously assumed that the rule of ethics to be applied to a lawyer's advocacy is the same where he acts for private interests against the public, as it is in litigation between private individuals.

The Patman filibustering did not always produce testimony so telling. There were times when Patman resurrected issues he had regarded for years as being profoundly in conflict with the public interest, though some had only an indirect relationship to the bill being considered. For example, on August 11, 1965, during the appearance of William McChesney Martin, chairman of the Federal Reserve Board at the time and a man Patman considered to be a tool of the banks, Patman got into a debate with Martin over the fact that the Federal Reserve System had been answering to no one but itself. Patman inserted into the record of the committee hearings "A bill to restore the authority of Congress over expenditures by agencies of the United States having jurisdiction over bank mergers, and for other purposes," i.e., the Federal Reserve System. One of Patman's long-sought goals was to throw a rein over the Federal Reserve and the Federal Deposit Insurance Corporation, each of which developed their own operating and expense budgets independent of Congress and each of which was supporting the legislation Patman was now holding hearings on. After he had inserted his bill into the record Patman went on to lecture Martin on the meaning of constitutional government (a lecture Martin obviously did not need but was compelled to listen to as he sat in the witness chair) and suggested that the Federal Reserve System Martin headed was itself "a money trust and a most vicious kind of money trust" that can manufacture money without being audited by anyone at all—a statement basically true so far as auditing is concerned.

For a while, especially during September, it seemed as though Patman, aided substantially by committee member Paul H. Todd, Jr., a Michigan Congressman who had gone to great pains to understand bank merging in all its ramifications, and Congressman Charles L. Weltner, another astute member of the committee, might actually kill off the bill with his filibuster. But in October, 1965, a majority of his own committee met secretly, giving him no notice, and in a rump session "purported," as their action is characterized by a Patman aide, to report the bill out of committee. Patman, however, got wind of the session, showed up before those attending could flee, and adjourned it. In the bitter rhubard that followed, the House Speaker and the House itself became involved. But by February, 1966, the bill was adopted, becoming the Bank Merger Act of 1966, though not without substantial changes. For example, the Justice Department could not move to unscramble the thousands of bank mergers that had been consummated, which would have hardly been in the public interest anyway. But three of the merged banks that had promised to divest and then defaulted on their pledges were told to unscramble themselves. The three had been merged after the Supreme Court's decision in the Philadelphia merger case. However, the special forgiveness fought so hard for by Manufacturers Hanover, Continental Illinois, and the two banks in Lexington, Kentucky, was granted by the act. This was one reason the act became known to some of the press as the Manufacturers Home Relief Act. In fact, three days after its passage Manufacturers Hanover sent a letter to its stockholders suggesting they tell Senator Willis Robertson, the legislator who had introduced the bill, how much they "appreciated his attitude and efforts." The letter was interpreted widely as a suggestion to send a campaign contribution to Robertson.

The special relief, ironically, was obtained at an onerous price the entire banking industry was forced to pay, for the Bank Merger Act of 1966 stopped the bank merger movement in its tracks. While other industries could still merge and then wait for legal opposition, which the Justice Department is generally unwilling to initiate because unscrambling a merger injures everyone, bank mergers could be hung up almost immediately by the Justice Department merely by asking a court for a temporary injunction that was temporary until "all remedies are completed." Those remedies could take forever. In the opinion of a least one antitrust attorney, "The law that was passed was a very effective law. There hasn't been a major merger since that day."

One important reason was that the new law was soon tested in the Supreme Court, which delivered a decision on March 27, 1967. The banks involved were First City National Bank of Houston, which wanted to mate with the Southern National

Bank of that city, and the Provident National Bank of Philadelphia, which wanted to merge with the Penn National Bank, a neighbor. As usual, the Comptroller of the Currency approved both mergers after private deliberations, despite strong opinions from both the Federal Reserve Board and the Attorney General that the mergers would have serious anticompetitive effects—the key prohibition against merger under the Clayton Act and a prohibition the Comptroller is under strict instructions to consider. At issue was the procedure of the Bank Merger Act of 1966, specifically the right of the Attorney General to prevent a merger from happening "until judicial remedies have been exhausted," as its was phrased by the Court. It was difficult in the extreme to unscramble two banks after they had merged, the Court said. Thus, it concluded, "normal procedure therefore should be maintenance of the status quo until the antitrust litigation has run its course, lest consummation take place and the unscrambling process that Congress abhorred in the case of banks be necessary."

The effects, as Wright Patman pointed out to the House of Representatives just a few days after the Court's decision, were to make the findings of the regulatory agencies for banks less than "sacrosanct" and to untie the hands of the Justice Department. To be sure, mergers that were anticompetitive could sometimes be permitted. The need of the community for bank services could forestall legal action against a merger that wiped out the competition, but the burden of proof was on the banks. As it turned out, that burden was too much. With its hands untied, the Justice Department became a formidable cop on the beat and a prosecutor ready to go to court. In June, 1970, for example, a case involving two small banks in Phillipsburg, New Jersey, ended up in the Supreme Court, which again ruled against the banks. The case was considered a landmark, since it established the point that it made no difference how small the banks were if a merger between them would wipe out competition in their community. Even a dissenting opinion by Justice John Marshall Harlan affirmed this, for he wrote that "after today's opinion, the legality of every merger of two directly competing banks . . . no matter how small . . . is placed in doubt if a court . . . concludes that the merger produces a firm controlling an undue percentage of the relevant market."

The next collision between the Justice Department and the banking establishment came in April, 1971, when the giant Wells Fargo Bank in San Francisco announced it wanted to acquire the First Western Bank and Trust Company, a Los Angeles bank that had itself demonstrated a voracious appetite for other banks during the years of booming merger activity. Most of First Western was now owned by World Airways, Inc., but the important point was that the two banks were clearly in competition in scores of California communities. The banks argued that most Wells Fargo offices were in northern California, while more than half of First Western's offices were in southern California. Besides, they argued further, their size should be viewed alongside that of the Bank of America, which dwarfed even the combined bank. To this the Justice Department replied that it would block any merger of substantial competitors in the same local market to prevent the largest banks in a state or metropolitan area from acquiring dominant local position in markets throughout the state. On October 20, 1972, Wells Fargo and First Western decided not to merge.

That the bill was an effective preventative of anticompetitive mergers was proved again and again. Suits and threats of suits, blossomed everywhere. For example, in November, 1971, the Justice Department sued to prevent the merger of five Atlanta banks that would have become two subsidiaries of Citizens and Southern National Bank, the largest bank in Georgia. Almost monotonously the complaint said that competition would be substantially reduced. Just as monotonously the banks complained that they were being denied the right to expand as other businesses have expanded, and even the right to compete and to profit. But bankers being bankers, they had already begun a new tack.

The New Tack

EVEN AS they were being pursued through the courts by the Justice Department to keep them on the straight and narrow, the banks were turning to that old and favored device, the bank holding company. Not that the Justice Department flatly opposed its use to expand. The issue, as always, was one of competition: Were the banks and their holding companies quashing it? Indeed, the Justice Department time and again enunciated a policy that actually encouraged banks to use the holding company to expand into other markets. For a large bank to go into another market by starting up a branch in competition with local banks, or by buying up a bank that had not much more than a foothold, was the right way to expand. Invariably such expansion was in the public interest, since the invading bank usually introduced new competitive service, e.g., free checking or higher interest rates on savings. In at least one community an invading bank starting from scratch became a significant competitor merely by introducing savings accounts, something the entrenched bank had not wanted to bother with.

Such de novo entry has won the approval of both regulators and the Justice Department, and in recent years the Antitrust Division of the department has even promoted that kind of expansion through its director of policy planning, Donald I. Baker. Again and again Baker has stood up before bankers' meetings, spelling out what was in the public interest and what was not. It was only when large banks began systematically to acquire leading banks in local markets by means of the holding company device that opposition in the courts could be expected.

But a new, vital point had emerged. If a bank holding company took over a bank, the Justice Department argued, it eliminated itself as a potential competitor and thus the Clayton Act was again violated. It was a fine argument, one that some bankers failed to grasp, or accept, and again a Supreme Court decison was needed to impress them.

The case that emerged, the so-called Potential Competition Case, was filed in 1970 by the Justice Department in opposition to an acquisition proposed by the First National Bancorporation, Denver, which wanted to acquire the First National Bank of Greeley, Colorado, the community's second largest bank. The Justice Department argument was that the First National Bancorporation, a large and therefore able banking institution, itself would be eliminated as a potential competitor in Greeley if it were allowed to go through with its acquisition.

The broad fear of the Justice Department, as usual, was concentration. First National Bancorporation already had pulled some Denver banks under its mantle. Its attempt to pick up the bank in Greeley supported the Justice Department's contention that there was a trend developing among big-city bank holding companies to pick up outlying banks that were the largest or next to largest in their communities. From the point of view of the banks and their holding companies, this was a lot easier and cheaper than starting from scratch.

At first the Justice Department suit was dismissed by a federal District Court in Colorado, which said that the department had not shown that the acquisition would substantially lessen competition. The elimination of existing competition was not the issue, though, said the Justice Department in appealing to the Supreme Court in 1972. The issue was one of eliminating "potential competition." If a well-off bank holding company was a potential competitor in a banking market, but decided to buy a leading bank instead of jumping into a market on its own, then it was violating the Clayton Act because it had eliminated a significant potential competitor—itself. It was an argument that had been upheld by the Supreme Court in another case, one involving an industrial company, but it had never been brought against banking. Unfortunately, the Court could not make up its collective mind, and in a 4–4 vote reached in March, 1973 (Justice Lewis F. Powell, Jr., did not vote), left the issue hanging. Thus, it remained possible for banking in entire states to be dominated by just a very few banking organizations, as in the cases of Arizona, Oregon, and Hawaii. Even as the Supreme Court delivered its non-verdict, just two banking organizations in each of these states controlled from 70 to 80 percent of state deposits and were by far the largest of the banks. The Justice Department, however, had not given up, for it had cases pending at the time in Colorado, Washington, Connecticut, Virginia, and South Carolina, all based on the charge that potential competition was being eliminated by the banks in their grab for other leading banks. There was reason to be optimistic, too, since the Supreme Court had recognized the potential competition doctrine a number of times before as an appropriate basis for challenging a merger under Section 7 of the Clayton Act in other industries, e.g., beer, gas, detergents.

Nor was the Justice Department the only overseer stirred up. The Federal Deposit Insurance Corporation, in filing a brief as amicus curiae, revealed a study that showed that economies of scale, an argument often advanced by acquisition-minded banks, did not really occur as the overall organization grows. A single banking office, as it got bigger, did produce economies of scale as its business increased, because its costs dropped. But in an organization such as a multibank holding company, no real economies developed as offices were added to the organization. In a study of 972 banks the FDIC found that if multibank organizations increased their total number of demand deposit accounts by 10 percent, the cost of servicing the accounts increased at almost the same rate, 9.771 percent. Other functions of banks showed no economies of scale, though in some functions, e.g., business loans, costs rose only 8.761 percent when the number of accounts increased by 10 percent.

Still another study, one by the Federal Reserve, also suggested a big organization made up of many small banks had higher costs than large bank offices with the same assets. In other words, three banks operating in a $150 million market and having $50 million each as assets, i.e., their share of that market, had lower expenses than fifteen banks with $10 million each.

Oddly, the information was ignored by a majority of the Federal Reserve Board in a decision involving two Florida bank holding companies, despite a history of decision-making by the board that generally opposed moves by large banking organizations to pick up other flourishing banking organizations. In February, 1973, the governors of the Federal Reserve Board approved the merger of First Florida Bancorporation of Tampa, which controlled twenty-eight banks in Florida, with United Bancshares of Miami Beach, which controlled six banks. The combined holding companies would control thirty-four banks, $971.5 million of deposits, and 5.7 percent of all the bank deposits in Florida. The Justice Department commented: the merger "could trigger a wave of consolidations among other large Florida bank holding companies and would have a significantly adverse effect upon the competitive structure of banking throughout the United States." In fact, that wave was already rolling throughout Florida. Between 1968 and 1972, the number of bank holding companies rose from ten controlling 86 banks to twenty-nine controlling 307 banks. The deposits under holding company control had also risen, from $3.8 billion to $11.2 billion. Put another way, half the banks of Florida controlled two-thirds of the commercial bank deposits of the state.

The Federal Reserve Board decision stunned at least one of its members, Andrew F. Brimmer, a governor with a deep concern for the public interest. In a powerful dissent, Brimmer wrote an opinion that included his "strong conviction that the board would have denied the application," perhaps even unanimously, for Brimmer could see "no public benefits" in the union of the two bank holding companies. On the contrary, he said in a statement that supported the Justice Department position, "I believe that if this application were denied, it is virtually certain that First Florida would be attracted to the Miami market (the home base of United Bancshares) either de novo or a foothold acquisition." In other words, First Florida had eliminated itself as potential competition.

Despite a role that made it the heavy, the Justice Department's encouragement of banks to compete in markets inhabited by slothful banks, involved the department—and everyone else with a direct and indirect interest in banking—in a Pandora's box of problems that go to the very makeup of banking in the United States: specifically, the dual banking system, which has criss-crossed banking with rules and laws that overlap, confuse, and most important, prevent the kind of expansion that would benefit the public and banker alike.

No matter whether a bank is federally chartered by the Comptroller or chartered by a state authority, it must conform to the banking laws of the states. Unfortunately, much state legislation is protectionist. To expand outside their own states, even to expand within their own states, banks come up against a variety of laws that do little more than protect entrenched and often do-nothing banks. When virulent competitors, a term used by the Supreme Court, do turn up to compete, they are stopped by archaic laws. Up to 1973 fifteen states prohibited banks from opening up branch offices under any circumstances. (They were Arkansas, Colorado, Florida, Illinois, Iowa, Kansas, Minnesota, Missouri, Montana, Nebraska, North Dakota, Oklahoma, Texas, West Virginia, and Wyoming.) Fifteen other states permitted branch banking, but limited it to within local markets. (These states were Alabama, Georgia, Indiana, Kentucky, Louisiana, Massachusetts, Michigan, Mississippi, New Hampshire, New Mexico, New York, Ohio, Pennsylvania, Tennessee, and Wisconsin.) Seven state legislatures would not even permit a bank to start up a branch where existing banks had home offices or even branches. (These were Michigan, New Hampshire, New Jersey, New York, Oregon, Connecticut, and Washington.) As for multiple-bank holding companies, eleven states kept them out altogether. (These were Georgia, Illinois, Indiana, Kansas, Louisiana, Mississippi, Nebraska, Oklahoma, Pennsylvania, Vermont, and West Virginia.)

One result of all the legislation was that only thirteen states permitted both branching and holding company entry into bank markets in 1973. (These were Alaska, Arizona, California, Delaware, Hawaii, Idaho, Maryland, Nevada, New Jersey, North Carolina, Rhode Island, South Carolina, and South Dakota.)

Generally, the confusing array of laws stemmed from the fear in the 1930s that too many banks were a danger to themselves and to banking in general, since bank failures in those days were caused by general economic depression. It did not seem wrong at the time to protect local banks against competition and failure, and even to protect against themselves those banks that would expand at any cost. Today, though bank failures have been growing in number, the failures have been caused by insiders, not by general economic conditions. The national economy, obviously, has improved enormously since the 1930s, and as a result there has been a growing feeling that the time has come for more competition in all regulated industries, including banking. That feeling has been espoused by the Justice Department for example, and by regulators, both federal and state, and as a result state laws have been under attack as never before. The banks themselves have generally taken two courses while waiting for reforms that will be coming during the 1970s. Where state banking laws have restricted branching, the banks have used the holding company to buy up banks, and as a result the multiple-bank holding company has become an extraordinary force in banking. Where branching has not been restrictive, the banks have simply branched. In those states where branching and holding company entry alike have been prohibited either completely or on a limited basis, the banks await reform. For example, in New Jersey home office protection laws confined branching to three basic districts, but bank holding companies could and did operate across district lines to form statewide organizations that threatened to dominate. Legislation introduced in 1972, however, would allow virtually unlimited branching.

Perhaps the most significant reforms being introduced have been in New York, where the fear of the giant banks' will to expand is widespread. As in New Jersey, bank holding companies were permitted to operate on a statewide basis, and the pattern that emerged was one in which the major banks used the bank holding company device to open or buy up subsidiary banks in a number of areas around the state. The pattern was one especially used by New York City's Chase Manhattan Bank and the First National City Bank to open subsidiary banks in New York's fastest growing banking market, Long Island.

Branch banking in New York, again, was like New Jersey's, only there were nine districts instead of three. Bank expansion through branching was held to within those districts—with exceptions being made for banks based in New York City in 1960. Those exceptions involved letting New York City banks engage in reciprocal branching with banks in two nearby counties: Westchester, just north of the city, and Nassau on Long Island, just east of the city.

Beginning in 1976, however, New York will be permitting commercial banks to establish branch offices and to merge with other banks anywhere in New York—with the approval of the regulatory agencies. So far-sweeping are the reforms that mutual savings banks and savings and loan associations will also be allowed to operate on a statewide basis, thus freeing them, too, from competitive restraints based on geography. The thrift institutions, as they are called, are in fact a more potent threat to the commercial banks than is generally realized. Not only can they pay rates of interest on deposits higher than those paid by the commercial banks, but there has been a growing tendency to permit them to offer checking account services, something that has always been a monopoly of the commercial banks.

To be sure, statewide branch banking—even interstate branch banking, as proposed once by former New York Superintendent of Banks William T. Dentzer, Jr.—is not the complete answer for creating competition among banks. In California wide-open branch banking has produced a concentration in which eight bank holding companies and banks own nearly 2,500 of the more than 3,100 bank offices in the state. There is no question, of course, that the customers of California's big banks such as BankAmerica receive as good an array of services as offered by banks anywhere, in fact, even better. At the same time, the bank holding device has proved to be something of a bomb for small banks, whether or not branching is permitted. Even if a bank could branch, it might not have the capital to do so, but by being part of a multi-bank holding company it can actually raise the size of its loans and thus inject money into the local economy without going hat in hand as a country bank to a big-city bank whose interest in the local bank's economy might be minimal. Not all small banks are venal, slothful, and unmindful of the decay around them, and many of those that are not have joined forces with other banks. One such alliance is the Commerce Bancshares, Inc., a Kansas City holding company put together only in 1967, but which had more than twenty banks within its organization by early 1973. As an example of what kind of lending power this produces, one of Commerce Bancshares' affiliates, because it could utilize the credit of all the other affiliates, was able to set up a $4 million loan, though as an individual bank it was tied to a limit of $125,000.

Commerce Bancshares was only one of many regional bank holding companies formed by small banks in the late 1960s and early 1970s, and their emergence has had a substantial effect on the entire banking business. Besides a new-found independence and the opportunity to become the pillars of the community they have always claimed to be, the small banks for the first time have actually dampened the dominance of the money-center banks. A device once used to grab power, the holding company, now is probably being used for its best purpose, to further competition. Yet, beneficial to customers and local economies as the new competition might be, it also carries within it the problems endemic to concentration. For example, in North Carolina four bank holding companies control the state's banking, something that was not true even in the heyday of mergers. In New York, where the giant banks have been anxious for years now to get deeper and deeper into consumer financing, they champ at the bit, waiting to expand statewide in 1976. For example, the Chase Manhattan Bank, through its holding company, Chase Manhattan Corporation, announced plans in February, 1973, to open a Chase Manhattan in Albany, New York. In Virginia a handful of bank holding companies have done much the same as in North Carolina—though present services to bank customers are superior to those that existed before control became concentrated. One trouble with such concentration is that once a monopolistic position is attained, a bank holding company or bank can move at its leisure to increase services further, and it will tend to look to its own interests, its profits, before it does so. In addition, concentration bars other competitors from opening up banks on a small scale and fosters an atmosphere in which only the truly big and well financed can compete.

Admittedly the problems are complex, but there is optimism among legislators and some regulators. The banks now answer to the antitrust laws and, moreover, must respond to procedures that prevent mergers before the fact and not after when the mergers cannot be unwound. Benet Gellman, counsel to the House Banking and Currency Committee and a contributing architect of the laws that were passed to control bank mergers, summed up a feeling in 1973 that can be taken as a standard view: "There's no longer any great threat of big banks being able to merge with each other. That battle has been won. The Justice Department's doing a good job, a vigorous job in enforcement, and the regulatory agencies, with the exception of the Comptroller, are doing a good job. The Comptroller knows now, though, that he can't win. So far as the new concentration is concerned, it can be beaten back on a technical basis in the courts. This is really a technical matter. Gellman believes no new laws are needed: "The laws governing holding company acquisitions are identical with the laws on mergers between the banks themselves. The provisions of the laws are identical, and the issues are really the same."

Yet, the wars are not over. Not nearly. As Gellman says, "The big battle now is in the potential competition area. It's a matter of big banks largely in big cities taking over big banks in little cities. In other words, the movement toward statewide domination in banking over a period of time by a few banking systems is the next war."

10

In Trust

A STANDARD way of measuring bank activity is to look at bank deposits. Most commercial bank deposits are demand deposits, i.e., checking accounts, which are a means of making payments, collecting money due, and even a measure of the amount of money circulating in the economy. In a sense, bank deposits are a benign kind of measure, capable of reassuring regulators and legislators that the nation's banks are doing just the things they were designed to do. Deposits as a measure are also reassuring to stockholders of a going bank, since the growth of deposits, with which a bank's ability to lend is inextricably entwined, suggests the bank is aggressive and bound to make a profit on soaring loans demand. For the managers of a bank with growing deposits, higher salaries, stock options, and even a kind of glory as community spokesmen, to say nothing of influence in governments, are quite attainable. None of this is necessarily objectionable; in fact, it suggests a thriving industry whose description as nerve center of the economy is well taken.

There is another measure of banking, however, that is used because it measures activities that go on behind banking's closed doors. Still, enough evidence has seeped forth in recent years to suggest that if one side of the banking system is a nervous system constantly touching off various parts of the economy with well-placed jolts of money and credit, another side, the trust side of banking, is akin to a fifth column that has infiltrated American business to the extent that it gives banks enormous influence and control over publicly held corporations. At the same time, the extent of the assets held by bank trust departments (generally securities of one kind or another) is so great and bank officers in charge of the portfolios such go-go traders that some of the orderliness and liquidity of the stock market has disappeared. The sinister side of bank trading in the securities markets is that banks, unlike everyone else, do not have to reveal their market activities.

In July, 1968, Wright Patman, as chairman of the Subcommittee on Domestic Finance, turned over to the subcommittee's other members a staff report entitled *Commercial Banks and Their Trust Activities: Emerging Influence on the American Economy.* The report was one of a kind, the first comprehensive public study of bank trust department size, investment patterns, concentration of assets, and that very old curse of American commerce and one that had been outlawed to a large extent by the Clayton Act, the interlocking directorship. It revealed, for example, that once again, as in the early 1900s, the United States was afflicted with a money monopoly. Just as managements of U.S. corporations had a few decades ago wrested away control from stockholders (thanks to the dispersed and disorganized ownership of small investors), the banks had in turn wrested away control from corporate managements, or worse, were in league with them. Widely dispersed stock ownership permitted banks holding as little as 5 percent of a corporation's stock to exercise power that was tantamount to control.

At the time of the report, the trust departments of the 3,125 banks legally allowed to maintain trust departments held corporate and personal trust assets worth $253.3 billion. That was in 1967. In 1968 the figure was $283 billion, in 1970, $292 billion, and in 1971, $343 billion.

To understand the enormous size of the assets involved, that 1967 figure represented 41 percent of all the assets held by commercial banks at the time, $607 billion. Further, those assets were concentrated in the banks, though only trustees held legal title to most of them. A mere 50 banks out of the 3,125 surveyed controlled $139.4 billion, or 55 percent, of the total trust assets. Even worse, or better from the point of view of the banks in-volved, only 25 banks controlled 49.42 percent, or nearly half, while the top five banks, all of them New York banks, controlled 24.34 percent, or nearly a quarter.

In the years following the report of the Subcommittee on Domestic Finance the concentration grew. Fully half of the $292 billion of trust assets in 1970 was now concentrated in just twenty-one banks, rather than twenty-five, as had been the case in 1967, while five banks still held a quarter of the trust assets. The five were the same banks that had led in 1967: Morgan Guaranty Trust Company, Bankers Trust Company, The Chase Manhattan Bank, N.A., First National City Bank, and United States Trust Company. The concentration was especially heavy in the Morgan Guaranty, a Wall Street bank that has never re-acted kindly to inquirers and probably has done more than any other bank to sustain the secrecy and mystique of banking. The Morgan, as its banker chums sometimes refer to it, controlled 6.73 percent of all the trust assets in the United States, or $16.8 billion, in 1967. By 1969 that figure had been surpassed easily as the Morgan Guaranty took in tow $18.8 billion of trust opera-tions, continuing as the largest trust operation in the United States. But again and again the year-before figure was topped, and by 1972 Morgan Guaranty was controlling $22.8 billion in trust assets.

But concentration of assets and the shocking realization that once again a money monopoly was present was only one of the eye-opening revelations of the subcommittee report in 1968. An-other survey published in the same report, a survey of forty-nine banks, disclosed a myriad of incestuous interlocking directorships among banks and corporations that defied comprehension. The banks surveyed were large ones, holding more than 54 percent of all trust assets, meaning that with holdings so extensive that they had thrust themselves into virtually every major industry of the country. Further, in the ten cities that were the homes of the banks surveyed, those banks held from 79 to 99.9 percent of all the trust assets in their own metropolitan areas.

As the report showed, the forty-nine banks had managed to place 768 of their own men on 286 boards of the 500 largest industrial corporations in the United States, averaging almost three bankers for each industrial corporate board. They had also planted 73 directors on the boards of 27 large transportation companies, another 86 on 22 of the largest utilities and 146 on the boards of 29 of the largest life insurance companies. In the case of the insurance companies (an industry that competes with banks in soliciting savings and making loans), simple arithmetic showed an average of five bankers holding seats on their boards. Individual industries the banks had infiltrated especially were mining, food, textiles, clothing and apparel, paper, publishing, printing, chemicals, rubber, cement, steel producers, manufacturers of electrical transmission, heavy machinery and communications equipment, aircraft manufacturing, railroads, trucking, airlines, retailers, utilities, and major insurance companies. In other words, just about every important industry of the United States had been penetrated; the banks had violated that line between commerce and banking as thoroughly as possible, for they not only were holders of vast quantities of securities but also were creditors of many of the corporations whose boards they were influencing and controlling.

The situation, as the report revealed it, induced recollection of a warning by President Woodrow Wilson decades ago when alliances between bankers and businessmen had resulted in a series of restrictive laws, including antitrust laws. Wilson had said:

> The great monopoly in this country is the money monopoly. So long as it exists, our old variety and freedom and individual energy of development are out of the question. A great industrial nation is controlled by its system of credit. Our system of credit is concentrated. The growth of the nation, therefore, and all our activities are in the hands of a few men who, even if their actions be honest and intended for the public interest, are necessarily concentrated upon the great undertakings in which their own

money is involved and who, necessarily, by every reason of their own limitations, chill and check and destroy genuine economic freedom. This is the greatest question of all, and to this statement must address themselves with an earnest determination to serve the long future and the true liberties of men.

In the six decades or so since Wilson spoke those words they have either been forgotten or treated as mere high-flown rhetoric and not the call to high purpose they were intended to be. The Patman list, a chart and tale of control on pages 427–36 is an abridged version of the original Patman list, but even as a sample it serves to show what was happening. Eight banks held 12.8 percent of all the stock of the Pennsylvania Railroad and there were thirteen interlocking directors on the board, i.e., bankers sitting on the railroad board and vice versa. Six banks held 15 percent of all the stock of United Air Lines, and there were two interlocking directorships. American Airlines, with 7.5 percent of its stock in the hands of six bankers, had five director interlocks. One of the most glaring examples of banker infiltration was Trans World Airlines: just three banks held 21.4 percent of TWA stock, while three other banks, apparently because they held less than 5 percent of TWA stock (the Patman list did not list actual percentages below that) were involved in three interlocking directorships. Throughout the industry the control of banks, through stock control especially, was plain to see. Five banks controlled 12.1 percent of Eastern Airlines, while three other banks holding less than 5 percent, had interlocks. The Chase Manhattan Bank, all by itself, held 11 percent of Northwest Airlines and 6.7 percent of Western Air Lines. In nearly every case the banks had the right to vote the stock as they saw fit.

Much the same pattern showed up among life insurance companies. Three banks held 21.7 percent of the stock of Aetna Life, and they, along with two other banks, had eight interlocks with the Aetna board—a number that was still well below the twelve director interlocks that six banks had with the Equitable Life

Assurance board, the ten interlocks with the Metropolitan Life board by eight banks, and the seventeen interlocks with Penn Mutual by seven banks.

Equally disturbing were the links between banks and the press, especially the financial press. The ubiquitous Morgan Guaranty held 9.7 percent of the common stock of the Dow Jones Company, Inc., publisher of the *Wall Street Journal*, and had a director interlock with the Dow Jones board. Morgan Guaranty also controlled 5.6 percent of a preferred stock issued by *The New York Times*. (Though Morgan had no interlock with the *Times* board, its neighbor bank a block or two away from Broad and Wall streets, the Chase Manhattan, did.) Morgan Guaranty also owned 8.1 percent of the common stock of Time, Inc., and again, though not represented itself on Time's board, was undoubtedly reassured that banking's interests would be looked after by the presence of another fellow banker from up the street, the Chemical Bank New York Trust. Morgan Guaranty was deeply involved with the press and other publishing ventures, for it also held 9.9 percent of a stock of McGraw-Hill, publisher of *Business Week* and other trade magazines and books, as well as 11.4 percent of the common shares of Harcourt, Brace and World, another book publisher.

The bank with the real lock on book publishing, however, was New York's First National City. It held 8.7 percent of the stock of Prentice-Hall; 7.5 percent of the stock of Allyn & Bacon, Inc; 12.8 percent of the stock of Charles E. Merrill Books, Inc.; 10 percent of Wadsworth Publishing; 7.6 percent of Harcourt, Brace and World; 23.4 percent of Doubleday and Company; and 5.8 percent of McGraw-Hill preferred stock. For sheer concentration in a single publishing company, however, no bank could best the 61.3 percent of stock held in A. S. Abell Company, owner of the *Baltimore Sun*, by the Mercantile-Safe Deposit and Trust Company, Baltimore.

There were other areas of American commerce in which the banks simply gobbled up a company's equity. For example, the

Noxell Corporation hardly seemed a public company anymore, with 23.7 percent of its common stock held by the Maryland National Bank of Baltimore, 40 percent by the Equitable Trust Company, and 1.1 percent by the Mercantile-Safe Deposit and Trust of Baltimore. Even Noxell's other securities (those that were not common stock) were in the hands of the banks to the extent of more than 13 percent, and there were three interlocking directorships.

One bank, the Cleveland Trust Company, had even accumulated 35 percent of its own shares in trust accounts, thereby assuring management of the bank that it could not be challenged successfully by any disgruntled stockholders.

As revealing as any part of the report were the sections indicating that though many banks held less than 5 percent of a company's shares they nevertheless had a substantial number of interlocks with the boards of some of the nation's most prestigious companies. For example, there were six interlocking directorships between banks and Union Carbide Corporation. New York's Manufacturers Trust alone was involved in three. Bank interlocks characterized the boards too, of Monsanto Company, Dow Chemical, Allied Chemical, and Olin Mathieson Chemical. In another major industry, oil, the interlocks were equally well represented. Two Chase Manhattan directors held seats on the board of Standard Oil Company of New Jersey and four bank interlocks existed on with Mobil Oil's board—the banks involved being First National City Bank of New York, two seats; Bankers Trust, also of New York, one seat; and First National Bank of Boston, also one seat. Texaco, a company whose reputation for avoiding inquirers is much like that of the Morgan Guaranty, also had four interlocks with Jersey Standard. Gulf Oil, perhaps because Pittsburgh's Mellon National Bank and Trust held 17.1 percent of Gulf's common stock, had only that bank interlocked on its board—in four seats. Indeed, in the oil industry the list of interlocking directorates went on and on: Standard Oil Company of Indiana, seven interlocks; Continental Oil, five; Sinclair, two;

Union Oil, two; Cities Service, two; Atlantic Richfield, three; Marathon Oil, two; Standard Oil Company of Ohio, five.

The situation was not exactly ad infinitum, but its extent was enough to make anyone pause. In all, the forty-nine banks surveyed had reported 8,019 director interlocks in 6,591 companies, an average of 135 companies for each bank. As the report pointed out, just the industrial companies involved accounted for 60 percent of all the industrial sales made in the United States and 70.5 percent of all the industrial profits.

The conflicts of interest as revealed by the report were rampant. For example, some banks controlled such large stockholdings in major corporations competing against each other that the subcommittee report raised the point of "serious potential problems of restraint of competition."

Relationships, too, were rarely a one-way street. Officers of the corporations involved turned up often enough on one or more bank boards, as they still do. In some cases, too, especially where insurance companies were involved, the insurance companies' investable funds were used to buy the securities of the bank. For example, Houston's Lincoln Liberty Life Insurance held from 15 to 41 percent of the stock in six Texas banks. Bankers Life and Casualty of Park Ridge, Illinois, held 192,666 shares, or 96 percent of the stock, in Citizens Bank and Trust, Park Ridge.

Once before, in the very early 1900s, the intimate relations of banks and commerce based on interlocking directorships had been spotlighted. That was in a report by the House Banking and Currency Committee under Representative Pujo. Banks then, too, had made alliances with the major corporations of the United States through interlocking directorships and Woodrow Wilson, under whom as President the Clayton Act had been passed, had included a prohibition against them, but, as mentioned earlier, the prohibition seemed to exclude bankers.

More than fifty years later the same kind of control was occurring. In some cities the banks were the most important single economic force. The cities named were Cleveland, which was dominated by the Cleveland Trust Company; Baltimore, dominated by the Mercantile-Safe Deposit and Trust Company; Hartford, dominated by the Connecticut Bank and Trust Company and the Hartford National Bank; and Pittsburgh, dominated by the Mellon National Bank.

One of the major reasons banks could accumulate control of enormous blocks of stock and insert themselves on the boards of corporations was the growth of employee benefit plans as against the growth of personal trusts. With the growth of these new trust funds banks took a more powerful hand, even taking legal title and keeping voting control for themselves. Economic historians have said that one result has been an evolutionary change in who runs American business. Many years ago control belonged to the owners, but then passed to management because of the dispersion of many small owners of stock. But now the banks run American business, the new theory goes, because of the enormous trust power they have, combined with their lending power. By controlling vast pools of investments they have become, even though only trustees, the real power—relegating even the owners of the assets to being merely receivers of cash dividends or payments of one kind or another.

Besides the issues of concentration, the reduction of competition, the incestuousness of interlocking directorships, and the usurpation of control that rightfully belonged to others and not to the banks as trustees. there was also the issue of the impact on trading in the securities markets. For about a decade financial institutions of various kinds have accounted for two-thirds or more of the trading in securities on the markets; yet banks, which dominate such institutional investing, have never had to reveal either their holdings or their trading activities, mainly because of the privacy traditionally and legally accorded personal trusts. That privacy, however, for a number of reasons needs to be discontinued. First of all, the nature of the trust has changed considerably; now employee benefit plans, not personal trusts, dominate. Being go-go traders in a market, their domination works to the disadvantage of all other investors, especially since the banks are able to act on the basis of inside information gained by virtue of their interlocking directorships. As might be expected, the banks deny it, but there exists substantial evidence to affirm that they do receive inside information and do act on it, as in the case of the Penn Central, a tale that will be told below.

In their new-found power as trustees, the banks have also become capable of initiating and maintaining a vendetta in retaliation against a corporation that had the temerity to covet one of their own. The vendetta (described in Chapter 5) developed against Leasco Data Corporation, the company whose young leader Saul Steinberg rashly decided to try to take over the Chemical Bank New York Trust Company, the same bank that has fired away at its critics for years as enemies of the free enterprise system. In January, 1969, an eleven-man "task force" organized by Chemical Bank from within its own ranks, from among Wall Street's investment bankers (First Boston Corporation; also Hornblower and Weeks, Hemphill, Noyes; and Kuhn, Loeb and Company), and from among members of a law firm (Cravath, Swaine and Moore) discussed ways of driving down the price of Leasco stock. In the sell-off that followed, the price of Leasco stock dropped from $135 to $99 in just four days between February 3 and February 7, 1969. That drop, however, was only the beginning. Even after a chastened Steinberg gave up his abortive attempt and apologized, the banks were relentless in the sale of Leasco. By 1970 Leasco stock had been pounded down to $7 a share, much to the bewilderment of independent shareholders who had held on because of the company's reasonably good earnings outlook. Stock transfer records indicated that "institutions," i.e., the banks, had dumped Leasco stock in enormous quantities, a dumping from which the company still had not recovered in 1973, for even then the stock languished at $14 a share despite an earnings outlook of $2.25 a share. By Wall Street's most used measure of whether to buy a security, the price/earnings ratio, Leasco stock was selling very low, a little more than six times earnings. Support for the argument that the banks were engaged in a vendetta came from the banks themselves, as a submissive and thoroughly subdued Steinberg sought their favor. In mid-1972 Steinberg tried to persuade them to forgive and forget, but the banks, though they said they had forgiven, were not about to forget, at least not for now. "They thought they would buy the stock, but not right now," Steinberg dolefully said. "They had misgivings, which stemmed from the Chemical Bank era." And then, hopefully: "In time, one or two bank trust departments will buy Leasco and many others will then follow."

The sell-off of Leasco and the subsequent vendetta is merely a paragraph compared to the long tale of the banks and the Penn Central. No vendetta was involved this time, but the story is one that has become a strong argument for the separation of commercial banks and trust operations, for a prohibition against interlocking directorships, and for the public disclosure, even on a daily basis, of trust and other bank trading in the securities markets.

It was on June 21, 1970, that the Penn Central, the nation's largest railroad, filed for reorganization under the Federal Bankruptcy Act. For months it had been clear that the Penn Central was in financial trouble. On April 22, 1970, for example, the Penn Central's parent holding company, the Penn Central Company, reported a loss for the first quarter of $17 million, largely caused by a $62,709,000 loss attributed to the railroad itself. But on April 28 the company announced it would bring out a $100 million debenture offering, paying, it was announced on May 15, an interest rate of 10.5 percent. Together, the events suggested a company that was, to be sure, struggling, but was still healthy enough to continue operating.

But then on May 28, 1970, the Penn Central announced it was postponing its public debenture offering. Instead, it announced on June 2, the First National City Bank of New York would head a group of seventy-four banks that would apply for a government guarantee on a loan of $225 million. The public offering would not succeed, it was realized, and the banks would step in if the government would guarantee payment. It was a bad sign, but even up to June 9 many newspapers were reporting that although Penn Central was a company deeply mired, it was still alive and kicking. In fact, on June 10, following meetings between Penn Central executives and various officials of the United States government, meetings that had been going on since May, it looked as though loan guarantees for $200 million at least would be forthcoming. But then on June 19 government support for the loan guarantee was withdrawn and Penn Central collapsed.

Up until the week before the collapse an investor in Penn Central might well have stayed on—indeed, those of a speculative bent might well have bought in, as many did for months and years after the collapse, for even in bankruptcy the stock of the Penn Central was still being traded. That is, an investor might have stayed with Penn Central stock on the basis of public information. If he had known, however, what was going on behind the scenes, he might well have fled, as nine banks and other financial institutions had done, being privy to other information.

On May 22, 1970, Chase Manhattan started selling its shares of Penn Central in large amounts, as Bail-Out, the text and table insert on pages 425–26, shows. On that date Chase Manhattan disposed of 134,300 shares, according to statistics gathered by the House Banking and Currency Committee, and by the week's end had disposed of a total of 286,600. In the following week the announcement came that the group of seventy-four banks would lend $225 million if they could get government guarantees, but by this time, and just a day after the Chase Manhattan had stopped selling, the Morgan Guaranty Trust began its own wholesale disposal of Penn Central shares. Between May 29, the day after the Chase Manhattan selling subsided somewhat, and June 1 Morgan Guaranty sold 44,900 shares. Between that date and June 11 it sold 299,200 shares. Then, as the chart shows, the Continental Illinois National Bank and Trust Company took up where the other two banks had left off. On June 12, a Friday, it disposed of 108,950 shares, then on Monday sold off another 56,100 shares. At week's end it had dumped 290,950 Penn Central shares.

Substantial as these figures are, they were only part of the dumping by the three banks (and other institutions that were not banks). Between April 1, 1970, and June 19, 1970, the latter date being only two days before the announcement of Penn Central bankruptcy, Chase Manhattan sold 436,300 shares, accounting for 22 percent of all trading in one five-day period. Morgan Guaranty Trust sold 391,575 shares, and the Continental Illinois National Bank and Trust 332,550 shares. Though they were not alone in dumping, the three banks together sold 1,160,-425 shares.

The banks denied to a House Banking committee that there was any wrongdoing, that they had acted on inside information, that their interlocking directorships were a source of secret information. Yet the fact was the banks sold in secrecy, and they were privy to a series of events and meetings that were not made public, the result of close-in relationships. For example, Penn Central owed the Chase Manhattan Bank $50 million, making the bank a major lender and giving it the right to put a man on the committee that was negotiating with the government for guaranteed loans. Obviously, a place on the committee was a sensitive position. Further, Stuart Saunders, the chairman of the Penn Central at the time, was a member of the Chase Manhattan Bank's board of directors. As for Morgan Guaranty, it, too, was a major creditor of the Penn Central with $35 million outstanding. It also had a director of its own board serving as a director on the Penn Central board. Continental Illinois had no interlocking directorships with the Penn Central, but it did have $23 million coming to it that had been lent to the railroad, and it, too, was a member of the committee talking to the U.S. government, specifically the Treasury Department, about backing up bank loans to the Penn Central.

The inside relationships these facts suggest put the banks in a position of knowing a lot more about Penn Central than was public knowledge. A comparison of what was known publicly and what was known privately supports the idea that tacit relationships do indeed provide insiders in banks with valuable trading information. For example, though the postponement of the Penn Central $100 million debenture issue was not announced publicly until May 28, 1970, Penn Central's chief financial officer, a man named David Bevan (who was a director of Philadelphia's Provident National Bank, a seller of 43,933 shares), met with representatives of the group of banks that planned the $225 million government-backed loan on May 21, a week before the public announcement, and revealed it to them. In a hearing before the House Banking and Currency Committee, David Rockefeller himself denied that the bank had acted under any stimulus except those publicly known. Yet on the day after the Bevan meeting, May 22, the Chase Manhattan Bank alone sold 134,300 shares of Penn Central. It was not until May 27 that the full Penn Central board itself was told of the decision to kill off the debenture issue. On that date Chase Manhattan sold 31,700 shares, after selling 32,100 the day before and 53,200 the day before that. On the next day, the day the public would be informed of the decision, Chase Manhattan would sell another 35,300 shares.

It was at that same board meeting on May 27 that the members were told the Penn Central would not market any more commercial paper (it was having trouble selling its paper, anyway), and that the first-quarter deficit for the railroad exceeded expectations by $30 million. There was more, but the point is these developments and the decision on the debenture issue, vital though they were, were not revealed to other stockholders of the dying Penn Central, but only to the board, sixteen of whose members were affiliated in one way or another with banks holding huge amounts of Penn Central stock as well as its debt.

In their rebuttals the banks have insisted that the wall between their commercial, or lending, side and their trust departments is a thick one rarely breached. Many banks, in support of this claim, even show internally distributed memorandums. Memorandums, however, sometimes conceal actual practice, and the latter suggests that the wall is breached at will. For example, the Chase Manhattan Bank and its chief executive, David Rockefeller, were adamant that a separation of the bank's commercial side and its trust side was a real one. Yet in 1965, as it developed in testimony taken in 1971 before the House Judiciary Committee chaired by Emanuel Celler, this was not the case in at least one very substantial instance. A vice president and loan officer of the Chase Manhattan Bank, Roy T. Abbott, had helped Gulf and Western, an acquisition-minded conglomerate corporation, develop a long line of credit with Chase Manhattan and other banks. But part of the price, besides the usual interest rates and other terms, was that Chase Manhattan be assigned trusteeship of Gulf and Western's headquarters employee pension and savings plans, despite protests from more than a score of other banks that would have lost out as trustees of employee benefit plans among G&W subsidiaries. The assignment, was insisted on by Chase Manhattan. The tie-in, which is something frowned on by the Justice Department, also included Gulf and Western's acceptance, which it gave willingly, of the transfer of all the accounts of its subsidiaries to Chase Manhattan and even assignment as stock transfer agent and distributor of corporate dividend payments, assignments that produced substantial fees.

The bank apparently restrained itself somewhat, for it did not insist on putting a director on the Gulf and Western board (the records show Chase Manhattan had none of its own men on the Gulf and Western board, despite the clubbiness indicated by a whole series of letters between bank executives and Gulf and Western executives). The records show that there were only three interlocking directorships on the Gulf and Western board—a figure that pales beside that for the board of the Penn Central Transportation Company (the name of the railroad as distinguished from its holding company, Penn Central Company). In

fact, the Penn Central Transportation board was a nest of interlocking directorships—thirteen in all in 1968. The company's
chairman, Stuart Saunders, might even have been called a multiple
interlocking director, serving as he did as a director of the Chase
Manhattan Bank, a director of the First Pennsylvania Banking
and Trust Company in Philadelphia, a director of the First National Exchange Bank of Virginia, and a director of the Philadelphia Saving Fund Society. John T. Dorrance, a Penn Central
Director, was also on the board of the Morgan Guaranty, as well
as being chairman of the Campbell Soup Company. Still another
Penn Central director, Thomas L. Perkins, was a director of
Morgan Guaranty and a lawyer associated with the firm of
Perkins, Daniels and McCormack. John M. Seabrook, another
Penn Central director, was a director of the Provident National
Bank in Philadelphia, also chairman of International Utilities, a
conglomerate holding company. Paul A. Gorman, president of
the Penn Central Company, was a director of Bankers Trust in
New York, while Gaylord P. Harnwell, the president of the
University of Pennsylvania, was a director of First Pennsylvania
Banking and Trust Company as well as Penn Central. Indeed,
First Pennsylvania's own chairman, William L. Day, since de-
parted from the post, was himself a director of the Penn Central.

Besides the interlocking directorships between the Penn Cen-
tral board and bank boards, the great majority of Penn Central
Transportation board members were directors of other corporate
boards. Saunders, for example, was affiliated with five other cor-
porations, including U.S. Steel, Georgia Pacific, and the Equitable
Life Assurance Society. Bevan, the chief financial officer of Penn
Central, was on the boards of nine other corporations, including
Allegheny Ludlum Steel, Madison Square Garden, and Borden,
Inc. The aforementioned Thomas L. Perkins was affiliated with
American Cyanamid, Duke Power, and General Motors.

And so it went. Though there were a few exceptions. Carlos
J. Routh, for example, chairman of the board of the Pittston
Company and director of Penn Central, had no other banking or

corporate affiliations. Nor did E. Clayton Gengras, chairman of the Security Corporation, and R. Walter Graham, Jr., a medical doctor.

One of the defenses of bankers and of corporate executives against criticisms of interlocking directorates is that theirs is a closely knit society of men of great ability, who are few in number and not to be found just anywhere. The assertion is open to question, however, since it can be argued that only the powerful, the rich, the favored, and the familiar are called on by American business to serve on corporate boards. It can be argued, too, that that society is basically conspiratorial and incestuous in an intellectual sense and that certain signs of power, e.g., being a corporate matchmaker, building a corporate empire, or being the head of Standard Oil or Sears, Roebuck, are the measures determining admission, not mere ability, which is actually in bountiful supply. But even if the argument were real that special abilities are needed and are scarce, it dodges the issue, which is that even an ingrown society of directors, such as we have today, can disclose decisions publicly—unless the directors are self-serving and have premeditated reasons for secrecy. This is the gist of the critics' argument, in fact. The opposition to interlocking directorships and all the wrongs they have produced has not been opposition to freedom to operate within the free enterprise system. Rather it has been opposition devised to help maintain the free enterprise system, for interlocking directorships can work to suffocate a company while maintaining the narrow interests of the directors. From 1963 to 1969, for instance, the board of the Penn Central continued to pay out dividends ($213 million) at a time when the railroad had extraordinary need to buy capital equipment, improve its maintenance of way, and pay off its lenders. Since its directors had to know of the railroad's financial plight—one director did fight a lonely, losing battle to change course—the presence of directors without a vested interest in dividends payments might have made a difference, for in those years the railroad became less and less a viable company.

The bankers who serve in such conflicting roles on the Penn Central and others as well have realized the conflict involved. Unfortunately, no changes have come, as even a random sampling of corporate boards would show, for bankers appear again and again as corporate directors. In 1971, for example, Richard P. Cooley, chief executive of Wells Fargo Bank, was a director of United Air Lines' sixteen-man board, as was William M. Jenkins, chairman of Seattle's First National Bank. Chrysler Corporation carried on its board Raymond T. Perring, chairman of the Detroit Bank and Trust Company, John H. Coleman, deputy chairman of the Royal Bank of Canada, and J. Richardson Dilworth, of the Rockefeller Family and Associates.

That national purveyor of hamburgers, McDonald's Corporation, could also boast a well-known banker, Allen P. Stults of Chicago's American National Bank and Trust Company, but more significantly, president of the American Bankers Association in 1972. The Textron Corporation, though it had only nine directors during 1971, had three bankers on its board. City Investing Company, a conglomerate corporation, had two bankers on its board: Eben W. Pyne, a senior vice president of First National City Bank in New York, and John L. Gibbons, an adviser attached to the Fiduciary Division of New York's Chemical Bank. Gibbons, in fact, was a member of the company's executive committee and thus had a direct hand in determining the company's policies. An industrial corporation, Wheelabrator-Frye, had a man from the Mellon National Bank in Pittsburgh on its board, while Armstrong, a manufacturer of home building materials, had two bankers on its board, one from Bank of America in San Francisco, the other from Union National Bank in Pittsburgh. The Budd Company, a maker of automobile components, had as a board member the chairman of the Girard Trust Bank, Philadelphia.

But if evidence exists that the interlocking directorship is still very much a going thing, evidence also exists that banks are becoming more and more aggressive traders in the various stock markets—the exchanges, the over-the-counter markets, and the third market in which dealers buy and sell securities listed on the stock exchanges.

In January, 1973, for example, a Federal Reserve Bank of New York study suggested that banks were accounting for an ever greater share of trading in the markets and further that rather than being investors in a true sense, they were in-and-out traders whose activities caused exaggerated rises and falls in prices. The banks were price-aggressive, buying at extraordinary rates when prices were rising, thereby sending prices up even more, then selling en masse and often in large blocks when prices were falling. Thus the banks were a disruptive influence in the stock markets, and their buying and selling were detrimental to other investors who had not had access to the information that bankers could wrest out of corporations on whose boards they sit.

The banks have continued to do all this in secret. To be sure, in recent times a few have disclosed their stock holdings in a handful of corporations, but both the gesture and the lists are deceptive, and dodge the issue of timely disclosure. The lists are in annual reports, which generally appear in the spring following the year being reported, and thus hardly constitute a timely revelation. Further, the lists are generally of blue chip stocks, such as American Telephone and Telegraph. It is a safe bet any given time that practically every bank would be carrying the shares of such blue chips. In 1972 one-third of the $6 billion stock portfolio of New York's Manufacturers Hanover consisted of ten stocks. Among them were General Electric, IBM, Standard Oil of New Jersey, Sears, and Eastman Kodak. The list, chock-full as it was of so-called investment grade stocks, suggested that the bank was far from being a go-go trader. Obviously, it failed the test other institutional investors must pass—full disclosure.

Another New York bank, First National City, tried a little different tack in what was also an exercise in minimal reporting. On March 6, 1972, the bank announced that it was breaking with industry tradition because "a company's sensitivity to its corporate responsibility is now an integral part of the bank's investment criteria." These words of high purpose, however, were accompanied by an annual report from the bank's Investment Management Group purportedly revealing crucial information. For instance, the bank disclosed the names and number of shares in forty-two corporations held by a common trust fund it supervised, but altogether the total market holdings were $95,968,634, or less than a tiny 0.6 percent of the $14.3 billion in assets managed by the bank.

Nor was any trading information published, though First National did say that the same stocks might be sold for some accounts and bought for others. The report carried other listings, including the holdings of a representative pension trust, the bank's twenty-five largest stock purchases, its twenty-five largest sales, and its hundred largest holdings—all of which revealed nothing of true consequence, e.g., trading activities. Actually the disclosure of such limited information, which is an improvement over no disclosure, is a practice that has sprung up since the appearance of the damaging report by the House Subcommittee on Domestic Finance, and was devised to quiet critics and to suggest that banks are not secretive. This is far from true, for most banks are closed to inquiries about trust activities—or anything else bankers regard as no one's business but their own.

The practice may also have been begun to head off legislation prohibiting secrecy and interlocks. Undoubtedly the banks were not encouraged to mend their ways voluntarily by the failure of legislation that would have prohibited interlocking directorships among a long string of financial institutions and cast a glare of light on bank trading in securities. The legislation was H.R. 5700, sections 2 through 9 of which, introduced by Wright Patman, would have prohibited interlocks. Section 12 of the same bill would have required banks to report annually to the Federal Deposit Insurance Corporation (the legislation actually was framed as an amendment to the Federal Deposit Insurance Act) their holdings of securities as fiduciaries, and to make the reports available for public inspection. The banks would also have had to include information disclosing their voting authority, i.e., whether actual beneficiaries had anything to say about which way the bank voted, and just how they voted the proxies of others. Did the banks solicit information and views from the true owners of the securities, or did they go their own way? Another section limited banks to holding no more than 10 percent of a stock.

Unfortunately, H.R. 5700 was too ambitious; its catchall nature produced a variety of feeling, and during hearings held before the House Banking and Currency Committee, on April, 1971, it failed to get the widespread support it needed. Even by 1973 no House action had been taken. Besides the prohibitions on interlocking directorships and secrecy, it also proposed prohibitions against banks taking equity kickers from businessmen when granting loans; it regulated insider loans; it prohibited brokered deposits, a reason for some banks going broke (as discussed in an earlier chapter); it prohibited giveaways to attract deposits; and it called for 100 percent insurance of state and local government deposits by the Federal Deposit Insurance Corporation. Many witnesses favored a net as wide as H.R. 5700 for banks in the light of past history. The Securities and Exchange Commission not only favored forced disclosure of bank stock market transactions, but even maintained the legislation should have included more stringent controls. It suggested that the SEC itself should be given the increased control rather than the FDIC, since the SEC was better able to determine what was pertinent in securities trading. It was not an illogical contention, especially in the light of an SEC study just concluded on institutional investing, a study, incidentally, that also found banks tended to concentrate investments in relatively few stocks. But the squabbling over who would be in charge also dimmed the chances of H.R. 5700.

If the hearings on H.R. 5700 failed to produce reform legislation, they did produce unusual admissions of favoritism. William B. Camp, a regulator who has consistently sympathized with the positions of the commercial banks, complained that the law was "too drastic and would unduly disrupt accepted business practices." Besides, he complained inaccurately (it did) H.R. 5700 did not cover "interlocks between commercial banks, savings and loan associations and other types of financial institutions." And how about preventing interlocks among those institutions "in actual competition with each other?" It was testimony that ignored the vast amount of evidence dug up by the House subcommittee that pointed to where the real ills were. Other financial institutions were not the issue, either. Finally, Camp suggested there was a need to "preserve regulatory flexibility . . . to prevent hardship and unnecessary restriction." He was especially opposed to the sections in the proposed legislation that would have forced the banks' market activities out into the open. To reveal publicly the name, class, value, number of shares held, the voting rights of the banks, how the banks voted in the previous year, he claimed, would produce no benefits to justify the costs, either to the banks or to the government (i.e., the FDIC, which would house the statistics gathered). The very massiveness of the information, Camp insisted would prevent its being utilized.

Inevitably, with the appearance of David Rockefeller on May 3, 1971, the sellout of Penn Central stock by Chase Manhattan and other banks was discussed. Rockefeller, who was accompanied by Herbert P. Patterson (whom Rockefeller fired as president of Chase Manhattan in 1972), denied that his bank had used inside information or even clairvoyance, the latter means suggested by Patman in questioning Rockefeller. Rather, his bank's investment department had used the same sources everyone else used, public information and the work of securities analysts. But then Rockefeller revived an old theme based on expediency, so old it was used by Alexander Hamilton in insisting on granting favors to close associates in return for their support in founding a central bank. Rockefeller himself, when he had been a member of a Commission on Money and Credit, had come "to realize that in dealing with issues of such enormous complexity, there are inevitably trade-offs that must be taken into account. One must consider," he said very early in his opening statement, "whether the potential for abuse is sufficiently grave as to outweigh the benefits to the community, and then come up with the most practical proposals consistent with the public interest. It is my hope that this committee will consider these factors in examining the provisions of H.R. 5700." It was a clear call for privilege cloaked in an invocation of "public interest."

Ignoring the massive evidence of the subcommittee on the trust activities of the banks, Rockefeller said, "The proposals to forbid interlocking directorates in varying situations seem to be based on the questionable assumption that interlocks are inherently evil, that they are always and under every circumstance contrary to the best interests of the public." This was not the case, of course. Interlocks presented those involved with a conflict, ipso facto, and the banks were already fallen angels, as the evidence suggested. Interlocking directorships, Rockefeller insisted, gave banks and other corporations the opportunity to draw on the major business minds of the country, though he failed to point out that the chummy relationship that results also eliminates many innovative minds and that a closed, ingrown ruling class can develop—as it has. Indeed, though the nation is rich in educated, well-off, intelligent individuals, Rockefeller claimed his bank would be managed by only inside directors, even "retired individuals," unless he could call on a list of men whom he clearly thought of as his peers. Among them he named Ralph Lazarus, a department store retailer; Charles Myers, a textile manufacturer; Douglas Dillon, an investment banker and once Secretary of the Treasury; and John Connor, once Secretary of Commerce. "In the final analysis, major reliance must be placed on the uncompromising integrity and good sense of corporate officers and directors," Rockefeller said. "Rather than taking it for granted that everybody is dishonest, I believe a more tenable assumption would be that individuals will act with integrity."

Rockefeller also referred to the Clayton Act, written long ago partly to prevent interlocks but which permitted exceptions. For example, the act permitted a corporate executive to be on the boards of two competing banks if the banks were some distance apart geographically. Presumably the distance between the two banks took care of the problem of competition. Obviously, though, the writers of the law had smaller banks in mind than Chase Manhattan and the First National Bank of Chicago. Each competes, theoretically and probably in fact, for the same business, both loans and trust. Yet in 1972 John E. Swearingen, the chairman of Standard Oil Company of Indiana, was a member of both boards. At the same time, Gordon M. Metcalf, the chairman of Sears, Roebuck, was on the boards of First National Bank of Chicago and the First National City Bank of New York, with the latter bank having at least 9,000 shares of Sears stock in its trust accounts. Perhaps the prize for exploiting a loophole based on geography, however, should go to the Chemical Bank and the Bank of America, which in 1972 had on their boards Augustine R. Marusi, chairman of Borden, Inc. Though Bank of America's headquarters is in San Francisco, it maintains a large international operation on Broad Street in New York, just off Wall Street. Chemical Bank, too, maintains its headquarters just off Wall Street, and is just a few minutes' walk from the Bank of America building.

In his testimony Rockefeller said that one of the more potent forces of bank regulation, the Federal Reserve Board—more particularly, its chairman, Arthur F. Burns—was "not persuaded that a case has been made for further broadening of the restrictions in Section 8 of the Clayton Act on interlocks with banks."

Actually, this was not the case. In a letter written to Wright Patman on December 16, 1970, Burns had committed himself and the Federal Reserve Board to a broad overhaul of Section 8 of the Clayton Act, which would have barred the great majority of interlocking directorships among financial institutions, including commercial banks and others. Burns did agree with Rockefeller that interlocking directorships were not inherently wrong and evil. "They may be good for the corporations involved and the public they serve," he even said, since bankers have the "experience and expertise to encourage high performance." But he also felt that interlocking directorships may impair competition.

The significance of the interlocking directorship and the operation of bank trust departments is that a morality problem exists, one that was perhaps best expressed by a member of the House Banking and Currency Committee during his questioning of David Rockefeller. The member was Richard T. Hanna, a Congressman from California, who approached Rockefeller with this longish statement:

> I have been privileged to sit on this committee for eight years now and I have noted that we are one of the real dramatic centers in this Congress. Drama is made in situations which have had antagonists and protagonists, and drama is made when you bring morality into this kind of confrontation. I note that today is no exception. . . .
>
> In the morality of the thing, it seems to determine as it always does in human action what are the intentions and what are the acts. I notice that those who are able to describe what they are doing by their intentions, as long as their intentions are good, focus on their intentions. Those who are the actors focus on the legality or what they presume to be the goodness of their acts. Now I have also noticed that the opportunity as provided by society—and the capabilities held by man are very limited—there are few instances when people do good with good intent. I have also noticed that men, being the creatures they are and wanting the love and affection of their fellow man, that there are very few instances in which you will find men doing evil with evil intent.
>
> So this leaves us in a situation in which we either have men of good intention doing evil or men of evil intention doing good. It seems to me that I am not in a position either by temperament or by wisdom to question the chairman's [Wright Patman] good intentions. In fact, I subscribe to most of them and I would to all except humility prevents me from this extreme.
>
> I am persuaded that I can't accept all the purifications that you have poured upon the bank's division and its personnel, Mr.

Rockefeller. I simply don't want to be pulled into the maelstrom of the drama, and I don't want to associate myself either as a protagonist or as an antagonist. But I am going to continue to carry a rather heavy concern about what is being done. In my definition of good it would be the public good, and there are some serious questions as to whether the decisions being made in your bank—many times I am sure the intentions are unquestionable— but the results raise the question as to whether or not in the long run and in the full scope of what your decisions affect, whether it is entirely good in the sense of public good. I think that—and you were saying that you had examined some incompatability, so perhaps you have given some thought to this yourself. So I think if these hearings are going to make a contribution, they may make a contribution and widen the vision of the bank in making their decisions as to what really ends up as the public good, and forget a little bit about the fact that what you are doing is legal and that your intentions are good and if we don't find that you are doing that, we are going to have to change what you are doing so it isn't legal. That is what our job is all about.

PART FOUR

Your Friendly Banker

11

True Tales of Banks and Business

THERE IS a popular image bankers like to project, an image that appears time and again in the advertising of banks, in their promotional material, in public statements, and even in textbooks supplied to schools. It is an image that depicts, first, a dynamic economy, but one that would be limping badly if it were not primed by a friendly banker always standing by with great wads of money. By spreading a little here and more there, in a manner similar to a very old story about loaves of bread and fishes, the banker keeps everyone going. Only when the risk is too great does he step back, but the refusal is kindly and paternal, for he is saving the bank's, and therefore its depositors', hard-earned money, and even the potential borrower from his own foolhardiness and certain failure.

For his services the banker asks very little. A mere 6 percent is the number most frequently bandied about. The law of supply and demand, that golden rule of the free enterprise system, determines the interest rate, as does the credit-worthiness of the borrower, not arbitrary decisions of bankers. Even in some of the worst days of inflation, in 1973, the prime lending rate of banks, which is the lowest rate and is granted to the most credit-worthy customers, bumped its way only to a mere 9¾ percent.

In the light of this benign image who would impugn the

banker, especially after seeing the smiling, satisfied farmer in nationally televised commercials urging his brand-new bank-financed tractor onward through unconquered fields; or after seeing the auto repair shop owner smiling through his grease-smeared face, secure in the knowledge that his good, gray full-service bank was behind him? How can anyone criticize thousands upon thousands of bankers who meet each year in convention, literally beneath yards and yards of American flags, and who precede their meetings with the strains of "America the Beautiful" and enormous scenes of bloody, but victorious American battles?

To an extent, the image projected by the banks, which through just one agency (Foundation for Full Service Banks) spend $3.5 million a year on it, is true. American commerce is indeed financed by banks, as any schoolboy knows. But the comparison ends there, for like so many myths, the hard facts are embellished until something not essentially true results.

The evidence suggests that far from being a benign figure helping all comers, much less the multitudes, the banker tends to allocate money where it will do him the most good. In times of tight or scarce money supplies, usually when the economy is thriving and everyone wants to borrow, bankers maintain their lending to business, while other areas of the economy, housing and local government, for example, go without. The reason is that these sectors cannot afford the soaring interest rates demanded by bankers at such times. This indifference to putting money where it is socially needed, money that is acquired to a large extent from the Federal Reserve System at low cost and not just from the banks' own depositors, is one argument in the book of critics for a national policy of credit allocation, administered perhaps by the Federal Reserve Board.

As for the interest rates levied on the money shifted and maintained in the business side of the economy, they are high. It is a rare corporate bird who gets money at that well-publicized rate called the prime rate. The prime rate, in fact, is applied so rarely that among many banks it may not even exist as a going charge. Even among the giant banks of the nation any measure of who gets the prime remains a mystery. New York's First National City Bank, for example, applies it only to ninety-day transactions and says it "is impossible to determine either the number of such loans or the amount involved." Similarly the Chase Manhattan Bank has said it is not possible to develop material determining and identifying the number of receivers of loans at the prime rate or the amount of money lent at that rate. Chase Manhattan insists, however, that it "probably has as many, if not more, prime rate loans on its books as any bank in the country." But that statement leaves an inquirer back where he started. How many such loans are made? Some kind of vague understanding begins to seep through, with the bank's admission that the prime rate is merely "a benchmark," and that "it would not be accurate to characterize loans made at prime as being in any way a majority portion of our business, either in terms of numbers of customers or in lending volume." Either only a few companies get loans at the prime rate, or none at all.

The prime rate, then, is virtually a fiction, and the rates most often applied are considered by most people as usury. A bank may lend at a fraction of a point or a whole point or two above the prime, indeed much more. But that is only the beginning. It nearly always will require a corporate borrower to leave part of the loan on deposit at the bank in a noninterest-bearing account. Banks call this a "compensating balance," and one effect is to increase the banks' yields. Another effect is to provide the bank with a club or a way of blackmailing corporate borrowers, by the tacit threat to withdraw the line of credit unless other services of the bank are bought. Many banks, as was pointed out in the preceding chapter, look for control over the employee benefit funds of corporations, and expect a transfer of that business when a corporation borrows. Many banks insist, too, that the accounts of subsidiaries be transferred to them, at the expense of other, competing banks. Many also insist that insurance be taken out against the loan and hint that one of their own subsidiaries can issue the policy. On top of all this, the typical loan to a corporation, the so-called term loan in which maturity occurs after one year, carries clauses permitting interest rates to rise and fall along with the prime rate. The effect is an open-ended rate of interest in favor of the bank.

That the prime rate, and overall interest rates, are becoming a center of major controversy, the result of bank selfishness, was brought home in February, 1973, when a number of banks raised their prime lending rate from 6 to 6¼ percent, only two months after the rate had risen from 5¾ percent. A very short time later the rate went to 6¾ percent. The moves promptly brought on the wrath of President's watchdog Committee on Interest and Dividends, whose chairman, Arthur F. Burns, was also chairman of the Federal Reserve System. For months during 1972 the Federal Reserve System had pumped money into the banks at bargain-basement rates, hoping in its reluctance to raise rates to the banks that it would not feed the psychology of inflation, and hoping, too, that the banks would not raise the rates they charged. So cheap was the money ladled out by the Federal Reserve that banks figuratively lined up at the door for it, foregoing other sources that had become expensive, relative to the Federal Reserve charge of a little more than 4 percent. But the Federal Reserve gesture went for nothing. After holding down artificially the cost of money to the banks, Burns asked the banks raising their prime rate—there were four—to explain the need for a raise in detail. The four banks were the Franklin National Bank, New York; the Bank of New York; the First Pennsylvania Banking and Trust Company, Philadelphia; and the Girard Trust Bank, Philadelphia. Said Burns, ". . . The committee has requested each of these banks to provide full information on recent changes in costs and earnings, together with any calculations that they may have made which they feel justify their announced increase in the prime rate on business loans." The request had no precedent, but clearly the banks had put their own interests ahead of the national interest, ignoring a plea from President Nixon for voluntary restraints and even a threat by Congress to pass mandatory controls on interest rates. In a matter of days three of the banks relented, with only First Pennsylvania, headed by John R. Bunting, defying the chairman of the Federal Reserve. Only a bitter confrontation between Burns and Walter Wriston of First National City Bank in New York prevented that bank from letting its prime rate "float" upward. Yet there was a real question of whether Burns had won anything.

In the figurative back rooms of the nation's largest banks the actual interest rates on commercial loans were raised anyway, even as the highly publicized prime rate remained at 6 percent. Term loan rates were tied both to the prime and to "other market rates" by one large bank, while short-term rates were calculated on "an estimate of what the prime rate would be if that rate were permitted to move." The reaction was a graphic example of what it was bankers really considered—their own well-being—and the cost of money to borrowers had risen after all. It just wasn't out in plain view.

Generally banks defend this attitude with the argument that they must remain "viable," a term that is a favorite of corporations everywhere attempting to justify overly rich profits, but a word the dictionary defines merely as an adjective meaning capable of living. Banks, however, as the preceding chapters show, are not content with merely being capable of living. Inevitably, it almost seems, the real goal of their lending is control, and not the viability of the borrower—which may be the borrower's goal when he asks for a loan.

One of the clearest examples of banker control over a corporation is that of Eastern Air Lines, a company whose total long-term debt, including both bank loans and debentures, totaled $951 million dollars in May, 1972. Banks like to lend money to airlines, since these corporations have an unusually large cash flow, i.e., retained earnings and depreciation, the latter produced by huge charges against income based on the length of time aircraft can be used and their initial price. But the banks do not lend their money, even to airlines with vast cash flows and obviously good collateral, without acquiring a great slice of say-so. In Eastern's case, it has meant placing on its fifteen-man board six members who are bankers or closely associated with banks. (The directors and their affiliations in May, 1972, were: Harry Hood Bassett, chairman of Southeast Banking Corporation, and the First National Bank of Miami; Roger C. Damon, former chairman of First National Bank of Boston; James A. Elkins, Jr., chairman of the First City National Bank of Houston; Clifton W. Phalen, chairman of the executive committee, Marine Midland Banks, Inc., New York; Edward D. Smith, chairman of the First National Bank of Atlanta; and Harper Woodward, an associate of the Rockefeller Family and Associates, New York.) Significantly, five of the bankers (all except Phalen) were members of the board's executive committee, meaning they were the architects of policy for Eastern.

In May, 1972, Eastern Air Lines, Inc., sold two million shares of stock to the public for $54.2 million, an offering that came on top of all its debt. Anyone who bought the stock, priced as it was at $27⅛ a share, would have bought into a company whose debt was so great that in the late 1960s a sharp rise in interest costs contributed to a substantial decline in net income. On top of that, Eastern's creditor banks had imposed a series of onerous restrictions on dividend payments, so onerous that even when the airline had $64.5 million on hand in March, 1972, out of which it could have paid dividends, it could use only $19 million. Even this meant nothing, for the banker-dominated board of Eastern has not declared a dividend in so long the last one does not appear on the usual records of such things. Nor are things likely to get better. Between 1973 and 1977 Eastern will be paying out to its lenders anywhere from $36.4 million to $75.3 million a year. With its flight equipment mortgaged to banks and insurance companies, and even its aircraft leases mortgaged as collateral, Eastern is also subject to indenture provisions requiring it to maintain certain levels of net worth, working capital, and a whole series of ratios such as assets to debt.

The plight of Eastern Air Lines lends support to the theory originated by Benet Gellman and later espoused by the late A. A. Berle that control of corporations, wrested away first by management from stockholders, now has been wrested away from management by banks.

But control is not always practical for a bank to aspire to, especially among the giant conglomerate corporations of the United States, and sometimes in the give and take of lending a bank must be satisfied, as in the case of the relations between Chase Manhattan Bank and Gulf and Western Industries, with mere fees and profits.

The two, banker and conglomerate, first met in 1963. Only five years before, in 1958, Gulf and Western had been a relatively small conglomerate with $84 million in sales and a net income of $27,000. It had been born in 1934 as a manufacturer of automobile bumpers, but did not become acquisition-minded until it was acquired in 1956 by Charles G. Bluhdorn, still its chief executive. Bluhdorn became a millionaire as a commodities dealer, especially in Brazilian coffee. By 1957 Gulf and Western, known then as the Michigan Plating and Stamping Company, had made its first acquisition, and by November, 1958, had also changed over to its new name. Between then and 1966 Gulf and Western made fifty-nine acquisitions. By 1971 the figure had risen to ninety-two. But for all its acquisitiveness, it remained a relatively minor figure in the conglomerate movement until it met the Chase Manhattan Bank in 1963. As it happened, a Chase Manhattan loan officer had tried to retrieve an account lost to another bank as the result of a Gulf and Western acquisition. By January 10, 1964, Gulf and Western had been granted a $500,000 line of credit by Chase Manhattan, which less than two weeks later was raised to $1 million, then in June to $6.5 million, and finally to $28.5 million in December of the same year. Besides itself, Chase Manhattan Bank had persuaded five other banks to participate. Almost immediately the tempo of Gulf and Western acquisitions picked up, as did the size of the acquisitions. In 1963, for example, prior to its alliance with Chase Manhattan, the company made only nine acquisitions, which ranged in price from $9,539 to $3.18 million. In 1964 there were eleven acqustions, and prices were as high as $9.3 million. It was in 1965, however, that Gulf and Western made its first truly major move, the acquisition of New Jersey Zinc, consummated in February 21, 1966, and costing $171 million. By October 19 it had bought Paramount Pictures for $130 million, picking up a handful of companies in between for $2 million and $3 million each. In 1967 Gulf and Western bought eleven companies, including Desilu Productions for $62.7 million, and in 1968 reached a new peak with sixteen acquisitions. These included Consolidated Cigar for $168.8 million, Universal American Corporation for $152.7 million, and Associates Investment Company for $318 million. Early in 1973 it initiated its takeover attempt of the Atlantic and Pacific Company. Gulf and Western did fail to acquire some of the companies it coveted, especially those larger than itself. Among these were Sinclair Oil, Armour and Company, and Allis-Chalmers. Gulf and Western even bought 1.6 million shares of Pan American World Airways, lending the impression (one that it denied) that it wanted that airline. Despite its few failures, by the beginning of 1972 Gulf and Western was a wide-ranging conglomerate corporation whose sales prospects for 1973 were expected to exceed easily the $1.67 billion of 1972.

It is clear from the records that Gulf and Western had an intimate relationship with Chase Manhattan Bank in what was clearly an accumulation of companies for the sake of accumulation. No economies of scale were expected by Gulf and Western's own management as the result of its acquisitions. Nor were the goals synergistic, i.e., a cooperative effort by the sum of Gulf and Western's corporate parts to produce an effect superior to the parts going it alone. The companies picked up were irresistible fruit in the eyes of Gulf and Western's management, which saw its acquisitions as "ripe for picking."

The Chase Manhattan Bank's role in Gulf and Western's parade of acquisitions was a major one. Besides arranging lines of credit at its own window and at those of other banks, it lent $83.4 million to Gulf and Western on September 10, 1965, for the purchase of New Jersey Zinc. The loan, in the form of an unsecured demand note, was let at 5¾ percent, and Chase Manhattan also was paid $200,000 as a fee for out-of-pocket expenses just eleven days later on September 21. Two months later Chase Manhattan was repaid with the proceeds of a $100 million loan to Gulf and Western that Chase Manhattan had arranged with itself and eleven other lenders.

There were other instances of Chase Manhattan's unfailing willingness to lend, especially short term, in which the money was used to buy portions of the stock of companies soon to be acquired. But the "imaginative" lending of Chase Manhattan in the New Jersey Zinc acquisition apparently overwhelmed Gulf and Western's Bluhdorn, and he promised that "Chase will figure permanently in their banking position."

The interest on loans for acquisitions, in addition to fees, was only part of the largesse. Despite the screams of protest from the banks that lost out, the banking business of Gulf and Western's acquisitions went to Chase Manhattan, as did advance information on proposed acquisitions of the conglomerate. Monthly withholding taxes, as well, were deposited with Chase Manhattan as compensating balances, and the vice president who started it all, Roy T. Abbott, moved from Chase Manhattan to Gulf and Western, from which point he made the arrangements to transfer the accounts of the subsidiaries to Chase Manhattan. In 1965 Abbott also helped arrange to make Chase Manhattan the transfer agent for Gulf and Western stock, a job that could be extremely lucrative, considering the vast acquisition program of the corporation. Time and again, far more often than in most corporations, the stock ownership of Gulf and Western was turned over, and each time it was, Chase Manhattan would do the job—for a fee. But Abbott was concerned whether his former employer was making enough as Gulf and Western's stock transfer agent and in October, 1967, asked whether the business was profitable enough. According to an internal memorandum of Chase Manhattan, Abbott suggested that if profits were not high enough it would be better not to raise fees, but rather to increase Gulf and Western's compensating balances. In effect, this meant Gulf and Western would be lending money to the Chase Manhattan Bank at no interest. Abbott also steered the accounts of Gulf and Western's subsidiaries into Chase, occasionally taking them away from a giant competitor or two as well as country banks. For example, the $400,000 account of Famous Music Corporation was transferred from Chase Manhattan's neighbor, Chemical Bank. Another account, in the name of O. and S. Bearing, totaling $430,000, was moved from the National Bank of Detroit. Once when Paramount Pictures, a subsidiary of Gulf and Western, had failed to open accounts in the Hong Kong office of Chase Manhattan, a vice president of the bank, Harold A. Young, sped a letter off to Abbott saying "we are anxious to have this account, so anything you can do to get things moving for us will be very much appreciated." Soon two accounts were opened in the Hong Kong branch of the Chase Manhattan.

Chase Manhattan was appointed transfer agent for Universal American, another Gulf and Western acquisition, and nowhere in the public record is it indicated that competitive proposals were ever asked for. In May, 1967, Abbott told Thomas P. Hill, Chase Manhattan officer, that the bank would become transfer agent for South Puerto Rico Sugar, a subsidiary of Gulf and Western, simply because the bank was already the transfer agent before Gulf and Western took the company over. A meeting was held on August 10, 1967, between Abbott and officers of the bank to determine how much more business South Puerto Rico Sugar should give over to the bank. A rival bank, the Royal Bank of Canada, had had the account first, and the purpose of the meeting was to divide up the pie, though as far as it is known, the Royal Bank was not at the meeting. Its branch in the Dominican Republic had had a lock on South Puerto Rico Sugar's banking business, but now was going to have to share it. The participants at the meeting determined that "the most reasonable solution appears to be a 50/50 split." The determination assumed, however, that the Royal Bank of Canada would retreat from what was termed "its inflexible position," and apparently it did, for South Puerto Rico Sugar opened an account with Chase Manhattan.

Still another bank, the Union Planters National Bank of Memphis, Tennessee, had to be told "the facts of life" once, as the episode was described by Martin J. Logan, another Chase vice president, in a letter to Abbott dated May 21, 1968. The subsidiary involved this time was Stax/Volt Records, for which Gulf and Western had paid a little more than $2.3 million. Union Planters was a correspondent bank of the Chase Manhattan Bank, depending on the New York giant for services it could not give its customers on its own, such as help with a big loan. The man who was told the facts of life was Fred Pendergrast, a vice president of Union Planters, who had complained about Stax/Volt banking business going to his bank's correspondent, Chase Manhattan. Soon after his protest the facts-of-life letter was written by Logan at Chase Manhattan to Abbott at Gulf and Western. Among other things, it pointed out the relative small size of Union Planters, that it was after all, as its loans, deposits, and capital suggested, not much more than a regional bank. It was clearly a good, big regional bank and Chase Manhattan's "highly valued correspondent for many years," one whose services Chase Manhattan would be "pleased to recommend." But the letter pointedly finished with a statement of Union Planters' capital position, its loans, and its deposits. Abbott responded with a letter of his own on May 23, 1968, and assured Logan that Union Planters National Bank would "receive every consideration," but added, "Of course, as you explained to Mr. Pendergrast, our money mobilization efforts may result in some reduction in their balances, but you may be sure that anything we do in Memphis will mean our first thinking of the Union Planters." In the vernacular, it was a "kissoff." What Logan meant by "money mobilization" was taking accounts away from the Union Planters and giving them to Chase.

It meant that Union Planters would lose out to the Chase Manhattan.

To be sure, it was the policy of Gulf and Western to seek out major banks besides Chase and to establish major lines of credit with them. But, in general, the policy produced an extremely lopsided concentration of business, for no subsidiary of Gulf and Western was permitted to borrow on its own, which eliminated more than 1,000 banks from being lenders to any part of Gulf and Western. Those subsidiaries wanting to borrow had to go through a bank designated by Gulf and Western, an approved bank, unless the subsidiaries could find local banks that provided a broad array of services. But covenants in some of the loan agreements that Gulf and Western had with its lending institutions prohibited subsidiaries from borrowing money except directly from the parent company. In fact, the company's own manual for executives directed subsidiaries to borrow only from Gulf and Western itself or from another subsidiary. The effect, as noted by the Antitrust Subcommittee of the House Committee on the Judiciary, was a "concentration of Gulf and Western's borrowing relationships with major banks located primarily on the East Coast. Although Gulf and Western and its subsidiaries do business with 1,008 banks located in all 50 states, Gulf and Western had credit lines as of July 31, 1969, with only 23 banks." At the time, Gulf and Western's lines of credit with the twenty-three banks totaled $196.7 million. Nearly always, the banks on the top of the list, including Chase Manhattan, could approve or disapprove of new acquisitions. Even so, this was not as bad as the control of Eastern Air Lines. Gulf and Western frequently negotiated exemptions to covenants that got in the way of its acquisition program. It has paid some kind of a dividend since 1964 and occasionally an acquisition raised the price of its own stock as well as that of the company being acquired. At year's end in 1972, even though it was more than $990 million in debt and was facing maturities of $44 million to $52 million in each year for the next four years, its board rather than its bankers, as at Eastern, was still in control of its operating executives.

Gulf and Western maintained, and the House Antitrust Committee conceded, that without the banks Gulf and Western could not have grown so. But that growth, based as it was on a 53,396 percent increase in debt over ten years or so, has produced a company highly leveraged with debt. In other words, like Eastern, it has become so burdened with the need to meet interest payments that its financial position can deteriorate even as the banks' position grows stronger. Little by little, ownership by shareholders is being converted to ownership by banks. For example, in 1960 long-term debt represented a little over 23 percent of Gulf and Western's long-term capitalization. Common stock ownership represented more than 76 percent of the total capital. In 1965 the ratio went to 44 percent long term and common stock equity to 55 percent. By 1968 the lenders' percentage of the capitalization was 60.7 percent and common stock equity was 32.4 (a ratio that stayed roughly the same as the decade ended). Since those who control the capital of a corporation control its destiny, it becomes clear how much the banks have increased their control over Gulf and Western. At the same time, the control of the holders of common stock has receded, as has the value of their stock. In 1969, when there was only one Gulf and Western merger, the company's stock fell from about $60 a share to $13.25 and the value of the common shares decreased by $836 million. In fact, at one point the stock price fell as low as $9.75. One reason was a sharp dropoff in earnings per share, caused to some degree by high interest payments on debt.

During the relationship between Gulf and Western and the Chase Manhattan Bank many questions of ethics arose. During questioning by a House antitrust panel it turned out that Chase Manhattan was privy to inside information regarding Gulf and Western's plans for acquisitions. More important, the information was available to many bank employees. The bank had written and distributed prohibitions against using inside information, but no mechanism of control of information had been devised and time and again the stock price of a company about to be acquired would rise sharply before public announcement of the acquisition.

It was common knowledge that Gulf and Western paid well above the going price, and inside knowledge of an acquisition was more than just a little valuable. At one point in 1966 Roy Abbott, by this time a senior vice president of Gulf and Western, agreed to enlarge upon the merger and acquisition information he was supplying Chase Manhattan. A memorandum signed by a Chase Manhattan officer, Bruce A. Crocco, supports this: "Roy also agreed to keep us better informed concerning proposed mergers and acquisition and important investments, i.e., notifying us prior to announcement in the newspapers."

Another ethical, indeed unlawful, issue also arose during the association of the bank and the conglomerate. The issue was reciprocity, in which two companies buy each other's products on the basis of an agreement rather than on the basis of the products' merits. Despite policy prohibiting the practice, reciprocity still was discussed by bank officers, especially by Abbott. As a bank officer in 1965, he wrote to Gulf and Western's chief executive, Bluhdorn, suggesting, in the opinion of the House antitrust questioners, "opportunities for reciprocal dealings" in the automotive industry. A report by the Antitrust Subcommittee also raised the issue of block booking in connection with Paramount Pictures. In block booking, a practice that is illegal under the Sherman Act, the license or sale of a copyrighted article is tied to the acceptance by the same customer of another copyrighted article. In the case of Paramount Pictures, the report said, "Peter Lengyel, Global Credit Department of the Chase Manhattan Bank, recorded a discussion that Harold Young [also of the bank] and he had with Roy Abbott, senior vice president of Gulf and Western, and Richard Spence, assistant vice president of Paramount, about Paramount's distribution methods that appear to require a tie-in of poor pictures with good pictures." Then the committee report quoted the Lengyel memorandum, which recognized the power of block booking: "Dick Spence stated that movie production is not at present and generally has not been a profitable operation. It is only from the sale or lease of films to TV where money can be made. Spence thinks that their actual movie production business can become profitable. This is possible in part to: ... (b) Development of better distribution methods. ... While block programing is not legally allowed, block programing is where the movie studio will make the film exhibitor take some 'B' pictures otherwise he can't get the 'A' pictures; it is nevertheless a factor in getting a company's pictures shown."

The concept of block booking turned up again, this time in a meeting attended by a number of the bank's officers and by Bluhdorn himself. On February 10, 1967, Gordon Gund, a member of the Global Credit Department of Chase Manhattan, recorded the conversation at a luncheon attended by Bluhdorn and Abbott (now with Gulf and Western), and Robert Schell, Thomas Hill, Harold Young, and himself from Chase Manhattan. Bluhdorn, according to the record, said that in buying Paramount he was buying a bank because of the worth of the film library. Negotiations had been concluded with a major television network to lease thirty-two films for $23.3 million. In making the deal he had made the network accept along with so-called locomotive films (the kind that pulled in large audiences) freight cars (the parlance for "B" pictures and reruns). As might be expected, Gulf and Western denied before the subcommittee that it had engaged in block booking.

Some critics of banks say it was only because of the strength of the Gulf and Western management group, which stayed in control, that the company did not suffer the fate of the Penn Central and go under because of debt.

On January 3, 1972, another House committee, the Committee on Banking and Currency, released a staff report that concluded that the involvement of "major financial institutions in the affairs of the country's largest transportation company prior to its bankruptcy in June, 1970," raised the question of whether it was necessary to limit the participation of banks on corporation boards. It further said that the financial assistance banks provided for a diversification program made them as much as the

Penn Central's own management responsible for the disaster that followed. So close were the relationships between bankers and the Penn Central board that the committee report concluded, "It was almost as though everyone was part of a close knit club in which Penn Central and its officers could obtain, with very few questions asked, loans for almost anything they desired both for the company and for their own personal interests." As testimony taken by the committee showed, the bankers sitting on the Penn Central board asked practically no questions and "simply allowed management to destroy the company, to invest in questionable activities and to engage in some cases in illegal activities." The banks, in turn, got what they wanted, the Penn Central's lucrative banking business. "The attitude," said the committee report, "of everyone involved seemed to be, while the game was still going on, that all these dealings were of benefit to every member of the club, and the railroad and the public be damned."

Basically, what had happened was that the Penn Central had used bank loans to finance a diversification program that turned out to be a disaster, then found itself without credit when it needed cash to run its railroad. The committee report then raised the question of whether banks made available massive amounts of credit to friends in high places, such as Penn Central, but put smaller, lesser-known corporations through a mill.

With Penn Central, the banks seemed content to exercise little control over the direction taken by management, whose strange actions made it highly profitable for the banks to remain mute. During most of the 1960s, for example, the Penn Central Transportation Company continued to pay enormous dividends, which often represented great percentages of its net income for the year. In 1963 it paid out 74.7 percent of its net as dividends. In 1964 the percentage was 58.7 percent; in 1965 89.9 percent. Then in 1967 it paid out more than twice as much as it earned, 232 percent of its net income. If this seemed absurd, the behavior became even more absurd in 1968 and 1969, two years when the railroad ran at huge deficits and yet paid $41.9 million in dividends the first year and $91.6 million the second. Penn Central's actions grew more extraordinarily ruinous. In 1968 Penn Central paid out $55.4 million dollars in dividends, a figure far higher than the $33.5 million paid out when dividends equaled 232 percent of its net income the year before. Then in 1969 Penn Central paid out another $43.3 million in only nine months. In the seven years 1963–1969 the railroad had paid out $215.7 million, while the average *loss* per year was $2.5 million.

All the while Penn Central was making these very high and uncalled for dividend payments it was borrowing in ever-increasing amounts at ever-increasing rates of interest. Though the purpose of much of the debt was to acquire for Penn Central's holding company nonrailroading, such as private jets and real estate, the dividend payments came out of cash provided by the loans at rates varying from 4.6 percent in 1963 to 10 percent in 1969. Thus it cost the Penn Central $57.3 million just in interest to pay out $215.7 million in dividends, according to estimates of the House Banking Committee staff report—which did its figuring not on the usual basis of compounded interest, but on the basis of simple interest. Dividend payments were finally halted in the fourth quarter of 1969, and in June, 1970, the Penn Central filed for bankruptcy.

Some of the two dozen or so banks that had lent the money were the biggest in the nation. Among them were First National City Bank, which was far ahead of every other bank as a creditor with $386 million as of December 31, 1969. Some months later First National City would lead a contingent of banks to Washington to argue—unsuccessfully—for a government guarantee of $200 million on further loans. Some other banks which Penn Central owed substantial sums to were Fidelity Bank, Philadelphia, $64.8 million; the Provident National Bank, $57 million; Girard Trust, $49.4 million; Bankers Trust, $26 million; Mellon National Bank, $25.8 million; Chemical Bank, $19.5 million; Morgan Guaranty Trust, $90.8 million. More than a dozen others were owed sums ranging from $1 million or so to $12 million.

Many of the banks, as mentioned in an earlier chapter, also controlled shares in the Penn Central and had their own men on the board. Thus the banks were levying charges of interest on the parts of loans that went for dividend payments, and at the same time accepting great chunks of those dividends as payments on the stock they controlled. For example, the Morgan Guaranty Trust, while being owed $90.8 million, also held and voted 849,275 shares at one point, or 3.4 percent of all the outstanding shares of the Penn Central. Two Penn Central directors, Thomas L. Perkins and John T. Dorrance, Jr., were also affiliated in one way or another with the Morgan Guaranty, according to the subcommittee report. Another bank, Chemical, while holding $19.5 million of Penn Central debt, also held 721,119 shares, or 3 percent of the stock. And so it went. Manufacturers Hanover, with $13.1 million of Penn Central debt, held 469,439 shares. The Chase Manhattan Bank, with $7.8 million of Penn Central debt, held 436,699 shares—all the while the chairman of the Penn Central, Stuart T. Saunders, was a member of the Chase Manhattan board. There was also the Provident National Bank with $57 million on loan to the Penn Central. Though the Provident disclosed no stockholdings, it had had on its board David C. Bevan, a director of the Penn Central, but more important, Penn Central's financial vice president and the chief architect of the affairs of the railroad and its holding company as well. Sitting on the board of Provident, too, was John M. Seabrook, another Penn Central director, also chairman of International Utilities and a strong supporter of the merger in 1968 that created the Penn Central in the first place.

Indeed, the most damaging conclusions of the House Banking and Currency Committee report were those relating the role of the banks in creating the Penn Central in the first place and the "rubber-stamp role" of the bank-dominated board that resulted from the merger.

The Pennsylvania Railroad and the New York Central were merged in 1968, ostensibly to create a combination of giants that would solve transportation problems in a vast area of the United States, for the railroad that emerged was the biggest ever. But from the beginning the proposed merger was never intended to produce a super-railroad. Actually it was nothing less than a financial transaction designed to bail out the financially pressed Pennsylvania Railroad. In the early 1960s, when the merger was merely a subject for discussion, the New York Central board and its chief operating executive, Alfred Perlman, were cool on the idea. Joining Perlman were Allan P. Kirby, the chairman of the Central's executive committee and head of the Alleghany Corporation, the Central's largest stockholder. These men were, in turn, joined by Robert Odell, a San Franciscan who was a director of the Wells Fargo Bank, who became the only board member of the merged company to propose ousting the Penn Central management led by Stuart Saunders and David Bevan. Before the merger Odell had regarded the Pennsylvania Railroad, with Saunders in charge, as a company not in the financial shape that the New York Central was in. Odell regarded Saunders as having "questionable managerial ability," and argued as well that the merger of the two railroads would produce a company too complex to be controlled by mere men. The merger proposal was pressed hard, however, by the Pennsylvania Railroad board of directors, which, as it turned out, had powerful allies on the Central board. Among these were Isaac B. Grainger, retired president of New York's Chemical Bank; Seymour Knox, chairman of Marine Midland Trust of Western New York and a director of other Marine Midland banks and corporations; and Dr. R. Walter Graham, Jr., of Baltimore. Finally, there was John M. Seabrook, "who had been put on the New York Central board in 1965," according to the House Banking and Currency Committee report, "at the request of Howard Butcher III." Butcher was a member of the Pennsylvania Railroad board, and also controlled large portions of securities issued by the Central. Another member of the Central board said he had had the impression that Seabrook became a member of the Central board to promote the merger wanted so badly by the Pennsylvania Railroad board, a statement that along with other evidence the House Banking and Currency Committee took to mean that Seabrook was in fact "an agent of the Pennsylvania Railroad in promoting the merger with the New York Central as a member of the Central board." At this time, after 1965, Seabrook was a close associate of Butcher's and was a member of the board of the Provident Bank of Philadelphia, along with David Bevan, the Pennsylvania Railroad's financial vice president. Thus those most interested in putting together the merger were not railroaders, as Perlman was, but men whose interests were predominantly financial, more specifically, banking.

Less than two weeks before the merged railroads went into bankruptcy in June, 1970, as the Penn Central, a holding company involved in real estate, executive jet aircraft leasing, and other industries not connected with railroading, a worried Treasury Department and a handful of Congressmen met to try to avert the coming insolvency. Weeks before the meeting the Treasury Department had called in no less than 122 bank officers representing over seventy of the nation's largest banks to plan a rescue operation, and on June 2, 1970, an application had been filed for a so-called V-loan guarantee with the Federal Reserve Bank of New York.

In the lead was the First National City Bank, which actually filed the application and which had the most to lose. Under the terms of the guarantee, it would be the Navy Department, of all things, that would do the guaranteeing. In the House of Representatives the chairman of the Banking and Currency Committee, Wright Patman, turned to the history of the Defense Production Act. In 1950 he had helped write the act to help small and medium contractors increase their manufacturing capability for defense. Since Penn Central in no way qualified, he could find no reason for the United States to prevent the Penn Central from going into insolvency. Despite repeated calls from the Department of Defense, specifically from David Packard, Patman remained adamant and the guarantee was denied.

That it was even considered seriously is a testament to the power of the banks in the Nixon administration, especially in the Treasury Department and the Department of Defense. Though guaranteeing $200 million, the government later would have had a place in Penn Central's creditor line equal only to the other creditors. It was also admitted by Penn Central and representatives of the Treasury Department that the $200 million (taxpayers' money) would have been lost, for the Penn Central would have gone into bankruptcy anyway, which raises a serious question about the Treasury Department's role as an effective keeper of taxes.

All the deliberations were in secret, with the details being available only to an elite of corporate, financial, and government executives. It was on June 17, 1970, three days before the Penn Central went into bankruptcy, that a report of its financial situation was completed by the Federal Reserve Bank of New York, though not made public. The report concluded that even with a guaranteed loan, the Penn Central would have gone into bankruptcy anyway by October, 1970. Thus, the government, i.e. the Department of Defense, had material in its file by June 17 showing the guarantee was questionable. One of the more pertinent clauses in the Federal Reserve Bank report was the statement that a $50 million loan, the so-called Chemical Bank loan, was due on June 11, 1970, but that Penn Central had been unable to market a $100 million debenture issue two weeks earlier. Presumably the $50 million that was due would have been paid by the guaranteed loan and eventually absorbed by the taxpayers. And that would have been only the beginning. Other payments were due, too. Hundreds of millions of dollars in maturities and payments were past due, about due, or due in the near future. The Federal Reserve Bank of New York estimated that Penn Central's cash needs, not only for the railroad company but for all its companies, could exceed a half-billion dollars. Nor was there any likelihood of early repayment or even any payment at all. The guaranteed loan would have provided, the Federal Reserve Bank said, no significant relief; it then added it "would not have recommended approval" either. Over in the Rayburn Office Building, Wright Patman had been refused a copy of the report, but that very fact led him to believe something drastic was wrong.

This was not the only time that the banks went to the Treasury Department, where they had many friends and sympathetic associates, for guarantees on loans whose risks banks are expected to take.

The case involving Lockheed Aircraft Company, which has been referred to earlier in this book, has become a classic. This time a bill was introduced into Congress. On the surface its purpose was to put a guarantee behind a loan of $250 million to major corporations being supplied emergency credit by banks. But the real purpose was to guarantee $250 million to Lockheed Aircraft, which the banks refused to lend without the guarantee.

Hearings related to the bill (H.R. 8432) began in the House Banking and Currency Committee on July 13, 1971. A total of twenty-four banks representing one-third of banking assets in the United States had already lent Lockheed $400 million, but now they were about to cut off Lockheed's credit. The alternative to a guarantee was bankruptcy for the aerospace company. So broke was Lockheed that without the additional $250 million it had asked for from the twenty-four banks it would be unable to continue building its L-1011 TriStar commercial jet transport, and would, in fact, go bankrupt. At least, that was the contention of Lockheed's chairman, Daniel J. Haughton, in testimony before the committee. The $1.4 billion already invested in the TriStar would go down the drain, as would the jobs of 17,800 Lockheed employees and 16,000 subcontractor employees. Lockheed itself, a major defense contractor, would disappear without the loan.

The company's troubles were rooted not so much in its commercial business as in its defense business, more specifically, its disputes with the Defense Department over contracts to build the C-5A Galaxy air transport plane, the AH-56A armed helicopter, a propulsion system for a short-range missile, and a number of ships. Lockheed lost its arguments and a great deal of money as well. The after-tax loss of Lockheed in 1970 was $83 million and the company's net worth declined to $235 million in a two-year period. Meanwhile, a new set of troubles arose. In England Rolls-Royce, the builder of the engines for Lockheed's TriStar commercial jet, went into bankruptcy and canceled its contract. Faced with the situation of having an airplane to build—three airlines had already ordered it—but no engines, Lockheed was in a desperate situation. If it did not build the TriStar, bankruptcy was inevitable, since too much had already been invested in it. But now that it had to start from scratch on an engine, Lockheed's financing needs had grown from a total of $600 million (it had already received $400 million from the twenty-four banks it was borrowing from) to $750 million. Haughton figured he could raise $100 million by asking his airline customers for increased advance payments, and then ask the banks for the other $250 million.

But the banks balked. There would be no money lent without a government guarantee. It was a posture that raised the ire of Wright Patman and many other Congressmen. For want of $250 million, an amount the banks "could walk away from without critical impairment," as it was expressed by Chauncy J. Medberry III, chairman of Bank of America, a major aerospace and defense company would disappear as a viable organization. It was estimated 34,000 jobs would be lost, as well as $700 million in business generated among suppliers, whose own employees would be laid off. An investment of $263 million by the customer airlines of the TriStar would also be lost, and the banks would stand to lose the $400 million they had already invested. The government itself would lose $500 million in tax revenues, and with Lockheed eliminated as a plane builder for the world's airlines, the United States trade balance, already in decline, might easily suffer further. On top of this, more than 56,000 investors in Lockheed common stock, 80 percent of whom were small investors, that is, average people, would also lose out.

There were those who said let Lockheed go into a reorganization. If that happened, only the management, led by Haughton, would be vanquished, while the aerospace company would limp on, as the Penn Central has in bankruptcy. But that solution ignored the major point. Why would the banks not lend the money needed by Lockheed? Were the banks not required to act in the public interest? Did they not have special privileges to accumulate funds to soak up losses, as Patman pointed out? What they were really after, he said, was a risk-free arrangement in which they would get the profit from the loans, while the taxpayers accepted whatever losses might occur. The banks had been allowed, Patman charged, to put aside a bad debt reserve as a charge against earnings, reserve on which no taxes were paid. That bad debt reserve was an amount equal to 2.4 percent of their loan portfolios. But while writing off that 2.4 percent, the banks had been experiencing loan losses equal only to 0.2 percent, a figure that suggested an enormous subsidy for the banking industry. By Patman's reckoning, the twenty-four banks that had refused the Lockheed loan had made over a billion dollars this way. "There is no excuse for the banks accepting this subsidy," he said in haling before his committee the most senior executives of all twenty-four banks, "if they are not willing to meet their responsibilities to make 'venture' loans. It is silly to suggest tacking a government guarantee on top of a bad debt subsidy. The bad debt reserve provision of the tax law should be repealed if the banks are unwilling to make these types of loans without insisting on a double guarantee from taxpayers." The kind of reserve Patman was referring to appears in the annual reports of the banks, and in some cases the sums involved are substantial. The loan loss reserve of the Morgan Guaranty Trust Company, for example, was more than $113.7 million at the end of 1971. The loan loss reserve of the Chase Manhattan Bank on the same date was $305 million, a figure comparable to the preceding year's $304 million despite substantial charge-offs by Chase in the bankruptcy of the Penn Central. The

Chemical Bank's reserve for loan losses was $123.1 million, while that of the BankAmerica Corporation, the nation's largest bank, was more than $276.1 million. First National City, the nation's second largest bank, had put aside $304.7 million as of December 31, 1971. Thus, just these five banks, all of whom were among the consortium of twenty-four banks that refused to make the Lockheed loan without a government guarantee, had put aside well over $1.1 billion in loan loss reserves that were tax free. In the prior year, 1970, all twenty-four banks had put aside well over $2.1 billion; at the going corporate tax rate of 48 percent, the subsidy was more than a billion dollars.

The banks responded through two of their number, Medberry, the Bank of America chairman, and William H. Moore, chairman of Bankers Trust in New York. As their testimony unfolded, it seemed that the banks already envisioned Lockheed in bankruptcy, with or without the $250 million, though it was not said this way. In written testimony Moore said the loss reserves were permitted the banks "to encourage the establishment of adequate reserves, not to justify the making of imprudent loans. It would be extremely irresponsible for bank officers to make unduly risky loans in reliance upon the existence of these reserves. These reserves," he said, "offer no solution of any kind to Lockheed's credit problems." (One bank, however, San Francisco's Crocker National, said that the loss reserves had been intended as federal tax policy to write off loans like those to Lockheed.) Moore's bank had calculated that Lockheed's debt at the end of 1970 was over a billion dollars, but that this could be increased to as much as $1.5 billion. It was plain that the banks feared Lockheed would be unable to pay the debt. They had been told by the Department of Defense that unless they, the banks, helped out, Lockheed's only recourse was bankruptcy. The trouble was that possible losses on defense contracts would cripple Lockheed's cash flow, and thus its ability to repay loans.

It was vital that Lockheed be saved, Moore said, as a spokesman for the two dozen banks, but what was needed was a show of confidence by the government: "No one company can stand the risk. No bank, or no group of banks, no matter how large, could take such a risk." None of the risks would disappear, Moore admitted, if the government took a hand and guaranteed $250 million more to Lockheed, but the "ingredient" of a government guarantee was critical. The risk would not be accepted alone, even though, as Haughton, Lockheed's chief executive, had pointed out to the committee, everything lent had been covered with collateral, such as real estate, and substantial collateral would be available for the extra $250 million needed. The response of the banks to this was that under the auctioneer's hammer the collateral would not be enough.

In the end the banks prevailed and the guarantee was granted, for the issue got down to something very basic, which was this: Should federal help go to a corporation whose bankruptcy could stir up such enormous consequences for so many—for the company itself, for its employees, stockholders, suppliers, and practically everyone connected with it? On that basis, the answer could only be yes. But the granting of the guarantee raised another significant question, this one about banks: Did they really have the right, with so much at stake among people and institutions, to flee from Lockheed, even if in their opinion it was going down into bankruptcy, especially since any one of the banks, as they admitted, could have absorbed the entire $250 million loss without much difficulty? The banks' attitude has also raised the question among some members of Congress of whether the banks feel they should finance only what they can control or what will produce the greatest return for them and then leave the riskiest financing to the taxpayer. (Since the financing guarantee of Lockheed, two other companies, Grumman Aircraft and Litton Industries, as a result of the government's refusal to pay defense contractors for cost overruns, have filed for what Representative Lee Aspin, a Wisconsin Democrat, has called welfare). In the summer of 1972, a year after the hearings over the Lockheed loan guarantee, Lockheed was in the black.

Presumably the banks were being paid as payments came due, and in fact Lockheed still had $150 million it could draw on. Meanwhile, orders for its TriStar commercial air transports were at 159 and rising. Haughton and his cadre were still at the top of Lockheed's management, which some congressional spokesmen say, was the real reason the banks had refused an unguaranteed loan. The relationship just was not chummy enough to suit the banks. By mid-1973, as TriStar deliveries mounted, Lockheed was healthy if not robust—though there was public talk that a diminishing market for jet transports might cause it to merge—perhaps with Boeing Company. It may have been that the incentives for dealing with Lockheed were just not great enough for the banks, for the fact is they demand more and more these days when they lend. Recently they have begun demanding equity kickers in a sharp break with their role as lenders to others. At times, the banks have asked for a percentage of net profits; at other times, a share of the net sales, or have tied their return for a loan to a rise in the market price of a borrower's stock. Banks explain these practices by saying they give them a hedge against inflation, while at the same time permitting them to levy lower interest rates on the loans that are tied to equity kickers. Generally, asking for equity kickers is confined to smaller businesses for the banks themselves are often part of the largest businesses, and if a bank owns a share of a corporation, its attitude toward lending will be different than if it has no ownership. It is in the mortgage area, however, that banks insist they require equity as a return for lending, for a fixed rate of return in long-term mortgages leaves the lender a victim of inflation and thus results in erosion of mortgage portfolio values.

Banks also argue that borrowers frequently ask them to change repayment schedules, to stretch out amortization, or even to waive interest payments. In such cases, some banks insist that a hook be given them on future earnings of the borrower as a kind of bonus. It this is the position taken by David

Rockefeller of the Chase Manhattan Bank. So, whether some additional role to that of lender would have made Chase Manhattan and other lenders of Lockheed more amenable financiers probably will never be learned. Today no one will discuss it, at least no one among the bankers who were there.

12

True Tales of Banks and People

I T H A S only been since World War II that commercial banks, with the exception of a handful whose most conspicuous member was Bank of America, have showed any interest in the wants and needs of people. Before, the banks, especially the commercial giants, preferred to deal with commerce, lending money in wholesale lots and providing credit and other services usually to businesses. Banking was more profitable that way. Lending to consumers was costly, since the amounts needed were relatively small and the cost of servicing consumer debt and other services to individuals relatively high.

But two things that happened in the United States after World War II are responsible for some changes. Despite a series of recessions the postwar period was characterized by prosperity and consumer spending grew to become a major and fundamental prop of the economy. Recoveries from recession, in fact, often hinged on what the consumer would do, spend or save, and many an economic forecast hung on his decision. Invariably, it was to spend. In fact, the pent-up desires of consumers for a whole list of wants including homes, cars, appliances, clothes, and even travel outpaced their current incomes and they became willing seekers of debt.

Ordinarily the banks would have turned them away, but now there was a reason to encourage them. That reason was the arrival of the computer, which along with its so-called software was capable of retaining and bringing forth on electronic command vast quantities of information from all areas of the country. This opened the way for banks to lower their costs and indulge themselves in what was clearly a seller's market.

At least two things resulted. By the 1970s the commercial banks had become the largest single source by far of consumer installment credit. (By 1970 the banks' share of all such lending was 42 percent, and it is expected to be 45 percent by 1975.)

At the same time, they abused their borrower customers to an extent that is hard to believe. Consumers became extraordinary sources of profits. Indeed, their borrowing and demand for bank services is behind the drive of the banks to expand branch banking by means of the holding company in the 1970s. Yet exploitation, including inhumane, sometimes brutal, collection practices, has been a lingering characteristic of relations between banks and their consumer borrowers.

For instance, banks charged rates of interest on loans that were clearly deceptive in appearance and usurious in fact. In December, 1970, a date chosen at random, many of the nation's banks were advertising consumer installment loans up to $5,000 at rates advertised as between 5½ and 6 percent. The true rates were much different from those advertised, however, the real annual percentage ranged between 12 and 13 percent. Either the banks subtracted, or discounted, the interest in advance, or the interest computations were made in such a way as to produce higher interest payments than those suggested by the advertised rates.

Such deception was only one of the ways banks jiggered interest rates to raise their own yields. Merely by requiring that repayment begin the following month after a loan was made raised yields, since the borrower did not have access to the full amount he borrowed for the full length of the term, say three years. In reality, he began paying it back almost immediately. Meanwhile the banks got money back they could relend to other borrowers. Obviously, it would be fairer if the principal lent were due on the final date the loan is due—one year, two years, three years, whatever it may be.

Banks have been known to refuse to disclose interest rates, at least voluntarily. A few years ago New York's First National City Bank was promoting its Checking Plus, a bank-inspired device to get people to overdraw their checking accounts by as much as $5,000. In its advertising First National City never revealed that the check writer who overdrew would pay an annual interest rate of more than 12 percent. Nor did the bank reveal that the checking accounts had to be overdrawn in multiples of $100, else a greater rate would be charged. If someone needed only $50 more than he had in his checking account, interest was applied as though he had overdrawn $100. Thus the rate of interest in that particular case would be 24 percent. At the same time, the bank still had the $50 not borrowed but charged for, and could lend it to someone else, thereby increasing its take even further. That was not the last jab, however. On top of all this, the bank still levied a $3 charge for being overdrawn.

The practice, incidentally, was uncovered by a Ralph Nader task force, which uncovered other things as well. It discovered, for example, that the tie-in sale, a frowned-upon and illegal practice in which banks require borrowers to take other services of the bank before a loan is granted, was very much a part of lending to individuals. Nader informed the House Banking and Currency Committee of the practice and suggested that banks be required to inform customers of their right to credit without having to take other services. The practice wasn't even hidden. First National City actually assigned point values for its various services—e.g., checking, Master Charge credit card, savings accounts—and awarded those points as incentives to employees who successfully cross-sold services when someone inquired about a loan.

Perhaps one of the more fascinating examples of how banks have manipulated interest rates to increase their profits has been the double standard for computing those rates. When banks were lenders of money, they applied interest on the basis of a 360-day year. When banks were borrowers, as they are when they accept savings from customers, interest was applied on a 365-day basis.

It was an outrageous practice in the view of a Chicago lawyer named Harold Perlman, who in 1970 asked his bank, the First National Bank of Chicago, how it justified such computations. It was nickel and dime grabbing, as Perlman pointed out. The reply of Perlman's bank was as outrageous as its practice. It said it had always done business that way, but it would refund its overcharge, providing Perlman took his business someplace else. Perlman's reaction, however, was not to go to another bank, at least not right away, but to go to court and to inform the House Banking and Currency Committee chairman, Wright Patman, of the practice. In April, 1972, the Chancery Division of the Circuit Court of Cook County, Illinois, sustained Perlman's right to continue his suit as a class action, and denied the bank's motion for dismissal. Perlman himself had only $5,000 involved in a suit costing him a far greater sum. If he won, the banks computing interest two ways would be liable for millions. Meanwhile, Patman asked the Federal Reserve Board to conduct a survey to determine how widespread the practice was. The survey results shocked a generally unshockable Patman, who had been wrestling with the banks for decades. The practice was widespread, and, Patman learned later, was uniquely a practice of United States banks. Neither European nor Canadian banks engaged in the deception. To its ever-lasting embarrassment, the American Bankers Association had to admit it was not even aware of the practice. In fact, in the spring of 1971, after Patman had publicly disclosed the results of the Federal Reserve survey and even inserted them into the *Congressional Record,* the ABA president at the time, Clifford C. Sommer, labeled Patman's statements as "untrue" and "entirely misleading and inaccurate." That was several weeks before Sommer had looked over the actual findings and realized the practice did exist and was as widespread as Patman had said. He sent his regrets for the statements he had made. Earlier the ABA had been adamant in saying that the "only way a borrower could wind up paying an extra five days interest is if, for example, he renewed the same 90-day note four times."

The position of many banks when their usurious practices are uncovered is to respond with a statement, the gist of which is that it is still cheaper to borrow and deal with them for other financial services than to borrow from a finance company, Basically, the argument is true, as figures developed by the Federal Reserve Board show. In the spring of 1972, for example, finance companies were charging an average annual interest rate on consumer loans of more than 21 percent. The average loan was for over $1,000. More typical, however, would be a rate well above that, as pointed out by Morton Silverstein, the producer and writer of the television documentary "Banks and the Poor." One case documented by Silverstein showed a finance company lending $800 to a consumer, and charging him an annual rate of interest of 25½ percent over a three-year period. And that loan was a standard one. Many borrowers paid far higher rates, as in Maryland, where a 36 percent maximum was legal.

As the numbers suggest, bank interest rates, though hardly low and even usurious, have not been as high as those of finance companies, even when the banks have engaged in self-dealing practices that increase their yields. But what the banks do not say is that they themselves push small borrowers toward the finance companies by refusing credit to low-income wage earners —and then lending money to the finance companies on which to operate. In at least one well-documented instance a commercial bank in Virginia named the Crown Savings Bank financed the operations of loan sharks. Banks have said it is good business practice to make a single loan to a finance company, rather than deal in hundreds of thousands of loans. But this attitude ignores human need and is regressive. High interest rates stop anyone with any sense from borrowing, while those who borrow accept a kind of servitude. The banks neatly ignore the fact, too, that 95 percent of the borrowers who end up in the clutches of finance companies pay back their loans.

The conclusion that banks are indifferent to human need is inescapable (not all banks, of course, as a later chapter will show).

The indifference that has permeated much of the industry is perhaps best illustrated by the collection practices of banks when borrowers have been overdue in making payments or in default.

As disclosed by the same Nader report that revealed some of the lending practices of the First National City Bank, the collection practices of the bank were not always of a kind that suggested the bank was dealing, first, with people, and second, with customers on whom it made a profit. The process of collection from a debtor, say one who was overdue on a Master Charge credit card payment, began with a letter from a computer suggesting reasonably enough it was "only fair" to repay the overdue amount. Soon another letter went out which threatened, in effect, to wreck the borrower's credit rating. This was followed by a "Stop Credit Order" which notified the borrower, who might not have received any of the earlier communications through no fault of his own (the bank did not check). This time the computer, going its electronic way, said that all "charge privileges were suspended," that "all our associate establishments" were being notified, and that legal action was about to commence.

At this point, the computer had done its job, and now First National City Bank's employees personally took a hand. As the Nader task force discovered by talking to borrowers, some of the employees were polite. After all, the borrower was still a customer, a very good one if he paid all the interest and fines that were accumulating. Strangely, despite the computer's canned threats of ruining credit reputations, the "nice" employees, as they were described by the borrowers, nearly always offered more money. One man who defaulted on a $2,500 loan, was offered a long-term consolidation loan, but said, "I couldn't accept it in good faith." Though the consolidation loan usually reduced monthly payments, total interest would be higher than before, and thus the borrower would be ever deeper into debt.

But for every "nice" employee of the bank there was one who was "nasty," the task force discovered. One man who was in debt for $2,000 was not at home when a telephone call went out from the bank's Collection Department. The man's eighty-four-year-old grandmother answered, and when she told the bank's representative that her grandson was not at home, was called "a lying old bastard." But this was only the beginning of the harassment. The bank made calls to the man's family at other times, and even pressured references. Only when the borrower threatened First National City Bank with a lawsuit did the harassment stop.

Still another borrower reported he had received abusive telephone calls from the bank as often as two or three times a week after falling behind in payments due on credit card purchases. What follows is the conversation between the borrower's roommate, not the borrower, and a representative of the bank, as repeated in the task force report:

> BANK REP: Mr. Jones?
> ROOMMATE: No, this is his roommate.
> BANK REP: Is Mr. Jones there?
> ROOMMATE: No.
> BANK REP: I don't believe you.
> ROOMMATE: Who's this?
> BANK REP: This is the First National City Bank. Mr. Jones owes us $500, and we want our money or he'll be in trouble. Tell Jones to call us as soon as he gets in.
> ROOMMATE: Can't you be a little more polite?
> BANK REP: Mind your own fucking business.
> > *Click*

Not many weeks after the harassing telephone calls, the borrower, Jones, paid off his loan.

Usually if such harassment failed, the bank threatened to call a borrower's employer. It was a potent weapon indeed, for though New York State law and federal law each prohibit firing an employee for garnishment of wages, which is what the bank asked, employers often violated the law and discharged the employee. Under this kind of threat, the employee usually borrowed money to pay back the bank. These facts, incidentally, were supported by a study of New York City borrowers that showed that their employers had been contacted by their bank creditors. Ten percent of those interviewed in the study had lost their jobs because of the threat of garnishment.

But even with all the threats and harassment, First National City still needed the courts. The task force reported it filed as many as sixty lawsuits a day. In one year, 1969, the bank filed more lawsuits against delinquent debtors than all the other banks in New York together. Some were for tiny amounts, in one case for as little as $11.72. A lawyer familiar with the bank's collection attitude said, "The bank is very hard-nosed, you know."

Yet the suits themselves were a legal farce, for the bank's lawyers turned out from 6,000 to 9,000 lawsuits a year, and as might be expected in so great production, a large percentage of the defendants were never even notified legally, as they must be under the adversary proceedings of the law. The bank's attorney was rarely familiar with the complaints he signed, and there was evidence that many complaints ended up in the sewers of the city, so little ($3.50) was paid process servers. But the process servers filed affidavits that service had been accomplished and First National City became such a constant user of the New York courts that it even hired its own clerk to work in the record room of New York's Civil Court to do the bank's filing work.

In at least one case, the Nader report said, the bank had defamed the reputation of a borrower all over the country by appropriating the balance in his checking account. The defendant in a suit brought by the bank had received an unsolicited credit card from First National City Bank and both he and his wife had used the card to make purchases. But then the two were divorced, and the husband, after making several payments, left a balance of $300 for his former wife to meet. But she declined to make the payments, with the result that First National City closed out the husband's checking account, then sued for a balance of $70 that was due. In accepting the unsolicited credit card, no agreement had been reached that the bank could appropriate the borrower's checking account, but the bank explained to the borrower's lawyer that it "always did things this way." The borrower then filed a counterclaim, charging that his credit had been defamed, since checks he had written to creditors in various places of the United States had been refused payment. Among the bank's lawyers there was agreement that there was neither a clause in the contract nor a statute to support the bank's move against the borrower.

It would be unfair to say, of course, that only First National City Bank of New York has such brutal collection practices. Banks do not answer questions about such practices, and only fragments of information, generally supplied by borrowers, exist to support the contention that they are less than kind. Yet enough exists to raise eyebrows.

In the television program "Banks and the Poor" one of the more invidious practices of banks, involving both lending and collection, was depicted. The scene was Philadelphia, in which a loan default can end up in the sale of the borrower's home, even though the debt may be a small one. Once a month, on the first Monday, people can lose their home in a sheriff's sale for not paying debts, and the resulting human misery has been extraordinary.

Mrs. Elizabeth Riley's home was the collateral for a $1,500 loan. Though she had reduced her debt to $157.69, or about 10 percent of the original total, her house went on the sheriff's auction block. The bank she had borrowed from had threatened to take her home, but Mrs. Riley, not believing any creditor would force the sale of collateral so great in relation to the amount due, had not resorted to "drastic action," like asking a relative for help.

Then there was the case of Mrs. Pickett, a homeowner, a registered nurse, and a woman who maintained three separate bank accounts at Philadelphia's First Pennsylvania Bank and Trust Company. One day Mrs. Pickett became ill and entered a hospital. After being discharged she was again away from her home in West Philadelphia to attend a funeral in South Carolina. Soon she was delinquent in her payments on a loan taken out at the First Pennsylvania, but according to her own account, never more than two months behind. For her delinquency, according to "Banks and the Poor," she received the following note from a bank collector: "We might as well write these notes to an animal or some illiterate, they would have the same effect on them as they do on you. You can afford to go to South Carolina but you can't pay your bills. You're fantastic, Mrs. Pickett, only an idiot would do something like that." The bank apologized, saying the collector was young and inexperienced. Yet neither the incident nor the attitude of the message writer was unique. A man named Robert Charles had fallen behind $40 on an installment contract three years before the Pickett incident, and received a note similarly abusive. The bank's defense in his case was that there were three years between the two incidents, suggesting abusiveness was a rarity among the hundreds of thousands of loans made, and that the bank had apologized to Mr. Charles, too. Mr. Charles, however, denied that he had ever received an apology. An organization named the Consumer Education and Protection Association also disputed the bank's contention that abuse was rare. It said it had brought "numerous cases of unethical behavior to the attention of First Pennsylvania and other Philadelphia lending institutions."

The fact is that the ethics behind some bank actions are more than just questionable; they can be shocking and disgusting. This is especially so in what are called holder-in-due-course transactions. Only a handful of states have laws against this doctrine, the effect of which is to use the laws to keep borrowers in servitude. Under it, merchants can sell the shoddiest of goods to customers, get their signatures on a contracts that guarantee payment, then sell the contracts to the banks. As former New York City Commissioner of Consumer Affairs Bess Myerson Grant pointed out many times during her tenure, banks bought installment contracts and insisted on payment, no matter what the circumstances. Often the debtors had signed installment contracts in good faith, but then found the merchant they were dealing with had sold them defective, even useless goods. The banks that bought up the contracts, however, were legally exempt from any claims and the debtors found themselves paying for a dead horse. In fact, in New York payment was due the banks even if the goods were never delivered. The only recourse was a lawsuit against the seller, which is something most people buying on such credit terms cannot afford. In some cases, especially home repair schemes and door-to-door sales, the company has disappeared, making even a lawsuit impractical.

This arms-length stance of banks has been discovered time and again, as when banks have freely given over private information about their customers. Once, in 1972, a Justice Department spokesman disclosed in a Senate hearing room that the Federal Bureau of Investigation had examined the bank accounts of individuals without their consent merely by asking the banks involved. Presumably the banks weighed the power of the individuals involved (Jane Fonda, the actress, and Benjamin Spock, the pediatrician and author, among others) vs. the power of the FBI, and permitted a violation of basic constitutional rights. Jack Anderson, an investigative news columnist, testified as well, saying that informants within the FBI had told him that the practice of putting checking accounts of individuals under surveillance was widespread. Thus the banks had accepted the business of customers, but abandoned their fiduciary responsibility to those customers to keep their business with the banks confidential.

The attitude of banks toward those who are lenders to banks, i.e., depositors, has not been much different from that toward borrowers. The bank's own well-being has come first, always.

Banks have paid their depositors as little as possible, and in the case of checking accounts, nothing at all. This is why so many corporate treasurers have taken their surplus funds out of banks, which say that federal law prohibits them from paying interest on checking accounts. This is true, but the banks could easily lobby to change the law. Instead, in the spring of 1972 they lobbied against permitting a number of savings banks in Massachusetts and New Hampshire from paying interest on accounts that in effect were checking accounts. Rather than pay interest, many banks levy a charge on checking accounts, thus not only borrow without paying any interest, but also charge their lenders for the privilege. Only in recent years have the commercial banks begun to take to the idea of paying interest on checking accounts—money they receive free and lend out at substantial rates. But again, the well-being of the banks has been the motive, not the needs of the depositors, for the banks are itching to draw funds away from such thrift institutions as savings banks, savings and loan associations, and credit unions, all of whom are burgeoning as a result of paying depositors interest on their money and generally lending funds where they are permitted by law at rates more reasonable than those of commercial banks. To be sure, savings deposited in commercial banks draw interest, but it has generally been lower (usually fixed so by law) than that paid by the other financial institutions.

Checking accounts represent free money for the commercial banks. A ban on paying interest on checking accounts began in 1933. The idea was to prevent banks from getting into wars of competition by paying ruinously high rates to attract deposits. The fear was that the banks would not be able to find loans with yields high enough to cover the interest outlay. Thus the ban was really aimed at precluding competition. Supposedly it would curb the power of big-city banks to outbid small country banks in acquiring deposits, but in that the ban succeeded not a whit, for the big banks offered services no small banks could match, e.g., larger loans.

When they have paid interest on deposits, as in savings accounts, the banks have nearly always tried to create the illusion that they were paying higher rates of interest than they were. At one time, for example, it was standard practice to compound interest quarterly, but then the practice of compounding interest from day of deposit to day of withdrawal was introduced. The difference actually paid was tiny.

Some banks even boasted of compounding interest each second of the year, but again they were promoting an illusion designed to fool people. A $10,000 savings account for which the rate of interest was 5 percent earned $512.67 a year on the basis of daily compounding. Compounded on the basis of seconds, the interest was $512.71, or four cents more. Compounded quarterly, incidentally, the payment was $509 a year.

It is probable that despite the abuses associated with personal loans and the trickery in interest rates no activity in consumer lending shows the banks' attitude better than does the home mortgage. Inevitably in times of tight money, i.e., when corporations call for great amounts of credit, housing gets very little of the supply of money on hand simply because corporations can pay more for the funds available. The practice deserves special criticism, for studies have shown that the banks are sucking in money from individuals in their geographic area, then lending the money out to business. All the while, the borrowing corporations themselves have been leaving less and less of their own money with the banks in the form of checking accounts, as they used to do. The criticism is especially significant since in the 1970s, as a result of liberalized laws on branching, especially through the holding company, the banks will be expanding into areas they have been prohibited from entering. Thus an even greater portion of the savings and wealth of consumers, the very ones who require housing, will be used to further the goals of U.S. corporations. At a time when the goals of corporations, and of the banks themselves, are directed abroad to a great degree, it would be ironic indeed for consumers to be financing such business when their own needs go by the boards.

But even when money is available for home building, it is distributed prejudicially and accompanied by abuses that the mortgage holder is expected to regard as normal.

First of all, banks will not lend to just anyone. Generally, the borrower must be white, male, and have an unusually good income. Women are only occasionally granted mortgages, a bias, incidentally, that extends as well to the personal loan field. It was not just that women earn less than men, but their sexual habits could keep them from qualifying for loans. In February, 1973, U.S. Senator Harrison A. Williams was planning to introduce legislation eliminating sex discrimination in loan-making, and revealed that some lenders were asking as a condition for a loan that a woman submit a doctor's certificate certifying she was using an accepted method of contraception. Certification that the woman was incapable of bearing children was also acceptable.

It was an insulting invasion of privacy, as Senator Williams said, but it was not unusual, even where laws prohibiting such discrimination already existed. In New Jersey, for example, a banker in a medium-sized city refused a couple a home-improvement loan, though the combined income of the two was easily enough for them to pay back the loan. Even a substantial discounting of the wife's income, another general practice, was not enough. The woman could become pregnant any time, the banker said, after a 60 percent discounting had been computed. The woman replied that she could not become pregnant, since she had had a hysterectomy. Bring in your medical records, the banker said, and the loan application will be reconsidered.

Blacks and other minorities go through something a great deal worse. Blacks' income and employment are far below those of whites, and thus bankers look more closely at their ability to pay and the risks involved. Reality demands this. Yet discrimination based on race, color, religion, and origin of birth exists, as evidence compiled by a bank regulator or two suggests. Banks have denied that there is outright discrimination, but such statements have become absurd even in the eyes of bankers themselves, and some are granting loans and mortgages on the basis of factors keyed more to income and fiscal habits than to race and religion. The First Pennsylvania Bank and Trust Company in Philadelphia grants loans on the basis of applicants' answers to a series of questions, none of which are tied to race or religion. The questions are assigned point values and an accumulation of points, say fifty-five out of a possible hundred, produces the loan. The only major variable is the bank's ability to lend. In times of tight money, it may take sixty-five points to get a loan.

The Bank of America has taken Americans of Mexican origin literally by the hand and escorted them through the facades of the bank's branches in an effort to erase a very real fear of entering such places. But as mentioned previously, this bank was founded early in the century for the benefit of a minority in San Francisco, Italian immigrants who were discouraged from entering bank doors, and has roots among consumers. Unfortunately, enlightenment is still a long way off for most banks, as is suggested by the reaction to a decision of the Federal Deposit Insurance Corporation. In 1972 the FDIC, which is a regulator as well as an insurer, required banks and other mortgage lenders to file data which included the racial characteristics of loan applicants, and to write down on the recorded tract numbers of the property. The idea was to determine whether origin or religion were factors in a refusal to lend, and to determine whether particular areas, especially in the nation's cities, had been red-lined by the bankers. In such districts people well qualified to borrow would have been discriminated against merely for living where they did. Up to the time the FDIC was announced, bankers merely had to advertise they were four-square disbursers of credit. All they had to do was print a symbol on their mortgage advertisements representing them as "equal housing lenders," and publish statements that they invited loan applications on that basis. The FDIC announcement of its new rule produced a round of violent reactions from bankers who accused the FDIC, among other things, of knuckling under to radicals, activists, and do-gooders.

Cynics might say that the FDIC should have let well enough

alone and left minorities in a position where they could avoid the clutches of the banks, since there were some loans, mortgage loans especially, that might better be avoided. The inability of minority members of the population, and low-income whites as well, to raise the down payment on a house, generally 25 to 33⅓ percent, was a blessing in disguise, for a mortgage is not much of a privilege, whether the mortgage holder is a minority member or an affluent Caucasian with origins reaching back to the *Mayflower*. The cynics would not be far wrong. The home mortgage is undoubtedly one of the most onerous lending instruments an individual ever agrees to, since its clauses are stacked against the home buyer. The conditions and terms, in fact, may well be more onerous than those required by loan sharks, who, after all, only ask that they be paid back at very high interest rates. The banks ask much more.

The cost of a mortgage in terms of its interest payments is enormous, rivaling loan shark rates. It is not merely a matter of paying a bank 6 or 8 percent, though the latter percentage is usurious. Such percentages actually are mere camouflage. As every homeowner with a mortgage knows, the interest paid is shocking in size, for the banks front-end load it. Typically, a homeowner carrying a $35,000 mortgage at 6 percent, an interest rate regarded as nominal these days, would pay his banker $10,000 in interest in the first five years and have reduced his principal debt only by about $3,000. In that five-year period it would not be possible to reduce the debt with a large lump-sum payment without accepting prepayment penalties. Thus the banks ensure they will strip off every pound of flesh they feel is due them. Before a mortgage is burned, in fact, a mortgage holder will pay in interest about one to one and a half times the amount borrowed. Thus interest costs easily outstrip the costs of building a home, the labor, the building materials, even the land.

Vast interest payments are only the beginning, however. Most banks are notorious grabbers of nickels and dimes, forcing their borrowers into paying any number of related costs. One of these is the closing cost, something the bank, as seller, i.e., of a loan should pay, but which the homeowner, as buyer, pays. Closing costs cover the cost of appraising a property (which either the builder or the bank should pay for). Closing costs also include payment to the bank's attorney, a true predatory charge, since the attorney has been employed by the bank to look after the bank's interest. Besides, the homeowner may already be paying a fee to his own attorney. On top of this gluttony, the cost of surveying the site of a home has been shifted to the home buyer as have the recording fee and even title insurance. All of these clearly are costs that should be borne either by the home developer, or builder, or the lender. But the two have been working in league for generations now to produce what is nothing less than a stacked deck.

Then there is the escrow account, a device that is plain financial villainy. Simply described, escrow is money homeowners pay to their banker-lenders to pay the homeowners' property taxes. Bankers insist on escrow being part of the terms of a mortgage, saying that the escrow account the bank sets up insures payment of taxes. Since homeowners as a group are among the most riskless borrowers anywhere, this is nonsense. The real motive of the banks, as always, has been to enhance profits. Escrow accounts pay the homeowner, whose money it is, no interest at all. Bankers have argued that they cannot pay interest because their own costs are rising sharply, and though this may be true, it is irrelevant. Banks make money on the spread between what they pay for money and what they can charge to lend it. Not to pay interest on such accounts is unconscionable, especially considering the way banks exploit the escrow. It is not just that the banks lend the escrow. The money is lent out in a way that raises the costs for the school or township to whom it is due.

Banks do not always pay taxes for the homeowner when the taxes are due. Payments are made at the end of any grace periods that exist, for the banks tend to squeeze every last bit of interest they can out of the escrow they have lent. Meanwhile, the taxing districts, e.g. school districts, in order to meet current bills at about the time taxes are due are forced to go back to the banks themselves to borrow. They obtain what are called tax anticipation notes, and in applying for them schools and other public taxing authorities are in effect borrowing their own money, since they are dealing with the very banks that are withholding it. Thus escrow produces interest directly for the bank when it is lent out, and it produces interest and income indirectly when the banks lend money to local taxing agencies that have not been paid what is due them. The result is substantial permanent rises in property tax rates and assessments to produce revenues in place of the monies withheld. The one who pays for it all, of course, is the homeowner.

It would not be unreasonable, incidentally, to change the terms that give banks tax free liens on homes, and to pay property taxes in a proportion represented by the principal amounts of the mortgages held. For example, where a bank was assessed for purposes of levying taxes at $50,000, and a bank held a $30,000 mortgage, then the bank would pay three-fifths of the annual property taxes levied. As the home owner's equity increased, his share of the taxes would rise of course, while the bank, as its mortgage principal was returned, would pay a declining share.

It is doubtful that reform will be coming soon, though some homeowners with mortgages have recently begun to insist on paying their own taxes. Generally, though, most mortgage holders continue to hand money over to the banks for escrow, and even attempts by legislators to require the banks to pay interest have failed. In New York State, for example, where bankers hold extraordinary sway over what will be legislated, bill after bill to force payment of interest on escrow accounts comparable to interest payments on savings accounts has never even come out of the legislature's banking committees. Even a bill introduced to force the banks at least to pay school districts the amounts due them no later than five days after the due date failed to get out of committee. As a result, many banks still wait the full grace period, which in New York is forty days, and the schools must borrow to keep going.

Probably any reforms will benefit the bankers even more. For example, in recent years banks have been pressing hard to install a variable interest rate on mortgages. In some areas of the United States mortgages have already been written with a variable rate as part of the terms. Under these terms, interest moves up and down in line with interest rates in the open market. In periods when interest rates generally are declining, home buyers pay less interest, but when rates rise, generally the mortgage holder is required to pay more interest to his bank.

The banks and other lenders, realizing that varying the monthly payments due would raise alarms, have devised a technique that is intended to seem painless. Instead of varying the actual payments, it is the maturity, or length, of the mortgage that varies. Thus instead of a home buyer taking down a twenty-five-year or twenty-year mortgage, the length of time would be open-ended.

The peril of the variable rate is clear. The history of interest rates for decades now has been one of driving upward thrust, from rates as low as 2 and 3 percent three and four decades ago to 8 percent and higher. Interestingly, too, the variable rate system has been in effect for years in Great Britain, a country where new home-building activity has certainly not been proceeding at a boom rate. The variable mortgage interest rate benefits only one side, the lender, since home buyers would pay more for their loans and would not know when they would be out of debt. Also, lenders in the mortgage market would stop competing since they would have what amounts to a guaranteed income.

Yet despite the obviously onerous conditions for home buyers that variable rates represent, some regulators of lenders look on it favorably—which suggests which side they identify with. One such agency, the Federal Home Loan Bank Board, determined in 1972 that the variable mortgage loan rate was a good thing.

The FHLBB regulates the savings and loan companies, who are not banks, of course, but are a major factor in home-building loans. The agency's chairman, Preston Martin, proposed a plan under which the interest payments themselves would be raised from time to time—or lowered. This proposal would clearly help lenders more than borrowers, since it inevitably would inflate the price of a home. It would be just one more condition of the home mortgage, whose terms are becoming more onerous with the years anyway—especially since 1970, when a new version of the so-called standard mortgage form appeared.

The form was written by two agencies, neither of which can be said to have a direct interest in the individual home buyer. One of them, the Federal National Mortgage Association (Fanny Mae), was a privately-owned, though government-controlled, company that purchased mortgages from original lenders, such as private mortgage-lending companies. The other agency was the Federal Home Loan Mortgage Corporation, another quasi-public corporation created by Congress to trade in mortgages issued only by banks and savings and loan companies. (Actually the two agencies, or companies, did much the same thing, but the banks and savings and loan companies refused to deal with Fanny Mae because mortgage-lending companies are competitors of the banks and savings and loan associations. The intramural fighting reached a peak and resulted in duplicate companies.)

What turned up as a new standard mortgage form after the rewriting was enough to send some critics of lenders into spasms. Prepayment penalties would become standard rather than negotiable, and so high that it would not be worthwhile to try to pay off a mortgage ahead of time or even to refinance a mortgage at a lower rate. The lenders would be prohibited from paying interest on escrow, giving them a windfall estimated at $100 million a year. If a home burned down, the proceeds from fire and other insurance would go not to the homeowner but to the mortgage lender, who would then apply the money toward his mortgage. The homeowner would then be forced to finance the repairs, whose interest costs would be well above the mortgage interest rates, as borrowers of home improvement loans know. If after purchase a house proved to be unhabitable, the lender and any-one else who may have bought the mortgage could continue to demand payment. The new form even included what has been called by Ralph Nader, one of those who opposed it, a "dragnet" clause. Under it, not only would the homeowner's house and its built-in fixtures be mortgaged, but free-standing appliances as well, including drapes and venetian blinds.

The one-sided mortgage form, as forty or so consumer or-ganizations found out when they protested, was written this way supposedly to stimulate mortgage lending. But the mortgage form was so one-sided U.S. Senator William Proxmire felt compelled to call it a disgrace. The mortgage form did, however, tend to underscore the approach of those who regulate lenders, an ap-proach in which the desires of the regulated industry are given priority over basic human need. Both the Federal National Mort-gage Association and the Federal Home Loan Mortgage Corpora-tion were dealers in mortgages who bought them to free the money of the original lenders to write even more mortgages. In this way, money was pumped into the mortgage market for the construction of housing. But in writing the mortgage form the two agencies had revealed whose interests came first. The home-owner would benefit to the extent that more money for mortgages would be available, but the terms of the mortgage form were more a liability than a benefit. When consumer advocates attempted to intervene their complaints were rejected.

To ignore human need, or to set it last, has not been unusual among the regulators of lenders, however. Lenders have even been allowed to exploit the misery of mortgage holders while official agencies looked on benignly, or even participated in the exploitation, as a tale of mortgage lending that emerged in the summer of 1972 during hearings of the Senate Antitrust and Monopoly Committee showed.

The chairman of the committe was Senator Phillip Hart, a

Michigan Democrat, and the tale that unfolded before him was as sordid a story as any. A number of the nation's most powerful lenders, including the Chase Manhattan Bank and the Manufacturers Hanover (as well as the Metropolitan Life Insurance Company and the Prudential Insurance Company), turned out to be financiers of private lenders who were writing mortgages for ghetto dwellers—mortgages that had been planned to go sour and put the home buyer in default.

Usually, it would begin in the office of a real estate agent who had persuaded people financially incapable of paying for a home to buy one anyway. The home itself was always a rundown building in a ghetto. The agent had no interest in the homebuyer's needs, income, or much else. Basically, he was a body hunter who had made arrangements with shady mortgage lending companies to finance the broken-down homes, and at the same time develop false credit ratings for the home buyer. The ratings were used to convince the Federal Housing Administration, a regulator that issued mortgage insurance, that the home buyer was a good risk. At times, FHA inspectors who turned up to look over the home being mortgaged were bribed, since many of the homes were clearly nothing more than shacks not worthy of a mortgage. In fact, the state of disrepair was an important factor in the scheme, for it assured the new homeowner would be unable to meet his mortgage and tax payments on top of repair costs. Inevitably, the mortgage was foreclosed and the homeowner evicted. Foreclosure, of course, was the goal, since the mortgage lender then collected insurance from the Federal Housing Administration.

As in the case of personal finance companies, some of the mortgage companies involved in the scheme were financed by the major banks. One New York City mortgage company named Eastern Service Corporation was indicted for fraud in connection with its mortgages, and in the course of events revealed that one of its major backers was the Chase Manhattan Bank. The bank, according to testimony, extended Eastern Service a line of credit of $20 million and even bought some of the company's mortgages. Manufacturers Hanover, as well, obtained mortgages from Eastern Service, on behalf of Metropolitan Life, while Prudential picked up $14 million worth of Eastern Service mortgages. As always, the banks, when asked, insisted they had not known they were dealing with a company whose practices were bad enough for prosecutors to seek indictments and win convictions. In one case, charges of bribing FHA inspectors were upheld.

If the home mortgage represents an example of how banks disregard human need, another credit instrument, the charge card, represents the view of many bankers that the affluent and near-affluent members of the population are ripe for exploitation. For the credit card was something not really needed, and is a prime example of what it is that businessmen and bankers mean when they say a thing is not bought, it is sold.

The banks began to sell the credit card hard for at least two reasons. They were handling a burgeoning volume of checks, which was raising their costs. The use of credit cards could reduce the load and take the banks a long step toward that cashless society they desire—one in which bills would automatically be deducted from paychecks. At the same time, the credit card would be a revenue producer.

The pitch that went out to consumers in bank promotions was that the credit card was convenient, which it was. Cardholders did not need to carry large amounts of cash, an argument that went over well in cities with populations of muggers. Millions of retail stores and other commercial businesses accepted credit cards for payment, meaning that impulse buying was highly possible and that cardholders could take advantage of sales. None of this meant that cardholders could overextend themselves. Not at all. Lines of credit were established, say of $500, and only the bank could raise the limit. No payment was due until a month or so after the billing date.

The appeal of all this was great, both to individuals and to businesses that joined up. In 1970 there were 35.9 million cardholders in the United States, compared with 6 million in 1967. More than 8.6 million of those 1970 cardholders were active accounts. Among the 869,500 merchants signed up to handle one bank card or another sales volume charged to the cards totaled $4.1 billion. From a mere 286 banks participating in charge card credit in 1967, the number rose to 5,360 in 1970. By 1973 there were more than 10,000 banks in the charge card business. Interestingly, the number of cardholders had declined from 35.9 million to 27.5 million, and the banks were engaged in a massive campaign to increase their number.

There are two major bank charge cards, Master Charge and BankAmericard. Master Charge is the service mark of the Interbank Card Association. In one recent survey more than 5,500 banks were members of the association, which was established in 1966 to permit people with Master Charge cards to buy from merchants affiliated with any other bank in the association.

BankAmericard is a charge card issued on a franchise basis by banks that are members of National BankAmericard, Inc. Often a large bank or two is used to issue licenses to lesser banks, as in New York, where BankAmericards carry the imprint either of the Chase Manhattan Bank or Bankers Trust.

Whether the bank credit card is a good thing, aside from its conveniences, is still debatable. One question that might be asked is whether a goal sought by the banks, reduced costs, was important enough to change the spending patterns of an entire society that was not really demanding change.

There was a time, too, when it was considered a virtue to be prudent. For a businessman on an expense account, a credit card is an obvious convenience, but for an average individual to be tempted to buy because of a credit card resting in his wallet is something else again. There are no figures available to prove that people are spending more than they should, unless a lower savings rate is indicative. But in promoting self-indulgence the banks, along with American Express (a full-fledged bank itself abroad), Carte Blanche, and others, have undoubtedly persuaded people to spend where they would have thought twice about paying cash. Being able to take advantage of a sale, for example, suggests that fact. Further, in the process of promoting spending the prices of goods and services have been inflated. The credit card may have helped merchants finance the credit purchases of their customers, but the cost of inserting the bank between merchants and their customers has added to the selling price of goods and services.

Banks have argued that their data processing systems were more efficient than those of the merchants and therefore the cost of their credit was cheaper and should not raise, but lower prices. To this there were at least two rebuttals. First, many department stores continued to issue their own credit cards. Second, the hundreds of thousands of small merchants signed up by the banks never had a credit structure. In fact, the reason many aligned themselves with bank credit was to obtain financing they could not afford before. Once they started paying the bank a fee or a percentage, they raised prices to absorb the cost.

At the other end, those cardholders who do not pay their bills on time pay a finance charge of 18 percent. Banks have encouraged this kind of late payment, for it is a loan at a high rate of interest.

The credit card also represents an instrument that at times has worked against economic policies of the government requiring spending restraints. In 1973, when the United States trade balance showed a deficit of billions of dollars, the result of so many dollars going abroad for the purchase of foreign goods, currency speculators, whose numbers included banks with offices abroad, traded their dollars for stronger currencies, such as the Japanese yen, the Swiss franc, and the German mark. The American dollar was devalued, and to help restrain spending, especially spending for foreign goods, it was even proposed by Representative Wilbur Mills, chairman of the House Ways and Means Committee, that taxpayers due a large rebate after filing their income tax returns in April, 1973, be given the option of buying a high-yield bond. It was a clear call for prudence in spending.

All the while, however, credit cards were being promoted heavily by their vendor banks, which were involved in a major drive to build cardholder lists. People everywhere suddenly received in the mail applications for BankAmericard (or American Express or Carte Blanche). Considering the ready acceptance of credit cards by most merchants, from airlines to sellers of French wines and Japanese television sets, the promotion was hardly needed at the time. Conspicuous consumption, despite being in opposition to government policies combating inflation and deficit trade balances, was heavily encouraged by the credit card promotion.

The credit card is also something of a discriminatory instrument that draws a line between that part of the population with more money than the other part. Credit cards are issued only to people earning a minimum salary. In the case of BankAmericard, it is $8,000, a figure that would eliminate, in conjunction with other criteria, about half the population. The criteria draw even sharper lines separating vast segments of people. For example, cards are not issued to women as easily as they are to men, though the banks and other agencies deny this by introducing confusing criteria, e.g., women generally do not hold jobs as long as men, which is true enough, but this criterion supports the point of discriminatory treatment. Blacks come by credit cards harder, too, though bank spokesmen say this is because the income of blacks lags behind that of whites. This, too, supports the point of discriminatory treatment, since basing the issuance of a card on income is itself discriminatory.

Credit in modern times is more than just the privilege of paying for something later. A credit card can be viewed as a badge; the lack of one a stigma. Moreover, credit is part of someone's reputation.

If this is so, then even the poor, it has been argued, are entitled to a credit card, limited though it might be in spending power. Banks, after all, already impose limits. Simply because people do not have as much economic power as their neighbors does not mean they should not be able to project an image of good credit standing, even though limited.

Limited use of the mail service or even the telephone is not the same as denial. There is still a great variety of telephone service, depending on economic means, including party lines with a dozen subscribers. Even a variety of postal service keyed to ability to pay is available. But a credit card is not available to many people. A recent survey shows that only 10 percent of those people earning $3,000 a year or less have a bank charge card. To be sure many people do not want cards, and there are many who should not have them. That, though, is not the point. Credit cards have replaced money at many levels of society, leading some critics of the banking system to say that the cards should be issued by the government.

In a day when hotel desk clerks look on registrants with suspicion if they are cash customers, even to the point of recording driver's licenses and the like, while credit cardholders are whisked to their rooms, the credit card becomes a discriminatory instrument. In the early 1970s, when airplane hijackings became a serious threat, customers of airlines who paid for their tickets in cash were subjected to special searches that credit card customers were not subjected to. In addition, credit card holders, at times, pay hotel room rates lower than those applied for cash customers.

Banks have never given much serious thought to the consequences of their credit cards, which they view simplistically as something that will reduce their costs, induce people to borrow, and pave the way for the cashless society. Irresponsibility is not too harsh a charge. When the idea of bank credit cards first caught fire among bankers, the banks mailed out cards in massive numbers, especially to people who were already customers of the banks, even though the cards were not requested. The technique was similar to one employed in the 1920s when the banks raided the lists of the savings account customers to build a list of names for the sale of stocks.

In the late 1960s the banks were trying to build lists of cardholders, and founded their own credit card structures to beat each other to what seemed like a lucrative market. It did not turn out that way, however, and abuses occurred. In tempting people to indulge themselves, First National City Bank sent out untold numbers of unsolicited credit cards, then found itself enmeshed in thousands of court suits to force cardholders to pay bills. When purchases were made by thieves who stole the cards from mailboxes (especially in New York, where mailbox theft is common), the bank tried to force those whose names appeared on the cards to pay the bills. Though the cardholders were not legally responsible, the bank hammered away at them anyway with letters and threats of legal action, hoping perhaps by the overwhelming power of its name to force payment. In an attempt to create legal grounds where there were none before, one bank even sent out a form that required people who did not want cards to say so by marking the form in a prescribed way. Not to mark the form produced an unwanted credit card, and an assertion by the bank that the card had been asked for. Thus there was legal responsibility for the payment of bills no matter who made the purchases.

Eventually the banks were coralled by federal legislation, and credit card solicitation became a relatively peaceful activity. But, as always when it came to the banks, it took an act of Congress to stop them. On the matter of cardholder liability, Section 133 of the amendment to the Truth in Lending Act, which became effective January 25, 1971, limited the liability of cardholders in unauthorized use of credit cards to $50. Under certain conditions the cardholders were not even responsible for the $50. Meanwhile, other sections of the legislation required the banks to spell out well in advance all the conditions. It also required that the banks reissue only cards requested by cardholders or cards that were used after acceptance of the original cards.

By this time, the banks had accepted responsibility for theft. Some began using photos of the holder on the cards. All of them imprinted beginning and expiration dates on the cards and placed on "hot" lists those cards that failed to reach holders. All of these measures could have been taken earlier.

The banks even installed computers at the end of their hot lines from point-of-sale terminals. The insertion of a credit card in a network terminal, say in a restaurant, would set off warnings in seconds.

But such networks seemed to emphasize the conspicuous consumption that some critics have said the credit card induces. Why not, they say, pay cash for a dinner or a dress? No computer must whir miles away; the restauranteur or dress shop owner does not have to give up part of his profit (or raise his prices) to cover the bank charges. Nor does the diner or dress buyer have to confront a bill one day or weeks hence. A receipt, perhaps to support a tax deduction, is available from anyone who sells something. The only one who really profits from having the credit card inserted between the buyer and the seller is the bank.

13

More True Tales of Banks and People

THE BANKS are not unaware that some of their harshest critics say there is an absence of consideration for human need in many of their dealings with the average man. A great many bankers are not ready to wrestle intellectually with such charges, and often defend themselves by saying the present banking system has little room for considerations that transcend profit and loss, risk and collateral. Some bankers are venal, and refuse even to debate the issues that bother critics, one of which is why does the banking system serve only those people with money, charging and extracting more from those least able to pay and giving decent service and low cost only to those who can pay most easily? Why are bankers as cruel as their actions suggest?

A few banks, fortunately, are examining the conflict, and some are even trying to do something about it. At times, their efforts are aimed at bringing people into the mainstream by getting them jobs—an effort that acknowledges, obviously, the inflexibility of banking as a distributor of money and credit to everyone on an equitable basis. Some bankers are opening their minds to criticism, thus making a start on attacking the problems that keep them remote from much of the population.

When the public service television program "Banks and the Poor," was screened, it was roundly attacked and in many communities bankers succeeded in blocking the film. In Richmond,

Virginia, for example, the Virginia Bankers Association, after seeing a preview of the film, prevented it from being shown locally,
according to a vice president of the association. Though the television station, WCVE–TV, was affiliated with National Educational Television (NET), a public service network, its seventy-
five-man board had six bankers on it, and Marchant Wornom of
the Bankers Association said that a decision was made not to
show it. In sharp contrast to this attitude was that of the City
National Bank and Trust Company of Columbus, Ohio. Though
the bank's chairman, John G. McCoy, felt "Banks and the Poor"
was one-sided, he admitted that "some of the abuses discussed
are real," and actually took out a half-page advertisement in
Columbus newspapers advising residents to watch a scheduled
second showing. Unfortunately, that second showing was blocked
by the operators of the NET station in Columbus, officials of
Ohio State University. It might be expected that those connected
with a university would endorse journalistic freedom, but after
receiving complaints from "representatives of local financial insti-
tutons," Ohio State canceled the showing. *American Banker,* the
daily newspaper of banking, reported that Dr. John T. Bonner,
vice president of Ohio State's education services, had not seen the
film before canceling it, but had talked "to several friends in the
financial community who were," as Bonner was quoted, " 'dis-
traught over the showing.' "

Despite such efforts to block the disclosure of facts that illus-
trate the yawning gap between banks and the poor, some banks
have been attempting to bridge that gap themselves. Citizens and
Southern National Bank of Atlanta, one of the South's biggest
banks, has been involved in the "Savannah Plan" since 1968, a
wide-ranging program aimed at helping the poor and near-poor.
It was the kind of program many bankers have paid lip service
to, but never really undertaken—a community effort involving
the bank as the catalyst, urging business, church, school, and
other community leaders to contribute their services. No government help was asked for, and when it was necessary the bank

itself laid out both money and time, and broke many of the rules of lending previously considered inflexible.

Part of the program, which was conceived by Mills B. Lane, president of Citizens and Southern, involved establishing lower credit standards, careful interviewing coupled with debt counseling, and "appropriate collection techniques" for home improvement loans among basically uneducated, unsophisticated slum dwellers. The bank determined that such people needed special protection from builders and merchants, and rode herd on contractors. It investigated them itself, instead of maintaining an arms-length stance, as so many banks do, and it supplied personnel with Polaroid cameras to record progress, or the lack of it. No funds were disbursed, in fact, unless contractors had satisfied both the homeowner and the bank that work had been completed satisfactorily. Even work done by a homeowner himself could be financed if the bank's interviewer had "enough faith in the borrower to lend the money." As for collection, the emphasis was placed on "helping the borrower to find a way to pay," not on abusing him. "Handling of weaker credit risks than usual was a normal course of events" under the Savannah Plan, and slow paying habits were discounted. Instead, the bank relied on intensive interviewing and counseling by their employees, who were required to make personal visits to the homes of borrowers, not as a banker demanding payment, but as a counselor.

To be sure, the loans were made at standard interest rates, which in this time of high interest rates can be hard or even impossible to live with. But the bank paid a dividend which worked as an incentive. It initiated a spring cleanup of slum debris, and in 1968, for example, the first year of the Savannah Plan, got 10,000 volunteers to collect 150 tons of debris from 109 Savannah blocks. The bank was instrumental in persuading business and government to lend trucks to cart away the debris, and in getting ten miles of new chain-link fence to replace what had broken down. In one year, 1969, the bank itself hired painters to paint all the houses in a two-block area in which the cleanup had been best, then provided paint to volunteer painters. The cost to the bank was about $100,000.

By 1970 the cleanup program had spread to forty-seven other cities and towns of Georgia, so successful had it been in Savannah. By now, though, Savannah was far ahead. Seven banks had initiated programs to build twenty-two playgrounds. Small business loans to low-income citizens were burgeoning, as were loans for second mortgages, funds from which were used to make down payments. Interestingly, Citizens and Southern found a way to get around federal law that prohibits national banks from granting second mortgages. It merely formed the Community Development Corporation, a wholly-owned subsidiary that was not a bank and could therefore lend money for second mortgages. Though CDC was profit-oriented, it was viewed by the bank as a research vehicle to find ways to commit money to high-risk, low-income people. Such people rarely accumulated enough money to make down payments on homes and businesses, but often, as the bank discovered, they were able to maintain payments within budgets for homes. Many of the businesses founded this way, as case histories showed, produced a cash flow that more than took care of repayment to the bank. An employee of the Savannah Electric and Power Company who sold used cars in his off hours became a used car dealer—and an employer of ten people. A bus driver told CDC of his ideas for founding a dry-cleaning business and got a loan for $14,000. An ex-Marine who was a cook on a tugboat got $5,000 to open a restaurant that proved so popular that he expanded his physical facilities, then started up a bakery, a taxi company, and finally another restaurant.

Perhaps what was most significant about the Citizens and Southern Savannah Plan, or Georgia Plan, as it later became known, was that it was a banker who started it. Like most bankers, Mills B. Lane had been conservative politically and felt that the people his bank helped, generally blacks, should be kept segregated. In his middle fifties, however, Lane worked closely with blacks in Jamaica when a Citizens and Southern subsidiary bank,

Jamaica Citizens Bank, was founded. He came back from Jamaica committed to an outlook of "emphasizing what a person is, not who he is." Obviously, such an outlook transcends color. The South, as well as the rest of the United States, has a large poor and near-poor population of many origins, and Lane's approach could easily be adopted by bankers everywhere. "Low-income people need money," Lane has said, "and the banks have got to provide it."

Though they may not be expressed quite that way, similar sentiments course through the spoken attitudes of some, though not all, of the executives of the largest bank in the country, the Bank of America. From the day of its founding by A. P. Giannini at the turn of the century as the Bank of Italy, the Bank of America has had a kinship with the ordinary man and woman. Dismayed by the indifferences of San Francisco's commerical banks to his countrymen, Giannini founded a bank that succeeded almost at once.

Giannini had what might be called a good thing going for him. Since he was well known in the Italian community where he had been a wholesale dealer in produce, his Italian brethren flocked to his bank. After a few years of swift growth Giannini's was clearly a competitor of the larger banks in the city. Yet he remained wedded to the idea of the soft loan and sympathy for people under stress. Thus it was consistent for him to use the bank's lending power to help rebuild San Francisco after the fires and earthquake of 1906. In doing so he accepted an unusual degree of risk, for who had much collateral after the quake and the fires?

But Giannini saw banking as something more than amassing deposits and lending them out at the greatest return. He believed the banker was a pillar of the community, not its master, and not just in name but in deed. No banker should stay remote from his environment.

Today the Bank of America is as much a wholesale lender of money to commerce as are other major banks. In many cases it is a larger lender. It has also gone abroad to finance international trade. But unlike other commercial banks, especially those of the East which wanted little to do with the average man until he seemed a good market, the Bank of America has deepened and strengthened its roots among small businessmen and individuals. Though it is now the biggest commercial bank in the United States, it is also one of the largest savings banks. Its savings and time deposits represented more than 60 percent of all its deposits in 1970, and the ratio has changed little since. In that year $9 billion of the bank's deposits belonged to individuals whose average account totaled only $1,400. The number of accounts held by the bank—8.5 million, including checking and savings, in 1972—also suggested extraordinary grass-roots contact.

That contact has had its benefits, not only for the bank and its depositors, but for the housing industry as well. In the late 1960s, when credit became tight, commercial depositors withdrew money from banks, as usual, to put it where it would draw the greatest returns. This occurred, too, at the Bank of America, but the stay-put, solid character of individual accounts prevented a severe money squeeze even as commercial accounts were transferred. One result was that the Bank of America continued to infuse money into home building at a time when home building ordinarily would be cut off. In fact, a special home-building program for the disadvantaged, a program into which $140 million was pumped and 8,000 loans let, continued to get funding on a priority basis. At the same time, normal mortgage lending increased drastically, rising from $375 million in 1970 to more than $848 million in 1971.

This, and other statements and deeds, suggest what is generally felt about the Bank of America, even among the harshest critics of banking, that its management has not really strayed too far from the Giannini creed. To be sure, today's Bank of America executives are more in the mold of the modern corporate executive, but what Giannini felt intuitively and acted on emotionally, these men have accepted intellectually.

In the spring of 1970, for example, Alden W. (Tom) Clausen, president and chief executive only since the previous January, suggested to an audience at New York's Economic Club that the United States was "dedicated to the eradication of poverty, the rebuilding of our cities, the rejuvenation of housing that is rapidly obsolescing and inadequate, the raising of educational standards for all our people, the elimination of environmental pollution and I hope the continuation and expansion of a private economy that has spawned our incredible level of material well-being." The issues were clear enough, Clausen said, and he added, "Now gentlemen, I submit to you this evening that each of these national goals requires money. Our financial mechanism will be called upon to generate the necessary credit and capital to provide the motive force for these national goals. It is not idle therefore to underline the fact that failure of our financial mechanism to meet these needs spells doom for some, or all, of these national goals."

Words of high-flown purpose have been uttered by bankers before, of course. Nor was Clausen even remotely suggesting that he was a sympathizer of liberal causes. On the contrary, he and other executives of the Bank of America, even those with unabashed sympathies for the disadvantaged (which does not necessarily mean only the blacks of the nation, but the Mexican Americans, the Orientals, the Indians, and the poor whites), are opposed to the belief that big business should be made some kind of convenient devil. But they also believe the banking system can be made to work more broadly, and thus they refuse to lash out at critics, and instead have instituted programs of aid that are keyed to the budgets of the poor, the near-poor, and even people with middling to good incomes, but who do not represent rich markets. There are few giveaway programs.

For example, the special housing program for the disadvantaged is not based on low-interest loans. It is based on reduced collaterals, suggesting that confidence in the borrower's will to repay is a major factor. Reflecting a policy of trying to gear borrowing to income, the homes built with funds lent by the bank have been generally smaller than the norm, averaging 750 square feet, one and a half baths, and just two bedrooms.

Few of the bank's programs rely on government subsidy, either. A loan program conceived for disadvantaged medical students was announced in June, 1971, in cooperation with the American Medical Association and the Guggenheim and Sloan foundations. The program involved $12 million of the bank's money and was designed to double the number of minority group doctors in California in a few years. Students were lent up to $4,500 a year under the program, but could borrow no more than a total of $12,000 during four years of medical training. The two foundations paid the interest on the loans during the four years of training, and the bank's principal was paid back only after the student entered medical practice, or approximately eight years after the first advance was made by the bank.

Loans to small businesses also have been sought out by the bank, which was the first bank in California to support the Small Business Administration's Project Own, into which the bank had put $15.6 million by March, 1972. In March, 1969, the bank formed Opportunity Through Ownership (OPTO), a San Francisco corporation into which it put $700,000 as capital, then persuaded six other banks to put up the rest of the $2 million needed. At month's end, in March, 1972, OPTO had lent more than $2 million. In May, 1970, the bank joined eight other banks to form the Los Angeles Job Development Corporation, providing $757,000 of the initial capital of $2 million. By May, 1972, $1.3 million had been lent.

The Bank of America has also been a ready buyer of bonds issued by communities to finance control of air, water, and land pollution. In the 1960s it was the underwriter to over $600 million worth of such bonds, despite declines in the bond markets. By doing so it not only became the largest underwriter of state and municipal bonds in California, but it also assured the issuers that there would be a market for such issues. At times, especially when the market for such bonds was weak, the bank was unable to resell them, as underwriters normally do.

Such lending does not produce maximum returns. In housing, for example, the counseling required by the disadvantaged, the paper work, showing people how to convert rent payments to equity payments (i.e., ownership) in a home, raised costs substantially above the ordinary. On top of that, the bank had to contend with a default rate as high as 13 percent, "a fantastic rate," as one executive described it, compared with the norm of 1 to 1.5 percent. Still, the bank believed it was necessary to forego some profits, not only in its home-building programs but in other soft-loan programs, e.g., student loans. Even straight-out donations were part of the policy, and the bank, besides giving to the likes of the Red Cross, committed its money to such social ventures as the U.S. Olympics, the opera, and children's playgrounds. The training and development of American athletes ordinarily gets Bank of America support by the diversion of part of the bank's commission from the sale of its traveler's checks. In 1971 the bank made an additional outright grant of $130,000. At about the same time it was converting bank parking lots to playgrounds, it was also sponsoring productions of San Francisco's opera.

Its social effort, however, has not been confined to soft loans and donations. There have been at least two other major aspects. One is represented by the so-called set-aside program, under which 8 to 10 percent of the bank's purchases have been made among minority-owned businesses.

The other aspect has been the bank's own employment policies. In the fall of 1972 the Bank of America had reached population parity in tis employment with respect to minorities. Just about 23.5 percent of the bank's payroll was going to minorities, i.e., blacks, Orientals, and American-born Mexicans, thus matching the 23.5 percent minority makeup of California's population. As the bank phrases it, "an affirmative action" employment program was also being developed for women—another minority that was already being treated on an equal basis in loan applications.

It would be easy enough to be cynical about the the Bank of America, since the bank, as a commercial lender, has engaged in practices found questionable by a number of critics, as earlier chapters show. The bank is also more vulnerable to violent opposition. Its thousand or so branches were, in fact, targets for arsonists during the protests of the late 1960s when about a hundred were partly destroyed. Thus it can be said that because it is so vulnerable, the Bank of America is almost forced to do something.

Two things argue against this attitude, however. One is the heritage of Giannini. The other, perhaps far more important, is the bank's willingness, even insistence, on critically examining what it is doing—something few banks anywhere will do. Early in 1972 Clausen formed a public policy committee composed of seven members of the bank's board to review and monitor social policies. The committee, Clausen said publicly, was to "act in a practical, constructive way to advance the bank's effort in the social field." At the management level the bank then appointed from among its most senior ranks a tough-minded former loan officer named G. Robert Truex to develop policy. By the fall of 1972 Truex had not yet developed new policies or additions to old ones, but he had articulated a set of problems, the solutions to which could become policy. His introspective criticisms were the kind of thing heard only occasionally among bankers, and went well beyond the platitudes generally spoken, as, for example, in this comment on banks and women:

> One of the kinks in our system is that we discriminate against women, as in the business of granting credit. There's no question that we've been doing it. Now I don't mean with particular malice. But people have long believed that a young woman eligible to bear children is for that reason not of the same quality credit risk as a young man of the same age. So we haven't given credit to women as freely. This hurts especially divorced women with no credit records, so we are developing a system for permitting the

reporting of credit records of married women so if the women should become divorced they'll have credit ratings, and be able to get new credit; for a credit card, for instance.

Truex is not especially fond, either, of the results of Bank of America's housing program for the disadvantaged, for reasons that no bank public relations man would ever bring to public attention. As he says:

Sure, during the last credit crunch we specifically instructed our people not to slow down these loans. Right now, in the fall of 1972, we've poured out $140 million into this home loan program. Nobody knows whether we've accomplished our objective or not. So what I'm trying to find out is whether we have. And if we haven't, what must we do to correct it? But the first thing that I realized when I began to look at this program is that what we were doing was perpetuating ghettos. We had set out boundaries around certain areas—ghettos—I wish there were another word. We were making loans to people . . . we literally were sending guys from door to door asking people if they would like to own the house they were renting. We'd be glad to help them; we'd take them through the steps. This person representing the bank would take this prospective buyer to the bank—many of them had never been in a bank, they were afraid to go in—and work out the loan for them. But what we had done, as I say, we had assured they would stay in this ghetto. So now, we've expanded the program. Now we are making such loans anywhere in the state of California; we can't do business anywhere else. And we've added forty branches that have the training and the capacity to make this kind of loan, so that now there isn't any point in the state that is more than thirty-five miles away from these branches that can make these loans. Now, how it is going to work out? I don't know, because one of the things that we haven't done properly on that particular program is that we have not done the proper job of counseling. People that have never borrowed money really do not understand in many cases the responsibility that they undertake when they borrow money. Frankly, they just don't realize sometimes that they have to make payments every month. And in our zeal to get the job done we have really not counseled borrowers to the extent we should have, with the result that we've got those delinquency problems, which are problems for the bank, and which are problems for the borrower. We take losses, for example, because the delinquencies can go as high as 12 to 13 percent a month.

There are some problems, social problems that have become issues, that Truex has not been able to cope with to any great extent. One of these is pollution. What exactly is the bank's role here? Should the bank refrain from lending money to a corporation because it is a flagrant polluter; in effect, make a reduction of pollution one of the terms of a loan? "I don't think so," Truex has said. "Sure, we'd love to have a program like that, but we're just not smart enough to develop such a program. Everybody pollutes. Every single one of us that drives an automobile or makes anything. We're just not sage enough to be able to develop the standards by which to judge who is a polluter and who isn't a polluter—and we have given the whole subject considerable thought. One of my colleagues likes to use the facetious example of the loan going to the guy who develops a new cure for cancer, but he's been dumping his chemicals into the stream behind his laboratory."

Under some conditions, however, the Bank of America has sided against some of its best customers, not by taking a position against them but by refusing to support them. In the election of 1972, when farm produce laborers led by Cesar Chavez were opposing a proposition on the ballot that was supported by the vegetable producers, their employers, the bank took a neutral stance. Since the days of Giannini it had financed the producers, and in 1972 was financing 40 percent of the agriculture in California. Chavez expected the bank would support the producers, but instead it took a neutral position in a public announcement. It was an act that brought the approval of Chavez, at least.

Involvement in politics is a disturbing thought for Truex, who is still not sure this is what a bank ought to be doing. "Frankly, it's brand new, and it kind of scares me a little bit. I am a little bit hesitant about big corporations ascribing to themselves this kind of power. I don't know whether we should be spending time or effort influencing the way people vote. Either way. It really concerns me. Down the line if you had some wrong-minded guys making decisions, this kind of power could be used against the public interest."

Truex, of course, was referring to open declarations of interest, not the subterfuge that has been associated with the political power of banks for many, many years.

Openness, though, is part of the new social policy, which informally is stated this way by Truex: "I believe the way to get to solutions of problems is to be open-minded and talk about it. If you're making a mistake, admit it, but at least allow yourself to be convinced that you might be wrong. Talk about things. Hammer out solutions. You don't do it by hiding behind anything."

It would not be unreasonable to contrast this with an attitude reflected by an executive vice president of New York's First National City Bank in a speech delivered January 12, 1972, to New Jersey's Department of Banking and the Conference of State Bank Supervisors. After implying that criticism of corporations and banks was mere "fad" and "fashion," the executive, James D. Farley, then said, "Corporate social responsibility is certainly one subject that has accumulated a thick coating of sugary rhetoric. A lot of well-meaning people both in and out of the business community have lately been advising corporations to become involved. Involved in what is the crucial question." After stomping verbally on consumerism, glossing over the abuses that caused its rise, Farley suggested that consumerism takes much of its vitality from the outrage we all more or less share against the shoddy practices we encounter. "In some ways, it is a species of blind revenge against the system with a capital S. There are those who regard consumerism as a wrecker's ball aimed at the superstructure of American business. And I, for one, am not entirely disposed to shrug off that concern as hysterical. Certainly a good many ill-conceived nostrums have been advanced in the name of consumerism by those who appear to regard the American economy as a kind of gigantic Tinker Toy. In our own industry, for example, the enduring fantasy is that credit can be made abundantly available at low interest rates by waving a legislative wand."

It is not known whether First National City Bank has ever said that it would forego profits for human need. A search of the public record reveals nothing. The bank has said, however, through its chief executive, Walter Wriston, that it sought profits of 15 percent a year, a rate any corporation would be proud to attain. Whether the banks' executives have ever indulged in examination of their own industry and corporation is also not known, for again the public record reveals little and the bank, typically, when confronted with such questions refuses to answer them. Its response to issues that stir people, say pollution, and tumble-down housing, is to bemoan their existence in slickly written booklets intended to leave the impression of a concerned institution. Invariably, the booklets are exercises in hand-wringing that conclude that the poor are poor, or the air is dirty, or most New York housing is not fit for human habitation.

When the bank has become involved, in the rebuilding of slums, in drug addiction programs, in educational programs, in day-care centers, its involvement is minimal and usually confined to giving advice. Most important, the bank does not take the lead, as in the case of Atlanta's Citizens and Southern and San Francisco's Bank of America (these, incidentally, are not the only ones with substantial, meaningful programs). First National City's procedure, according to its own publications, is to wait for government to take the lead, and indeed put up the money required or at least agree to reimburse the bank for any outlays that might be a bit risky.

A case in point is First National City's participation in the rebuilding of New York's housing. At one time in 1972 the bank disclosed it would "provide" nearly $250 million for housing in New York during the two-year period 1971 to 1972. The money would be let for the construction of apartment buildings at various locations, but one thing was consistent no matter where the housing was to be built. Some sort of government subsidy and guarantee was always involved, and the initiative to build was not the bank's but various private and nonprofit or New York City agencies'. There was no foregoing of profits by the bank. Despite a stream of public relations announcements the bank was really operating on the basis of business as usual. Typical was the $5 million it lent to Redeemers Homes, Inc., a nonprofit group founded to provide apartments in Brooklyn. The bank's role was to make a twelve-month construction loan in an arms-length arrangement. At the end of the twelve months New York's Housing Authority would buy the buildings and the bank would get its money back. Meanwhile, the entire program was guaranteed by the Department of Housing and Urban Development, a federal agency.

In another building program First National City lent funds for the construction of housing sponsored by a pair of nonprofit private civic organizations. In this case, the Federal Housing Administration insured the entire loan, thereby eliminating any risk at all to the bank. Then the federal government even subsidized the interest payments on the permanent financing.

That First National City's involvement with people is limited is supported by other programs the bank itself tends to point to as examples of its good deeds. In December, 1971, the bank disclosed it had lent $600,000 for a day-care center. Again, however, the bank was merely a business-as-usual lender. Under a New York City program designed to stimulate the building of new day-care centers, New York's Department of Social Services furnished funds for leasing the day-care centers from their builders, guaranteeing them a "fair" return on their investments. The city then turned the buildings over to local community groups to operate. The bank's part was a short-term profitable lending transaction, nothing more.

Still another example of First National City publicly claiming community participation when its participation was minimal occurred early in 1972. The federal Office of Education awarded a grant of more than $300,000 to establish a pilot project in Monroe, New York, a community not many miles from New York City, to study ways of improving teaching and administrative techniques. The money for the study came from public funds. The bank's personnel executives had helped design the proposal submitted to the government for the funds. The bank's investment was unknown.

Even greater reliance was placed by the bank on the federal government (which most banks prefer to verbally flog rather than compliment) when First National City became a founding sponsor of a coalition to combat the serious problem of drug addiction. The "coalition" is a favorite device of major corporations faced with calls to help out with social problems. Typically, they emerge with a name suggesting vigorous action. In this case, the name was PACT, for Provide Addict Care Today, and presumably it was thought up by someone familiar with words that stir people, i.e., someone in the bank's public relations department. PACT's main purpose, as some cynics had prophesied, turned out to be "to encourage major support from the federal government for deserving programs." Among its earlier activities was the hosting of a luncheon or two to acquaint New York's business leaders with PACT and to ask them to join labor and civic groups in the drug rehabilitation program.

Meanwhile, the real business of the bank went on as usual.

PART FIVE

Power

14

Banks as Lobbyists

I T W O U L D be hard to find an important or even not-so-important banker today who would not scorn the efforts of banking's lobbying groups, especially the American Bankers Association. Most directly the scorn would stem from banking's defeat in 1970 in opposing legislation that would close the loophole of one-bank holding companies, and again in antitrust legislation that put banks under restraints that surpass those governing the rest of American commerce.

Yet the scorn is not really deserved. Bankers have operated under such privilege that the effort to corral them received widespread support, including some from President Nixon. Some form of legislative restraint was inevitable. The bankers might as well have tried to hold back the dawn.

But the defeats were bitter medicine because bankers have had enormous ability to influence legislation. Their disenchantment with their lobbyists, especially the ABA, was the disgruntlement of men used to getting their way. In both the bank holding legislation and the antitrust legislation that halted bank mergers, the activities of the banks were so effective that the legislation nearly died. At times, their lobbying produced acrimony not ordinarily seen among the nation's legislators, both in the House and in the Senate. The tale of the lobbying effort shows how banks have infiltrated both the legislative and the administrative bodies of the United States government.

There is no question, as the available documentation shows,

that many staff advisers and lawyers employed by Congress and by the administration, especially in the Treasury Department (one of the regulators of banks), have gone over to the banks, taking with them knowledge of the legislative process that could be learned only in government. When similar defections have occurred in American industry, corporations have sued the employees and even got court orders forbidding them to work for a competitor or to sell trade secrets.

In 1956, when President Eisenhower signed the Bank Holding Act of that year into law and gave the Federal Reserve Board the power to regulate all bank holding companies except those with just one bank as a subsidiary, he objected to the loophole. The objection was well taken, as an earlier chapter in this book shows. The loophole was eventually plugged, but not before fourteen years had gone by. The success in plugging the loophole is a tribute, ironically, to the vast influence of the banks and their lobbyists. Though the Federal Reserve Board had recommended year after year, beginning in 1958, that the loophole be plugged, the recommendations were virtually ignored. In 1966 amendments introduced by Wright Patman in the House were rejected by the Senate, which had always been especially receptive to bank interests. In the two years (1968–1970) that it took to get the Bank Holding Act of 1970 passed, the opposition was formidable.

Some of the earliest opposition appeared in the form of an administration bill, which was generally less restrictive than a bill authored by Patman. The administration bill was put together by Charls E. Walker, an Under Secretary of the Treasury, who had once been an executive of the American Bankers Association. Though he denied at the time that his bill was written to head off Patman's, it was accepted by lobbyists for the banks and Congressmen alike that this was its purpose.

During the hearings held before Patman's Banking and Currency Committee, Representative William Widnall, a New Jersey Republican, introduced the administration bill, insisting that the

Committee consider it as well as Patman's. Then he actually organized a majority of Patman's own committee to rewrite Patman's bill to conform to the administration's.

Behind the scenes the bank lobbyists were well organized. One organization, named the Association of Corporate Owners of One Bank, was campaigning for no legislation at all. It had been organized by John H. Yingling, a lobbyist who had been tracking the members of banking committees for half a dozen years and who attended more committee meetings than some members. More significant as a suggestion of Yingling's effectiveness was that he had been a former chief clerk of the Senate Banking and Currency Committee between 1956 and 1960. Besides organizing his association, Yingling was also employed by First National City Bank of New York, which had little faith in the lobbying abilities of the American Bankers Association.

That organization, however, was also laboring to kill the Patman bill. It sent its president at the time, Nat S. Rogers, to speak, but Rogers, in the eyes of some very big bankers, made the error of agreeing that perhaps some kind of legislation, preferably the administration's bill, might be necessary. The ABA had also organized its "contact" bankers, men selected from all the geographic locations of the United States, to support the administration bill, especially that provision dividing the regulatory responsibilities governing bank holding among the three regulatory agencies of the banks—the Federal Reserve, the Comptroller of the Currency, and the Federal Deposit Insurance Corporation. The aim was to secure a troika of regulators, one of whom (the Comptroller) the banks could count on as sympatic (the Federal Reserve had been a tough taskmaster and the FDIC was not exactly probank either). The idea was that a divided authority would give the banks the opportunity to avoid tough interpretation, even if Patman's bill was the one that passed.

For a while it looked as though the banks' lobbyists would have their way. In November, 1969, Representative Widnall's rewritten version of the Patman bill was the legislation that Patman himself took to the floor of the House after his committee hearings were ended. The lobbyists relaxed. In past years they had usually lost their fights in Patman's committee, then had to wait until bills went to the House or the Senate floor to repair the damage. This time Widnall had made that unnecessary. But then Patman, turning the tables, transformed the Widnall version of his bill back into his original proposal in just four hours of work on the floor of the House, as discussed in the chapter on one bank holding.

The lobbyists denied they had been asleep. A Bankers Trust lobbyist named Alexander Christie (many of the major banks maintained their own man in Washington) had said to his employer that "the bill was too good to be true." In other words, reversals should be expected.

The ABA, though it has since been the chief target of banker chagrin and charges of ineptness, supposedly was aware, too, since it urged its contact bankers to write in support of the committee bill Patman took to the floor, and even spelled out bit by bit the strategy Patman might use. The banks also tended to credit the effectiveness of lobbies opposed to them, e.g., insurance agencies whose business would be taken over by the banks without the restrictive legislation, for their defeat. But Congressmen said that the banks had a poor image, the result of their charging high interest rates and not releasing enough money for the home mortgage market. Banks had a general "bad odor," as one of their own phrased it.

The cause, however, was far from lost; the bill would go to the Senate. The Senate Banking Committee over the years had been a kind of training ground for lobbyists, as a rundown of its graduates suggests. Among the lobbyists registered at the time for banks or banking interests were at least five one-time staff members of the Senate Banking and Currency Committee. Yingling had been chief clerk of the committee between 1956 and 1960. Donald L. Rogers, a lobbyist for the Association of Registered Bank Holding Companies, had been assistant counsel for the committee between 1953 and 1958. James B. Cash, a lobbyist employed by the American Bankers Association in the one-bank holding issue, had been a committee staff member between 1955 and 1961. A fourth man, Lewis G. Odom, had been staff director of the Senate Banking Committee between 1967 and 1968. In the one-bank holding issue he was a lobbyist for C.I.T. Financial Corporation, a conglomerate corporation that had picked up a large bank and would have been a major beneficiary of the Williams Amendment, which would have exempted many conglomerate corporations from bank holding regulation and thereby gutted the bill. A fifth lobbyist was Matthew Hale, a former general counsel for the Senate committee, now a lawyer for the American Bankers Association.

Such men gave the banks new confidence, as did the sympathy for their position that existed among some members of the committee itself. That sympathy was demonstrated more than once but an example as good as any was the dispute over a key phrase of the bank holding bill. From the beginning Wright Patman had fought to define strictly which businesses bank holding companies could get into and had, in fact, developed a laundry list. Patman would also have required the acquisitions of the holding companies to be "so closely related to the business of banking as to be a proper incident thereto." That language, incidentally, was precisely the same as that used in the Bank Holding Act of 1956, the one that had allowed the one-bank loophole. To gut the new Bank Holding Act of 1970, which plugged the loophole, the banks' lobbyists fought hard to convince the Senators to replace the Patman language with words permitting the bank holding companies to get into any business "functionally related" to banking. It was the heart of the bill, John H. Yingling, the lobbyist for First National City Bank, said.

It was easy enough to see why. The language preferred by the banks was another loophole. It was language that had never really been defined, a new phrase that lawyers could wrangle over forever as the banks applied their own definition of "functionally related" to whatever businesses they sought, and expanded into commerce as they saw fit. The phrase preferred by Patman, i.e., "closely related," forced the banks to stay closer to home, and was already a working, legal definition, since it had been used in the 1956 Bank Holding Act. Andrew F. Brimmer, a governor of the Federal Reserve Board, saw the phrase favored by the banks as being more lenient. For example, banks might well be entitled to get into the insurance business, an area the Federal Reserve Board, as administrator of the 1956 act, had not generally permitted. It might well have permitted them to get into mutual funds, property leasing, travel agencies and other businesses that would have presented a basic conflict and from which Congress and the courts had tried to exclude banks.

Yet when it came down to a vote in the Senate Banking and Currency Committee "functionally related" won out eleven to four. Voting for the banks' phrase were Senator John Sparkman, chairman of the committee; Thomas J. McIntyre, a New Hampshire Democrat; Harold E. Hughes, an Iowa Democrat; Alan Cranston, a California Democrat; Walter F. Mondale, a Minnesota Democrat; Ernest F. Hollings, a South Carolina Democrat, Wallace F. Bennett, a Utah Republican; John G. Tower, a Texas Republican; Charles H. Percy, an Illinois Republican; Robert W. Packwood, an Oregon Republican, and Charles E. Goodell, a New York Republican. Those who voted for the more restrictive language, "closely related," were Edmund S. Muskie, a Maine Democrat; Harrison A. Williams, a New Jersey Democrat; Edward W. Brooke, a Massachussetts Republican; and William Proxmire, a Wisconsin Democrat.

Oddly enough it was one of those who had voted for the more restrictive language, Senator Williams of New Jersey, who introduced an amendment that would have nullified the entire act. The effect of the amendment would have been to exempt conglomerate corporations that held banks as subsidiaries. Many corporations had picked up a bank, which was somewhat different from the tail-wagging-the-dog exercise that occurred when such banks as Chase Manhattan organized holding companies and made themselves a subsidiary in order to get into businesses ordinarily denied them.

The difference, however, was not enough, and an uproar followed. It was charged that the Williams Amendment was much too similar to the draft of an amendment circulated by Robert Oliver, a lobbyist for Sperry and Hutchinson. That company, best known as the issuer of "green stamps," was a one-bank holding conglomerate corporation. One of the most adamant foes of the amendment was Senator Proxmire, who at one point was reported as referring to the amendment as the "green stamp amendment." Other objectors were the Federal Reserve Board and the Justice Department. J. L. Robertson, vice chairman of the board, said that "the approach of the amendment is totally inconsistent with the act." There was no reason, he said, "for treating a conglomerate bank holding company any differently." The potential evil of combining banking and nonbanking still existed. From the Justice Department came the opinion that the difference was slight between a bank holding corporation dominated by a conglomerate corporation and one dominated by a bank. The amendment would negate the intended effects of the Bank Holding Company Act. The danger was the transfer of economic power from banking into other activities. Not surprisingly, Under Secretary Charls E. Walker, the former ABA executive, said that "enactment of the Williams Amendment would not defeat the basic purpose of the legislation." How many corporate conglomerates would benefit from the amendment was difficult to determine, but at one point more than two dozen seemed bound to. Among them were Tenneco, Inc., which owned the Houston National Bank; New York's National Lead, which owned the Lake View Trust and Savings of Chicago; Sperry and Hutchinson, which owned the State National Bank of Connecticut in Bridgeport; the Signal Companies, which owned the Arizona Bank of Phoenix; Gulf and Western Industries, which owed the First Bank and Trust Company, South Bend; and General American Transportation which owned the LaSalle National Bank of Chicago.

All the banks on the list had a net worth under $50 million, the cutoff point of the Williams amendment, though more significantly the deposits of the individual banks, the real measure of strength, were as high as $375 million. Corporations with assets above that $50 million figure would have to divest.

The lobbyists of corporations owning banks with a net worth over $50 million sought to amend the legislation to give them a great deal of time to divest, specifically ten years. This was the goal, in fact, of Lewis G. Odom, a former Senate Banking and Currency Committee staff director, who was chief lobbyist for C.I.T. Financial Corporation. C.I.T. owned the National Bank of North America, whose net worth at the time was over $100 million, and would be forced to divest. Odom, in fact, wanted the law to grant ten years automatically, then give the Federal Reserve as the regulator the option to grant another three years. In the print of the bill that emerged from the committee this, as well as a series of other modifications wanted by C.I.T., had been written in. In a so-called markup session the divestiture term was reduced to five years, but later it was put back to ten years.

The intrusion of bank lobbyists into legislatures, especially the Senate of the United States and its banking committee, has been going on for so long that it has come to be regarded as accepted practice. It was the Senate that exempted holding companies from the 1956 Bank Holding Act—an exemption that supposedly would help small-town banks stay in business, but one which the big banks pounced on and used to advantage.

The bank lobbyists have even written laws to be introduced into the Senate, knowing that as long as Wright Patman was chairman of the House Banking and Currency Committee, this was not possible there. The Senate was a different matter, however, as in the case of a bill carried on the Senate docket in the summer of 1972 as S.3652. The bill would have blocked the efforts of state governments to raise taxes paid by banks, which pay far less to state and local governments than do their industrial counterparts. It was written by the American Bankers Association, and though damned by a Senate staff study as "the most unconscionable example of special interest legislation," according to news accounts at the time, it was nevertheless introduced by Senator Wallace Bennett, a Utah Republican and a member of the Senate Banking Committee. In August, 1972, Senator John Sparkman, chairman of the committee, scheduled executive hearings on it that were closed to the public.

One of the more unusual tales of relationships among a Senator, bank lobbyists, and banks involved Senator A. Willis Robertson, a Virginia Democrat who was Sparkman's predecessor as chairman of the Senate Banking and Currency Committee. It was Robertson who in April, 1965, introduced legislation that would have exempted banks from the antitrust laws (see Chapter 8). The bill came to be known among some members of the press as the Manufacturers Hanover Home Relief Act, since that bank and a handful of others were the chief beneficiaries of the legislation. In turn for enactment, the entire banking industry was saddled with antitrust restrictions far more onerous than anything that existed before. So delighted, however, was Manufacturers Hanover with the legislation that the bank wrote to all its stockholders suggesting they say "thank you" to Senator Robertson for introducing it. The bank had reason enough to be grateful. Just one month before the legislation was introduced, a Federal District Court in New York had ruled that the merger of Manufacturers Trust with the Hanover Bank was in violation of both the Sherman and the Clayton antitrust acts. The bill introduced by Robertson got the bank off the antitrust hook.

In June, 1966, Robertson, who had been appointed to the Senate in 1946 to fill a vacancy and faced virtually no political opposition in three subsequent elections, was again due to campaign for return to his office. The chairman of his finance committee was Richard S. Reynolds, Jr., a member of the Manufacturers Hanover board, and this time Robertson faced opposition from within his own party. The man opposing him for the party nomination was a Virginia state senator named William B.

Spong. Robertson saw no favoritism in having bankers support him: "Naturally I appreciate the fact that bankers think I have done a good job," he said to a Virginia audience during the campaign. "Some of them are kicking in a few thin dimes, but they don't expect me to do anything other than what I have been doing." Earlier Robertson had said, "They [the bankers] simply think I know more about banking than any other member of the Senate or the House as the result of my experience in that field."

Spong's position was this: "I believe that voters should know in detail, before they vote on election day, who is contributing how much to a candidate's campaign. The voters should know whether any candidate is beholden exclusively or largely to any special interest groups. The public has a right to know many things so it can form a judgment. . . . What are the interests that back his reelection campaign?"

The bankers, meanwhile, were rallying to Robertson. The president of a Virginia bank asked all his directors to contribute to Robertston's campaign. This followed the letter of R. E. McNeill, Jr., chairman of the Manufacturers Hanover Trust, to stockholders in Virginia and elsewhere to support Robertson. Charles Emmet Lucey, a lobbyist for the banker merger bill, became a research assistant of Robertson's. J. Harvie Wilkinson, Jr., chairman of the State-Planters Bank of Commerce and Trust in Richmond, became treasurer of Robertson's campaign finance committee. Indeed, a Robertson campaign banner was strung between two buildings of Wilkinson's bank in the heart of Richmond. Weeks before the campaign got under way a group of bankers from various parts of the nation gave a testimonial dinner for Robertson, during which he was praised by Homer J. Livingston, chairman of the National Bank of Chicago, as someone who had "left an indelible mark on the institutions that govern the nation's economy." (It was a phrase that could have been used just as aptly to refer to Wright Patman.)

One of the especially interesting stories of Robertson's run for reelection involved Charles Emmet Lucey, the lobbyist who became Robertson's research assistant for the length of the campaign. Lucey was hired by Robertson on April 21, 1966, as a campaign researcher. During 1965, the year in which the antitrust legislation had been introduced and passed, Lucey had been a "counsel" of the Manufacturers Hanover Trust. More important, though Lucey had been a registered lobbyist since April 8, 1964, as an employee of the Support Group for Progressive Banking, according to records of the Clerk of the House, Robertson's two top aides denied knowing this. The two were William B. Foster, Jr., administrative assistant, and Robert B. McNeil, legislative assistant. Lucey, in fact, had said he intended to remain a lobbyist "through the 1966 legislative year and indefinitely thereafter." Yet in June, 1966, Lucey, McNeil, and Foster said Lucey was no longer a lobbyist. "I'm just here helping out," Lucey said. The Support Group for Progressive Banking was supported by banks in the major cities of the country. Lucey was one of two lobbyists employed by the group to lobby for Robertson's bill. The other man was John H. Yingling, who worked for the organization, according to records, between 1964 and 1965.

The political campaign became an acrimonious intraparty battle, one reason being the brute power some bankers seemed impelled to employ. An advisory board member of the Bank of Virginia, identified as Dr. Russell M. Cox, resigned after receiving a letter from the bank's chairman, Thomas Boushall, who asked him "irrespective of party affiliation to send me a check" for Robertson's campaign. Another officer of the bank who was also a board member had announced at an April, 1966, meeting that the bank intended to raise $82,000 to help Robertson's reelection. The bank officer, who was unnamed in reports of the incident, had said that he intended "to be forceful with the people in our bank," and would "twist arms as hard as necessary." Robertson responded to this report by saying that he himself had "never twisted the arm of any banker to contribute one red cent to this or any previous campaign." For his part, Boushall said, "I make no apologies for raising money for Willis Robertson." At the time, however, the Federal Corrupt Practices Act forbade corporations from making contributions to candidates for federal office.

Soon the candidates clashed directly. Robertson said Spong was financed by labor unions and would be a puppet of Senator Robert F. Kennedy of New York, if elected. Spong had received about $300 from a labor group, but no money had been received from Kennedy or the Kennedy family. A total of $100,000 or so was expected from a variety of sources, and Spong fired back a challenge that Robertson reveal his own sources of funds. On June 16, 1966, Robertson learned that Virginia's bankers, who had organized the Virginia Bankers for Robertson, had raised far more than a few dimes so far, in fact, had come up with $30,000 (a sum that grew to $56,000). Robertson said he was unaware of this.

At this point, Spong became a serious threat. An unknown early in the spring of 1966, he was about to topple one of the more powerful men in Congress, who though seventy-nine was as physically and mentally agile as ever. The bankers' support was backfiring. The buttons, the automobile bumper stickers, the money they had raised despite a law forbidding them to engage in politics, were all being used by Spong in verbal attacks. Spong scorned Robertson's statement that he did not know that Emmet Lucey had been a bank lobbyist when he hired him as research assistant. "A United States Senator," said Spong, "should never allow himself to be in a position where his business is handled by those closely associated with special interests whose conduct he must oversee in the public interest." Late in June, 1966, just two weeks before the primary date of July 12, the issue of aid from out-of-state banks arose, as Spong renewed his challenge to Robertson to reveal his sources of funds. Robertson's campaign manager, State Senator E. E. Willey, responded by saying that no disclosure would be made before the primary date. Spong charged that out-of-state banking interests, including the Manufacturers Hanover Trust and the Chemical Bank in New York, were raising money to support Robertson. Then Spong threw a bomb. Using a transcript of an interview in which Robertson had appeared on a Washington television station. Spong quoted Robertson as saying, "It's gotten to be tough—the expenses—so what is the result? Under this system you've either got to be a rich man or else you've got to take money from some group that expects something in return." Perhaps it was the flailing of a drowning political candidate, but reproductions of newspaper articles showing Spong associating with blacks were mailed to voters. Soon political forecasters were saying Spong would win—despite support for Robertson from Virginia's powerful Byrd family organization. On July 12 the forecasters were proved right. Spong defeated Robertson in a victory that shook Virginia's political organization to its core. The issue clearly had been Robertson's special interest in banks.

The infiltration of banks into the legislative process by means of their lobbyists goes on, of course, despite the destruction of a lone Senator. Yet there is reason to be hopeful, for the banks' tendency to overkill has been working against them. Staff assistants in the Senate are beginning to examine banks' evolvement into some sort of incestuous role, as suggested by Timothy D. Naegele, a lawyer and an assistant to Senator Edward W. Brooke of Massachusetts. Naegele has warned bankers in speeches that they tend to overplay their hands. Lobbyists may provide legislators with carefully developed, intelligent arguments, Naegele has said, but when all the lobbyists are on one side of an issue and then are joined by government administrators, including regulators, as in the case of the one-bank holding legislation, they jeopardize their chances. In a reference to Senate aides who easily went over to the other side, Naegele said that members of Congress were questioning people who flipped between one conflicting role and another. And congressional offices were being staffed by younger individuals who did not covet jobs with industry associations, but were possessed of idealism. It can only be hoped that this is true, for the evidence is hardly overwhelming so far.

Lobbying, in fact, is one of Washington's biggest businesses, and law firms that lobby flourish. Among those considered part of the banking lobby are Covington and Burling; Corcoran, Foley, Youngman, and Rowe; Clifford, Warnke, Glass, McIlwain and Finney; Arnold and Porter; Leva, Hawes, Symington, Martin and Oppenheimer, and Metzger, Noble, Schwartz and Kempler.

Despite the sneers of many of the bankers it serves, the American Bankers Association is also stronger. It has reorganized and presumably has become more effective since moving to Washington from New York after its humiliating defeat on the one-bank holding issue. The ABA has 300 regular employees in its Washington headquarters and can call on 1,000 volunteer bankers throughout the nation to serve on committees that produce overwhelming amounts of information favorable to banking interests. The ABA also has patched up some of the differences between the big banks, which were hurt the most by passage of the one-bank holding legislation, and the small banks, many of which were threatened by the appearance in their market areas of subsidiaries of the holding companies of the big banks. The big banks saw the ABA as defending the small banks, and even founded a competing organization, the Foundation for Full Service Banks. Based in Philadelphia, the foundation spent most of its $3.5 million budget for advertising programs extolling the virtue of so-called full-service banks, a phrase that can be taken to mean big banks. Late in 1972 the foundation was brought into the ABA fold.

Much of the reorganization of the ABA was the work of Willis Alexander, its executive vice president and the successor of Charls Walker. It was Alexander who finally brought the ABA to Washington from New York, though the idea had been discussed for years. One strong point in his arguing for the move must have been the fact that when the one-bank holding bill was rewritten on the floor of the House of Representatives by Wright Patman, no one in the New York headquarters knew about it until the following day. In fact, as a staff man who was there recalls it, "communications between New York and Washington had broken down to such an extent that no one knew there was even a risk. Everybody was caught completely flatfooted and they blamed it on the Washington staff which over the years had become a law unto itself."

Today the ABA presence in Washington represents one of the biggest lobbies, if not the biggest, in terms of numbers of people. In the opinion of one staff member, it is rivaled only by the American Petroleum Institute, another organization that moved from New York to Washington for more or less the same reason, i.e., to increase its effectiveness.

Alexander is a vastly different executive personally than was his predecessor, Walker, who was characterized once or twice by staff members as a "showboat." Though as chief operating executive he has been very much the formulator of policies and strategies, Alexander has remained in the background, a shadowy, string-pulling figure who has propelled the presidents of the ABA into the spotlight. Once president himself of the ABA, between 1968 and 1969, Alexander played out his role in the shadow of Walker, who maintained a highly visible position in the job of executive vice president. Critics of Walker's style within the ABA say that Alexander, a man who avoids talking to writers, resented it when as president of the ABA he was overshadowed by Walker. The men elected to that post were, after all, bankers by profession, capable of discussing bankers' needs. Alexander himself had been a banker in Trenton, Missouri.

Walker, on the other hand, had never been a banker. Staff men who worked for him said he was not "an organizational man," though he was outstanding at making his influence felt in the administration, especially in the Treasury Department. Walker, in fact, yearned to be Treasury Secretary, associates have said, but was passed over because of "some kind of personal clash with the White House staff that kept him from making the grade with Nixon." Walker's main strength was being "helpful on legislative strategy," and it was granted that "Charley knew the Hill better than anybody else. He was more than just an articulate spokesman; he was thought of as the spokesman for the entire banking industry."

After Walker went to the Treasury Department as Deputy Secretary, bankers were put in the limelight by the ABA under Alexander. In 1972 the banker was Allen P. Stults, president of Chicago's American National Bank and Trust Company. In 1973 the banker elected to the ABA presidency was Eugene H. Adams, president of the First National Bank of Denver. Stults was one ABA president who admitted in public it was impossible for him to answer a question in a few words, and in many ways he was refreshingly frank. He made many of his fellow bankers uncomfortable, in fact, for he seemed to go out of his way to come up with an answer, even when he could have avoided one. Once, as his term was ending, he was asked by a newspaper reporter, "What is the biggest problem or the biggest challenge for banking in the year ahead?" It was a question made to order for rhetoric, but Stults responded with some hard facts. A presidential task force known as the Hunt Commission had made seventy or eighty specific recommendations for reform in banking, and issued a report developed in part by Charls Walker. The ABA did not know what it would do about the recommendations, many of which would change the financial mechanism of banking drastically, e.g., by letting savings banks and savings and loan associations offer checking accounts. But a position would be arrived at in thirty days. Continuing without prompting, Stults admitted that banking generally had a technical capability in the business of credit cards that was way ahead of what the public wanted, implying, without realizing it perhaps, that the credit card, to convert a much-used saw, was an idea whose time had not yet come but which banks were insisting on pushing anyway. Finally, Stults said, "I think the greatest problem which, as you grab it here will bulge out there, is the extent of our social responsibilities as separate from our business responsibilities. The manner in which we serve the financial needs of the economy, I think, is something for which we have almost always gotten the highest grades."

But Stults despaired of bankers' capability to resolve the problems of human need, though accepting the responsibility: "In regard to this other area, while it is our responsibility and we do recognize it is our responsibility, precisely how you go about trying to be helpful in solving something that probably in the history of the world will never be solved, it will be just a matter of making progress."

But despite the frank talk of an ABA president or two, the policies of the ABA are such that true inquiry, at least at headquarters, is discouraged.

Support for this appears in the narrative of a newsman, Charles Gardner, who made the jump from being the Washington bureau chief of McGraw-Hill World News (a large news-gathering organization that feeds news to dozens of McGraw-Hill magazines, including *Business Week*) to the ABA soon after it moved to Washington. Gardner was acutely aware that the ABA had an image of not caring about the public interest, but believed, mistakenly, that Alexander's reorganization of the ABA meant new policy. Gardner at one point suggested that it would be good public relations for the ABA to demonstrate its new role by taking positions on worthwhile public issues that had nothing to do with banking. "I suggested," he said, "that the banking industry pay some attention, for example, to President Nixon's ideas for revamping the administrative side of government, the new scheme of the cabinet, consolidating departments and so forth." Gardner even talked over the idea with Allen Stults "to see if he was interested in making this a mark of his presidency of the ABA. He was interested enough to accept being named to an advisory committee of citizens, a kind of citizens' lobby. But when we went through the routine of trying to get a formal position endorsed by the association, and I went to a couple of committees of bankers, I found out this was going to be shot down in a hurry. There were lots of reasons, but the general feeling was that, well, why should we do it; we have enough battles to fight without taking on other people's. If it antagonizes one legislator friendly to banking's interests in general, then it is not worth the whole candle."

Gardner shot back that banking's interests would not be harmed, that the criticism of legislators was that bankers had hardened, unreconstructed positions, generally negative, and could be counted on to oppose virtually anything. "I can drag out pages of testimony by the score showing legislator critics of banking saying, 'You guys don't do anything but come up the Hill and say you're opposed.' "

Gardner next proposed giving newsmen an open, welcome reception but this idea, too, failed to win acceptance. "I thought they ought to open up the place considerably. One of the things that bugged me was this low profile of the staff. I didn't believe the staff ought to be one of low profile. They ought to be on a day-to-day basis with top bankers, not carrying suitcases to the airport. Basically, the staff was required to butter up egos. I thought instead of having a tightly structured press office and all questions funneling into some guy who funnels back answers, if he can find them, especially answers for the financial press, which generally knows what it is looking for, we ought to distribute to the press a little guide showing who's expert in particular areas. Most calls involved just routine questions, anyway. If there were a policy question involved, it could be referred to someone dealing with policy. Someone higher up the line. Well, that was shot down for some reason I never learned. Willis just said, we're not going to have everybody in this place talking to the press. He really misunderstood the whole thing."

Gardner left the ABA in less than six months, his disillusionment complete and thorough (though they gave him an extra half-year's salary when he departed). It was not only the staff that was muted; the ABA disapproved also of bankers who spoke out. "Guys like Stults or guys like Bunting [John R. Bunting, chief executive of the First Pennsylvania Bank and Trust, Philadelphia] who were willing to get out and fight and talk and express themselves about anything; they were regarded as some kind of freakish, publicity hounds. They weren't regarded as citizens participating in a debate taking place in their country." From the ABA Gardner went to the International Monetary Fund in Washington, where he develops and edits new publications and the *IMF Survey*.

That the ABA views the press as something to control and parcel out news to is confirmed by the routines of the ABA annual convention—for example, the one held in Dallas in October, 1972. Few major publications covered the event, regarding it as a no-news convention, though press conferences were scheduled at a rate of two or three a day and thousands of bankers showed up, including the mightiest of all. The press conferences produced a numbing amount of innocuous information, much of which the average reporter preferred not to inflict on his readers. In the pressroom, where rows of desks, typewriters, and chairs were arranged as they might be in a schoolroom, the press relations employees of the ABA sat behind desks in the manner of schoolteachers while young female assistants filled mailboxes assigned to each reporter with news releases that often were suffocatingly trivial—e.g., 21 billion personal checks were written in the United States in 1972. The news releases also described the structure of the ABA, the finding of a survey that the size of a bank is related to the size of its community, and the finding of another survey that communities need industries in their midst. The texts of speeches given by bankers on the floor of the convention were also made available, but the text of a speech by Mayor Richard Lugar of Indianapolis was not. A man concerned over the rot spreading among the cities, Lugar had said that "power and money must flow to the point in the cities that need it." He called on the bankers "to rally the troops" for the "alleviation of human need and the quality of life," for they were the ones who possessed the degree of sophistication needed.

For the most part, the press covering the convention, which was basically an orgy of drinking and eating, broke down into three parts. There were the newspaper and television reporters who had lucklessly been assigned to the convention for periods ranging from a few hours to days. Enthusiastic, generally intelligent, often young, and anxious to do a job of informing their readers and viewers, they were forced to wander in a maze of information they were hard put to fathom or relate to their readers. As a result of this, and often the reporters' own ignorance of banking, they seldom asked the pertinent and even the necessarily impertinent questions. For example, one day Earl L. Butz, the Secretary of Agriculture, turned up as the principal speaker at a press conference. At the time, in October, 1972, the Nixon administration had disclosed the enormous wheat purchases by the Russians. No one asked, however, what the role of bankers would be in the wheat purchases. The emphasis, instead, was on speculation that the major grain dealers in the United States had made windfall profits. As events in 1973 showed (and it could have been anticipated), the windfall actually went to the bankers, since everyone involved, farmer, shipper, grain handler alike, was borrowing extraordinary amounts all the while interest rates were rising and the banks were getting their money from the Federal Reserve at unusually low rates. Farmers who borrowed perhaps $100,000 in normal times were into their banks for $1 million.

The second group of newsmen at the convention were those who either were publishers themselves or worked for trade journals and magazines that generally danced to the bankers' tune. Such publications faithfully reproduced many of the ABA releases and the spoken words of its leadership, and acted almost as a Greek chorus, crying in print for the bankers when things were going wrong and laughing when things were right. Invariably, the members of this group were invited to the private parties of the bankers. As far as could be observed, they never asked a banker a question that could be interpreted as hostile.

The third group, much in the minority, were those newsmen able and ready to ask pertinent questions. These included the banking reporter for *The New York Times,* H. Erich Heinemann; the banking reporter for *The Wall Street Journal,* Ed Foldessey;

the financial editor of the *Christian Science Monitor,* Richard Nenneman; and others from publications in the major cities. Almost always, the hard, probing questions came from these men. It was one of them who asked Allen P. Stults, the retiring president of the ABA, how he reconciled the findings of a Harris poll commissioned by the Foundation for Full Service Banks that gave bankers a good image with the argument of critics saying banks are failures in attacking minority problems. The question got down to who was right and who was wrong. Said Stults, "I would suggest when you don't know what the problem is, there is no way of knowing whether it is being solved or not being solved." Another time, a reporter asked, "Do you think the banks have any responsibility to reach out other than through lending to help the poor?" "I surely do," said Stults, adding, "I think that banks can be the leaders."

Though such questions might well be expected from *The New York Times,* a paper that has demonstrated its position in liberal causes, to hear them posed by a trade newspaperman would be unusual to say the least. Most trade papers are mere forums for the industries they cater to, publishing articles reflecting industry interests and carrying advertising of manufacturers serving the industry. In the case of banks, it would be typical for a trade paper to carry the speech of a major figure upholding banking as a part of the free enterprise system whose rights were being stripped away by hostile legislators; facing the speech might well be an advertisement by a manufacturer of bank vaults.

Banking, however, unlike most industries, does have one truly informative trade paper, the *American Banker,* a daily newspaper published in New York that its editor, Willard C. Rappleye, Jr., operates as a "community newspaper" for bankers. The *American Banker* carries much of the news of its industry, but Rappleye sees banking as "a community badly informed by its own press," and thus the full text of a Ralph Nader speech not necessarily complimentary to banking will be carried by the *American Banker.* More important, Rappleye views his newspaper as a competitor of the general daily newspapers that cover topics that appeal to bankers, so he aims to provide detail in a volume general newspapers have no room for. In doing so, Rappleye makes sure his reporters tell his readers "what they ought to know as well as what they want to know. We are reporters *to* them, *not for* them." To do this Rappleye avoids hiring reporters with an addiction to bland facts. His financial editor, Ben Weberman, was the financial editor of the *New York Herald Tribune,* and can talk to bankers on their own, sometimes exotic, levels. Some of Rappleye's reporters are young and idealistic and display a decided liberal bent. One of these is William Zimmerman, who, Rappleye says, brings bankers "tidings they do not know, but in our judgment they have to know." Tall, sparely built, and constantly projecting an air of eager inquiry, "Zim" was handed the unenviable task of developing news of blacks that bankers would read without canceling their subscriptions. "We were late to discover cities in trouble," Rappleye says ruefully. "But we decided, well, we'll talk to the blacks. And we'll talk to the banks. In developing coverage we assumed that both were trying. Our questions were: How are they doing? Is it all working? Zim was told to go turn over the stones, and he was one of the guys who made it kosher for bankers to talk about blacks at all. Bankers don't like his questions. They're also nervous at the start. The blacks didn't trust him, either. But he is earnest and the black guys have realized that while he is not their patsy he cares about them." But besides being earnest, Zim, as a Jew, is conscious of what it is to be out of the mainstream. Besides, his wife is Puerto Rican. Typically, he once asked an ABA president at a press conference for an opinion of the terms of a loan contract worked out by the American Civil Liberties Union, compared with the harder terms of the bankers' standard contract. His answer was a plea of ignorance regarding the ACLU terms.

The *American Banker* did not always take such a liberal stance. When Rappleye arrived from *Time* magazine, where he had been Dallas bureau chief and later national economic correspondent in New York, the *American Banker* was a "friendly" paper with a large payroll. Reporting standards were low, and Rappleye set to work hiring young, dedicated newspapermen. In his view, the *American Banker*, which had been founded in 1836, was "the record," and as such would publish everything bankers had to know. "We are not in the scoop business, though," Rappleye admonished his reporters who were recruited from the dailies and the wire services. His newspaper, in fact, will sit on a story until it can be done thoroughly, and in that sense is far superior to many dailies. Rappleye admits that his 14,000 circulation, among bankers in the highest echelons, was achieved by being compatible, too. "We sugar-coat some things so we won't raise their hackles. We don't do this to make friends, but to gain respect for our newspaper. We don't speculate." The sugar coating is likely to appear especially when shenanigans are disclosed. Instead of big black headlines, the *American Banker* does a detailed reporting job, as it did when Wright Patman disclosed the conflicting role played by bank trust departments.

One of the *American Banker*'s more valued investigative reporters, James S. Byrne, wrote a series of seventeen articles on bank trust departments and interlocking directorships, interviewing in such depth that the reprint alone was a booklet of forty-seven pages. Though all the abuses were touched on, the bankers' side of things was told as well. Byrne was also charged with discovering the extent of bank involvement in social problems, and like Zimmerman had a definite liberal bent. In the spring of 1973, Byrne joined Tax Analysts and Tax Advocates, a public-interest tax law firm in Washington that supplies analyses of tax inequities to newsmen.

As Rappleye suggests, he really has no competition. Banking is not a subject that editors of general news take to. Other interests, sports, for example, receive much more coverage than banking, or even all of business. On the *Houston Post*, for instance, in October, 1972, there were six people writing and editing the business pages. One of these "laid out" the pages, e.g., that is, determined positions and length of stories, so only five people were actually developing information for publication. On the other hand, the newspaper's sports section had a staff of thirty or so, by one reporter's reckoning. Even the number of editorial people covering the society pages dwarfed the number assigned to business and financial coverage.

The *Post*, of course, may well have been reflecting what its editors felt their readers were interested in reading. Yet, as newspaper readers know, financial and business pages are edited as though only businessmen and the professionals in finance, e.g., bankers, are interested in subjects that affect the lives of everyone.

Part of the problem, too, has been that the reporters assigned to business, especially banking, soon discover their own inadequacies. By the time they do begin to understand the effects of business and finance on the everyday lives of the population, they are elevated or promoted and the process starts all over again. The result is that "the press does not do a good job on banking," in the opinion of a banking reporter of many years and one whose right to make the judgment is unquestioned, but who prefers to remain anonymous. "Many of the reporters simply do not know the subject," he says. But the fault is not all theirs; nor is it their editors', either. Bankers stop seeing reporters who are not friendly, especially if they work for smaller publications. They wouldn't dare try stopping a reporter say from *The New York Times* or *The Wall Street Journal,* but they definitely put the heat on reporters from lesser publications. The reporters' calls aren't returned. There are delays in answering inquiries on the pretext of being busy. The p.r. men don't invite them to press conferences (these generally aren't worth much anyway, but they go to fill the pages of some papers).

The tendency of the press not to examine the "pervasive importance" of banking has long been a puzzle to legislators involved in banking, on both the state and federal levels. The work of a legislator, indeed the legislator himself, is often slighted by superficial coverage. Wright Patman, for example, has dealt in such fundamental issues as interlocking directorships, antitrust

law, one-bank holding, and housing, but in the stories of many
reporters who pretend they know the man and his work Patman
comes off as a "gadfly" and a seeker of low interest rates. An
attorney who has helped Patman write much of the legislation
banks abide by suggests that the press is immersed in day-to-day
issues. The lawyer, Benet Gellman, believes the problem lies in
the fact that the issues in banking are so fundamental "they do
not get the kind of attention they should. It's not the fault of the
press, the daily press." But Gellman also believes there is a part
of the press that is not immersed in daily news events and should
get involved with banking. "I think the other side of it is that the
guys who do understand it, who are capable of realizing banking's
pervasiveness in our society, are the very people who have prevented investigation, research, and even reform proposals from
getting off the ground. I think some of the press certainly under-
stands banking, especially some of the business press. But some-
how banking gets by. But not only because of the press. In fact,
the main thing is that the people who have the capability of
making this into a very important public policy issue, the Brook-
ings Institution and the Ford Foundation, for example, never do.
It's very, very peculiar that it is never regarded this way. There
are few major studies combining banking, the economy, and society. There are no institutions driving in that direction. Once I
asked an economist who'd been in his profession for twenty-five
years whether he had ever seen or heard of a study on the effect
of lending practices, availability of capital, on innovation and
competition in the business world, something we are clearly in
need of today. He had never even heard of anything like that.
Nobody even talks about doing something like that. There are no
professors in universities that I know about who are planning a
study like that. It's appalling; yet it's a fundamental thing. You
cannot grow as a business unless you have capital. Where do you
get capital? From these institutions. Who controls these institutions? What are their motives?"

A lawyer who has also had training in the fields of economics,
political and legal philosophy, and international affairs, Gellman

despairs that the "liberal free enterprise" as represented by a generation now gone from power or no longer alive—Senator Estes Kefauver, Emmanuel Celler, Louis Brandeis—is fading badly before "more monopoly and more concentration" than ever. "The reason, I think, is that the fundamental question, the fundamental key to this whole thing, is the banking system. It's been ignored by everyone. Economists don't write about it; they don't investigate it; they don't research it." As one who would himself be glad to expose the role of the banks, Gellman tells this story of how banking and agencies that pertain to it, in this instance the Federal Reserve Board, are ignored by writers, investigators, and researchers, even those with great skills.

"One of the best, most experienced reporters in Washington once wrote an article for the *Columbia Journalism Review* with a truly good point of view. He was saying that one of the most important, far-reaching functions of the government was virtually free of coverage by the press. This was the regulatory agency. Not just one. All of them. The article listed seven of what were the most important agencies. Actually, two of them were quite obscure. The list included the Maritime Administration. But nowhere on that list, nor anywhere else in the article, was the Federal Reserve Board even mentioned. That's a hell of a reflection on the perception of an otherwise very good journalist. His criticism was well taken, but he left out the most important regulatory agency of all in terms of impact on the economy, in fact, on the entire country. It was unbelievable. Here was an agency that determines interest rates, the quantity of money, that enforces the truth-in-lending laws, determines bank acquisitions, what businesses banks can go into, the entire range of economic matters of crucial importance to the economy of the country. And it isn't even recognized to be important enough to be covered by the Washington journalism corps."

Gellman agrees, however, that the Federal Reserve Board has successfully wrapped itself in a mystique that discourages inquiries, and at times has defied inquirers—Gellman's boss, Wright Patman, learned long ago.

15

Banks and Legislators

BEING A legislator of laws under which banks have to live is likely to be an acrimonious and difficult task, unless a legislator chooses to side with the banks. The official transcripts of bank legislation hearings are thick with statements by legislators toadying to witnesses who represented a powerful bank. Happily, many passages of testimony do suggest a legislator was perfoming his task, i.e., representing the broad public interest and his constituency, unmindful of the economic power the man before him represented.

Unfortunately, the record also suggests, very strongly, in fact, that only a handful of men will dare to oppose bank interests, which generally are the same as those of the general public only rarely and by coincidence. Many legislators are in awe of bank power, as this sample of toadying suggests.

It was April 17, 1969. The hearings of the House Committee on Banking and Currency were under way, and Wright Patman, the chairman, had just finished raising the issue of Secretary of the Treasury David Kennedy testifying on the one-bank holding bill even as he continued to be a stockholder of substance and a receiver of income from the Conill Corporation, the bank holding company he had formed when he was chief executive of the Continental Illinois Bank and Trust Company. Patman had raised the specter of serious conflict of interest, which would dog Kennedy long after he had departed from the government, but Kennedy simply refused to discuss it. In the usual routine following interrogation by the chairmen of House committees, the members took their turn in asking questions. One of them, New York's Representative Seymour Halpern, began his questions with these remarks: "First of all, I wish to express my unyielding faith in the character, the utmost of confidence in the integrity of our distinguished Secretary of the Treasury. Our nation is fortunate to have a man of your stature, sir, your wisdom, your ability, your dedication, to be at the helm of our great Treasury Department." Such statements obviously are bald flattery.

Ostentatious respect is only one facet of the relationship between some legislators (a minority) and the banks. Many lawmakers own an interest, perhaps through stockholdings, in banks and other financial institutions, e.g., bank holding companies, savings and loan associations. In June, 1972, 101 members of the House of Representatives reported such interests. Seven of those were members of the House Banking and Currency Committee, which initiates banking legislation. The seven were William Chappell, Jr., of Florida; Tom S. Gettys of South Carolina; William S. Moorhead of Pennsylvania; Thomas M. Rees of California; Henry S. Reuss of Wisconsin; Robert G. Stephens of Georgia; and Leonor K. Sullivan, of Missouri. All were Democrats. Ownership was sometimes hardly large enough to sway the thinking of the legislators, but this ignores the main issue of permitting a conflict to exist at all. There was also the fact that some Congressmen served on the boards of their banks. Furthermore, Congressmen by the score had voted on bank legislation despite their interest as stockholders and directors, in violation of a House of Representatives rule requiring members to abstain from voting when their private interests are involved. Violating the rule did not mean necessarily that the Congressmen voted in favor of bank interests. It did mean, though, that they were content with the appearance of conflict. As the list on page 415 shows, many of those same Congressmen who had reported stockholdings and directorships in banks were returned to Congress in the 1972 elections to serve during 1973 and 1974, two years in which major reform legislation concerning the banking structure of the country was to be considered.

The rules of the Senate generally are less strict than those of the House, and information about Senators is therefore less readily come by. Senators, for example, do not have to reveal their financial conflicts of interest; few do so voluntarily. But a list worked up in recent times has shown that at least a handful were serving as directors of banks, despite criticism by the American Bar Association that the duties of a Senator are clearly in conflict with the duties of a bank director, who among other things is required to attend board meetings, bring business to the bank, and determine policy. The list, which was developed by Morton Silverstein, the producer and writer of "Banks and the Poor," showed the following Senators to be bank directors, according to various standard references: Allen J. Ellender, a Louisiana Democrat; Clifford P. Hansen, a Wyoming Republican; Daniel K. Inouye, a Hawaiian Democrat; John L. McClellan, an Arkansas Democrat; John O. Pastore, a Rhode Island Democrat; Winston L. Prouty, a Vermont Republican; and William B. Saxbe, an Ohio Republican. A look down the roster of the 93rd Congress meeting in 1973 disclosed that Hansen, Inouye, McClellan, Pastore, and Saxbe were still holding office.

Many legislators are also lawyers, a situation that may suggest to lawyers that they should be legislators as well. Such aspirations, however, have led such men into deep conflicts, which they have tended to ignore. In recent times, despite a report by a committee of the American Bar Association recommending that Congressmen sever their associations with law firms that have banks as clients, the evidence is that the lawyers-legislators have been reluctant to do so. For example, in 1970 the following Congressmen were associated with law firms with bank clients: Tom Bevill, Edward G. Biester, Jr., J. Herbert Burke, William C. Cramer, Robert V. Denney, Robert N. Giaimo, Sam M. Gibbons, Charles R. Jonas, Speedy O. Long, William M. McCulloch, Thomas J. Meskill, Alexander Pirnie, Richard H. Poff, John J.

Rhodes, David E. Satterfield III, John P. Saylor, Garne E. Shriver, Burt L. Talcott, John C. Watts, and Lowell P. Weicker, Jr.

Seven of these men also disclosed in 1972 that they owned an interest in a financial institution of one kind or another. They were Giaimo, Gibbons, Jonas, McCulloch, Poff, Rhodes, and Saylor. One of them, Gibbons, was also a member of the House Ways and Means Committee, the committee that originates legislation controlling the income taxes banks will pay.

In the spring of 1973 a House of Representatives listing of those men who returned to office after the 1972 elections showed that only half of them were back at their desks. They were Bevill, Biester, Burke, Giaimo, Gibbons, Rhodes, Satterfield, Saylor, Shriver, and Talcott.

As mentioned, the Senate does not have the same strict rules of disclosure as the House. But in his "Banks and the Poor" Silverstein developed a list of Senators associated with law firms that had banks as clients as of the date of the program which included: Abraham A. Ribicoff, the Connecticut Democrat; Edward J. Gurney, the Florida Republican; Hugh Scott, the Pennsylvania Republican; and William B. Spong, Jr., the Virginia Democrat who toppled Senator Willis Robertson, chairman of the Senate Banking Committee, in a campaign citing Robertson's close attachment to banking. In 1973 all but Spong were back in their seats in the Senate.

As every voter knows, one of the assets of a legislator is an ability to deliver speeches. It is an ability that serves him well, not only during his campaign but also while he is in office, for many organizations tender invitations to speak for a fee. Banking organizations are no exception and sometimes their fees are substantial. In 1971, for instance, in speaking before financial groups fourteen Senators earned well over $34,000 as honoraria. The leading speaker by far was Senator John Sparkman, chairman of the Senate Banking Committee, who made nine speeches before banking groups and received $11,200. Well behind him was Senator Robert Dole, who received $4,500 for speeches.

No one can say, of course, that accepting honoraria, which is what money is called when legislators make speeches for it, is going to sway the voting habits of a legislator. Too much is at stake, including the legislator's own integrity. Sometimes, though, the banks overreach, becoming so cocksure that they have infuriated the very men they wanted to reach.

One of the more blatant examples of this occurred just prior to the elections of 1970. In October the *American Banker* in a story written by James S. Byrne disclosed the a Bankers Political Action Committee (BankPac) would be distributing $200,000 to members of Congress who were up for reelection. The money would not go to just anyone, however. Only forty or so men who were members of key committees would be supported. At the time, Ralph L. Stickle, executive director of BankPac, said the money would be distributed among only those incumbents the bankers favored, specifically members of the House Banking and Currency Committee, the Ways and Means Committee, the Rules Committee, and the Senate Banking Committee. Wright Patman, chairman of the House Banking and Currency Committee, was not one of those chosen for support by the bankers. "I doubt if we would give him very much," Stickle had said to writer Byrne. Patman's reaction to BankPac was to write a letter to Attorney General John Mitchell asking for an investigation of the political fund-raising activities of commercial banks, as the banks might be violating both "the spirit and the letter" of federal laws that barred direct campaign contributions. The details, according to Patman, of how those banks raised their political funds in violation of the Federal Corrupt Practices Act have been told in Chapter 4, including the refusal of the Justice Department to follow through on prosecution. The distribution of those funds is another side of that story that also bears telling. In Patman's view, and it was a view generally accepted, that distribution was nothing less than a blatant attempt to "weaken the one-bank holding bill," which was to go before the Joint Conference Committee on November 18, 1970, in a series of meetings that were some of the most acrimonious ever. By November 1, 1970, BankPac, which was formed with the support of the American Bankers Association, had distributed $35,000 to twenty-one of the thirty-five members of the House Banking and Currency Committee and $15,500 to four Senators, according to a BankPac report filed with the Clerk of the House. The largest contribution of all, $5,000, was given to Senator Harrison A. Williams, Jr., a New Jersey Democrat who was a member of the Senate-House conference that would meet in joint sessions. Williams was also the sponsor of the Williams Amendment in the one-bank holding bill as it came out of the Senate, and which would have gutted the whole bill in the opinion of just about everyone connected with the bill. The BankPac report said that the money was sent to the "Harrison A. Williams D.C. Committee," a money-raising group in Washington, and that the committee's address was Suite 352, Old Senate Office Building, Washington. That address was the office of Senator Williams, who was running for reelection that year.

Contributions of $4,000 each went to Senators Harry F. Byrd, Jr., of Virginia, Roman L. Hruska of Nebraska, and Winston L. Prouty of Vermont. Only Byrd served on a committee dealing directly with banking legislation. But $2,500 was reported sent to Senator Edmund S. Muskie, a member for years of the Senate Banking Committee. Muskie, like Williams, was up for reelection. Suggestive of the view banks held of Senator William Proxmire was the absence of his name on the BankPac report. Proxmire had fought hard for a one-bank holding bill and was the lone dissenter of one Senate version favoring banks in a seventy-seven to one vote. He had also put some of the teeth in the Bank Merger Act, a law that stopped mergers between truly big banks in its tracks.

Wright Patman's Banking and Currency Committee seemed a very special target. The BankPac report showed that among its thirty-five members, twenty-one had been sent political contributions. Patman, of course, was absent from the list. But three of the largest contributions ($2,500 each) went to Representatives William B. Widnall, of New Jersey, Albert W. Johnson of Pennsylvania, and J. William Stanton of Ohio. Widnall was the ranking minority member of the Patman committee, and his opposition not only to the substance of Patman's banking legislation but also to Patman's style suggested strongly he was in basic philosophical opposition to the chairman.

Other members of the committee whose names appeared on the report were: Representatives Thomas L. Ashley of Ohio; Robert G. Stephens of Georgia (who was running unopposed); Charles H. Griffin of Mississippi (he retired in 1972); Chester L. Mize of Kansas (defeated in 1971, partly, it was believed, because of the disclosure of bank support); and Garry E. Brown of Michigan. All of these were reported as receiving $2,500 each. Another committee member, Nick Galifianakis of North Carolina, was given $2,000, while $1,500 each went to Representatives Lawrence G. Williams of Pennsylvania, and Chalmers P. Wylie of Ohio. An amount of $1,000 each went to Representatives Richard T. Hanna of California; Frank Annunzio of Illinois; Thomas M. Rees of California; William Chappell, Jr., of Florida (he left the House Banking Committee in 1973); Michael J. Harrington of Massachusetts; Florence P. Dwyer of New Jersey; Benjamin B. Blackburn of Georgia; and William O. Cowger of Kentucky.

As might be expected staunch supporters of Patman were opposed by the bankers. The *Washington Post* disclosed that Representative Joseph G. Minish, a New Jersey Democrat who often sided with Patman on the issues, was facing a Republican candidate, James J. Shue, who had received $2,500 from C. Douglas Dillon, a former Secretary of the Treasury. Minish was reelected, however, as he was again in 1972.

On November 2, 1970, the day after the BankPac report of campaign contributions was disclosed, Washington was chockful of angry lawmakers. Many of the legislators had never received the funds BankPac said it had sent them. Moreover, some said, if they had received them they would have sent them back, for acceptance would violate the Federal Corrupt Practices Act.

An aide to Senator Harrison A. Williams denied that a $5,000 contribution had ever been received. An angry Representative Lawrence G. Williams said he had never received an offer from BankPac and threatened a suit. Though Leonor Sullivan denied receiving "even five cents," a check for $1,000 did arrive in her mailbox. It was returned. By November 2, 1970, the ire of some legislators had reached substantial heights. But not all.

A new BankPac report showed that eleven of the twenty-one members of the House Banking and Currency committee who were on the original list had returned their checks. The remaining ten had not. Among those who kept the money were Representatives Brown, Rees, Dwyer, Ashley, Griffin, Harrington, Stephens, Blackburn, and Chappell. Those who returned it were Galifianakis, Johnson, Mize, Annunzio, Stanton, Reuss, Sullivan, Wylie, Cowger (who was defeated in the election that year), and Widnall.

In the Senate Roman Hruska returned the check he had received, as did Senator Harrison Williams. Senators Byrd, Muskie, and Prouty held onto their BankPac checks.

A final report of BankPac disclosed, in fact, that though a hue and cry went up over its activities, thirty-seven Congressmen and six Senators had accepted $167,000 in contributions in the last few days before the elections of 1970. At year's end, after the elections were over, a final BankPac report showed that thirty-four more candidates, incumbents all, had been given last-minute donations, for on election eve BankPac found it had excess funds and ended the year with a $120,000 surplus.

To observers it seemed that the legislators were merely furious at the stupidity of BankPac in its insistence on following a procedure that could cause them nothing but embarrassment. Some legislators were genuinely outraged at what they saw as unlawful activities by BankPac. But others were merely chagrined at the bankers' display of stupidity in campaign giving, especially in insisting on an untried procedure when a tried-and-true one existed for giving money.

As every legislator knows full well, the technique of giving money is simple and works this way: A lobbyist can send a check, say for $10,000, to a campaign committee, accompanying the contribution with instructions for distributing special amounts to particular candidates. One legislator might be designated as the receiver of $1,000, another the receiver of $2,000, and so on. When the time comes for the contributor to file a report, as required by law, he can state only that he gave $10,000 to a committee. At the other end, the candidates, when they file statements with Congress, can say only that they have received money from a certain committee. Thus the committee acts as a device shielding both sides.

The BankPac group displayed another unprofessional tendency, which was to send money out without first checking with a candidate or someone designated to receive his money. In many cases, BankPac not only failed to call, it failed to ask the candidate when it did call how he would like the contribution handled. At least one Congressman who was defeated in the 1970 elections claims the publicity from BankPac beat him. Representative William Cowger, who lost by 211 votes, blamed news stories reporting the first BankPac report for his defeat. (Cowger was one of those who sent back the BankPac money.) One of the most irate was Lawrence G. Williams, who survived the election in 1970. Williams' name was one of those appearing in a BankPac list of recipients, but a check had never arrived. If it had, Williams would have returned it. On November 13, 1970, Williams received a letter from BankPac's chairman, William McKee, offering his "deepest apology." This was accepted, but then a month later Williams received a letter from Stickle, BankPac's treasurer, saying that a $1,500 check, one never received by Williams, "has been returned to us and we have notified the Clerk of the House." Angry almost beyond description, Williams asked for and got an investigation of BankPac by a special House subcommittee.

Undismayed by all the furor it had caused, BankPac went

blithely on. In 1972 it told the *American Banker's* Washington bureau chief, Joseph D. Hutnyan, it was going to be raising more money and becoming a "professional" lobbyist. A new man, William A. Glassford was executive director and would be working full time in a permanent office being opened in Arlington, Virginia. Its goal in 1972 was $500,000. In its new-found professionalism, Glassford said to Hutnyan, BankPac certainly would call the candidates it favored before sending the money over the next time.

The influence of banks is not confined to the national legislature. In Texas that influence evolved into downright corruption of a number of legislative leaders by Frank Sharp, whose Sharpstown bank was closed by his shenanigans (see Chapter 1). In New York the pervasiveness of the banks has been felt by every legislator who has ever arrived in Albany, the state capital. Only a very few, however, have tried to bring it to light and even oppose it.

One of these has been Franz S. Leichter, a New York assemblyman representing the 69th Assembly District in New York City's borough of Manhattan. The home of the nation's largest banks and some of its most willful bankers, New York has a history of sordid tales involving the banks, especially in their earliest years when they tried to eliminate one another as competitors. A man whose constituency approves of his tendency toward reform, Leichter was disturbed by a number of relationships he discovered in the state capital. Especially disturbing was the conflict among legislators in both houses who were members of the banks committees. According to Leichter's count (taken in 1971), nine of the twenty-two members of the New York Senate Banks Committee and five of the twenty-two members of the corresponding committee in the Assembly were shareholders, officers, and directors of banks of the lending institutions for which their committees originated legislation. "The whole concept was wrong of having legislators regulate an industry in which they are personally involved," Leichter said. "It raised a serious question of conflict of interests." One Republican member of the Senate Banks Committee, a man named Leon E. Giuffreda, owned stock in a Marine Midland Bank and in Bankers Trust. A company of which he was president and a director also owned stock in the two banks. Another member of the committee, John H. Hughes of Syracuse, was a trustee of the Onondaga County Savings Bank as well as the bank's attorney. Hughes was also chairman of the Senate Judiciary Committee, as well as a member of committees on codes, corporations, finance, insurance, and rules. An assemblyman named Alfred A. Lama of Brooklyn held more than $5,000 in Central State Bank stock. He was, as well, a director of that bank and of the Northport Federal Savings and Loan Association. And so it went. Another Brooklyn committee member was a director of a savings and loan association. A committee member from Syracuse named Tarky Lombardi, Jr., owned "less than $5,000" worth of stock in the First Trust and Deposit Company of Syracuse; less than $5,000 worth of stock in Lincoln National Bank and Trust Company; and more than $5,000 worth of stock in Lincoln First Banks. Lombardi was also a director of the Lincoln National Bank and Trust Company of Central New York.

In Leichter's view conflict was unavoidable. A measure was introduced in the New York legislature to give the state's Bank Board discretion to set rates on mortgage loans to individuals. The state's usury law that put a limit of from 5 to 7.5 percent on mortgage loans was due to expire. To tie mortgage buyers to market conditions for money would have meant far higher costs to homeowners, opponents of the new proposal said. Those favoring it said that without the new proposal there would be little money for mortgages when money was tight. Leichter's point was no matter who was right, men with a vested interest in lenders should not be legislating on such matters. Thus he introduced the following resolution to amend Assembly rules: "No member shall serve on any committee which has jurisdiction over bills concerning a state agency or industry or business regulated by such agency if he or a member of his immediate family is an employee, officer, director or stockholder of any such business in the State of New York, or if he has a financial interest in any such business, or if he represents any such business in a professional capacity or is a partner in a firm representing any such business in a professional capacity, or if he has rendered within the past eighteen months any service for compensation to any such business." As reported by *The New York Times,* the resolution "stirred scarcely a ripple," and was promptly bottled up by the Rules Committee. Undeterred, Leichter has been reintroducing his resolution year after year.

The legislators explain their reluctance to face this issue of conflict with the usual pat answers of people in such a position. William T. Conklin, chairman of the Banks Committee and a director of a savings and loan company, said that a banking-business background gave him and others expertise in a highly complicated field that helped them make the best judgments in the public interest. Of course, this is not necessarily so. Many men have understood the banking mechanism and its structure, but were not especially concerned with the public interest. And expertise can be bought easily enough, from any of the hundreds, perhaps thousands, of consulting firms and individuals plying that trade today. On top of that, it is quite possible to understand without having a bank background.

The conflict of the state legislators did not stop with stock ownership and associations with banks. It was a known fact that banking's lobbyists were themselves so accepted as associates in the state capital that they literally hung their hats in legislators' offices. The legislators said they were provided with expert knowledge by the lobbyists. "We welcome the explanations of all interested parties," said Lucio F. Russo, Banks Committee chairman (and incidentally, neither an officer nor a shareholder of any bank). In Leichter's view, however, this closeness to bank lobbyists has permeated legislators' own thinking with a "banker philosophy." Nor has any consumer advocate, so far as is known, been asked to hang his hat in a legislator's office.

Leichter has also fought a long-established practice of the banks to give employment to former state officials and staff members of the state Department of Banking. A bill of his would amend the law to provide that "for a period of two years after an employee of the Banking Department has left, he shall not accept employment from a banking institution under jurisdiction of the Banking Department." One reason for the bill is that the Banking Department of New York has unusual power over the track of banking legislation, perhaps even more than the legislators. For over a hundred years there has been a strict prohibition in New York against bank officers being permitted to buy bonds of their own banks below par. A bill reported out in 1969 by the Banks Committees would have changed this. It was initially beaten. But then the Banking Department attorney spent a mere two days lobbying for the bill, and it was passed. The department, of course, answers to Nelson Rockefeller, governor of New York, a man who brooks no challenges from any of his appointees. When William Dentzer, a state banking superintendent, exercised some independence, he was fired summarily by Rockefeller in 1972. The governor is the brother of David Rockefeller, whose Chase Manhattan Bank is about to spread its branches throughout New York after lobbying hard for a bill that will permit statewide branching. "As far as the public is concerned," Assemblyman Leichter has said, "we could get along without the Banking Department and just let Chase Manhattan take over its functions." It was not the Chase Manhattan lobbyist, said Leichter at the end of the 1972 session of New York's legislature, but another who said publicly that his influence was such that he "didn't buy lunch for the legislators of New York. I buy the legislators."

PART SIX
Patman

16

Warrior from Patman's Switch

THE POWER of the banks to sidetrack the legislative process is so widespread that legislators everywhere have felt it almost as soon as they have taken their seats either in their state capitals or in Washington. Bank political power has never consisted of mere lobbying. It has been, instead, crushing pressure applied to the legislative process from within the government and from without. It has been so pervasive that seasoned legislators have generally warned Young Turks to give the bankers what they wanted for the sake of peace. Banking became, as Thomas Jefferson had feared, a shadow government not answerable to anyone but itself and a central bank, currently the Federal Reserve System, which is autonomous and determines the course of banking. To get their way, bankers infiltrated the government, including the Treasury Department, bank regulatory agencies, and Congress, and even manipulated the wills of Presidents.

Patman was born in Patman's Switch, Texas, a switching point for the Katy Railroad in Morris County, the son of a struggling farmer. His family had migrated from Georgia, and when not farming the land they operated grain mills or country stores. Patman recalls his very early life in Texas this way: "My father was a farmer and earned a little extra by repairing cotton gins, but we were always poor. Neither of my parents had much education, but my mother was an ardent student of the Bible. She told me never to use the Lord's name in vain and I never did." As a young man Patman sold insurance and worked as a sharecropper at times to put himself through law school at the Cumberland University in Tennessee. Between 1917 and 1919 he was in the army. Returning home, which was now Texarkana, Patman entered politics. He became a crusading district attorney when a murder a day was routine, then became a member of the Texas House of Representatives. Patman was as tough a campaigner as he was a district attorney. Campaigning for the legislature, he referred to his opponent, the incumbent, as "the rat and gopher candidate," after his opponent had used a rat and gopher control program for farmers as one of the reasons he should be reelected.

When he arrived in Washington from Texarkana, Texas, in 1929 as a fledgling Congressman, Wright Patman, too, was told, as he recalls it, "not to do anything against the banks. The banks can cause you trouble." If a Congressman ignorant in the ways of banking had to say "anything about money, just say 'Federal Reserve.' Have nothing to do with banking. They can run you into the dirt."

But Patman had an abiding respect for the legislative process, as well as a passionate fondness for the little man whose interests he has always measured against national issues and legislation. Besides this, he brought such vigor to his causes that as a crusading district attorney he had to be protected by the Texas Rangers against Chicago hoodlums who had been brought in by local criminals to murder him.

A man with such views and energy had to meet head-on with the establishment of the day. And he did. Almost immediately. For Patman took up the cause of the veterans of World War I.

The story actually begins while Patman was still in Texas. On March 18, 1924, the House passed a Soldiers Bonus Bill, which provided not a bonus but a tricky annuity of certificates that would be paid to the veterans in full only after twenty years. The certificates could be cashed by taking them to a bank, but a veterans who did so would have to accept a substantial discount. The banks, in turn, could keep the certificates for the full period and collect the full amount. From the first, beginning in 1922, the Soldiers Bonus Bill had tough going, being subjected to five vetoes by four Presidents until the time the bonus was finally paid in full in 1936. The initial bill was passed over the veto of President Coolidge in May, 1924, amidst a feeling in Congress that the soldiers of World War I had been paid so little they were owed additional compensation. Some Congressmen even viewed the bonus as back wages.

With the crash of the market in 1929, the onset of the depression and unemployment (which reached 13 million by 1932), the Bonus Bill took on new significance. If the certificates could be cashed for the full amount, it would not only put money into the pockets of veterans desperately in need of money, but it would also increase spending and give the economy a much needed lift. The cause was a natural one for a legislator who viewed the bonus as money rightfully belonging to the veterans and saw his task as forcing the government to pay it. Like other new legislators at the time, Patman had to wait through a lame-duck session of Congress before he could claim the seat he had won in the election of 1928 from his opponent, a man named Eugene Black. Thus Patman did not get to the floor of the House until March 1929. But rather than waiting quietly in the wings, he used the time to learn the rules of the House and the techniques of the legislative process. He also let his views be known.

It was time well spent. In a Republican Congress working in tandem with a Republican administration a freshman Democratic Congressman would likely be treated with indifference. But Patman ignored the traditions that kept young Congressmen from introducing bills and introduced one to pay the Soldiers Bonus in full. So well had he learned the rules that when the Senate threw it back to the House, he was able to revive it and force it back to the Senate, where it passed, only to be vetoed by President Hoover. But in 1931 Hoover relented and half the veterans' bonus —$1 billion—was paid. But Patman was not satisfied with half a loaf and introduced a new bill to pay the veterans the rest of their due. This would not be passed for five more years, in 1936, and then only when Congress overrode a veto by President Roosevelt.

That Patman's bills continued to go through the House and Senate and then to the White House was a tribute to his perseverance and legislative skills unrivaled by any other junior Congressman. Patman had learned the rules of the House so well that he was even the cause of a change or two. After he twice resorted to discharge petitions, gathering the signatures of House members to force his bill out of committee, the House leadership changed the rules of the discharge petition, increasing the number of signatures needed to force release from one-third to a majority of House members. Patman also paid a personal price for his persistence, as the Republican-led, and then even the Democratic-led, Congress broke tradition and denied him his rightful appointment to the Banking Committee. In the days when Patman was first elected, a winning congressional candidate not only replaced his man in office, but also took the defeated Congressman's place on the various committees. Patman's opponent in 1928, Eugene Black, had been a member of the Banking Committee, but the appointment was denied Patman, who wanted it badly. It was not until the late 1930s that he was finally assigned a place on the committee. The delay was sufficient under the seniority system of the House to deny him the chairmanship of the committee until 1963. (Granted his rightful appointment, he would have been chairman by 1949.) The Congressman Patman eventually succeeded in the chairmanship was Brent Spence, a Kentuckian who was reported to be fond of saying, "I never cast a vote that would not be concurred in by the American Bankers Association."

In the early years of his fight for the Bonus Bill Patman's opposition in the Hoover administration was centered around Andrew E. Mellon, Secretary of the Treasury. Mellon was an extraordinarily rich man who had once remarked with unintended foresight that "It is always a mistake for a good businessman to take public office." Mellon was sixty-six when he became

Secretary and one of the richest men in the United States. Paradoxically—one newspaper said it was because he came from
Pittsburgh—he was an unknown when he became a member of
President Warren Harding's cabinet in March, 1921, as Secretary
of the Treasury. Mellon's obscurity was seen as an asset, according to an adviser of Harding's, who said that only a magician
could have made so many millions so quietly. Mellon, perhaps,
fairly enough, was compared to Alexander Hamilton because
both men put the banking mechanism ahead of everything else
in government. Mellon apparently agreed with the comparison, or
at least was an admirer of Hamilton's, for he kept a painting of
him in his office.

Mellon's position on the Bonus Bill was stiff opposition to full
payment. It was a position concurred in by the nation's banks,
which stood to make windfall profits from the premature cashing
of the certificates by the now jobless veterans. In Patman's mind
the certificates represented a device for shortchanging the veterans;
he had felt from the beginning that the bonus ought to be paid
outright, and then with interest. Considering the shape of the
economy between 1930 and 1932, he could not understand
Hoover's veto, which had been exercised on the advice of Mellon.

Mellon himself, according to a biographer of the period, was
an enormously wealthy banker who had underwritten Republican
party campaign costs one year by $1.5 million. He was a cabinet
officer who had continued in office under the succeeding Republican adminstrations of the 1920s, and he was a man who had had
virtually no contact with the average man and his problems. Yet
Mellon was a darling of the press, especially the business press
and in particular those publications controlled by a publicist
named C. W. Barron. Mellon had been "showered with adulation"
by such men, even though he had been "a party to strike breaking, breaking a competitor, and corrupting a legislature," according to the biographer. He had stood for tax reduction for big
business, and to make up what he gave away to business he
wanted to double taxes on documentary stamps, charge a tax on

bank checks (two cents) to be paid for by the customer, put a tax on post cards (two cents), and put a license tax on vehicles. He had fought hard for the repeal of business taxes, and, in fact, President Coolidge in 1924 staked his campaign on the Mellon Plan. This would lower the surtax on business profits from 50 percent to 25 percent, and its logic, as quoted by Mellon's biographer, was that "wealthy men will not pay one-half of their income to government, so tax them at what they will pay." Though the Mellon Plan also reduced the tax rate on personal incomes under $4,000 from 4 to 3 percent, much greater reductions were allowed for higher incomes. Mellon's main point was that business was being stifled, that it needed capital to invest, and he basked in references in the press comparing him to Alexander Hamilton. Meanwhile, the opinion of the so-called radical press that it was people, not business, who needed purchasing power went unheard. Senator James Couzens said that business already was spending for expansion, thus refuting Mellon's main point that expansion was being stifled. Couzens argued that money put into public roads and schools was as productive as private investment. A magazine said that private industry produced essentials, giving as examples chewing gum, jewelry, cosmetics, and yachts. For his part, Mellon responded to Couzens' criticism by getting out his tax return, which Mellon could do as Treasury Secretary, and showed Congress that Couzens himself, as a retired businessman, had an income of $1 million a year but paid no taxes. Senator Robert LaFollette, a liberal of the day, concluded that Mellon represented a principle that suggested "wealth will not and cannot be made to bear its full share of taxation. He favors a system that will let wealth escape."

LaFollette's words were prophetic. At first, with LaFollette in the front of the fight, the Senate reduced the surtax on business not to 25 percent, as Mellon wanted, but only to 37½ percent. The Mellon Plan itself was defeated, and the inheritance tax was put at 40 percent (yield: $100 million annually) Mellon was furious. The inheritance tax alone would hit him hard personally.

But then on October 18, 1925, Mellon· came up with a new plan. LaFollette was dead now and the opposition faded. The maximum surtax on business would be 20 percent. The basic income tax would be 5 percent instead of the 2 percent favored by the Democrats. The gift tax would be repealed. On October 23, 1926, the plan, which had passed both Houses of Congress, was signed by President Coolidge. Mellon had cut the tax load of the rich, it was estimated at the time, by $700 million. The inheritance tax, which he had tried to have repealed, might as well have been, for it was cut to 2 percent.

In 1932, in the House, Patman had reached a conclusion similar to that reached by LaFollette years before, and his response was that of the tough fighter he had become. On January 6, 1932, he rose in the House and said, "Mr. Speaker, I rise to a question of constitutional privilege. On my own responsibility as a member of this House, I impeach Andrew William Mellon, Secretary of the Treasury of the United States, for high crimes and misdemeanors and offer the following resolution." In substance, Patman's resolution quoted from the Code of Laws of the United States, one section of which put clear restrictions on the Secretary of the Treasury "carrying on," either "directly or indirectly trade and commerce" while holding the office. Patman said, "The said Andrew William Mellon has not only been indirectly concerned in carrying on the business of trade and commerce in violation of the above-quoted section of the law, but has been directly interested . . . since taking the oath of office. . . ." Mellon, said Patman, was the owner of a substantial interest in more than 300 corporations worth more than $3 billion. Mellon owned ships subject to Coast Guard examination and seizure, but the Coast Guard answered to the Secretary of the Treasury. Mellon's ships also had to pass through customs, but United States Customs also answered to and its personnel was hired by the Secretary of the Treasury. How, asked Patman, could Mellon serve two masters? Mellon had general superintendence over tax collection, and was also the boss of the Commissioner of Internal

Revenue—all the while Mellon was developing tax proposals. In fact, many corporations owned substantially by Mellon had received large refunds at "his direction." The Secretary of the Treasury was also "ex officio chairman of the Federal Reserve Board," but a section of the law prescribed that no member of the Federal Reserve Board could own stock in a bank. Mellon still did. Mellon was even in the whiskey business, Patman charged, taking "his share of the proceeds from the sale of whiskey" all the while he was Secretary. The charges went on and on. Secretary Mellon controlled the construction of public buildings, and was directing that aluminum be used more extensively—while he was privately the "principal owner" of Aluminum Company of America, a company that had a "monopoly" on the business.

Patman's resolution, H.Res. 92, asked for impeachment. When he was finished the House was in a uproar. But two weeks later, on January 13, 1932, the House Committee on the Judiciary met in a "preliminary examination" to determine whether to recommend a full investigation to the House. The committee's chairman was Hatton W. Sumners, a fellow Texan who was generally friendly toward Patman. Patman's real support in the committee came, however, from Fiorello H. La Guardia, a New York Congressman who would later become mayor of New York City. In delivering summaries of the evidence he had accumulated over a three-year period of research, Patman faced two of Mellon's lawyers, A. W. Gregg and D. D. Sheppard.

As it turned out, Mellon never did appear before the committee, for at a critical point in the proceedings he resigned as Treasury Secretary. The announcement came at a dramatic time, at the noon hour on January 19, 1932, just after the Judiciary Committee had recessed to go into executive session. At the White House, President Hoover called in reporters to announce that Mellon was leaving Treasury and was being appointed Ambassador to the Court of St. James. On February 5, 1932, the appointment was confirmed by the Senate. The impeachment proceedings were dropped, but to Patman Mellon's resignation was vindication of his charges.

During the hearings Patman had made a strong case. He related how the statute he was bringing to bear against Mellon had never been successfully amended since its enactment in 1789, despite many attempts, to exclude the Secretary of the Treasury. Many of the amendments actually had made more employees of the government vulnerable to being charged. A letter produced by Patman revealed that though Mellon had sold his stock in the Mellon National Bank, from which he resigned as president in 1921, he still owned a substantial amount of stock in Gulf Oil Corporation, the Aluminum Company of America, the Standard Steel Car Company, and "other business corporations." He owned enough, in fact, to give him working control of these companies. Mellon also admitted to having owned a part of A. Overholt and Company, a company he said had been liquidated before he became Treasury Secretary. Mellon had resigned his directorates, but Patman maintained that he still remained "indirectly concerned," which was forbidden by the statute. To Mellon's assertion that he had divorced himself from banking, Patman pointed out that the Aluminum Company of America owned shares in the Union Trust Company of East St. Louis, Illinois. At one point, after Patman had said Gulf Oil Corporation, which figured its "resources" at $760 million even after the stock market slide, was buying up distressed companies with its surplus, Mellon's attorneys tried to hold his statements to those in the resolution. The Judiciary Committee chairman, Hatton Sumners, said, however, that he could not "hold the investigation . . . within the bounds that would be proper in a court proceeding." Of necessity, "there is considerable latitude allowed." Patman then went on to show tha tthough Mellon had, as he said, given up his directorates, a brother with whom he had "been very close and intimate" had not given up his directorates all the time Mellon was Treasury Secretary.

Next, Patman showed through letters and depositions that

Mellon owned 15 percent of Gulf Oil (a brother owned another 15 percent) and that Gulf owned about forty ships of American registry. Mellon's lawyers argued that Mellon's shares in Gulf Oil and in Aluminum Company of America did not constitute control, and thus Mellon did not "own" the two companies.

Within the committee acrimony and accusation based on party affiliation erupted, as when Patman expressed a belief, after being challenged by Republican members to take his charges to the Attorney General, that he could get no satisfaction there. "If the Department of Justice will let him violate the law and run roughshod over the laws, like I say he has done, and I am convinced he has done, what reason have I to believe that the department would prosecute him in a criminal action?" It was a statement that angered the committee's Republicans, and a verbal brawl ensued over Patman's status. Was it that of a witness, who could be chastised for his statements? Or was he a Congressman exercising a constitutional right to raise charges against a public official? Plainly, Patman was a Congressman doing his duty, said La Guardia in support of Patman and in countering an attack against him by Leonidas C. Dyer of Missouri and Earl C. Michener of Michigan. It was an important point, one that gave substance to Patman's charges against Mellon. It also formed the basis of an opinion from the chairman that Patman had the right to ask questions of Mellon's attorney, A. W. Gregg, an opinion strongly objected to by Dyer.

With this settled, Patman launched into tax refunds, pointing out that while in December, 1919, the Aluminum Company of American had asked for a tax refund of $6.8 million for the depreciation of its "war facilities" during World War I, after Mellon became Treasury Secretary the company asked for $18 million and was grantetd $15 million. "No man should occupy that position, where he could secretly pass upon these cases for his own concern," Patman said to the committee. Yet Mellon did more than that, according to Patman, who promised a witness in support of his charge that "the employees of the Bureau of In-

ternal Revenue are intimidated to the extent that they are afraid
to make a ruling or do anything that is detrimental to the interest
of Mr. Mellon's company, although the law might be violated."
Within the bureau the files pertaining to the tax returns of Mellon's interests were marked "This is a Mellon case." On top of
that auditors who did not examine returns "correctly" had them
sent back again and again.

Basically, Mellon's response, which was made through his attorney Gregg, was that he was not a direct owner of businesses,
but indirectly an owner through stock ownership. Said chairman
Sumner at one point, "Mr. Gregg, does it seem to you to be a
sensible construction of the statute to say a man who owns 99
percent of a business can escape the restraint of the statute by
incorporation? . . . Is there such magic in the act of incorporation
as to make him then a proper person to hold office as against
the statute?" The test, said Gregg, was whether the man was
active in the business. Further, an interest in a corporation can be
a straight-out investment and nothing much else.

With Mellon gone early in 1932, Patman had reason to be
optimistic over the passage of his Bonus Bill. The Republican
administration was still inflexible, but in May veterans from everywhere in the United States began arriving in Washington with the
intention of staying until Congress authorized cashing the Soldiers
Bonus certificates in full. By June 15, with 17,000 men camped
in Washington, the House passed Patman's bill. But on June 17
the Senate killed it. The administration offered the veterans
enough money to get home, but 2,000 refused to go, and on July
28, 1932, troops led by Douglas MacArthur drove the men from
their encampments in a gruesome display of government power.

But then on June 27, in Chicago, Franklin D. Roosevelt told
a National Convention audience of Democrats he had a New Deal
in mind. Privately he told Patman that his Bonus Bill was a good
issue to be used against the Republicans in the November elections, and in response Patman promised to campaign for Roosevelt, almost exclusively on the issue of the bonus payments. True

to his word, Patman stumped in forty-five states. But once elected, Roosevelt called Patman, who was still not a very important Congressman, to a White House meeting at which Roosevelt was shaping his legislative package. "It wasn't long," Patman recalls, "before I discovered why I was there at all. Roosevelt said, 'We'll have to submerge the Bonus Bill.' " Patman's response was a resolve to fight Roosevelt for the bonus payments. "I said, 'When I campaigned for you, I promised to get that bonus paid, and I'm going to try to do it whether you like it or not.' " It was a costly statement to make, since it put Patman in conflict with Roosevelt and the leadership of the House, which was represented at the time by its Speaker, John Nance Garner. Patman, however, had memories of the bonus marchers, with whom he had kept faith and whose right to camp out in Washington he had upheld, despite the actions of Douglas MacArthur. Patman reasoned that if the corporate lobbyists could camp in the Mayflower Hotel, the veterans had a right to camp in the streets. By 1936 Patman had won his fight, and the remaining half of the veterans' bonus was paid, over the veto of Roosevelt. Patman himself was consigned to that doghouse reserved for legislators who fail to follow the party line, and as punishment was again and again denied the place he wanted so badly on the House Banking and Currency Committee.

It was in 1936, too, that Patman found himself at odds with the Federal Reserve Board. Once again, the center of the storm was the bonus payments, and the issue was whether the Federal Reserve Board had the right to counteract the will of Congress through unilateral action. Almost immediately after passage of the Bonus Bill the Federal Reserve Board sharply cut back the money supply in the nation. Thus it neutralized the beneficial effect on the economy that was expected to result from the bonus payments and which was one of the main reasons Congress had passed the Patman bill. In Patman's mind the move linked forever the Federal Reserve Board with the bank's interests, rather than the public interests, for the banks also had opposed the bonus payments.

Patman's attitude toward the Federal Reserve hardened even more when he realized that it operated beyond the control of both the legislative and the executive branches. But, he has maintained since then, the Federal Reserve has even exceeded the powers of independence granted it, and has thwarted the will of legislators and administrations alike to keep the bank mechanism working when to the detriment of human and social priorities. Patman also raised the very real question of whether an agency created by Congress should thumb its nose at its creator. The kind of independence practiced by the Federal Reserve Board, he insists, is not ordained by the statutes creating it. And he is right. The agency was given the right by Congress to produce its own income outside the administration budget. (The Federal Reserve Banks of the nation and their branches are banks for bankers, operating on a profit and loss basis. Each Reserve Bank is a separately incorporated business with nine-man boards of directors elected by the banks they regulate, which are the stockholders. In 1970, for example, the earnings of the Federal Reserve Banks were more than $3.8 billion. After more than $41 million was paid out to stockholders, i.e., the banks who were members, and $321 million in operating expenses was deducted, nearly $3.5 billion was turned over to the United States Treasury. A surplus of $32.5 million, as is the custom, was held back that year.) But though it was given the right to develop its own income, the Federal Reserve System of banks and the Board of Governors in Washington was never given the right to refuse to be audited by Congress, which it has done for years. There has not been much question but that the Federal Reserve Board and the banks in the system have equated independence with secrecy. For example, it took Patman thirty years to get a look at the minutes of the powerful Federal Open Market Committee, which buys and sells government and other securities, and in doing so controls the money supply in the nation. By being a "nuisance," Patman got the Federal Reserve Board to agree to give him the minutes after five years, and then after only ninety days. Even so, the minutes are a sanitized and therefore meaningless version of what goes on—as are the vast majority of publications and news releases distributed by the Federal Reserve. Even the annual report, which the Federal Reserve Act requires to be a "full report of its operations to the Speaker of the House of Representatives," is hardly a revealing document.

Strong Presidents, such as Richard Nixon, have been able to take the agency in tow and get its cooperation on economic programs. But Nixon has had the cooperation of a generally affable man, Arthur F. Burns, the Federal Reserve Board's chairman since 1972. Besides, Nixon appointed Burns to the job so there must have been a meeting of the minds beforehand. And Burns has shown no hesitation about jawboning the banks, especially in his other role as chairman of the President's Committee on Interest and Dividends, for raising interest rates so as to adversely affect the President's economic policies.

Until Burns' arrival, the chairman of the Federal Reserve Board was William McChesney Martin, a man who has been credited with fouling up the economic policies of at least two Presidents, Lyndon Johnson and Harry Truman, and helping to cause the recessions in the eight years of the Eisenhower presidency. Many bankers considered all three Presidents "dunderheads" as far as economics was concerned, ignoring the fact that they were the elected heads of government and accountable for their policies. The Federal Reserve Board was accountable to no one except itself and those it regarded as its peers, i.e., the more powerful bankers of the nation.

When Martin was the head of the Board the war between him and Wright Patman, who argued the accountability issue, was inevitable. In Patman's view the Federal Reserve System and its Board of Governors were created as mechanisms, not policy makers, to handle credit. The credit of the nation belonged to the people and was a national and public resource. The people had the right to direct the use of that credit, meaning that social needs, not the needs of the mechanism, should come first. Thus Patman, as he has said, stood for "bringing the Federal Reserve back into the government to make it responsive to economic policy. It would be just another agency." The effort would have to be tandem effort by both Congress and the President, and the agency that would emerge would still have the two basic responsibilities of the Federal Reserve today, control of the money supply and regulation of the banks. "No one is suggesting," an aide to Patman has said, "that the President should enter into the regulatory function on a day to day basis, but the monetary side of things certainly is a part of the economic policy he is assigned to carry out." There is also the fact, documented many times, that the mystique-wrapped money market operations of the Federal Reserve have at times thrown the United States into recession and fed fire to a runaway boom. The simple fact is that the machinations of the Open Market Operations Committee, which is composed of seven members of the Board and the president of the New York Federal Reserve Bank, are not very precise. The mechanism of buying and selling securities and other financial bits of paper is an unwieldly one with lagging effects. The Federal Reserve actually is blamed by many economists, including some of its own, with causing the depression of the 1930s by its "stupid" monetary policies.

As good a view as any of the board was delivered by Wright Patman just before Martin retired as chairman:

> The Board is a creature of the big banks, particularly the New York City banks, and it is a captive of their will. They operate it. They pay no attention to anyone, to Republicans or to Democrats, or to what they believe. They think they are God. They seized power just like Castro seized Cuba. You take the marble palace down here on Constitution Avenue [the headquarters of the Federal Reserve and home of the Board of Governors in Washington]. Every three weeks, who goes in there to make these decisions? Twelve of the biggest banks [i.e., the Federal Reserve Banks] in America. They're not obligated to the public interest.
>
> Then there are these seven members of the Federal Reserve Board who are supposed to represent the public interest on the Open Market Committee. Those fellows meet in closed-door sessions, secret sessions. They don't make the minutes public for

years. And, incidentally, that's after all statutes of limitation have run out on any crimes that they have committed, you know. They're practically safe. So they determine how much interest shall be paid and they determine the volume of money. Now, two or three thousand bankers know that instantly. They can capitalize on that knowledge and information. But other people don't know about it.

Over the years Patman's outspokenness has been intended to some degree to overcome with its shocking power the indifference of the public and especially of the press to the shenanigans of the banks and the Federal Reserve. He has complained often that events that affect the economic life of everyone appear alongside the food advertisements or in other obscure areas of a newspaper. Thus over the years his conversations, especially those that oc- curred so often between him and Martin during committee hearings, have a salty air. Once he faced Martin with the fact that the Federal Reserve Banks were dues-paying members of the American Bankers Association, then said that "makes you a dues-paying, card-carrying member of that vicious lobby that you are supposed to supervise and do something about and make sure that they are not dishonest." The Reserve Banks had indeed been dues-paying members, giving over $100,000 a year, according to Patman. In 1971 they gave up their memberships.

One day in August, 1965, after Martin had finished making a statement favoring legislation to restrain the vast merger movement among banks, Patman accused Martin of being a tool of the banks, especially the New York banks, and the feud burst forth in acrimonious encounters that became standard. Martin had favored letting stand the mergers of the Manufacturers Trust and the Hanover banks in New York, despite the banks' reneging on their agreement to divest if a U.S. District Court in New York, as it did, found their merger illegal. The hearings were held over legislation that would, among other things, permit the merger and nullify the federal court decision. Martin had implied, too, under questioning by Paul H. Todd, a Michigan Congressman, that the regulatory powers of the Federal Reserve superseded the power of the Justice Department to challenge a merger between banks once the Federal Reserve had given its approval.

It was all Patman could do to restrain himself. When his turn came to question Martin, Patman attacked the "independence" of the Federal Reserve, saying it was tied to the apron strings of its most powerful member, the Federal Reserve Bank of New York. Before the exchange was finished, Patman had compared Martin to a piano player in a mining town whorehouse who had played his music downstairs for years without knowing about the vice upstairs. Patman's main point was accountability, or the lack of it:

PATMAN: Mr. Martin, I wanted to ask you some questions about these . . . supervisory agencies. The Federal Reserve not only claims and asserts, but they demand independence, which of course I do not concede. I still believe in the Constitution and I think that is in opposition to the Constitution, for the reason that the people framing it did a wonderful job. They wanted everything arranged in a way that the people who were elected to public office, the members of the House, could be defeated every two years, and the members of the Senate could be defeated every six years if they did not perform their duties faithfully and well. All public affairs were to be performed by the government and the citizens could hold these members responsible if they administered their duties improperly. The people could penalize them, could defeat them for office. They would have something to lose. A member of Congress has something to lose if he does not do the right thing. But an independent agency has nothing to lose. If you are correct in your assumption of independence, and there is no question in my mind that you are not correct, but that you feel like you are, you cannot be punished for any mistakes you make. The people cannot reach you.

MARTIN: You never let me forget anything, do you?

PATMAN: I beg your pardon.

MARTIN: I say you never let me forget anything.

PATMAN: I know, but we cannot punish you. Even if your acts are equal to high crimes and misdemeanors, we cannot do anything about it. You see, the Federal Reserve, when it was organized, comprised 12 separate banks. It was not a central bank . . . President Woodrow Wilson would not stand for a central bank.

I think if he were living today he would not be in favor of a central bank. So he would not permit a central bank to be organized, and we had 12 separate banks. But there were people who did not want this. . . . The big banks did not want it either. They did not want a thing to do with it. Then they commenced ways of getting control of it. They wanted Wall Street running this Federal Reserve banking system. I think they made it very plain that they wanted it that way. So in 1921, when Mr. Mellon came in as Secretary of the Treasury, he organized a Coordinating Committee: You remember reading about this Coordinating Committee, do you not?

MARTIN: You and I have been over it many times.

PATMAN: Yes, sir. And this Coordinating committee was without sanction of law. They had no power to do anything and Mr. Mellon wanted to do it anyway and he did. He organized the Coordinating Committee and he got all these 12 banks to agree that the Committee would run the whole show. That meant that the bankers were running it. Of course, they had no power to do it at all. Then when the Depression came along and members of Congress were willing to vote for anything anyone claimed would get us out of the Depression or make times easier, all of this banker domination over the people's money was written into the 1935 act. The result was a Federal Central Bank controlled by the bankers. And they wrote into the law something else that lets you way away from the people or any responsibility for your acts. They built a stormproof shelter with all the modern conveniences so that you could not be reached. They set up this Federal Reserve Board of seven members with 14-year terms, one selected every two years. That meant that the President had to be in office two full terms, eight years, before he could appoint a simple majority of the Federal Reserve Board's seven members. He would select three the first two years of his second term. Then only during his last two years in office, when he was in a lameduck status, could be finally have a majority appointed by him. [Patman then suggested that the two-term limit on Presidents worked as a device that prevented "people from having a voice over their own monetary system."]

MARTIN: Mr. Chairman, this is the first time I have ever heard the two terms for President used as a direct thrust at the Federal Reserve.

PATMAN: Oh, certainly it was.

MARTIN: This is the first time I have heard it.

PATMAN: It has been very effective, too. For instance, when President Kennedy had the opportunity to appoint a chairman of the Federal Reserve Board he felt at the time—I believe he did—that he could go out and select the best man in the United States. Many people did. But he could not. He had to select one of the seven on that board. And after he looked at the seven, he concluded that since Mr. Martin was the senior man, and had been there as [acting] chairman for a long time, that it would disrupt things to select anyone else. So he was a sort of captive. He had to take you.

MARTIN: This, Mr. Patman, is your story.

PATMAN: Yes, it is my story.

MARTIN: This is your story and you are entitled to it. Mr. Kennedy is dead and I cannot get him to say what he said and I would not dream of putting in the record what he said to me, but I think that President Kennedy was a truthful man and he did not give me the story the way you are giving it.

PATMAN: I know, but he was in a straitjacket. He could not do anything else. There you had the President of the United States without freedom of choice.

MARTIN: He went out of his way to tell me he was not in a straitjacket. That is all I am saying.

PATMAN: No freedom of choice. He had no freedom of choice. He had to take one of the seven. That is a difficult situation for the President to be in, but that is the truth.

MARTIN: Let me say this . . .

PATMAN: You say you are in favor of the President's having a chairman of the board whose term is coterminus with that of the President. I think you are to be commended for being forthright in your statement, and I am going to give you a chance, because we are going to attach it to this bill right here.

MARTIN: You and I have always been very good-natured about this and I will continue always to be good-natured about it, but I just do not want the record to leave the implication that President Kennedy was talking to me on the basis of being two-faced in what he was saying. I shall not go into the record of that conversation, but I was there and you were not. So you have your story and I have mine.

PATMAN: The only important thing about it is that he had to take one of the seven. . . . That is the truth, is it not, Mr. Martin?

MARTIN: I just want the record to show he did not have to take me.

PATMAN: Answer that yes or no. Isn't it a fact that he had to take one of the seven?

MARTIN: The answer is that under the law he had to take it. But I am making it specific that he did not have to take me.

PATMAN: No. But you were the experienced man. . . . Furthermore there were two new men on the board.

MARTIN: It happened in the days . . .

REP. WIDNALL (the senior minority member of the House Banking and Currency Committee): Is it not a fact that a member could have resigned and another new member been appointed?

PATMAN: But none of them offered to do that.

WIDNALL: This is your opportunity to tell what you know.

MARTIN: I am not going to draw on President Kennedy, who is dead and cannot answer.

PATMAN: It is not necessary. The only point I am raising is that Mr. Kennedy had to appoint one of the seven. That is the law. The law has been changed over the years, just a little bit here and a little bit there. But you know, this 90-year-old bankers lobby has been a pretty effective lobby.

MARTIN: It certainly is if it could get that two terms for President through. That is the first time I ever thought the bankers lobby was that powerful.

PATMAN: That is right. They are smart, you know, and they are working for just one thing, to help banks where they could and keep banks from being harmed where they could. . . . Now a member of Congress comes in for two years, four years or six years—in and out. They have 300 things to think about all the time. They are not just thinking about banking. But this bankers lobby is right here on the trail all the time. They get little things done here and little things done there. Finally, we wake up, we don't have 12 separate, independent banks at all. We have one bank in New York which runs the entire show. [The president of the Federal Reserve Bank of New York is a permanent member of the Federal Open Market Committee, the most powerful committee of the Federal Reserve Board. Presidents of other Reserve Banks serve one-year terms in rotation. At the same time a senior officer of the New York bank is appointed annually by the committee to conduct purchases of securities in the open market with the intent to affect the money supply and, therefore, credit. The New York bank also is the agent for the Federal Reserve and the Treasury that trades in foreign currencies, as it did during the dollar crises of 1972 and 1973. Since 1956 the president of the New York bank has been Alfred Hayes, a man who prefers the shadows and who came from the New York Trust Company, now the Chemical Bank and before that National City Bank. As well as a member, Hayes was for many years vice chairman of the Open Market Committee.]

MARTIN: I was reading the testimony the last time I was up here and you were developing this point about the New York bank, you know, how they ran everything and I had no control over Mr. Hayes. I found it quite confusing because earlier you said I was the most important civil servant in the world and here I could not even control one of my subordinates.

PATMAN: Well, you know, one time out in a western mining town, they had a grand jury investigation of a boardinghouse. This was the most important place in the community, of course. They had lots of activity there. Downstairs, they had music. They had a piano player. Upstairs, they had gambling and all forms of vice. The grand jury discovered that the piano player had been playing a piano downstairs there for four years without knowing what was going on upstairs. I just wonder if Mr. Martin has been playing the piano down here in Washington without knowing what is going on up in New York. The Federal Reserve Act says that the president of the Federal Reserve Bank in New York has complete control over that bank, that all of its officers and directors are subject to his supervision and authority. The law says that. It is written that way. You cannot write it any plainer. No regulation entered by Mr. Martin or the board can change the existing law . . . [but] the Federal Reserve Bank of New York runs the whole show, while the other 11 Federal Reserve banks do not even know the condition of their own accounts until the Federal Reserve Bank of New York advises them what their condition is. San Francisco, Atlanta, Dallas, all the rest of them, do not know what their condition is because all the books are kept by the Federal Reserve Bank in New York. All the bonds are kept there. All the business is done there. It is all done at the Federal Reserve Bank in New York. Now all this has happened over a period of time by just getting in little amendments here and there, apparently insignificant amendments, but when you add them all up, you have this thing in a condition where people do not have much voice in their monetary affairs. . . . In fact, you admitted to me, Mr. Martin, that if President Johnson had one idea about monetary affairs and interest rates and you and the Federal Reserve Board had another, you would prevail over the President of the United States. Did you not say that to me?

MARTIN: I said that—

PATMAN: You said that, that is right. Here you are, you are claiming more power than the President of the United States and he is elected by all the people. You are not elected by all the people.

The Federal Reserve was not the only agency regulating the banks that had taken power Congress had not delegated, as Patman indicated in an exchange that came just a few minutes later:

PATMAN: ". . . You say you have this independence and so do these other supervisory agencies, the Federal Deposit Insurance Corporation, and the Comptroller of the Currency. The Comptroller [William B. Camp] receives all this money from the banks he supervises and when he was up here before this subcommittee he said I have always believed true that old saying, "Whose bread I eat, his song I sing." I said I would like for him to elaborate on that. I have not yet gotten an answer from him, but that is the truth, I think. He is getting his money from these banks, all of it. He can spend that money any way he wants to. He can use the power of the Federal Government to make all the national banks pay into this fund. He can use that money for a world trip, and incidentally, he did. He can use it for anything. . . . He is just as independent as the Federal Reserve, and that is plenty independent. Then you take the FDIC. None of the FDIC assessments on insured banks are audited by the General Accounting Office. The Federal Reserve has never been audited by an independent auditor by the government or by the General Accounting Office. We do not know what you have done. We assume you have been honest, but we do not know. All the others are honest; but they are audited. And here is the FDIC, independent, too. It does not come to Congress for any appropriation. It is independent. Members of the Congress can be chastised by their constituents for permitting certain things to go on and we have to say "We do not know, we have no power over them." I just wonder whether these three agencies that are off to themselves and do not come to Congress are any different from other agencies. In other agencies, if they collect money, they have to put it in the Treasury and then the Appropriations Committee is compelled to appropriate that money so they can use it. That is the constitutional way of doing it. But these three agencies have gotten off to themselves and the only one now that has anything to do with these bank mergers [the subject of the hearings] is the Department of Justice that comes to the Congress like all agencies should. The American Bankers Association is now trying to get Justice out of the picture. In other words, they are trying to shoot the last policeman that is on the corner.

Patman stopped, then, telling Martin that once again, as he had so many times before, he was going to submit a bill to bring the Federal Reserve under the jurisdiction of the administration and the Congress.

In Martin, Patman saw a product of Wall Street. Martin had been president of the New York Stock Exchange. "There was real disagreement between the two men," an associate of Patman's has said. "Patman really felt Martin was trying to fool him. Trying to fool the Congress. Trying to use fluff public relations methods to run around the Congress. Patman felt Martin often lied. Martin often circled around Patman and lobbied with members of Patman's own committee in a manner that was not acceptable. It's true that these agencies always do a certain amount of lobbying. But Martin often used personal events within the committee to influence members and play one off against the other. You don't do that. Patman almost got personal with Martin, though that's not Patman's real style. He's given every agency head man hell at one time or another, but not in the bitter manner he did with Martin. It was not only the issue. It was Martin's style. He felt Martin was using unfair tactics and misleading, even lying. At least two studies show how central banks in other countries have policies that require them to respond to social needs. But before those studies Martin came up on the Hill and said that every country that has tried this has become a Communist dictatorship. This just wasn't true, as the studies show. Then he denied that central banks, like the Federal Reserve, took an active role in supporting the economic objectives of their countries. The truth is they did, as the studies showed again. Patman saw Martin not as a banker, which he wasn't; nor as an economist, which he wasn't. He saw him more as a political operator. The fact is he probably could have become a very successful politician. Patman especially disliked the way Martin would do such things as use the private dining room at the Federal Reserve to entertain key columnists and reporters. He used this device very carefully. The reporters were invited there, individually, and it was handled as a great honor. You could almost spot the guy that had been there. A week or two later there would come a great, glowing column about the wisdom of the Federal Reserve."

Since Arthur Burns became chairman of the Federal Reserve, Patman has harbored no such personal ill feelings. Philosophically, the same basic differences exist, but Patman trusts Burns, and as Patman's associate has stated it, "Martin and Burns may be very similar, say in their feelings about monetary policy, but Patman trusts Burns. He thinks Burns tells the truth and pursues his philosophical point of view honestly."

Contrary to what might be expected and to the image bankers themselves like to draw, Patman has no real dislike of bankers. He has said, "Bankers themselves are good people. You won't find any more bad apples in the barrel than you do in the congressional barrel or any other. I don't tackle them from that standpont, because there are good ones and bad ones. Some of them are real greedy, but some of them are not."

Yet Patman is not above pulling their tails. During hearings on the bill that would have guaranteed $250 million in loans to Lockheed Aircraft Corporation, loans the banks would not make without a government guarantee of payment, Patman forced twenty-four of the nation's most powerful bankers to answer to a roll call as schoolboys might. The incident occurred on July 15, 1971, and Patman was well within the rules of parliamentary procedure and tradition when he demanded that each banker state his name, occupation, and that he was authorized to speak at the hearing. Among those required to answer the roll call were such men as Donald M. Graham, chairman of Continental Illinois Bank, Chicago; Chauncey J. Medberry, chairman of the Bank of America; and John F. McGillicuddy, president of the Manufacturers Hanover Trust. The representative of the Chemical

Bank was asked to hold up his hand when answering the roll call, and when Norman Barker, Jr., president of United California Bank in Los Angeles, answered out of turn Patman forced him to wait, then to repeat himself.

Patman has recalled the occasion at times with relish: "Yeah. You see, I first said, let's have the twenty-four bankers stand up. All right, they stood up nicely. They were nice fellas. Then after they sat down I said, the assistants that you brought around to help you. Each one of them could bring one assistant. They were in the next row. They stood up. Then I said all of you here present in the hall who are connected directly or indirectly with the Lockheed case and interested in it, stand up, too. And all of the rest of them stood up."

A partisan of the banks has said that Patman was the only man who could cast the biggest banks in the role of underdogs. The statement is an exaggeration, of course, but it does suggest the vigor of Patman's lifelong campaign "to see people get a square deal."

17

Pushing and Shoving

AS A FIRE-EATER, Wright Patman hardly looks the role. Rather he projects the air of a kindly, though though alert, chubby grandfather whose roots go deep into American life. A Baptist, Shriner, Elk, Mason, Eagle, and American Legionnaire all rolled into one, he has what might be called a cherubic smile. His blue eyes are deep-set and gentle, and his voice is usually gentle, too, even when talking to bankers. A writer once compared Patman with Victor Moore, an actor who projected himself and the characters he played as "kindly, fey and fuzzy-headed." It is doubtful that Patman has ever been fuzzy-headed, yet there are times, especially during his committee hearings, when he seems unable to grasp the point. The consensus has been that this is a put-on, adopted as a defense mechanism against a committee whose members are frequently uncontrollable, for it is often they who are trying to make a point. Yet bankers who have been dealing with Patman for decades are split over whether he is fuzzy-headed or not. Some say flatly Patman does not understand banking. But some of the impression of fuzzy-headedness could come from the fact that Patman never shouts during committee meetings, though he himself is sometimes shouted at by his own committee members, apparently in an effort to impress him with what they are saying. Further, despite being unpopular with many of his colleagues, Patman will not say anything against any of them, at least not for publication. He leaves that to his admirers, who often do attack his enemies with

some relish. Patman has only kind words for Roosevelt, despite
the way Roosevelt used him back in the 1930s. Though his
committee members in their occasional revolt have resorted to
subterfuge and a secret meeting or two without him, he will not
comment, at least not bitterly, about it, for he feels they are his
colleagues.

In fact, sitting in his office in the Rayburn Building in Washington, where behind him an enormous window frames the Capitol (as in just about every movie on the FBI), Patman tends to
be expansive and generous. His harshest words are reserved for
the banks, and not all the banks at that. He rarely hits at the
Bank of America, though it does occasionally come under his
guns. His mail from bankers is such that he feels that half the
bankers of the United States are behind him, especially those in
control of moderate-sized banks. The big banks, particularly those
in New York, are his special target, since he feels they do not
serve the public interest. Patman agrees with what has been supported by important studies, i.e., the New York banks suck up
the funds of individuals in their banking areas, then lend the
money to businesses geographically distant at a high rate of
profit, while the local area goes without. It is a telling point. For
the New York banks to cap this social indifference with arrogance
raises Patman's ire.

The impunity with which such banks have raised interest rates
is a subject also likely to raise his ire, for he considers that the
way interest rates are raised, with the New York banks almost
invariably taking the lead, is almost tantamount to a conspiracy
that violates the antitrust laws. Banks may argue, of course, that
identical interest rates are merely a reflection of keping up with
the competition or responding to the laws of supply and demand,
even when the product is money.

Time and again Patman has asked the Federal Reserve to
close its windows to banks that are part of the "conspiracy" and
want to borrow from the Federal Reserve. On the surface, higher
interest rates have been explained away as a device for fighting

inflation, but it is a murky explanation at best, since inflation has run rampant in the United States even as interest rates have risen and bank profits have soared. For example, during the period 1965 to 1969 the prime rate went from 5 percent to 8.5 percent, a rise of 70 percent. There is no telling how much most borrowers pay, since only a relative handful of borrowers get the prime rate. In those same years the net profits of commercial banks rose from more than $2.5 billion to $3.4 billion, or 36 percent. Today, bankers are promising stockholders annual earnings increases of 15 percent.

Patman has always fought the vested interests. Bankers like to call him a populist and thus suggest he is the champion of a cause that died many, many years ago. Patman himself does not mind being called a populist. "A populist is for the people; well, I'm for the people," he has said. A better label might be watchdog, for like the populists of the past, he is not against capitalism and banking, only for its decentralization, and most important, for a fair shake for everyone.

From the beginning Patman's pushing and shoving in the House of Representatives got him into serious trouble with the leadership. It was not only the denial of a place on the House Banking and Currency Committee until the late 1930s. It was the denial of honors and other such gestures of splendid service as well. At home, however, in the eighteen counties that constitute the First District of Texas Patman is a folk hero who seems to have satisfied everyone. He has brought home "pork," as he calls it, through the construction of two arsenals, an army depot, and a lake that supplies water to local paper mills. He has personally helped blacks in his district to set up credit unions and has spoken out nationally against the erection of ghetto housing for blacks. He has even pleased many bankers at home who have feared that without Patman the major banks of the country, especially those in New York, would be opening up in Texas.

Patman's interests, however, have transcended those of his own constituency, and undoubtedly contribute to his position of folk hero far more than the pork. Despite little cooperation from his party leadership, he has sponsored and supported a long list of major legislation. Besides the Soldiers Bonus Bill, he was a co-author of the Robinson-Patman Act, legislation passed in 1936 which became known as the Golden Rule of Business. Its purpose was to protect small business from the predatory tactics of large business. It was typical of Patman. In the years after Patman was a co-sponsor of most of the legislation passed that affected small business. He was also the co-author of the Smaller War Plants Corporation Act of 1942, a bill that helped small manufacturers get contracts to produce war or essential civilian goods. He co-sponsored the Federal Credit Union Act, was the author of the Veterans Emergency Housing Act of 1946 and the Full Employment Act of 1946. He was the author of the Foreign Bank Secrecy Bill, which passed the House unanimously in May, 1970, and whose purpose was to control the use of foreign bank accounts to hide illegal earnings. Once when it seemed banks would become sellers of lottery tickets. Patman led the fight to prevent this, arguing that gambling and thrift hardly went together. In the late 1960s he led an investigation into abuses of tax-exempt foundations and became the leadoff witness in a congressional hearing that ended in the Tax Reform Act of 1969. Under the act, private foundations were put under tougher expenditures control. Patman came up with fascinating information, showing, for example, that the Ford Foundation spent half a million dollars a year on public relations; that the Rockefeller Foundation spent half as much on its New York office as it spent on charity throughout the nation.

Most important of all, of course, is that Patman has been the sponsor of virtually all legislation dealing with banks, savings and loan associations, and the financial community in general. Generally, he has fought for plentiful credit on reasonable terms, and as a result has been regarded merely as a man who wants low interest rates, especially by a press that has failed to take his real measure. To be sure, he has fought hard against high interest rates, since they are regressive and hurt those with the lowest incomes. He also introduced a House version of the Truth in Lending Act that was tougher than the one introduced into the Senate. And of course, he has been the sponsor for many years of H.R. 11, a bill that would shorten the terms of the members of the Federal Reserve Board, require audits of the Federal Reserve System's books, and require that the System come to Congress for appropriations as required by the U.S. Constitution. Patman has also supported proposals to require the Federal Reserve to allocate the nation's credit resources equitably so that small business, farmers, home buyers, and the general public "can have their fair share of lendable funds."

There are those in both major political parties of the nation who would agree with such a statement, yet Patman rarely has had the full cooperation of his own Democratic party. If anything, he has been duped by it, and despite remaining loyal to it, opposed by its most powerful members.

Among the Presidents he knew well there were Lyndon Johnson, Roosevelt, and John Kennedy, for whose election, it is said by some politicians he delivered the state of Texas. Whether Patman did or not, it was he who did deliver an audience of 100,000 when Kennedy spoke in Patman's home base of Texarkana and urged Kennedy the Catholic to discuss religion in a staunchly Baptist region whose population was not always friendly to Catholics. In describing Patman's stance toward Johnson, fealty would be a proper word. As it happened, the relationship proved to be a burden to Patman, whose association with Johnson made him vulnerable.

The relationship actually began with Johnson's father, Sam Ealy Johnson, a seatmate of Patman's in the 1921 Texas legislature. The two men were not close, but Patman told a reporter once that Sam Johnson was "an honest, straight-forward cowboy." It was a conclusion reached apparently more out of observation that association, however. Johnson admired Patman to the extent that when his son Lyndon went to Washington he advised him to emulate Patman, who had already made himself a major reputation. It was reported more than once that Lyndon Johnson said, "When I came up to Washington my daddy told me if you want to know how to vote, watch Wright Patman and vote like he votes because he always vote for the people." Johnson took the advice and aligned himself with the popular actions of Patman. At first. Then, of course, Johnson plotted the course that took him to the presidency.

It was in 1964, when Patman was unearthing information about the tax-free status of the private foundations, that his association with Johnson, and perhaps party affiliation as well, made him what one reporter described as a "fall guy." Five of the foundations that were more front than foundation turned out to be in Texas. Worse, many a Johnson associate was involved in them. There was more, though. When Patman unfolded the incestuous story behind interlocking directorships, sure enough, there again stood many associates of Johnson, his President and friend. On top of all that, Johnson generally bowed to the economic program called for by the Federal Reserve, and this helped neutralize the warrior in Patman. In an oft-told story Patman once went directly to Johnson on the matter of the private foundations to ask his old friend to send a message over to Congress to help Patman wage his fight. The President was reported by sources close to Patman to have said that it was time to "forget it. I'm going to be asking the foundations for several millions of dollars over the next few years to help my library." Patman's response is unknown. It can only be speculated that some of his subsequent refusals to attend luncheons at the White House where he had often been a guest of Johnson's, were caused by Johnson's urging to "forget it." Paradoxically, it wasn't till Johnson decided in 1967 not to run in 1968 and Richard Nixon, a Republican, succeeded him that Patman could become a more effective legislator than he had ever been. The restraint imposed on him because of his still close friendship with Johnson had been removed.

In 1963 Patman had finally won that long-coveted chairmanship of the House Banking and Currency Committee by outlasting his opposition, suggesting that the much maligned seniority system can not be all bad. Indeed, in 1973, he was the dean of both houses of Congress.

Patman's seniority has given him access to staff, a crucial need for an effective Congressman, through several committees— the Banking and Currency Committee, of course, of which he is chairman, but also through his membership on the Joint Economic Committee, the Joint Committee on Defense Production, and until recently, the Small Business Committee of the House of Representatives. On Capitol Hill, Patman's staff people are termed "good" by admirers, something less than that, e.g., "intruders in the legislative process," by opponents of Patman's ideas. The staffs of Patman, especially the Banking and Currency staff, have been criticized for being overly zealous, but the truth is that, like any effective staff, it responds to a man who is constantly pushing them. A "good" staff, in fact, will atrophy rapidly without constant pressure.

In Patman's case, the pressure has been near constant, and since 1964, when he was hired, that pressure has been conveyed to others by Paul Nelson, Patman's staff director. A New Yorker, Nelson holds a Ph.D. in economics from Columbia University and is the man who "bears the responsibility for what does or does not happen in the staff," according to an associate.

Nelson maintains liaison not only with Patman but with all the members of the House Banking and Currency Committee.

In the years he has been its director, Nelson has also built the staff. There is, for example, Jake Lewis, a tall, lanky writer knowledgeable in the ways of politics and Washington. It was Lewis who began writing and defining Patman's positions in speeches delivered by Patman and in releases. Lewis is the contact, too, for newsmen.

Whenever it is practical, the entire staff participates in the investigations, but often a single investigator is assigned to ferret out facts, particularly in special investigations. Benet D. Gellman,

for example, a Columbia law school graduate, left the Executive
Office of the President in 1965 and a job in the Office of Emergency Planning to become a member of Patman's investigative
staff. One of the foremost experts on banking law in the country
who is not beholden to bankers, Gellman has provided the substance for Patman's charges in such controversial issues as one-
bank holding, bank merger, interlocking directorships, and the
control over corporations being exercised by bank trust departments.

Patman's chief investigator is Curt Prins, a man who works
across the board but has also produced a great deal of material
in such areas as Federal Reserve expenditures, the Tax and Loan
accounts of the banks and housing program investigations. Patman's investigation of the foundations was supported by material
dug up by Mike Flaherty, a lawyer with an expertise in taxes, and
by Rick Barnes, a man with a background in accounting.

Occasionally, Patman uses a team of his investigators, as
when the committee began investigating the role of foreign and
domestic banking institutions in connection with campaign financing related to the Watergate affair. Involved were Paul Nelson, Jake Lewis, Curt Prins, and Davis Couch.

It is an intensely loyal staff that Patman has built, one whose
members cast soured glances at their counterparts in Senate committees who have gone over to lobbying for the other side. Though
maintaining a low profile publicly, occasionally, they have been
so active during hearings that the opposition, which was often
within the committee, complained about them doing work legislators themselves ought to be doing. When Patman dumbfounded
the banks in 1968 by going to the floor of the House of Representatives and rewriting his one-bank holding bill, he could do it
only because of his staff's work. Recollecting the event in his
Washington office, he has related this account of how he operated
with Nelson, Gellman, and Lewis standing by: "Well, here's how
it came about. These fellows here helped me. Some of my committee members, they knocked me over good. [Patman's bill had

been rewritten extensively by committee members led by William Widnall.] That was in committee. They just stripped the bill of everything that was good. They did it by amendment. And I had to take what was left, you know. And I asked for a rule on it. Well, we brought the bill out with these amendments, but all the things that were knocked out, well they came up fresh and new in the House. In the House we helped the members who wanted certain things done, and we got the bill written. We made offers on the Republican side, and we offered them on the Democratic side. When we got through we had the strongest bill ever offered. And it called for a roll call and only 24 members out of 435 voted against it."

Patman has also thrown a rope or two around the Federal Reserve, though a real corraling of the "Fed" undoubtedly will take the combined efforts of both Congress and the administration. There is no doubt, however, that Patman has changed the emphasis in the role of the Federal Reserve. As the lack of visitors at the Federal Reserve building in visitor-flooded Washington suggests, the Federal Reserve prefers to be left to itself. Those visitors who do turn up do not receive a welcome. But Patman has succeeded in dragging the Federal Reserve and its staff partly out of the shadows by making the board the guardian of things it does not want to guard (it would much prefer to concentrate on monetary policy). For example, the board is the agency responsible for protecting the public in a broad sense in the area of credit under the clauses of the Truth in Lending Act. The passage of the Bank Holding Company Act also thrust the Federal Reserve into the limelight as a guardian of the public interest. In Patman's view and in the view of some of his staff these acts have shoved Federal Reserve more into the economic regulation business. But it does not know it yet, and if it does, it is staying quiet.

Patman is probably the most formidable foe banking has ever had to face. Yet his successes in recent years have not been the result of his efforts alone. A rising tide of criticism against banks, the rise of consumerism, and even the spread of banks into other business activities have been significant. In the passage of bank holding legislation a substantial counterforce of businessmen appeared at hearings and wrote letters demanding that the banks keep their place, i.e., stay in banking. Insurance companies, data processing companies, travel agencies, and others turned up to fight the banks.

Unfortunately this does not happen often. Says Lewis, Patman's speech writer and press relations representative, "Usually there is no one on the other side. The banks come in, in numbers. Ralph Nader may come in. Now occasionally the AFL–CIO comes in. But there's very little on that side, the public side. The consumer side. The whole theory of the committee system in the Congress is that you have some kind of adversary system. But there is a lack of the adversary situation on financial legislation. And it really hurts. Until these consumer organizations start coming in and raising hell it will hurt and affect the guy on the street. The real test, too, of a lot of consumer organizations, say Common Cause, is whether they are going to take up the real, complex issues, the subtle ones that affect millions and millions of people."

Most newspapers and other publications fail to convey the issues, with just a handful of exceptions. One of these is the *American Banker*, which, interestingly, though written and edited for bankers, is praised highly by Lewis and the rest of the staff for its coverage. The lack of an adversary worries others as well as Patman. Senator Clifford Case, a New Jersey Republican, has gone so far as to sponsor a bill to form a consumer advocate to intervene in hearings.

As so often in his career, Patman's troubles even now begin with some of the more powerful members of his own party. In recent years one has been Wilbur Mills, chairman of the House Ways and Means Committee. Mills heads the committee that determines who shall be members of other committees. It is a powerful post, obviously. But tradition dictates that the chairmen of the various committees be consulted. Patman, however, has never been consulted by Mills over who was being assigned to the House Banking and Currency Committee. This lack of consultation has been critical, for frequently Patman has watched Democrats supposedly in tune with his thinking join Republicans to vote down his legislation. Once when Patman ran in a bill to audit the Federal Reserve, the Republicans on his committee voted solidly against it, while enough Democrats "on my side, whom the bankers can influence," voted with the Republicans. So often has this happened that Patman got his director of staff, Paul Nelson, to keep a tally. Nearly all those who had defected, he discovered, had been put on his committee after Mills had become chairman of the House Ways and Means Committee.

"All of them were put on after Mills was made chairman," Patman says. "So Mills, instead of being a great man for the public, has been a great man for the New York and Wall Street interests." If some bitterness comes through here it is because Mills seems to Patman to be a perpetrator of breakdown in the governmental process. He has accused Mills and the twenty-five members of the Ways and Means Committee of playing a game of footsy in which each member of the committee could have a bill of his choice brought to the House. "I made enemies," Patman admits, "but you see they were actually giving each of the twenty-five members of the Ways and Means Committee a bill of his choice. Each man could pick out a bill, and they would have a meeting, and all twenty-five of them would unanimously agree to report the bill to the House and recommend passage, and ask that it be passed by unanimous consent. They said all twenty-five members had looked into it, but what they didn't say was that every one of the twenty-five also had a bill. The bills ran into taxes and big money. Why, it's criminal, it's absolutely criminal. You can't have a government last too long if it intends to accelerate things like that."

Patman will not disclose their names, but as he looks over the members of his committees during the past sessions of Congress he says with certainty that "a percentage, I'm convinced, arrived here on the committee because of lobbying pressures from the trade associations, the banks, the savings and loan associations, and the others."

One of Patman's staff members suggests that the basis for assignment to a House committee these days is not "what the purists and the apologists for the House will tell you it is. That is, that it is done without any outside pressure. That this is one area no lobbyist would dare enter into. But this is false. They do. All the trade associations in Washington, whether it's banking matters or agriculture, or what have you, they watch the vacancies come up. And if they have a friend on Ways and Means, they call him and they get him to promote someone. And sometimes these members come in and they want certain assignments, and they lobby for themselves. They might have contact with the Speaker of the House. So there's a variety of ways they arrive here on the Banking Committee."

Mills does consult with other committee chairmen in the House, but it's doubtful he ever will with Patman. Mills was once a director of a bank in Arkansas, while sitting as chairman of the Ways and Means Committee.

Those who have watched Patman and Mills duel on the floor of the House accept that there is a philosophical difference between the two men that makes them dislike each other naturally. "I think that Patman," says one of these observers, "is very much a democrat with a small 'd'. He doesn't mind bringing up controversial matters and letting the chips fall where they may. He doesn't mind if he gets beat, either. Mills is one of these guys who likes to harbor power. If he can't get a majority he doesn't go for a vote. He'll sit there for two or three years and never put out a bill because he can't let the pressure get him. He's a manipulator. This closed-rule business, for example, of never going to the floor, of not allowing any amendments on bills. Patman has fought closed rules ever since he's been here. He's a much more democratic personality than Mills. I think this just bothers Mills. It's Mills' idea that he should not bring a bill up unless he has all the votes locked in. This makes his record look very good, and this is one of the reasons for all those press stories he gets. But he will never bring out controversial bills. Patman takes just the opposite view. He goes out there. As he did in the Bank Holding Company bill. Now Mills would have taken the committee bill and said this is the bill, and he would have defended it, not changed it, each step down the line." Patman has his own opinion of Mills, and recently expressed it this way: "Ever since he's been in, the taxes of the big corporations have gone down, down, down. Of course, the burdens on the poor have gone up, up, up." It has been Mills, of course, who has had control of tax legislation and reform bills in recent years, including the tax reform legislation of 1969. In 1973 he was calling for further "reform."

In August, 1973, Wright Patman reached his eightieth birthday at a time when he was serving his forty-fifth year in the House of Representatives. With his election in November, 1972, to his twenty-third term, he became the most senior member of the House (his old friend, associate, and monopoly hunter, Emanuel Celler, lost that place by failing to be reelected). Ahead lay one of the most intricate banking wrangles ever. A presidential commission, the Hunt Commission, had produced a report intended to be a plan for restructuring the entire banking industry, including savings and loans associations and mutual savings banks. All year Patman's staff had been quietly forming other ideas for restructuring banking, ideas closer to Patman's. The Hunt Commission had merely dealt with the mechanism. It would, for example, permit savings banks to offer checking accounts. But Patman was "unhappy with the whole thing," and if legislation based on the Hunt Commission recommendations were sent up in any form he was planning to counter it with his own concept of structuring.

He had gained, he felt, in terms of his committee members. Changes through retirements and transfers had given his committee what he considered "an attractive" group of young Congressmen. There was Andy Young from Atlanta, who had been an assistant to Martin Luther King in the Southern Christian Leadership Conference. There was Pete Stark, an ex-banker from Oakland who had sold out his banking interests and had become a force for reform in banking. There were also John Mokely of Boston and Walter Fauntroy of the District of Columbia. At the same time, Patman had lost members who at one time or another often joined the Republican minority.

The fight over reform in banking promises to be an extraordinary one in terms of its breadth and intensity. It is probable that Patman has never been in a better position to wage that fight.

PART SEVEN

Conclusion

18

The Reforms That Are Needed

I N D E C E M B E R, 1971, President Nixon's Commission
on Financial Structure and Regulation (the Hunt Commission) submitted its report for restructuring and regulating the commercial banks and a handful of other financial institutions, including savings banks, savings and loan associations,
credit unions, private pension plans, and life insurance companies. One of the myths that has hovered over the Hunt Commission report, a myth that is generally furthered by bankers, is
that its recommendations add up to reform.

The truth is something very different. As any dictionary defines it, reform means the correction of abuses and corrupt practices. The recommendations of the Hunt report, which were intended to be the basis of legislation sponsored by the Nixon
administration, would do no such thing. They would merely give
the banks and the other financial institutions the bits and pieces
of each other's markets that they have been craving for years. In
the name of competition and free enterprise there would be a new
division of the pie. For example, savings banks and savings and
loan associations, which have been restricted to making loans to
home buyers, would be permitted to make highly profitable consumer loans, the aim being to raise profits for the two lenders.
Credit unions would be given a whole array of consumer lending
powers, as well as permission to sell traveler's checks on the side.
The savings banks and savings and loan associations would also
be allowed to put their own money into investments in develop-

ment corporations, a recommendation that would drastically pros-
titute their role as lenders. Direct investment in real estate, either
alone or with "other organizations," would also be allowed.

As for the commercial banks, they would be permitted "to
invest in any assets in amounts to aggregate not more than 3 percent of total assets or 30 percent of capital, surplus and undivided
profits, whichever is less. . . ." That recommendation represents
an extraordinary loophole that could give the banks enormous
control over U.S. business. But that particular recommendation
was only the beginning. The Hunt Commission would permit the
commercial banks, their subsidiaries, and their holding companies
to manage and sell mutual funds—despite all the evidence accumulated since the 1920s that banks would best be kept out of
the securities business. In addition, the banks would be allowed
to get into the insurance business to a greater degree than they
are now.

Generally, the Hunt Commission's permissive recommendations would let the banks branch by starting from scratch, i.e., de
novo, which is a generally acceptable idea to critics. But the Commission would also let the banks merge and acquire, and it would
eliminate just about all the restrictions designed to prevent concentration, e.g., geographic restrictions.

The regulation of banks would be placed more in the tender
care of the Comptroller of the Currency (there would be a new
title), a figure who has invariably given the interests of banks a
high priority. At the same time, the Federal Reserve Board
would be allowed to retreat behind its veil of mystique, shedding
its regulatory responsibilities with only a few exceptions, e.g.,
bank holding, and regulate the money supply and such. "It is
wise," said the Commission, "to keep the central bank and its
decision-making responsibility in a basically insulated position
within the Federal government."

The way the Hunt Commission would go about loosening control over banks and shifting regulatory responsibility would be
through the creation of a number of new offices. The Comptroller

would become the Office of the National Bank Administrator, and though it would continue to supervise nationally-chartered banks, it would be severed from Treasury Department control. More important in view of its insidious nature, a recommendation of the Hunt Commission would free the National Bank Administrator from the control of its own government by permitting it to operate outside the budgetary control of the Office of Management and Budget. Financial supprt would come not from tax revenues, as is now the case with the Comptroller, but from fees paid by banks. (The recommendation recalls the words of one Comptroller, who said, "Whose bread I eat, his song I sing.")

Giving the Comptroller new, near-sovereign power was only a first step on the part of the Hunt Commission, which also recommended the formation of an office of the Administrator of State Banks to take over many of the regulatory and supervisory functions of both the Federal Reserve Board and the Federal Deposit Insurance Corporation. Like the National Bank Administrator, this office, too, would be free of control, developing its own operating funds from fees imposed on the banks it regulates.

Next, the Hunt Commission recommended the establishment of the Federal Deposit Guarantee Administration, another agency that would be free of any budgetary control, to "incorporate" the Federal Deposit Insurance Corporation, the Federal Savings and Loan Insurance Corporation, and the insurance function of the National Credit Union Administration. Two of its five reigning trustees would be the Administrator of State Banks and the National Bank Administrator. Under this recommendation the FDIC, an energetic regulator of banks, as Chapter 1 suggests, would lose its regulatory and supervisory functions to the Administrator of State Banks and be reduced to determining and collecting insurance premiums and to paying claims.

There were other recommendations, but the net result of the Hunt Commission's "reforms" for the regulation of banks would be the creation of a sovereign set of agencies free of "the constraints," in the commission's word, "imposed by the budgetary processes of the federal government which are necessary for tax supported institutions. . . ." Put more bluntly, it is a naked grab for power by the banks and other financial institutions of the United States whose influence and infiltration into the agencies that regulate them already is substantial, even overwhelming. If the Hunt Commission's recommendations were to become law, the rise of a separate sovereign power feared by Thomas Jefferson would have come about. Yet, in a mockery of the words, the Hunt Commission maintained that its recommendations in the regulatory area were needed to assure the banks "continued freedom of action in serving the public interest."

The Commission's engrossment with the well-being of the financial institutions was, in fact, almost obsessive. It worried, for example, that when interest rates rose sharply money flowed out of insurance companies, impairing the amount of capital they had to lend. It worried that an expanding Social Security system which had gone "beyond its original purpose—that of providing a minimum floor of economic security," would cause private insurance and pension plans "to suffer." The recommended medicine was tax deductions. Despite the abuses of bank trust departments in their securities trading, it recommended that only the twenty largest stock holdings in terms of market value be disclosed by banks, and then only once a year "with the appropriate regulatory agency," not to the public.

The disturbing thing about the Hunt Commission report was its disregard for the real issues, which have generally been ignored by the banking system of the United States. For example, it recommended that interest rates on mortgages insured by the Federal Housing Administration and the Veterans Administration be determined in the marketplace, forgetting that it was the market's disregard for human need that produced VA and FHA mortgages in the first place (to the ever rising profitability of lenders). The recommendation would clearly give the banks the privilege of having their cake, since FHA and VA mortgages are riskless (in fact, have been subjected to lender abuses), and eating it, too. It recommended the variable rate mortgage be adopted, and that Congress pass an insurance program against "interest rate risk to mitigate the problems faced" by lenders in times of rising interest rates. It suggested a special tax credit for investors in residential mortgages and called for the repeal of statutory ceilings on usury in connection with residential mortgages and the repeal as well of "legal impediments to the use of variable rate mortgages." All this was ostensibly in support of home building. But then, in a statement that could easily be interpreted as an accusation of failure by the banks, the Hunt Commission said, "In the event the mortgage financing is not adequate to achieve national housing goals, Congress should provide direct subsidies to consumers."

The Hunt Commission's original mandate was not to promote the welfare and the sovereign powers of banking. At one of its very first meetings the Under Secretary of the Treasury, Charls Walker, noted in a welcoming speech that the financial system of the United States had not been distributing money and credit as it should. "There is great significance in the allocation of funds," he said to the assembled commission, "and quite frankly it has meant that certain areas of high social priority have not received as much financing as the Congress and the people would like to see them receive." Walker also raised the allocation problem in another way, saying, "There is the question of the distribution of . . . savings among competing uses within an environment where I suspect there is going to be a lot more emphasis on the quality of life and high social priorities as contrasted perhaps with the last thirty or forty years."

The philosophies of the members of the Hunt Commission are not generally known, though their recommendations (only a few have been listed here) suggest concern for social need does not run deep—with one major exception, Lane Kirkland, who was secretary and treasurer of the AFL–CIO when he served on the Hunt Commission. In a sharp dissent to the majority recommendations Kirkland said, "Unfortunately, the commission, while giving lip service to the broader public interest, washes its hands of the problem and disclaims any responsibility for seeing to it that a fair share of the financial resources are allocated for social priorities.

"It recognizes, too, that free competition by itself does not allocate resources properly and that its role is to recommend an institutional framework conducive to achieving whatever social goals the Congress may determine. Then it walks away from the problem. Its recommendation in the area of social needs is that the problem be taken care of by Congress through direct sub-sidies and tax incentives for housing." Kirkland favored subsidies for low- and moderate-income housing, for water pollution cures, for medical facilities, and other socially desirable projects, but his point was that subsidies "by themselves do not fulfill our social needs." Subsidies do not fill the broad vacuum produced by "the tendency of the private financial structure to assign a higher priority to corporate enterprise and other preferred customers at the expense of programs and projects which are essential to meet the requirements of life in this country. . . ." The point was one ad-vanced many times by critics who have charged banks with suck-ing up the savings and surplus of people in their banking area and redistributing the funds to corporate and other favored bor-rowers at home and abroad. Studies support this point.

Kirkland also attacked another favorite tune of bankers when they are accused of lopsided funds allocations. Nearly always bankers respond to such accusations with calls for tax breaks or other incentives. Said Kirkland: "Tax incentives and credit simply provide another tax loophole, enabling mortgage lenders to get a tax benefit whether or not housing is stimulated. It will increase the profit of the lender without regard to whether there is any increase in housing."

No other members of the Commission expressed such senti-ments. Two members, William H. Morton, president of American Express Company, and Edward H. Malone, vice president—trust operations of General Electric Company, came out against tax credits for holders of residential mortgages, fearing distortions in credit flows in the nation that might hurt, for example, the municipal bond market. Morgan G. Earnest, president of a Earnest Homes, Inc., a home-building company, suggested the "commission had failed to come to grips with the overriding problem of providing a more stable flow of funds into the residential mortgage market."

Coming to grips with social need, however, may have been an impossible task for most members of the commission, since many, by virtue of their own position in life, might well have been unable to comprehend that need. Some were bankers, and it would be unlikely to expect solid reforms from them. As the following list shows, not a single member was a consumer advocate: Atherton Bean, chairman of the executive committee, International Multifoods Corporation; Morris D. Crawford, Jr., chairman, Bowery Savings Bank; Morgan G. Earnest, president, Earnest Homes; J. Howard Edgerton, chairman, California Federal Savings; Richard G. Gilbert, chairman, Citizens Savings Association; William D. Grant, chairman, Businessmen's Assurance Company; Alan Greenspan, president, Townsend-Greenspan and Company; Walter S. Holmes, Jr., president, C.I.T. Financial Corporation; Lane Kirkland, secretary-treasurer, AFL–CIO; Donald S. MacNaughton, chairman, Prudential Insurance Company of America; Edward H. Malone, vice-president, Trust Operations, General Electric Company; Rex J. Morthland, chairman, Peoples Bank and Trust; William H. Morton; Ellmore C. Patterson, chairman, Morgan Guaranty Trust; K. A. Randall, president, United Virginia Bankshares, Inc.; Ralph S. Regula, state senator, Ohio; R. J. Saulnier, professor of economics, Barnard College, Columbia University.

It was not as though there were no good, feasible proposals around for the commission to consider. The establishment of national goals and economic policies has been associated with the banking institutions of many countries, as a means of allocating credit to areas of the economy where it is needed. At least two recent studies show that central banks in most industrial countries designate certain sectors of their economies that must receive more favorable treatment from the central bank. In the United States such policies should logically emanate from the Federal Reserve Board, but in its lofty autonomy the Board has usually refused to participate in economic programs and policies of the federal government. Yet the Federal Reserve's actions in the money markets, say in the tightening of credit, have resulted in enormous and jagged distortions in the economy. Whenever interest rates are tightened, the corporate side of the economy usually has no trouble finding money to borrow, willing as it is to pay interest rates that are nothing less than usurious. Meanwhile, housing, agriculture, state and local governments, small business, and underdeveloped regions of the United States find that they must carry the burden of general monetary policies designed to deflate the economy. Thus, whether it admits it or not, the Federal Reserve does indeed make economic policies. Other countries refuse to accept such a situation. In Sweden, for example, the Riksbank (the central bank) fosters sectors of the economy that have been assigned preferred positions for the national welfare. One result is that even in periods when money is tight, a steady flow of funds goes to housing. The basic sources of the money are bond issues controlled by the Riksbank, but commercial banks are required to provide the credit needed to meet annual home-building needs. And the banks are not bludgeoned into participating. So-called sweeteners and various inducements make their participation voluntary. The result has been that despite a series of tight money periods in recent years a constant flow of credit has gone to housing in Sweden.

The Swedes are far from alone in allocating credit. Italy's central bank, the Bank of Italy, is a tool of government, and participates with other lenders in allocating credit. But the bank is a primary influence in monetary policy, and has been a supporter of "credit incentives" that include government guarantees and tax deductions for lenders as well as the subsidizing of interest payments by borrowers. In recent years the incentives have been used to help develop industry in the south of Italy.

Even in Japan, where banks and commercial interests have had their way for years, credit is allocated in accord with central goals rather than merely letting market mechanisms determine who will be granted loans and who will not. Japan's Bank of Japan, for example, adopted credit policies that favored those in foreign trade. In Germany policies of the Bundesbank produced what amounted to a subsidy for those in the export business.

It is not as though the Hunt Commission had no home-grown ideas to wrestle with either. Its leading dissenter, Lane Kirkland of the AFL–CIO made a detailed suggestion that was all but ignored. Besides direct subsidies for low- and moderate-income housing, Kirkland urged "the establishment of a National Development Bank and the mandatory allocation of credit to socially desirable projects. I would envision the National Development Bank as an instrument of the government, capitalized by the U.S. Treasury, with the authority to issue securities of its own. This bank would be authorized to make direct loans to state and local governments, public agencies, corporations, and individuals for social priority projects. It would also be vested with the authority to guarantee loans made by financial institutions for such projects.

"One way of allocating the available credit," Kirkland said in his dissent to the Hunt Commission's majority report, "is through imposition of an asset reserve requirement on the financial assets of all financial institutions. Such a requirement would channel a share of financial resources to social priority investments. Under this concept, the government would place a 100 percent reserve requirement on a portion of each financial institution's assets unless this portion is invested in housing or other social priority projects. If a financial institution did not invest the required portion of its assets in social priority projects, the shortfall would be left as a reserve with the government. Thus, a financial institution would have the choice of either making interest-paying loans in the social priority field or making an interest-free loan to the government. The asset reserve requirement would guarantee that a given percentage of financial resources would be funneled into housing and other priority investments. That percentage would be reviewed periodically and revised as needed. No financial institution would escape making priority loans or suffer a competitive disadvantage thereby. In times of tight money there would be an assurance of an adequate flow of funds into housing and other social priority projects."

Under Kirkland's plan, every financial institution would take part as a social priority lender, if not with direct loans, then by buying the bonds of the National Development Bank or the bonds of other private financial institutions that specialized in social priority lending.

Kirkland at the same time criticized the other members of the Hunt Commission for recommending that interest rate ceilings on deposits be removed. For decades commercial banks have been required to pay lower interest rates on deposits than those rates paid by savings banks and savings and loan associations which lend money in the residential mortgage markets. If commercial banks were to pay higher rates, Kirkland argued, the flow of funds to housing would be reduced even more than it is now.

In the months after the report of the Hunt Commission was sent to President Nixon, it became clear that the Commission had ignored real, necessary reforms in favor of tinkering, like a team of mechanics, with the mechanism of finance in a way that would favor the lenders. Despite the long list of ills that could be traced directly to the banks, especially the largest banks, of the United States, the Commission had been concerned only for the well-being of the industry, already fat, profitable, and highly influential and powerful. Despite the critical need to hobble the political power of banks, which have time and again since the founding of the banking system corrupted and undermined the wills of legislators in Congress and in the states, the Hunt Commission did not even raise the subject. In the name of competition, which bankers themselves admit does not exist today in the United States, it worked toward dividing up markets among financial institutions that were dissatisfied with their portion.

It is clearly time for Congress and state legislators to begin hobbling the political power of banks (and, indeed, of other major corporations capable of corrupting the political process for their own benefit). Banks especially should be prohibited from making any kind of financial contribution to political campaigns under penalty of jail terms for their officers. At the same time, bank lobbying efforts should be sharply restricted, even to limiting the number of people employed and the amounts of money spent. The massive amounts of money banks are able to spend on lobbying make a mockery of political democracy. Influence peddling, a growth industry in the nation's capital and in state capitals, also needs to be sharply restricted. Aides of legislators and banking committees must be prohibited from going over to the other side for at least a period of two years after leaving their posts in Washington or state capitals. All the information such men have learned while on the public payroll is not theirs to sell to the highest bidder. Private industry puts up with no such nonsense. Defecting employees (which is the term that should be applied to aides who leave Congress or the administration to take employment with bank and other powerful lobbies to sell what and who they know) need to be restrained by law from doing so. Bills that would do that must not be allowed to be bottled up in committees, as in the case of bills introduced in the New York legislature by Manhattan's assemblyman, Franz Leichter. Other legislators must pry them out and make them law.

To free the legislators themselves from the terrible vise of the banks, political campaigns need to be financed by the American taxpayer. A beginning already exists, since taxpayers can earmark one dollar of their federal taxes for the presidential election, either designating the party of his choice or directing the money into a nonpartisan fund for distribution by formula to the contenders in 1976. This idea needs to be implemented on

all levels of government to induce candidates who are not har-
nessed to bank and other interests to run for office. As Senator
Philip A. Hart has said, "This is one effective way to reduce the
influence that big-money interests have in government, whether
the party in power be Democratic or Republican."

Curtailing bank influence on the political process, however,
is only a beginning in the work that needs to be done. Despite
the arguments of bank apologists that bigness is not in itself evil,
the banks themselves are the living argument that big banks (and
other corporations) can produce evil. Can there be any doubt
that the trust departments of banks should be severed and made
separate, independent entities, especially in the light of the Patman Committee disclosures? At present, confidential information
clearly goes back and forth between those in charge of trust departments and those in charge of lending, and the inside information picked up by the lenders has been reflected in the activities
of the trust departments in the stock markets. On top of that, the
stock market itself has lost its liquidity, thanks to the go-go trading of the banks, and such former bellweather criteria as earnings
of a corporation have little to do with the price of a stock today,
so distorted has the stock market become. More important, the
banks alone trade in secret, though practically every other big
trader—mutual funds, college endowments, foundations—must
make at least some public disclosures about their market activities.

The incestuous relationship of the interlocking directorship
must be eliminated by federal law, too. The claim that only when
bankers and corporate managers sit on each other's boards can
intelligent, hard advice develop for managements to act on is a
self-serving lie. The United States abounds with people capable
of taking a far broader view than those ingrown views of bankers.
Many college professors, for example, have given truly pertinent
testimony before inquiring congressional committees, testimony
that is not tainted by a vested interest. The bulk of evidence suggests, too, that the banks have used the interlocking directorship
to infiltrate industry, while corporate managements have invited

the banks to feather their own nests at the expense of stockholders and the public. Happily, the inherent evil of the interlocking directorship is being recognized. In 1973 the New York legislature passed a bill making such directorships illegal among financial institutions.

It is hard, too, to understand why banks insist they need deposits totaling in the billions upon billions of dollars. Individual banks are limited by law in the amount they can lend, and truly huge lines of credit must be put together by groups of banks. Big banks thus serve the bankers, who can and do use their banks' size to awe everyone and to exercise power, political and otherwise. So intimidating are such banks to people that an executive of the Bank of America has said representatives of his bank have had to take people literally by the hand to get past the hardly imposing facade of a branch office. Congress needs to consider not whether banks should be broken down in size. That is long past due. Like the oil trust of generations ago, banks themselves have demonstrated the need. Only the maximum size left to a single management needs to be determined.

The regulators, too, must be part of a reform, but in precisely opposite the way recommended by the Hunt Commission. No agency in the United States should be allowed to act contrary to the national economic policies of the duly elected government, or flaunt its "independence" before the elected members of the House of Representatives and the Senate. Despite the Federal Reserve's disdain for the economic policies of past Presidents, the Federal Reserve's own record is highly vulnerable to criticism. No one who knows anything about the causes of the depression of the 1930s, the nation's worst, refutes the argument that it was by Federal Reserve policies. In more recent years the Federal Reserve Board's secretly reached decisions to tighten or loosen credit have extended booms to an unhealthy degree and made busts more painful. In the first quarter of 1973, as bank profits soared to record highs, the Federal Reserve Board stood by as the nation's major banks sent billions of dollars abroad in low-profit loans to foreigners, thus adding vastly to the supply of unwanted dollars abroad and helping to bring on a major currency crisis. One result, now history, was two devaluations of the dollar. All the while the banks were raising interest rates on loans at home, saying demand was at a peak, they were engaged in speculation against their own dollar, trading it for Swiss francs, German marks, and even gold, and thereby adding even more dollars to the overseas glut. Many foreign banks with branches in the United States did much the same as their U.S. counterparts, but the Federal Reserve Board merely lamented that it could not restrain a flight of dollars initiated by them. A governor of the board, Andrew F. Brimmer, was reported as saying, "The susceptibility of the U.S. banking system to influences originating abroad but which result in large capital outflows from this country remains a serious problem." More to the point, control over banking in this country, both by foreigners and by American bankers, must be put in the hands of the administration, which after all really represents the sovereign power of the United States. The Federal Reserve System and its Board were organized in more primitive times, when Presidents were not accustomed to drawing on the talents of men skilled in banking and economics and when the problems were of a domestic kind. In today's international scheme of things, the Federal Reserve cannot possibly operate, and its very independence works against it.

To put the banking system into the hands of political administrations, of course, is risky, since the banks have demonstrated time and again their ability to infiltrate administrations, most notably the Treasury Department, which supervises national banks. That infiltration could be stopped by a President less sympathetic than those of recent years to special interests, and by a watchdog Congress, one whose members are driven less by personal greed and ambition and more by personal conviction.

Such a President and Congress, incidentally, could be helped immeasurably by a more thoughtful press, one that was more of a watchdog; a press attracted less by a carnival atmosphere and more by substance. Some notable examples exist now, and the great measure of their success is the venom directed at them by the central figures whose depredations they have exposed. The lawyers of the land might also begin to assess which is more important: a win for a client over the public interest; or a win for a client in tune to and not in opposition to the national interest. Certainly the lawyers who are influence peddlers ought to be exposed as such, even if their activities are not illegal, so that they cannot hide behind a mystique and grow rich by working only for wealthy interests whose goals are often detrimental to the rest of us. In a land that is already divided over the inequity of things, such moves could have a cauterizing effect.

Within the administration no bankers or bankers' lobbyists should be appointed to key posts, at least until some of the taint of their former employment has been worn away. The laws of the United States forbid its individual citizens from reaching agreements with foreign nations; such laws should be read aloud to bankers who have come perilously close to breaking them.

There are those who say that the nationalization of banking would be a proper step today, and this thinking goes like this: The products of banking, money and credit, are crucial. Thus banking is a crucial utility. At the same time, the distribution of money and credit by the banks has been vastly selfish and inequitable, a point agreed on even by some bankers. That inequity has not been by malicious design, necessarily, but at least one of the highest-ranking executives in banking today has despaired that banking itself will ever correct the inequities. He has said that even if all the money in the land were divided equally among the population, 10 percent of that population would have 90 percent of the money in ten years. The thesis obviously assumes greater predatory ability on the part of a few individuals in the population to the detriment of the rest. If true, then that is all the more reason, perhaps, if not to nationalize, at least to regulate, banks intensively, to determine their returns, the interest rates they charge, the width of their profit margins, and so on. Bankers say they are already overregulated, and that supply and demand, the profit system, and free enterprise are doing the job that is needed. But the free enterprise system has not collapsed because power companies, airlines, and telephone companies are intensively regulated. They do what they exist to do, which is to provide service to all comers at reasonable and, nearly always, profitable prices. Less intensively regulated industries that are monopolies, most notably the investment and securities industry as well as banking, make extraordinary profits at times, taking the cream so to speak, but do not provide service to all comers at reasonable prices. In this sense, they are remote from the people indeed, and reform that brings them closer is surely warranted.

415

With an Interest in Banks

In June, 1972, 101 members of the House of Representatives revealed they had some sort of financial interest in a bank or other financial institution. Some of those members did not take their seats in the 93rd Congress, which met in 1973. The following list contains the names of those who did reappear:

Glenn M. Anderson	James R. Gover, Jr.	Carl D. Perkins
John M. Ashbrook	John Paul	J. J. Pickle
Jonathan B. Bingham	Hammerschmidt	Otis G. Pike
William G. Bray	Wayne L. Hays	Richardson Preyer
Jack Brooks	Lawrence J. Hogan	Melvin Price
James T. Broyhill	Chet Holifield	James H. Quillen
Joel T. Broyhill	Craig Hosmer	Thomas M. Rees
Omar Burleson	Edward Hutchinson	Ogden R. Reid
John N. Happy Camp	Richard H. Ichord	Henry S. Reuss
Tim Lee Carter	John Jarman	John J. Rhodes
Bob Casey	Robert E. Jones	Ray Roberts
William Chappel, Jr.	Manuel Lugan, Jr.	J. Kenneth Robinson
James C. Cleveland	John Y. McCollister	Paul G. Rogers
George E. Danielson	Robert C. McEwen	Edward R. Roybal
Glenn R. Davis	William S. Mailliard	Philip E. Ruppe
John Dellenback	Robert B. Mathias	John P. Saylor
David W. Dennis	Wiley Mayne	Herman T. Schneebeli
Edward J. Derwinski	Ralph H. Metcalfe	Joe Skubitz
Harold D. Donohue	William E. Minshall	Henry P. Smith III
Thomas N. Downing	Robert H. Mollohan	Robert G. Stephens, Jr.
John J. Duncan	G. V. Montgomery	Leonor K. Sullivan
Pierre S. duPont	William S. Moorhead	Roy A. Taylor
Edwin D. Eshleman	Thomas E. Morgan	Morris K. Udall
Frank E. Evans	John E. Moss	Victor V. Veysey
Joe L. Evins	John T. Myers	Charles W. Whalen, Jr.
Dante B. Fascell	William H. Natcher	Larry Winn, Jr.
Robert N. Giaimo	Thomas P. O'Neill, Jr.	John W. Wydler
Sam Gibbons	Otto E. Passman	C. W. Young
	Claude Pepper	

A Roster of Closed Banks

Name of Bank	Date Closed	Number of Depositors' Accounts	Deposits	Disbursed by FDIC	Liquidation Recoveries	Estimated Loss to FDIC
Rocky Mountain Bank, Lakewood, Colo.	1/30/69	6,716	$ 8,107,000	$ 3,016,052	$ 2,761,155	none
Citizens State Bank, Alvarado, Tex.	4/14/69	2,329	2,299,000	1,893,763	1,995,735	none
Morrice State Bank, Morrice, Mich.	5/5/69	1,759	2,167,000	1,404,282	559,989	$ 52,320
First State Bank, Dodson, Tex.	5/12/69	686	1,085,000	988,698	909,525	300,000
State National Bank, Lovelady, Tex.	5/28/69	2,030	3,814,000	3,148,114	2,757,685	200,000
First National Bank, Ursa, Ill.	8/20/69	1,655	1,798,000	1,495,241	1,203,168	350,000
Big Lake State Bank, Big Lake, Tex.	8/25/69	2,642	4,432,000	2,352,517	2,314,448	none
First State Bank, Aransas Pass, Tex.	9/2/69	6,459	10,489,000	7,490,175	5,087,761	322,891
First National Bank, Coalville, Utah	10/3/69	3,254	6,002,000	3,207,447	3,236,552	none
State Bank, Prairie City, Iowa	2/22/70	1,651	3,897,000	3,537,790	2,740,171	750,000

Name of Bank	Date Closed	Number of Depositors' Accounts	Deposits	Disbursed by FDIC	Liquidation Recoveries	Estimated Loss to FDIC
People's State Savings, Auburn, Mich.	4/18/70	8,068	9,940,000	8,241,032	6,204,082	3,000,000
Farmers Bank, Petersburg, Ky.	6/25/70	454	1,260,000	1,157,543	387,985	525,000
Eatontown National Bank, Eatontown, N.J.	8/7/70	9,764	15,912,000	13,561,000	8,695,068	2,800,000
First State Bank, Bonne Terre, Mo.	8/24/70	5,778	7,198,000	5,683,000	2,518,549	400,000
City Bank, Philadelphia, Pa.	9/3/70	1,940	8,829,000	8,828,858	5,046,061	1,000,000
Berea Bank & Trust Co. Berea, Ky.	10/8/70	3,312	5,420,000	5,281,276	2,148,375	10,807
Sharpstown State Bank, Houston, Tex.	1/25/71	27,300	66,771,000	31,088,577	1,960,530	24,000,000
Birmingham-Bloomfield Bank, Birmingham, Mich.	2/11/71	40,100	57,695,000	106,609,000	12,148,427	1,000,000
Farmers State Bank, Carlock, Ill.	2/17/71	1,101	2,077,000	1,688,561	150,715	1,000,000

Statement of a Looted Bank

CRIPPLE CREEK, COLO.

Assets

Cash and due from bank	$ 102,900
U.S. government obligations	52,000
Other securities	110,300
Loans *	664,700
Overdrafts *	260,100
Bank premises	11,200
Furniture and fixtures	9,400
Federal Reserve stock	3,000
Accrued interest	2,800
Prepaid insurance	2,700
Other assets †	143,400
Unlocated differences †	(77,600)
Total Assets	$1,284,900

April, 1971

Liabilities

Demand deposits	$ 520,900
Savings deposits	83,400
Other time deposits	631,500
Total	$1,235,800
Other liabilities	1,900
	$ 1,237,700
Valuation reserves	400
Capital stock	50,000
Surplus	50,000
Undivided profits	17,200
Net earnings	(70,400)
Total Capital Account	$ 46,800
Total Liabilities	$1,284,900

SOURCE: Federal Deposit Insurance Corporation.

* Loans and overdrafts are $664,700 and $260,100, or $924,800, equal to nearly 72 percent of indicated total assets. The heavy total of overdrafts came from checks totaling $290,000 being found in various places of the bank by examiners.

† Other assets account represents an amount which the Teller County treasurer represented as a shortage in the county's deposit accounts.

‡ Unlocated differences account was set up by auditors to facilitate the debiting and crediting of items for which proper entry was unknown, i.e., could not be determined. The total changed daily after the account was set up, as additional claims were presented by the bank's customers.

On the Day of Reckoning, Aug. 7, 1970

THE EATONTOWN NATIONAL BANK
EATONTOWN, N. J.

August 7, 1970

Statement of Assets and Liabilities

Assets	$15,700,752.67	Liabilities	$15,997,921.28
		Suspense account	43,807.44
		Nonbook cashier's	
Known		checks	2,920,888.23
shortage	5,760,004.76	Safekeeping items	637,981.37
Total	$21,460,757.43	Deposit items	54,800.00
		Total	$19,655,398.32
		Capital	$625,000.00
		Surplus	300,000.00
		Undivided profits	880,359.11
Total assets	$21,460,757.43	Total Liabilities	$21,460,757.43

SOURCE: Federal Deposit Insurance Corporation.

A Tale of Brokered Funds, Tie-In Loans, and Dead Banks

Date of Bank's Closing	Name of Bank	Total Deposits	Total Brokered Funds	Total of Tied-in Loans
5/5/69	Morrice State Bank, Morrice, Mich.	$ 2,167,500	$ 949,000	$ 455,063
9/2/69	First State Bank, Aransas Pass, Tex.	10,471,900	820,000	450,000
10/3/69	First National Bank, Coalville, Utah	6,002,000	1,000,000	614,503
2/22/70	State Bank of Prairie City, Iowa	3,896,900	848,000	615,595
4/18/70	People's State Savings Bank, Auburn, Mich.	9,940,100	2,725,000*	2,330,000
6/25/70	Farmers Bank, Petersburg, Ky.	1,257,600	737,000	482,400
9/3/70	City Bank, Philadelphia, Pa.	8,829,000	505,000	155,000
1/25/71	Sharpstown State Bank, Houston, Tex.	66,771,400	31,661,600	13,404,400
4/2/71	Bank of Salem, Salem, Neb.	606,000	80,000	45,000
12/30/71	First Community State Bank, Savannah, Mo.	3,488,500	324,575	362,397

* Not included in total deposits.

The banks above were all insured by the Federal Deposit Insurance Corporation, which sees a disturbing correlation between the use of brokered funds by bankers and bank failures.

SOURCE: Federal Deposit Insurance Corporation.

Bankers' Salaries * —and the Extras 1971 †

THE BANK	THE BANKER	SALARY	Retirement Income‡	THE EXTRAS		
				Profits from Options	From Profit Sharing§	From Dividends
BankAmerica Corp.	A. W. Clausen, pres.	$168,200	$ 89,000	$78,039‖		
	C. J. Medberry III, chmn.	123,350	72,247	84,246‖		
	Samuel B. Stewart, senior vice chmn.	127,000	55,970			
	C. H. Baumhefner, vice chmn., cashier	107,500	59,450			
	Rudolph A. Petersen, advisor	42,349	42,839			
	Louis B. Lundborg	46,875	33,002			
Chase Manhattan Corp.	David Rockefeller, chmn.	230,000	116,883		33,926	$790,706
	George Champion, chmn. (ret.)	——	101,217¶			
	Herbert P. Patterson, pres.	160,000	94,661**		25,444	
	John B. M. Place	135,000	79,661			
	George A. Roeder Jr.	135,000	76,146			

Bankers' Salaries (continued)

THE BANK	THE BANKER	SALARY	Retirement Income‡	THE EXTRAS Profits from Options	From Profit Sharing§	From Dividends
Chemical New York Corp.	William S. Renchard, chmn.	215,000	64,042	24,615††	176,913‡‡	
	Hulbert S. Aldrich, vice chmn.	170,000	53,088	20,773††	144,241‡‡	
	Howard W. McCall, Jr., pres.	170,000	52,161	12,690	148,762‡‡	
	Donald C. Platten	112,500	51,760	12,245	54,349‡‡	
Conill Corp. (Continental Illinois)	Donald M. Graham, chmn.	200,000			28,606	
	Tilden Cummings, pres.	175,000			24,981	
First Chicago Corp.	Gaylord Freeman, chmn.	248,600§§	0	§§		
	Edward F. Blettner, vice chmn.	177,919§§	70,313	§§		
First National City Corp.	Walter B. Wriston, chmn.	235,000	139,473	37,937	22,820	
	William I. Spencer, pres.	200,000	118,497	68,796	19,421	
	Edward L. Palmer, chmn. of exc. comm.	165,000	97,497	0	16,023	
	George C. Scott, vice chmn.	95,333	45,009	20,080	9,247	
	J. Howard Laeri, vice chmn. (ret. 9/1/71)	33,750	62,196	0	3,277	
First Pennsylvania Bank & Trust	John R. Bunting	126,538	52,332			
	John F. Bodine	82,500	36,300			

THE BANK	THE BANKER	SALARY	Retirement Income‡	THE EXTRAS		
				Profits from Options	From Profit Sharing§	From Dividends
Manufacturers Hanover Trust	Gabriel Hauge, chmn.	200,000	77,360			18,375
	John F. McGillicuddy, pres.	135,000	74,418			12,403
	Walter F. Thomas, vice chmn.	100,000	58,318			9,187
Security Pacific Corp.	Frederick G. Larkins, Jr.	180,000		6,670		
	William E. Siegel, vice chmn.	150,000		5,591		
Morgan Guaranty	E. C. Patterson, chmn.					
	W. H. Page, pres.					
	J. M. Meyer, chmn. (ret.)					
U.S. Trust Co.	Hoyt Ammidon, chmn.	182,412‖	55,687			
	Charles W. Buek, pres.	182,364	99,000			
Bank of Detroit	Robert M. Surdam, chmn.	140,000	91,305			
	Ellis B. Merry, chmn. (ret. 2/1/72)	135,000	50,323			
Wachovia Corp.	John F. Watlington, chmn.	177,916	136,500			
	Archie K. Davis, chmn. Wachovia Bank	99,166	81,250			
	Edwin P. Latimer, chmn. American Credit Co.	83,862	35,000			
	Bland W. Worly, pres., Wachovia Corp.	90,187	65,000			

Bankers' Salaries (continued)

THE BANK	THE BANKER	SALARY	Retirement Income‡	THE EXTRAS		
				Profits from Options	From Profit Sharing§	From Dividends
First Commercial Banks, (Albany, N.Y.)	Lester W. Herzog, Jr., pres.	86,297	45,596			
	Joseph S. Spaid, Sr.	75,000	21,516			
Western Bancorporation	Frank L. King, chmn.	105,000				
	Clifford L. Tweter, pres.	118,088		53,817		
Wells Fargo	R. P. Cooley, pres.	224,836				
	E. C. Arbuckle, chmn.	176,179				

* 1971.

† Some extras, such as the lending at prime rates to its officers by Albany, New York's First Commercial Bank, do not appear in the table for the obvious reason that they cannot be illustrated this way. Some salaries also include bonuses, breakdowns of which are not available. Other services that are in reality income include financial advice to bank officers, the construction and lease of homes for entertainment, and huge insurance policies.

‡ The figures in the column can often by synonymous with deferred compensation, which gives executives a tax break and increases retirement benefits. The money due continues to be paid to the bank executive's wife upon his death in many of the plans.

§ The figures in the column represent the bank's contribution to its profit-sharing plan.

‖ The figure is arrived at by computing Clausen's cost of $172,847 and his selling price of $250,886. Few executives actually lay out the money for stock optioned to them by their bank. Typically, the money to purchase is borrowed and then repaid upon the sale of the stock.

¶ George Champion, the former chairman of the Chase Manhattan Bank, retired March 1, 1969, receiving $101,217 annually for life. If his wife survives him she receives $50,608 during her lifetime.

** Herbert P. Patterson resigned in October, 1972, and was succeeded by Willard C. Butcher.

†† Includes options exercised during 1971 and January, 1972.

‡‡ Total for all years of bank employment up to and including 1971.

§§ Includes bank's contribution to profit-sharing plan.

‖‖ Includes bonuses.

Bail-Out

Between May 15, 1970, and June 19, 1970, the Chase Manhattan Bank, the Morgan Guaranty Trust Company, and the Continental Illinois National Bank and Trust Company bailed out of a dying Penn Central, as any prudent investor might. But the banks, as well as half a dozen other financial institutions, were not acting so much as prudent investors as insiders privy to information that was not public. That was the claim, at least, of the Subcommittee on Domestic Finance, a part of the House Banking and Currency Committee. On May 21, 1970, for example, the commercial lending side of the Chase Manhattan Bank learned that a $100 million debenture offer planned by the Penn Central was being canceled, meaning the Penn Central might be without badly needed capital. The next day, on May 22, the Chase Manhattan Bank's investment trust department sold 134,200 shares and continued selling stock all week long. When it let up, the Morgan Guaranty Trust started selling, then, in turn, the Continental Illinois National Bank. It was a sale of great coincidence, perhaps clairvoyance, commented Wright Patman, chairman of the House Banking and Currency Committee, when the banks denied any collusion, or even access to inside information. The wall between their trust departments and the commercial side of their banks could not be breached, they said. Thus when the commercial side learned of the debenture cancellation, a week before the public announcement, or just the length of time of the Chase Manhattan bail-out, it did not tell the trust department.

	NUMBER OF SHARES SOLD OFF		
DATE	Chase Manhattan Bank	Morgan Guaranty Trust Co.	Continental Illinois Bank & Trust
May 21	2,000	200	0
22	134,300	0	0
23	—	—	—
24	—	—	—
25	53,200	0	500
26	32,100	0	0
27	31,700	0	9,500
28	35,300	0	10,000

NUMBER OF SHARES SOLD OFF

DATE	Chase Manhattan Bank	Morgan Guaranty Trust Co.	Continental Illinois Bank & Trust
29	0	44,900	0
30	—	—	—
31	—	—	—
June 1	12,100	28,500	0
2	0	25,900	0
3	0	24,200	0
4	3,000	40,600	0
5	100	31,000	0
6	—	—	—
7	—	—	—
8	0	0	0
9	0	96,500	0
10	0	44,100	500
11	0	8,400	0
12	90,700	0	108,950
13	—	—	—
14	—	—	—
15	0	0	56,100
16	0	0	37,700
17	500	0	44,200
18	1,500	11,600	24,600
19	1,800	1,100	19,400

SOURCE: House Banking and Currency Committee.

The Patman List: A Tale of Interlocking Directorships and Control Through Trusts of U.S. Corporations

In a way, the Subcommittee on Domestic Finance of the House Banking and Currency Committee, which prepared a one-of-a-kind report called *Commercial Banks and Their Trust Activities: Emerging Influence on the American Economy,* might well have called it "Who Really Controls the American Economy?" A sample only of that vast report follows, and though it is material gathered in 1968, it is dated only in terms of precise percentages of holdings in the corporations listed or in the actual number of interlocking directorships shown. The names and the numbers may have shifted and changed somewhat in the years since, but the game still goes on. For what the report tried to show—that there was a concentration of assets among a handful of banks, that banks had access to inside information, that banks were engaged in incestuous interlocks among corporate directors—is all too true today. The banks, in effect, were using their place as trustees to gain control and to influence corporate boards. In fact, a study by the Federal Reserve Bank of New York in 1972 and 1973 suggests that if anything the intrusion of banks through their trust departments is growing, for trust assets controlled by the banks have risen from $253 billion, the amount estimated by the subcommittee, to $293 billion. The assets are also controlled by a very few banks, the same that appear in the abbreviated list that follows, though thousands of banks can legally maintain trust departments and do.

Ever since the appearance of the Patman List, which is what it came to be called, the banks have, as expected, refuted its conclusions, though the evidence consisted of a roll call of hundreds upon hundreds of corporations along with the lists of the banks holding directorships in them, stock through trusts, and voting rights. Banks have argued that 5 percent is not control, merely "influence," and thereby tried to reduce the dispute to a matter of semantics. The fact is that 5 percent of a corporation's common shares, which are usually the voting shares, means enormous influence, if not control. More than 5 percent (a situation not uncommon), say 10 or 12 percent, is tantamount to control—often because of the wide dispersal of share ownership in the United States among disorganized small investors. Anything over 12 percent (and there are many examples) generally means flat-out control and woe to the managements that do not heed the dictums of those with the votes, especially if they are banks.

Voting control is only half of the story, though. The other half is the interlocking directorship—the man from the bank sitting on the board, not by virtue, say, of his loans to the corporation, but by the fact of holdings built up in trust departments, holdings that really belong to others.

We have not abused our power, the banks have shot back at critics. But this is not really so, as the tale of the Penn Central in Chapter 10 suggests. But banks have also come to dominate trading in Wall Street in a way that is not healthy. In recent years they have revealed an aggressive trading nature that has produced extremes in prices of stocks, whether they are rising or falling. The result has been disorderly markets, not really reflecting fundamental values, but the current fears or manic state of bank trust officers charged with investing. The markets have risen sharply at times to heights forcing them to topple, then have plummeted to an oversold position that reflects a well-known phenomenon attributed to mutual funds—price aggressiveness. Thus the banks, which accounted for 38.5 percent of all institutional trading on the New York Stock Exchange in 1971—mutual funds and even insurance companies are tiny alongside bank trust assets—have hardly been following the prudent man rule, which in some states is required by law. In essence, the rule requires them as fiduciaries to seek reasonable income and to preserve capital. Banks respond to this by saying the owners of the trust want them, the banks, to become stock market performers, not investors.

The Patman List

The Corporation and the Bank	No. of Interlocking Directorates Held by All Banks	No. of Funds Managed by All Banks	Percent of Common Stock Held by Banks	Percent of Sole Voting Rights	Percent of Partial Voting Rights
Ford Motor Co.					
Manufacturers National, Detroit	4	11	6.9	0.2	0.0
Gulf Oil Co.					
Mellon National Bank, Pittsburgh	4	10	17.1	1.9	10.8
American Airlines					
Morgan Guaranty Trust, New York	5	5	7.5	6.4	0.3
American Smelting & Refining					
Morgan Guaranty Trust, New York	4	0	15.5	9.8	1.8
Boeing Company					
Chase Manhattan Bank, New York	2	4	8.7	7.2	1.3
Burlington Industries, Inc.					
Morgan Guaranty Trust, New York	1	2	14.5	9.5	1.3
Celanese Corporation of America					
Morgan Guaranty Trust, New York	2	4	7.5	5.4	0.5
Chicago & Northwestern Railway					
State Street Bank, Boston	2	0	13.8	0.1	0.0
Northwest Airlines					
Chase Manhattan Bank, New York	0	0	11.0	9.9	0.9
Atlantic Coast Line					
Mercantile-Safe Deposit, Baltimore	5	0	54.4	51.7	2.4
Western Air Lines					
Chase Manhattan Bank, New York	0	0	6.7	6.2	0.3

The Patman List (continued)

The Corporation and the Bank	No. of Interlocking Directorates Held by All Banks	No. of Funds Managed by All Banks	Percent of Common Stock Held by Banks	Percent of Sole Voting Rights	Percent of Partial Voting Rights
Aetna Life	8	0			
Hartford National Bank, Hartford			9.6	6.7	1.9
Connecticut Bank & Trust, Hartford			1.7	5.8	0.7
Chase Manhattan Bank, New York			5.0	4.6	0.3
Cleveland Cliffs Iron Co.	5	2			
Cleveland Trust Co., Cleveland			21.7	8.6	10.6
Island Creek Coal Co.	3	2			
Cleveland Trust Co., Cleveland			16.5	15.7	0.6
North American Coal Corp.	1	0			
National City Bank, Cleveland			41.0	2.0	0.0
Campbell Soup Co.	2	1			
Philadelphia National Bank, Philadelphia			6.5	0.0	0.0
Girard Trust Co., Philadelphia			5.4	0.2	5.0
Fidelity Bank, Philadelphia			8.3	0.2	0.0
H. J. Heinz	6	4			
Mellon National Bank, Pittsburgh			31.3	0.6	3.1
General Mills, Inc.	2	3			
Bankers Trust Co., New York			5.0	4.9	0.1
Pillsbury Co.	1	0			
National Bank of Detroit			7.0	3.9	0.3
Tasty Baking Co.	0	0			
Fidelity Bank, Philadelphia			12.3	12.3	0.0

Heublein, Inc.	2	1			
Connecticut Bank & Trust, Hartford			33.0	23.7	1.7
Pepsi Cola Bottling, Washington, D.C.	0	0	10.0	10.0	0.0
First National Bank, Chicago	1	0			
Vanity Fair Mills, Inc.					
Morgan Guaranty Trust, New York			11.9	9.5	0.8
Provident National, Philadelphia			27.9	0.0	27.1
Bobbie Brooks, Inc.	0	3			
First National Bank, Chicago			6.1	3.0	2.4
Cleveland Trust, Cleveland			26.9	0.1	26.8
Morgan Guaranty Trust, New York			8.2	7.7	0.3
Dow Jones Co., Inc.	1	0			
Morgan Guaranty Trust, New York			9.7	8.0	0.7
Booth Newspapers	0	1			
National Bank, Detroit			9.6	3.9	0.0
Detroit Bank & Trust			5.2	0.8	4.4
Time, Inc.	2	1			
Morgan Guaranty Trust Co.			8.1	4.1	0.7
Prentice Hall, Inc.	0	0			
First National City Bank, New York			8.7	0.8	0.0
Scott Foresman Co.	1	1			
State Street Bank, Boston			5.7	0.1	0.2
First National, Chicago			8.9	7.8	0.7
Northern Trust Co., Chicago			8.2	3.9	2.6
Butterick Co., Inc.	0	1			
Chemical Bank, New York			39.00	0.0	23.4
Harcourt, Brace & World	0	0			
First National City, New York			7.6	3.5	0.6

The Patman List (continued)

The Corporation and the Bank	No. of Interlocking Directorates Held by All Banks	No. of Funds Managed by All Banks	Percent of Common Stock Held by Banks	Percent of Sole Voting Rights	Percent of Partial Voting Rights
Morgan Guaranty Trust, New York			11.4	2.4	0.4
Olin Mathieson Chemical Corp.	1	3			
Morgan Guaranty Trust, New York			6.8	5.7	0.3
Richardson-Merrell, Inc.	0	4			
Chase Manhattan Bank, New York			10.4	10.00	0.2
G. D. Searle Co.	4	5			
Harris Trust, Chicago			30.5	15.5	14.6
Chase Manhattan Bank, New York			5.5	5.2	0.2
Noxell Corp.	3	0			
Maryland National Bank, Baltimore			23.7	0.0	23.7
Equitable Trust Co., Baltimore			40.0	0.0	40.0
Mercantile-Safe Deposit, Baltimore			1.1	0.8	0.2
Fuller Brush Co.	3	3			
United Bank & Trust			28.7	27.8	0.1
Betz Laboratories	0	2			
Morgan Guaranty Trust, New York			7.5	3.2	1.0
Girard Trust, Philadelphia			28.8	10.8	0.7
Provident National, Philadelphia			7.9	0.0	0.4
Medusa Portland Cement	3	4			
Cleveland Trust Co., Cleveland			18.5	12.5	3.6
National Steel Corp.	9	6			
Chase Manhattan Bank, New York			6.2	5.5	0.6

Mellon National Bank, Pittsburgh			6.6	2.9	1.0
Pittsburgh National Bank, Pittsburgh			8.3	3.0	0.7
Allegheny Ludlum Steel	4	4			
State Street Bank, Boston			5.2	0.0	0.1
Chase Manhattan Bank, New York			5.2	4.9	0.2
Mellon National Bank, Pittsburgh			5.1	2.7	0.5
Carpenter Steel Co.	2	2			
Girard Trust Co., Philadelphia			19.4	11.2	2.2
Northwestern Steel Fire Co.	1	1			
Continental Illinois, Chicago			34.6	17.3	0.1
Aluminum Company of America	3	4			
Mellon National Bank, Pittsburgh			25.3	4.1	16.4
Kennecott Copper	2	3			
Morgan Guaranty Trust, New York			17.5	10.5	2.6
Deere & Co.	1	11			
Morgan Guaranty Trust, New York			8.0	5.6	0.6
Anchor Coupling Co.	1	1			
Continental Illinois, Chicago			30.9	18.3	12.6
Reliance Electric	6	3			
First National Bank, Chicago			6.2	5.3	0.3
Cleveland Trust Co., Cleveland			14.0	9.7	2.9
Sunbeam Corp.	1	2			
First National Bank, Chicago			6.4	3.2	1.3
Chase Manhattan Bank, New York			8.5	8.1	0.4
Bausch & Lomb, Inc.	0	0			
Chase Manhattan Bank, New York			9.4	9.2	0.1
Xerox Corporation	2	0			
First National City Bank, New York			5.0	3.7	0.3

The Patman List (continued)

The Corporation and the Bank	No. of Interlocking Directorates Held by All Banks	No. of Funds Managed by All Banks	Percent of Common Stock Held by Banks	Percent of Sole Voting Rights	Percent of Partial Voting Rights
Morgan Guaranty Trust, New York			9.7	4.7	0.6
Penn Central	17	0			
Chase Manhattan Bank, New York			5.6	5.4	0.1
Morgan Guaranty Trust, New York			7.2	6.2	0.2
United Air Lines	2	1			
State Street Bank, Boston			6.8	0.1	0.0
Morgan Guaranty Trust, New York			8.2	6.0	0.4
Pan American World Airways	3	3			
Chase Manhattan Bank, New York			6.7	6.4	0.2
Trans World Airlines	3	3			
State Street Bank, Boston			6.2	0.0	0.0
Chase Manhattan Bank, New York			7.8	7.4	0.3
Morgan Guaranty Trust, New York			7.4	6.1	0.3
Columbia Broadcasting System	0	0			
Chase Manhattan Bank, New York			5.9	5.0	0.7
Panhandle Eastern Pipe Line Co.	0	5			
Chase Manhattan Bank, New York			5.6	4.6	0.6
Morgan Guaranty Trust, New York			5.8	4.4	0.2
Federated Department Stores	3	1			
First National Bank, Chicago			10.2	1.9	6.9
Sears, Roebuck	11	1			

First National Bank, Chicago	2	24.6	0.4	0.2
W. T. Grant Co.				
Connecticut Bank & Trust, Hartford	1	31.0	1.2	29.8
Morgan Guaranty Trust, New York		10.3	6.0	1.1
Purity Stores, Inc.	0			
Chase Manhattan Bank, New York	0	25.4	25.4	
Tiffany & Co.	0			
Morgan Guaranty Trust, New York	1	11.9	3.3	8.6
Household Finance Corp.				
State Street Bank, Boston	0	6.1	0.1	0.0
First National Bank, Chicago		8.5	5.2	2.0
Commercial Credit Co.	1			
Mercantile-Safe Deposit, Baltimore	0	6.9	3.2	0.9
General Finance Corp.	2			
First National Bank, Chicago	2	15.5	0.5	0.0
Northern Trust Co., Chicago		8.5	6.6	0.1
Connecticut General Life Insurance	9			
Hartford National Bank, Hartford	0	6.3	5.0	0.7
Bankers Trust Co., New York		6.4	6.3	0.1
Grey Advertising	0			
Morgan Guaranty Trust, New York	0	6.5	5.3	0.0
Newsday	0			
Morgan Guaranty Trust, New York		Class A...49.0	0.0	49.0
		Class B...42.5	0.0	42.5
Chicago Tribune	0			
Continental Illinois, Chicago		8.0	1.2	6.8
Hartford Courant	2			

The Patman List (continued)

The Corporation and the Bank	No. of Interlocking Directorates Held by All Banks	No. of Funds Managed by All Banks	Percent of Common Stock Held by Banks	Percent of Sole Voting Rights	Percent of Partial Voting Rights
Connecticut Bank & Trust, Hartford					
Detroit News	0	0	92.0	0.0	0.0
Detroit Bank & Trust, Detroit			16.1	5.8	0.0
Baltimore Sun	3	1			
Mercantile-Safe Deposit, Baltimore			61.3	27.0	23.4

Bibliography

Activities by Various Central Banks to Promote Economic and Social Welfare Programs. Staff report, Committee on Banking and Currency, House of Representatives, December, 1970. U.S. Government Printing Office, 1971.

Annual Report. Federal Deposit Insurance Corporation, 1970, 1971, 1972.

Annual Report. Federal Reserve Bank of New York, 1971, 1972.

Budzeika, George. "Lending to Business by New York City Banks." *The Bulletin.* Institute of Finance, New York University, September, 1971.

Citibank: A Preliminary Report by the Nader Task Force on First National City Bank. David Leinsdorf, project director; introduction by Ralph Nader. Center for Study of Responsive Law, 1971.

The Commercial Banking Industry, An "In" Study of Commercial Banking from the Industry Itself. Monograph by the Commission on Money and Credit, American Bankers Association. Prentice-Hall, Inc., 1962.

Commercial Banks and Their Trust Activities: Emerging Influence on the American Economy, Volumes 1, 2. Staff report, Subcommittee on Domestic Finance, Committee on Banking and Currency, House of Representatives, July 8, 1968. U.S. Government Printing Office, 1968.

Congressional Record: Proceedings and Debates Providing for Consideration of H.R. 8432, Emergency Loan Guarantee of 1971. Volume 117, No. 121, pp. H7444-7520. U.S. Government Printing Office, July 30, 1971.

Crosse, Howard O. *Management Policies for Commercial Banks.* Prentice-Hall, Inc., 1962.

Denton, Frank R. *The Mellons of Pittsburgh* (an address). Newcomen Society of England, American Branch, 1948.

Foreign Experience with Monetary Policies to Promote Economic and Social Priority Programs. Staff report, Committee on Banking and Currency, House of Representatives, May, 1972. U.S. Government Printing Office, 1972.

Friedman, Milton, and Schwartz, Anna Jacobson. *A Monetary History of the United States: 1867–1960.* Princeton University Press, 1963.

Golembe, Carter H. *The Economic Power of Commercial Banks: An Examination of the Reports of the Subcommittee on Domestic Finance Dealing with Banking Concentration and the Trust Accounts of Commercial Banks.* American Bankers Association, 1969.

Gordon, Thomas Francis. *War on the Bank of the United States.* Reprint of 1834 edition. Burt Franklin, 1967.

Growth of Unregistered Bank Holding Companies, Problems and Prospects. Staff report, Committee on Banking and Currency, House of Representatives, February 11, 1969. U.S. Government Printing Office, 1969.

Hall, George R., and Phillips, Charles F., Jr. *Bank Mergers and the Regulatory Agencies: Application of the Bank Merger Act of 1960.* A monograph commissioned by the Federal Reserve Board, 1964.

Hamilton, Alexander. *Argument of Secretary of Treasury on Constitutionality of a National Bank.* Treasury Department, U.S. Government, 1791.

Hearings to Amend the Bank Merger Act of 1960, before the Subcommittee on Domestic Finance, Committee on Banking and Currency, House of Representatives, August 11 to September 25, 1965, Volumes 1–4. U.S. Government Printing Office, 1966.

Hearings to Authorize Emergency Loan Guarantees to Major Business Enterprises, before the Committee on Banking and Currency, House of Representatives, July 13 to July 20, 1971. U.S. Government Printing Office, 1971.

Hearings on Bank Holding Company Act Amendments, before the Committee on Banking and Currency, House of Representatives, April 15 to May 9, 1969. Parts 1, 2, 3. U.S. Government Printing Office, 1969.

Hearings on the Banking Reform Act of 1971, before the Committee on Banking and Currency, House of Representatives, April 20 to May 4, 1971, Parts 1, 2. U.S. Government Printing Office, 1971.

Hearings on Charges of Hon. Wright Patman Against the Secretary of the Treasury, before the Committee on the Judiciary, House of Representatives, January 13, 14, 15, 18, 19, 1932. H. Res. 92. U.S. Government Printing Office, 1932.

Hearings in Investigation of Conglomerate Corporations: Government and Private Witnesses, before the Antitrust Subcommittee, Committee on the Judiciary, House of Representatives, May, 1970. Part 7. U.S. Government Printing Office, 1970.

Hearings in Investigation of Conglomerate Corporations: Gulf & Western Industries, Inc., before the Antitrust Subcommittee, Committee on the Judiciary, House of Representatives, July 30 to August 7, 1969. Part 1. U.S. Government Printing Office, 1970.

Hearings in Investigation of Conglomerate Corporations: Leasco Data Processing Corporation, before the Antitrust Subcommittee, Committee on the Judiciary, House of Representatives, October 15, 16, 22, 23, 1969. Part 2. U.S. Government Printing Office, 1970.

Hearings in Investigation of Conglomerate Corporations: Ling-Temco-Vought, before the Antitrust Subcommittee, Committee on the Judiciary, House of Representatives, April 15, 16, 22, 23, 1970. U.S. Government Printing Office, 1970.

Hearings in the Investigation in Crown Savings Banks Failure, before the Subcommittee on Domestic Finance, Committee on Banking and Currency, House of Representatives, July 20 to August 6, 1965. U.S. Government Printing Office, 1966.

Hoffman, William. *David.* Lyle Stuart, 1971.

Instruments of the Money Market. Edited by Jimmie R. Monhollon. Federal Reserve Bank of Richmond, August, 1970.

Investigation of Conglomerate Corporations. Staff report, Antitrust Subcommittee, Committee on the Judiciary, House of Representatives. U.S. Government Printing Office, June, 1971.

James, Marquis, and James, Bessie R. *Biography of a Bank: The Story of Bank of America.* Harper & Row, 1954.

Knox, John Jay. *A History of Banking in the United States.* Bradford Rhodes & Co., 1900, 1902. Reprinted by Augustus M. Kelley, 1969.

Kross, Herman, and Studenski, Paul. *Financial History of the United States.* McGraw-Hill, 1952.

Money Market Instruments. Research Department, Federal Reserve Bank of Cleveland, September, 1971.

O'Connor, Harvey. *Mellon's Millions.* The John Day Co., 1933.

Patman, Wright. *Banketeering, Bonuseering, Melloneering.* Peerless Printing Co., 1934.

Penn Central Failure and the Role of Financial Institutions. Staff report, Committee on Banking and Currency, House of Representatives, January 3, 1972. U.S. Government Printing Office, 1972.

Report of the President's Commission on Financial Structure and

Regulation (Hunt Commission Report). Commission on Financial Structure and Regulation, December, 1971.

Summary and Interpretative Analysis of the Report of the President's Commission on Financial Structure and Regulation (Hunt Commission Report). American Bankers Association, 1972.

Story of American Banking. Banking Education Committee, American Bankers Association, 1963.

Index

441

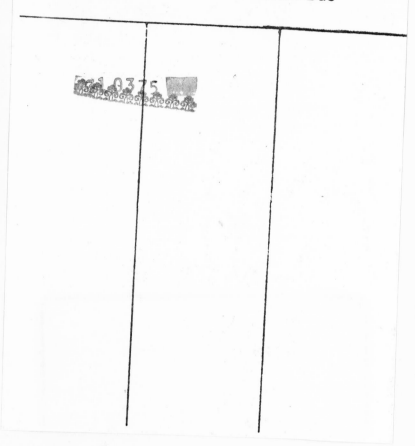